THE *Reformation Heritage Bible Commentary* is a unique series that promises to be a valuable resource for laity and preachers. The verse-by-verse commentary focuses on major topics, providing clear interpretation and devotional insight in keeping with how the Reformers approached Scripture, and emphasizing themes that were central in their teaching. This focused approach gives a clear reading of the text which engages one's mind and heart.

—The Rev. Dr. Rodney A. Whitacre
Professor of Biblical Studies
Trinity School for Ministry
Ambridge, Pennsylvania

Busy pastors and teachers of the scriptures need commentaries that are biblical, theological, and practical. Fortunately, the Reformation Heritage Bible Commentary series fulfills those requirements. The scholarship is reverent, demonstrating that the truths of the Reformation are relevant today just as they were in the 16th century. The volumes are accessible to a wide variety of readers, for it is written in a wonderfully clear way. I commend this work gladly.

—Thomas R. Schreiner, PhD
James Buchanan Harrison Professor of New Testament
The Southern Baptist Theological Seminary
Louisville, Kentucky

The Reformation Heritage series is a "Heritage of Reformation theology" now put at the fingertips of every serious Bible student, young or old.

This commentary helps anyone to dive deeply into the Scriptures, verse by verse, even word by word. I was blessed with its academic rigor in straightforward language, the sidebar articles explaining overarching Biblical themes, and the voices of the Reformers demonstrating again that this Good News of Jesus is a message for all times. If one yearns to know the unique message of the Scripture and its meaning for life, now and forever, then join me in having the Reformation Heritage Series in your library today.

—Rev. Gregory P. Seltz
Speaker, The Lutheran Hour

Reformation Heritage Bible Commentary promises to be an asset to the library of serious Bible students, whether layman or clergy. This series exemplifies the reformers commitment to sola scriptura, that the revelation of God's saving purposes is in scripture alone, which is primarily about Christ alone. The blend of overviews and insights from our protestant forefathers with exegesis and application from contemporary reformed theologians makes for an interesting read. Contemporary readers will also appreciate the devotional notes in these commentaries. Because the study of God's word is not just an academic endeavor, it engages the mind, heart and will of those who trust Christ for their salvation. While many modern commentaries seem to focus on the application of the scriptures, the intent here is gospel centered interpretation, resulting in devotional application. This is a work of serious scholastic intent combined with theological scrutiny and integrity. I am grateful for such a work and confident that it will be profitable for years to come in aiding the church's effort to know Christ more fully as He is revealed in holy scripture.

—Kenneth R. Jones
Pastor of Glendale Baptist Church, Miami, FL
Co-host of nationally syndicated talk show—White Horse Inn
Contributed to: "Experiencing the Truth", "Glory Road", and
"Keep Your Head Up"; all published by Crossway.
Contributed to Table Talk and Modern Reformation magazines
Frequent conference speaker

The Reformation of the church brought with it biblical insights that revitalized churches and radically changed the course of theological studies as giants like Luther, Melanchthon, Calvin, Chemnitz, and Wesley commented extensively on Holy Scripture. The new *Reformation Heritage Bible Commentary* is a one-stop-resource where the observations of these and other distinguished Reformation leaders are brought together around specific books of the New Testament.

—The Rev. Dr. R. Reed Lessing
St. Michael's Lutheran Church
Fort Wayne, IN
Longtime Professor of Exegetical Theology at
Concordia Seminary, St. Louis, MO

Reformation Heritage
BIBLE COMMENTARY

GENERAL EPISTLES

James | 1 & 2 Peter | 1, 2 & 3 John | Jude

Reformation Heritage
BIBLE COMMENTARY

✦ GENERAL EPISTLES

James | 1 & 2 Peter | 1, 2 & 3 John | Jude

CLINTON J. ARMSTRONG

CONCORDIA PUBLISHING HOUSE • SAINT LOUIS

Copyright © 2014 Concordia Publishing House
3558 S. Jefferson Ave., St. Louis, MO 63118-3968
1-800-325-3040 · www.cph.org

Manufactured in the United States of America

Library of Congress Cataloging-in-Publication Data

Armstrong, Clinton J.
    General Epistles / Armstrong, Clinton J.
        p.   cm. — (Reformation heritage Bible commentary)
    ISBN 978-0-7586-2765-0
    1. Bible. N.T. General Epistles. I. Armstrong, Clinton J.- II. Title. III. Title: General Epistles.
    BS2715.53.E54   2014

227'.077--dc23   2011044778

1 2 3 4 5 6 7 8 9 10   23 22 21 20 19 18 17 16 15 14

CONTENTS ◆

About This Series

The great reformers' influence upon the Bible's interpretation and application could not help but revitalize our churches. This is as true today as it was 500 years ago. This renewal happens in part because the reformers drew upon the insights of the Renaissance, which linked the medieval church back to her earlier roots in the ancient world. There the biblical texts sprang up. The reformers were among the earliest students to pursue classical studies, not only due to personal interest but especially due to the benefits such study brought to the study of the Bible. By reading the New Testament Scriptures in their ancient languages and context, the reformers dispelled many misunderstandings.

Second, the fires of controversy, which followed Luther's proclamation of justification by grace through faith on account of Christ alone, served to refine the study of Sacred Scriptures. So many ideas that medieval people took for granted or that were accepted based on human authority alone were tested and retested, leading to more careful study of God's Word.

Third, the reformers themselves taught with special insight due to their constant reading, study, translating, and preaching of the Sacred Scriptures. Their approach to the Scriptures and the insights they gained have continued to inform biblical studies even to the present day. For all of these reasons, Concordia Publishing House wished to produce a readable commentary series that would serve the current generation by sharing with them (1) insights from the reformers and (2) commentary that stemmed from their heritage.

In preparing this commentary, we drew upon the insights of the following reformers and heirs to their evangelical approach to teaching the Scriptures:

John Hus (c. 1372–1415)
Martin Luther (1483–1546)
Thomas Cranmer (1489–1556)
Philip Melanchthon (1497–1560)
John Calvin (1509–64)

John Knox (c. 1513–72)
Martin Chemnitz (1522–86)
Johann Gerhard (1582–1637)
Johann Albrecht Bengel (1687–1752)
John Wesley (1703–91)

Not every commentary in this series will include quotations from each of these reformers or heirs of the Reformation, since these authors did not all comment on Books of the Scriptures with equal frequency. Other reformers may be included, as well as citations of Reformation era confessional documents such as the Augsburg Confession and Westminster Confession. Readers should not conclude that citation of an author implies complete endorsement of everything that author wrote (heaven knows, these were fallible men, as they themselves acknowledged). The works of other significant Reformation era commentators are less available in English. We have intentionally stayed away from more radical reformers such as Andreas Bodenstein von Karlstadt, Ulrich Zwingli, and Thomas Münzer.

The commentary is not simply a compilation of sixteenth-century views but a thorough verse-by-verse commentary built from the reformers' approach of *Scripture interprets Scripture* and supplemented from their writings. Along with quotations from the reformers and their heirs, readers will also find quotations from some early and medieval Church Fathers. This is because the reformers did not wish to overthrow the earlier generations of teachers but to profit from them where they were faithful in teaching the Word.

Some readers will note that the writers listed above represent different branches in the Protestant family of churches, and they may wonder how compatible these writers will be alongside one another. It is certainly the case that the reformers held different views, especially concerning the Sacraments, biblical authority, and other matters. Some authors for the series may at times describe differences between the various reformers.

However, while it is true that these differences affect the fellowship and work of the churches of the Reformation, it is also true that the reformers shared significant agreement. For example, the great historian Philip Schaff noted, "Melanchthon mediated between Luther and Calvin" (*History of the Christian Church* vol. VII, second revised ed. [New York: Charles Scribner's Sons, 1894], 260). Early Reformation works like Melanchthon's *Commonplaces* and the Augsburg Confession served as models for the various traditions of Protestant confession and doctrine. What is more, as the writers focused on a particular biblical text for interpretation, they often reached very similar conclusions regarding that text. The text of Scripture tended to lead them toward a more unified expression of the faith. This is something I have described as "the text effect,"[1] which illustrates for

---

[1] *Friends of the Law* (St. Louis: Concordia, 2011), 136.

us a way in which the Bible brings us together despite differences and always remains the most important guide for Christian teaching and practice. In view of the 500th anniversary of the Reformation in 2017, I believe it is fitting for us to draw anew upon the time-honored insights of these great servants of God.

The Bible Translations

Among the translations for our commentary, we have chosen, on the one hand, what many regard as the finest English translation ever produced: the King James Version. The KJV is a product of the Reformation era, and although it is now more than 400 years old, it remains a most valuable tool for study. Along with the KJV, we are pleased to present the English Standard Version, which has rapidly become one of the most widely used modern English translations. The success of the ESV is due in part to the translators' efforts to follow sound, classical principals of translation very like those used by the KJV translators. The result is a very readable English translation that also allows readers to grasp the biblical expressions and terms that appear repeatedly in the Bible. Due to this approach, we find the ESV an especially helpful translation for Bible study. Our notes are keyed to the ESV, but we have placed the KJV in parallel with the ESV for easy comparison. Since the ESV text is based on the broad consensus of biblical scholars who have consulted the early Greek manuscripts, it differs at points from the KJV text, which was produced when fewer manuscripts were available for study. Where significant differences between the translations appear, the notes include comment.

Our Prayer for You

The following prayer embodies the sense of study and devotion we wish to convey to all who take up these commentaries:

Blessed Lord, You have caused all Holy Scriptures to be written for our learning. Grant that we may so hear them, read, mark, learn, and inwardly digest them that, by patience and comfort from Your holy Word, we may embrace and ever hold fast the blessed hope of everlasting life; through Jesus Christ, our Lord. Amen.

Rev. Edward A. Engelbrecht, STM
Senior Editor for Bible Resources

PREFACE

The General Epistles may be the most neglected books of the New Testament. Not addressed to a specific congregation or person, as are Paul's Letters, these seven books are sometimes seen as controversial. Five of them have historically been the subject of debate among Christians: do they even belong in the canon of Scripture? James has drawn scrutiny for its teaching about faith and works. Jude quotes from non-biblical books. Several are so short they seem easy to skip over.

And then there is the subject matter. These books address an astonishing range of topics including election, the office of the ministry, the antichrist, the fall of the angels, the role of the Christian in society, Christ's descent into hell, and our responsibilities toward others both inside and outside of the Church. These Letters certainly do not shy away from challenges!

In response to such challenges, some Christians seem to find it easier to avoid these books, or to focus exclusively on passages that they consider easy to understand. "I like what 1 John says about love . . ."

Dear reader, do not shy away from these books. We, who live in a challenging world, need God's Word regarding challenging topics. Read these books as we do read all Scripture: in faith. Read them in the context of the rest of Scripture and you will see that, like the rest of God's Word, these books are about our life in Christ. Read them in conversation with our forebears in the faith and you will see that they were blessed by these books. The General Epistles point us, who like our forebears are "elect exiles," to the work of Christ on our behalf, the blessings of the life that He gives to us, and the sure and certain promises of God.

Steven P. Mueller, Ph.D.
General Editor

AD	*anno Domini* (in the year of [our] Lord)	NT	New Testament
		OT	Old Testament
BC	before Christ	p.	page
c.	circa	pp.	pages
cf.	confer	St.	Saint
ch.	chapter	v.	verse
chs.	chapters	vv.	verses

Canonical Scripture

Gn	Genesis	Ec	Ecclesiastes
Ex	Exodus	Sg	Song of Solomon
Lv	Leviticus	Is	Isaiah
Nu	Numbers	Jer	Jeremiah
Dt	Deuteronomy	Lm	Lamentations
Jsh	Joshua	Ezk	Ezekiel
Jgs	Judges	Dn	Daniel
Ru	Ruth	Hos	Hosea
1Sm	1 Samuel	Jl	Joel
2Sm	2 Samuel	Am	Amos
1Ki	1 Kings	Ob	Obadiah
2Ki	2 Kings	Jnh	Jonah
1Ch	1 Chronicles	Mi	Micah
2Ch	2 Chronicles	Na	Nahum
Ezr	Ezra	Hab	Habakkuk
Ne	Nehemiah	Zep	Zephaniah
Est	Esther	Hg	Haggai
Jb	Job	Zec	Zechariah
Ps	Psalms	Mal	Malachi
Pr	Proverbs		

Mt	Matthew	Rm	Romans
Mk	Mark	1Co	1 Corinthians
Lk	Luke	2Co	2 Corinthians
Jn	John	Gal	Galatians
Ac	Acts	Eph	Ephesians

Php	Philippians	Jas	James
Col	Colossians	1Pt	1 Peter
1Th	1 Thessalonians	2Pt	2 Peter
2Th	2 Thessalonians	1Jn	1 John
1Tm	1 Timothy	2Jn	2 John
2Tm	2 Timothy	3Jn	3 John
Ti	Titus	Jude	Jude
Phm	Philemon	Rv	Revelation
Heb	Hebrews		

The Apocrypha

Jth	Judith	2Macc	2 Maccabees
Wis	The Wisdom of Solomon	Old Grk Est	Old Greek Esther
Tob	Tobit	Sus	Susanna
Ecclus	Ecclesiasticus (Sirach)	Bel	Bel and the Dragon
Bar	Baruch	Pr Az	The Prayer of Azariah
Lt Jer	The Letter of Jeremiah	Sg Three	The Song of the Three Holy Children
1Macc	1 Maccabees		
		Pr Man	Prayer of Manasseh

Other Books

1Esd	1 Esdras	Ps 151	Psalm 151
2Esd	2 Esdras	1En	1 Enoch
3Macc	3 Maccabees (Ptolemaika)	2En	2 Enoch
4Macc	4 Maccabees	Jub	Jubilees

Abbreviations for Commonly Cited Books and Works

ANF   Roberts, Alexander, and James Donaldson, eds. *The Ante-Nicene Fathers: The Writings of the Fathers Down to AD 325*, 10 vols. Buffalo: The Christian Literature Publishing Company, 1885–96. Reprint, Grand Rapids, MI: Eerdmans, 2001.

Bengel   John Albert Bengel. *Gnomon of the New Testament.* 5 vols. Edinburgh: T. & T. Clark, 1877.

Calvin   John Calvin. *Commentaries on the Catholic Epistles.* Rev. John Owen, Ed. Edinburgh: Calvin Theological Society, 1855.

Chemnitz   Chemnitz, Martin. *Chemnitz's Works.* 8 Vols. St. Louis: Concordia, 1971–89.

Church   Huss, John. *The Church.* David S. Schaff, trans. New York: Charles Scribner's Sons, 1915.

Concordia	McCain, Paul Timothy, ed. *Concordia: The Lutheran Confessions.* 2nd ed. St. Louis: Concordia, 2006.
Cranmer	*The Remains of Thomas Cranmer, D. D.* Rev. Henry Jenkins, ed. 4 vols. Oxford: Oxford University Press, 1833.
ESV	English Standard Version.
FC	Formula of Concord. From *Concordia.*
Gerhard	Gerhard, Johann. *Theological Commonplaces.* Richard J. Dinda, trans. Benjamin T. G. Mayes, ed. St. Louis: Concordia, 2009–.
H82	*The Hymnal 1982, according to the Use of The Episcopal Church.* New York: The Church Hymnal Corporation, 1985.
KJV	King James Version of Scripture.
Knox	John Knox. *Writings of the Rev. John Knox.* London: The Religious Tract Society, 1900.
LSB	Commission on Worship of The Lutheran Church—Missouri Synod. *Lutheran Service Book.* St. Louis: Concordia, 2006.
LW	Luther, Martin. *Luther's Works.* American Edition. General editors Jaroslav Pelikan and Helmut T. Lehmann. 56 vols. St. Louis: Concordia, and Philadelphia: Muhlenberg and Fortress, 1955–1986. Vols. 56–75: Edited by Christopher Boyd Brown. St. Louis: Concordia, 2009–.
MPG	Migne, Jacques-Paul, ed. *Patrologiae cursus completes: Series Graece. 161 vols. Paris and Turnhout, 1857–66.*
MPL	Migne, Jacques-Paul, ed. *Patrologiae cursus completes: Series Latina. 221 vols. Paris, 1844–80.*
NPNF2	Schaff, Philip, and Henry Wace, ed. *A Select Library of Nicene and Post-Nicene Fathers of the Christian Church*, Series 2, 14 vols. New York: The Christian Literature Series, 189099. Reprint, Grand Rapids, MI: Eerdmanns, 1952, 1961.
SA	Smalcald Articles. From *Concordia.*
Schaff	Schaff, Philip, ed. *The Creeds of Christendom with a History and Critical Notes.* 3 vols. 4th ed. New York: Harper, 1919.
SD	Solid Declaration of the Formula of Concord. From *Concordia.*
TLH	*The Lutheran Hymnal.* St. Louis: Concordia, 1941.

TLWA   Engelbrecht, Edward, comp. and ed. *The Lord Will Answer: A Daily Prayer Catechism Drawn from Holy Scripture, the Church Fathers, and Luther's Small Catechism with Explanation*. St. Louis: Concordia, 2004.

TPH   *The Presbyterian Hymnal*. Louisville, KY: Westminster/John Knox Press, 1990.

TUMH   *The United Methodist Hymnal*. Nashville, TN: The United Methodist Publishing House, 1989.

War   Josephus, Flavius. *The Wars of the Jews*. In *The Works of Josephus*. Translated by William Whiston. Peabody, MA: Hendrickson Publishers, 1987.

WDC   Scott, Robert, and George W. Gilmore, eds. *Selections from the World's Devotional Classics*. 10 vols. New York: Funk and Wagnalls, 1908.

Wesley   Wesley, John. *Explanatory Notes upon the New Testament*. 12 ed. New York: Carlton & Porter, 1754.

TIMELINE FOR THE NEW TESTAMENT

Anatolia, Greece, and Rome	Egypt and Africa	Dates	Syria, Canaan, and Israel	Mesopotamia and Persia
		4 BC	Angel appears to Zechariah (c. Nov 15; Lk 1:8–22)	
		3 BC	The Annunciation (inter Apr 17–May 16; Lk 1:26–38); John the Baptist born (Aug; Lk 1:57–66)	
	Holy family in Egypt	2 BC	Jesus born (mid Jan to early Feb; Mt 1:25; Lk 2:1–7); Magi visit; flight to Egypt (mid to late in the year; Mt 2)	
		1 BC	Death of Herod the Great (after Jan 10; Mt 2:19); return to Nazareth (Mt 2:19–23)	
		AD 6	Judas the Galilean leads revolt against Rome; Judea, Samaria, and Idumaea combined to form the Roman province of Judea	
		c. 10	Rabbi Hillel dies	
		11	Jesus in temple before the elders (c. Apr 8–22; Lk 2:42)	
Tiberius, Roman emperor		14–37		
Revolt in Gaul; grain shortages cause unrest in Rome		21		
		29	Baptism of Jesus (fall; Lk 3:1–2)	
		30	Jesus at Passover (c. Apr 8; Jn 2:20)	
		32	Jesus at Passover (c. Apr 15; Jn 6:4); Jesus arrives at Feast of Booths (c. Oct 14; Jn 7:14); Feast of Booths (Oct 17 or 18; Jn 7:37)	

Anatolia, Greece, and Rome	Egypt and Africa	Dates	Syria, Canaan, and Israel	Mesopotamia and Persia
Roman senators unable to pay debts; subsidized by Emperor Tiberius		33	Triumphal entry (Sun, Mar 29); Last Supper (Thurs eve, Apr 2); crucifixion (Fri, Apr 3); resurrection (Sun, Apr 5); ascension (May 14; Lk 24:51; Ac 1:9); Pentecost (May 24)	Jews of Parthia, Media, Elam and Mesopotamia travel to Jerusalem for Pentecost
	Ethiopian eunuch baptized, returns home (Ac 8:26–39)	c. 35		
		35–42		Revolt of Seleucia on the Tigris against Parthian rule
		36	Paul's conversion (Ac 9:1–31)	
Caligula (Gaius), Roman emperor		37–41	Josephus, Jewish historian, born	
	Philo of Alexandria leads Jewish delegation to Rome	c. 39	Caligula attempts to place statue of himself in Jerusalem temple	
		41	Martyrdom of James (late Mar; Ac 12:2); Peter in prison (Apr; Ac 12:3–4); Passover (May 4; Ac 12:4); Peter leaves Jerusalem (May; Gal 2:11)	
		41–44	Herod Agrippa I rules Judea	
Claudius, Roman emperor		41–54		
Peter on mission in Asia Minor (spr/sum; 1 Pt 1:1–2); [in Corinth (fall); at Rome (mid Nov)]		42	Peter in Antioch (May 41–Apr 42; Gal 2:11)	
		44	Herod Agrippa at festival in Caesarea (Mar 5; Ac 12:19); death of Herod Agrippa (Mar 10; Ac 12:21–23)	

Anatolia, Greece, and Rome	Egypt and Africa	Dates	Syria, Canaan, and Israel	Mesopotamia and Persia
		47–48	Paul's 1st missionary journey (Ac 13:1–14:28)	
Paul goes to Macedonia; Barnabas and John Mark go to Cyprus (mid May; Ac 15:36–16:10)		49	Conference in Jerusalem (Ac 15:1–35); Peter goes to Antioch (Feb; Gal 2:11); Paul confronts Peter (Apr; Gal 2:11)	
		49–56	[Peter in Antioch (seven years)]	
Paul's 2nd missionary journey (Ac 15:39–18:22)	Philo of Alexandria leads second Jewish delegation to Rome	49–51		
Paul's 3rd missionary journey (Ac 18:23–21:17)		52–55		
Nero, Roman emperor		54–68		
		55–57	Paul imprisoned in Caesarea (Ac 23:23–26:32)	
Paul's journey to Rome (Ac 27:1–28:16)		57–58		
Paul in custody in Rome (Ac 28:17–31)		58–60		
		62	Martyrdom of James, the Lord's brother	
Paul assigns Titus at Crete (Ti 1:5)		64–65		
Paul in Ephesus, where he leaves Timothy (spr–sum; 1Tm 1:3)		65		

Anatolia, Greece, and Rome	Egypt and Africa	Dates	Syria, Canaan, and Israel	Mesopotamia and Persia
	Tiberius Julius Alexander, of Jewish descent, appointed Roman prefect of Egypt	66		
		66–70	Jewish revolt against Romans	
Peter and Paul martyred		68		
Emperor Vespasian		69–79		
		70	Titus destroys Jerusalem temple; Rabbon Yohanan ben Zakkai at Yavneh Academy	Jerusalem Jews settle in Babylonia, which becomes the new center of Judaism
		c. 73	Fall of Masada	
Emperor Titus		79–81		
Emperor Domitian		81–96		
		c. 90–115	Rabbon Gamaliel II at Yavneh Academy	
Jews revolt in Cyprus	Jews revolt in Egypt and Cyrene	115–17		Trajan captures Mesopotamia; Jews revolt
	Founding of Antinoöpolis by Emperor Hadrian	130		
		132–35	Bar Kokhba revolt; death of Rabbi Akiva, Yavneh Academy leader who hailed Bar Kokhba as the messiah	

Israelite/Jewish Diaspora Settlements

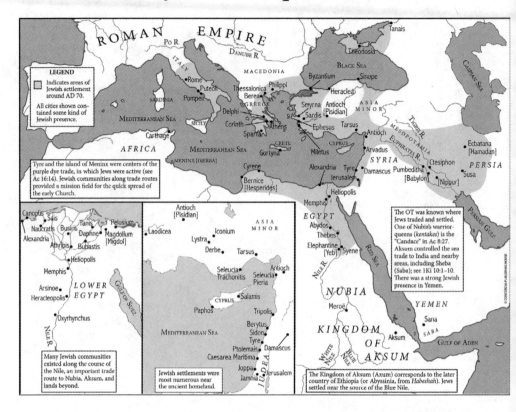

This map illustrates the spread of Israelites and Judeans from the Assyrian conquest and resettlement (722 BC) to the second Jewish revolt (AD 132–135). All cities shown contained some kind of Jewish presence. Trade routes provided the framework for expanding Jewish settlement. Close-knit communities allowed Jewish people to trade on stable credit throughout the known world and to stay in contact with one another.

The Diaspora also enabled the early spread of the Gospel as Paul and other Christian leaders visited Jewish settlements and preached that Jesus fulfilled the OT promises of the Messiah.

JAMES

INTRODUCTION TO
JAMES

Overview

Author
James, brother of the Lord

Date
c. AD 50

Places
The "Dispersion"

People
James; "the twelve tribes in the Dispersion"; rich and poor church visitors and believers; sick Christians; elders of the Church

Purpose
To impart the Lord's wisdom to the congregations dispersed among the Gentile nations

Law and Sin Themes
Must keep the whole Law; death; works required for salvation; sinners judged by Law as transgressors; faith apart from works is dead

Grace and Gospel Themes
Good and perfect gifts from the Father of lights; brought forth by the Word of truth; heirs of the Kingdom; counted righteous; the coming of the Lord, compassionate and merciful; forgiveness; because of Christ's death and resurrection, sinners are judged under the "law of liberty"

Memory Verses
The crown of life (1:12); the Father of lights (1:16–17); the tongue (3:1–12); fervent prayer (5:13–18)

Luther on James

In 1522, Luther made harsh statements about the Epistle of James. These statements have become notorious among scholars who have sometimes taken them out of context. The statements derive from Luther's frustration with opponents who used Jas 2 to attack what Luther had learned about justification and sanctification while carefully studying the Epistles of Paul. The chief problem is raised by the way James and Paul use the same terms (faith; law) and the same OT history (examples from Abraham's life) to illustrate very different points about the Christian life.

Critics have been delighted that Luther described James as an "epistle of straw" in 1522 and have used this statement as justification for launching attacks on other NT documents and doctrines.

However, a patient consideration of Luther's statements yields the following important points:

1. Luther's description of the Book changes. In some cases, Luther describes James as the work of an apostle (e.g., his postil of 1536; WA DB 41:578–90), but in other cases, he argues that it was not written by an apostle.

2. When Luther describes James as "straw," he is referring to its mundane, moral topics and not to its truthfulness. In medieval Wittenberg, straw was appreciated for its usefulness (e.g., Luther's mattress was stuffed with straw), but it was also characterized as having low value (cf. 1Co 3:12). So in his 1522 Preface to the New Testament, Luther is making a contrast between James and other NT Epistles and is not dismissing James outright.

3. In Luther's preface to James, he describes the Epistle as "a good book, because it sets up no doctrines of men but vigorously promulgates the law of God" (LW 35:395). But Luther also notes that the Book lacks teaching on Christ, whom the apostles were to preach.

4. Despite his strong opinion and suggestion that the Lord's brother James may not have written the Book, Luther retains it as a NT Epistle. He even cites it as authoritative teaching from God (see LC IV 122–24).

As the points above show, Luther was inconsistent in his opinions about James.

Luther wrote most harshly about James early in his career, while struggling against Rome and Andreas Carlstadt. Following the Antinomian Controversy, Luther showed new interest in the Epistle. In 1533, he urged Christians in Leipzig to hold to the Apology of the Augsburg Confession, in which Philipp Melanchthon provided a careful explanation of James's arguments about faith and works (Ap V 123–32), the issue in James that Luther found so troubling. During the ten years after Luther wrote his prefaces to the NT, we have no sermons on James from him. But in 1536, Luther wrote a postil commentary on Jas 1:17–21. He preached on Jas 1 in 1535, 1536, 1537, and twice in 1539. Although Luther never fully reconciled himself to the challenges presented by Jas 2, it appears that he became more comfortable with the Book in his mature years.

Below is a quote from Luther's 1522 preface. It is followed by a quote from his 1546 preface. These quotes are presented for historical purposes.

> In a word St. John's Gospel and his first epistle, St. Paul's epistles, especially Romans, Galatians, and Ephesians, and St. Peter's first epistle are the books that show you Christ and teach you all that is necessary and salvatory for you to know, even if you were never to see or hear any other book or doctrine. Therefore St. James's epistle is really an epistle of straw, compared to these others, for it has nothing of the nature of the gospel about it. (LW 35:362)

> Though this epistle of St. James was rejected by the ancients, I praise it and consider it a good book, because it sets up no doctrines of men but vigorously promulgates [*treibet*] the law of God.[1] However, to state my own opinion about it, though without prejudice to anyone, I do not regard it as the writing of an apostle; and my reasons follow.

> In the first place it is flatly against St. Paul and all the rest of Scripture in ascribing justification to works [2:24]. It says that Abraham was justified by his works when he offered his son Isaac [2:21]; though in Romans 4[:2–22] St. Paul teaches to the contrary that Abraham was justified apart from works, by his faith alone, before he had offered his son, and proves it by Moses in Genesis 15[:6]. Now although this epistle might be helped and an interpretation devised for this justification by works,[2] it cannot be defended in its application to works [Jas. 2:23] of Moses' statement in Genesis 15[:6]. For Moses is speaking here only of Abraham's faith, and not of his works, as St. Paul demonstrates in Romans 4. This fault,[3] therefore, proves that this epistle is not the work of any apostle.

> In the second place its purpose is to teach Christians, but in all this long teaching it does not once mention the Passion, the resurrection, or the Spirit of Christ. He names Christ several times;

---

[1] The translator does not consistently handle Luther's use of German *treiben*, but renders it negatively when Luther uses the verb regarding teaching the Law. Readers should note that Luther did not oppose strongly teaching the Law (e.g., nearly half of Luther's Large Catechism expounds the Ten Commandments).

[2] Melanchthon provided a very helpful explanation of the text in Ap V 123–32, which became standard among Lutherans.

[3] German *Mangel* often describes a lack of something, a weakness.

however he teaches nothing about him, but only speaks of general faith in God. Now it is the office of a true apostle to preach of the Passion and resurrection and office of Christ, and to lay the foundation for faith in him, as Christ himself says in John 15[:27], "You shall bear witness to me." All the genuine sacred books agree in this, that all of them preach and inculcate [treiben] Christ. And that is the true test by which to judge all books, when we see whether or not they inculcate [treiben] Christ. For all the Scriptures show us Christ, Romans 3[:21]; and St. Paul will know nothing but Christ, I Corinthians 2[:2]. Whatever does not teach Christ is not yet[4] apostolic, even though St. Peter or St. Paul does the teaching. Again, whatever preaches Christ would be apostolic, even if Judas, Annas, Pilate, and Herod were doing it.

But this James does nothing more than drive [treibet] to the law and to its works. Besides, he throws things together so chaotically that it seems to me he must have been some good, pious man, who took a few sayings from the disciples of the apostles and thus tossed them off on paper. Or it may perhaps have been written by someone on the basis of his preaching. He calls the law a "law of liberty" [1:25], though Paul calls it a law of slavery, of wrath, of death, and of sin.

Moreover he cites the sayings of St. Peter [in 5:20]: "Love covers a multitude of sins" [I Pet. 4:8], and again [in 4:10], "Humble yourselves under the hand of God" [I Pet. 5:6]; also the saying of St. Paul in Galatians 5[:17], "The Spirit lusteth against envy." And yet, in point of time, St. James was put to death by Herod [Acts 12:2] in Jerusalem, before St. Peter. So it seems that [this author] came long after St. Peter and St. Paul.

In a word, he wanted to guard against those who relied on faith without works, but was unequal to the task.[5] He tries to accomplish by harping [treiben] on the law what the apostles accomplish by stimulating people to love. Therefore I cannot include him among the chief books, though I would not thereby prevent anyone from including or extolling him as he pleases, for there are

---

[4] Luther's earlier version of the preface (1522) lacks this qualification. He at first dismissed James as not apostolic. In 1546, he characterizes the Book as not on equal standing with apostolic teaching.

[5] In 1522, Luther had continued, "in spirit, thought, and words. He mangles the Scriptures and thereby opposes Paul and all Scripture." These comments placed James outside of Scripture. Luther deleted these words for the 1530 edition.

otherwise many good sayings in him.[6] (LW 35:395–97; see also LW 4:133–34; 54:424–25)

Despite Luther's early, harsh opinions and influence as an interpreter, the Lutheran Church has held that James is rightly part of the NT, citing its authority in the Book of Concord.

Calvin on James

It appears from the writings of Jerome and Eusebius, that this Epistle was not formerly received by many Churches without opposition. There are also at this day some who do not think it entitled to authority. I, however, am inclined to receive it without controversy, because I see no just cause for rejecting it. For what seems in the second chapter to be inconsistent with the doctrine of free justification, we shall easily explain in its own place. Though he seems more sparing in proclaiming the grace of Christ than it behoved an Apostle to be, it is not surely required of all to handle the same arguments. The writings of Solomon differ much from those of David; while the former was intent on forming the outward man and teaching the precepts of civil life, the latter spoke continually of the spiritual worship of God, peace of conscience, God's mercy and gratuitous promise of salvation. But this diversity should not make us to approve of one, and to condemn the other. Besides, among the evangelists themselves there is so much difference in setting forth the power of Christ, that the other three, compared with John, have hardly sparks of that full brightness which appears so conspicuous in him, and yet we commend them all alike.

It is enough to make men to receive this Epistle, that it contains nothing unworthy of an Apostle of Christ. It is indeed full of instruction on various subjects, the benefit of which extends to every part of the Christian life; for there are here remarkable passages on patience, prayer to God, the excellency and fruit of heavenly truth, humility, holy duties, the restraining of the tongue, the cultivation of peace, the repressing of lusts, the contempt of the world, and the like things, which we shall separately discuss in their own places.

---

[6] In 1522, Luther had continued, "One man is no man in worldly things; how, then, should this single man alone avail against Paul and all the rest of Scripture?" Luther deleted these words for the 1530 edition.

But as to the author, there is somewhat more reason for doubting. It is indeed certain that he was not the son of Zebedee, for Herod killed him shortly after our Lord's resurrection. The ancients are nearly unanimous in thinking that he was one of the disciples named Oblias and a relative of Christ, who was set over the Church at Jerusalem; and they supposed him to have been the person whom Paul mentioned with Peter and John, who he says were deemed pillars, (Gal. ii. 9.) But that one of the disciples was mentioned as one of the three pillars, and thus exalted above the other Apostles, does not seem to me probable. I am therefore rather inclined to the conjecture, that he of whom Paul speaks was the son of Alpheus. I do not yet deny that another was the ruler of the Church at Jerusalem, and one indeed from the college of the disciples; for the Apostles were not tied to any particular place. But whether of the two was the writer of this Epistle, it is not for me to say. That Oblias was certainly a man of great authority among the Jews, appears even from this, that as he had been cruelly put to death by the faction of an ungodly chief-priest, Josephus hesitated not to impute the destruction of the city in part to his death. (Calvin 276–77)

Gerhard on James

At times there were likewise doubts in the Church about this Epistle. Eusebius, Hist. eccles., bk. 2, c. 23: "This Epistle, which is first among the catholic Epistles, is said to be the work of James. But one should note that it is not considered genuine . . . , for not many of the ancients mention it, just as they also do not mention that Epistle which is entitled "of Jude," though it, too, is one of the seven that are called 'catholic.' Nevertheless we know that these, along with the rest, are read publicly in many churches." . . . The same Eusebius, in Hist., bk. 3, c. 22, after his enumeration of the canonical books of the New Testament of the first rank, adds: "But the following are the ones spoken against, though they are well-known to many: the Epistle that is attributed to James," etc. . . .

Of the more recent writers, Cajetan (commentary on this Epistle) says: "It is still not very certain whether this Epistle is by James, the brother of the Lord. The salutation placed here is so pure that it is not in conformity with the salutation of any other apostolic Epistle. You see, it says nothing of God, nothing of Jesus Christ, nothing of grace, nothing of peace. Instead, it gives a greeting in the secular fashion. Also, the author does not call himself an apostle but only a servant of Jesus Christ." Erasmus, c. 1, Act., p. 199: "There has been some doubt about the Epistle of James." On James 5, p. 523: "Regarding this Epistle, though filled with salutary precepts, there once was doubt as to whose work it was. Nowhere does it appear to report that apostolic majesty and gravity, nor as much Hebraism, as one might expect from James, who was bishop of Jerusalem." . . .

Arguments to prove that this Epistle is apostolic, however, are not lacking. (1) Not only does it contain nothing unworthy of an apostle, but it also shows apostolic gravity and zeal in all things. (2) The Council of Laodicea and the third Council of Carthage quote it under James's name. (3) The following give their testimony to it: [lists ten Fathers], and as many as published a catalog of the canonical books of the New Testament.

These are the more significant arguments that are set forth for the opposite. (1) "The Syriac version attributes this Epistle to James, the son of Zebedee, the brother of John, for this is the way the inscription reads on the three Epistles, namely, of this one, of 1 Peter, and of 1 John. These three are the Epistles of the three apostles before whose eyes our Lord transfigured Himself, that is, James, Peter, and John. Yet that James was taken away from them by Herod at the beginning of the preaching of the Gospel (Acts 12:1). This Epistle seems to have been written a bit later, when the Gospel already had been preached among the nations among whom converted Jews had been scattered." Some people respond that because ten years, more or less, intervened between the death of Christ and the martyrdom of James, it is likely that within that period James wrote this letter to his Jewish brethren who were scattered after the murder of Stephen. Obviously, they take this "dispersion" to mean the one mentioned at the beginning of this Epistle. However, because (as Irenaeus witnesses in Adv. haeres., bk. 3, c. 1) the apostles began to consign their instruction to writing late, because they were at first intent upon the preaching of the Word, and especially because this Epistle is directed against the opinion of those who were taking Paul's instruction about faith alone justifying without works inaccurately, therefore it is not likely that this Epistle was written at that time when Paul had not yet begun to preach to the Gentiles nor yet to write his Epistles. Therefore it is more correct to attribute this Epistle to the other James, the son of Alphaeus, brother of Jude, otherwise called "the Less," whose cognomen was "Oblias," who later was bishop of the church at Jerusalem and whom Paul listed among "the pillars of the church" (Gal. 2:9). But Jerome points out (Adv. Helvid.) that that James was of the number of the twelve apostles and thus could have written a catholic Epistle. We must disagree, then, in this point from the Syriac version.

(2) "The author of this Epistle calls himself neither an apostle nor the brother of the Lord." We respond. Paul, too, in his Epistle to the Philippians, both to the Thessalonians, and to Philemon does not call himself an apostle of Christ, but either a servant, which James does also, or he adds nothing. Likewise, John adds the name "apostle" in neither his Epistles nor the Apocalypse. But Jude, too, who was beyond all doubt in the number of the twelve apostles, does not call himself an apostle but only the servant of Jesus Christ and the brother of James. As to why neither Jude nor James calls himself a brother of the Lord, the explanation can be given that they could have appeared to have honored themselves rather than Christ if they had called themselves the brothers of Him whose apostles and servants they were, especially if they were to do this in public letters written to their churches. In the epistle of Epiphanius to John of Jerusalem, which Jerome translated from Greek to Latin, James, the author of this letter, is called in clear words sometimes an "apostle," sometimes "the brother of the Lord."

(3) "This Epistle seems to conflict with justification by faith." We respond. In our article On Justification Through Faith [Commonplace XIX], § [191], we explained the genuine meaning of c. 2 in detail. Augustine, De fide et operibus, c. 14: "Because this idea had begun (that good works are not necessary), other apostolic Epistles—of Peter, John, James, and Jude—direct their thought particularly against this opinion, to affirm strongly that faith without works profits nothing, just as also Paul himself defined not just any faith by which one believes in God but that salutary and fully evangelical faith whose works proceed from love. And faith, he says, is something that works through love."

(4) "The salutation is not similar to the apostolic salutation." We respond. On the contrary, there is a similar salutation in Acts 15:23: "The brethren, both the apostles and the elders, to the brethren who are of the Gentiles in Antioch, Syria, and Cilicia: health [salus]." The apostles did not always use the same or a similar formula for greeting [salutandi] in their Epistles but would follow commonly accepted custom in this matter. One must not

judge that the person who speaks the greeting [salus] has omitted grace and peace, because there is no place for true health [salus] without grace and peace.

(5) "It preaches neither Christ nor faith because it teaches nothing about the way to obtain salvation through faith in Christ." We respond. On the contrary, it mentions Christ and faith several times: "Christ," when he calls himself His servant (1:1); when he calls Him the "Lord of glory" (2:1); when he mentions His coming in judgment (5:7ff.); when he commands us to pray in His name (5:14); and "faith," when he declares that "the testing of faith works patience" (1:3); when he teaches that "one must pray in faith" (1:6); when he teaches that, having grasped the word of truth by faith, we are born of God (1:18); when he orders us to "receive the implanted Word," namely, by true faith (1:21); when he forbids us to have faith in our acceptance of persons (2:1), that is, he requires us to have the sort of faith that has true love connected to it, which does good to all without a distinction of persons; when he claims that "the rich in faith have been elected by God" (2:5); when he teaches that we must demonstrate true faith "through works and from works" (2:14ff.); and when he teaches that "the prayer of faith will save the sick" (5:15). Yet all these passages speak about the true and saving faith that grasps the promise of the grace of Christ set forth in the Gospel for righteousness and salvation.

Moreover, the principal aim of this Epistle consists in refuting the false idea of those who were abusing the doctrine of gratuitous justification through faith to make it a license for the flesh. Therefore the author especially applied his instruction to this aim.

(6) "It calls the Law of the Old Testament 'the law of liberty' (1:25; 2:12), but Paul calls it 'the law of slavery' (Gal. 4:31)." We respond. In and of itself, the divine moral law is the law of liberty, but through accident, with respect to us, it is the law of slavery. Thus Stephen calls the Law in and of itself "living oracles" (Acts 7:38). Paul calls it through accident "the dispensation of death" (2 Cor. 3:7). . . .

(7) "He calls the Church a 'synagogue' (2:2), which is a custom foreign to the apostles." We respond. In Heb. 10:25 we have the expression ["meeting together"], drawn from Matt. 23:37: "How often have I wanted ["to gather together"] your children?" Some people refer to this the passage 2 Thess. 2:1, where the word . . .

is taken to mean the universal gathering of the devout on the Day of Judgment. . . . Moreover, words related to *synagogue* ("congregation") are attributed to the Christian people (Matt. 13:2; 18:20; John 11:52; 20:1; Acts 4:31; 11:26; 14:27; 15:6; 20:7).

(8) "The author of the Epistle gives testimonies from the Epistles of Peter and Paul. Therefore he was not one of the apostles but one of the disciples of the apostles." We respond. In this Epistle, some statements similar to those that occur in the Epistles of Peter and Paul are found, but that is so far from diminishing its canonical authority that, on the contrary, it proves its authority. In Isa. 2:3 and Mic. 4:1, completely similar statements occur, yet no one doubts the canonical authority of these prophets.

(9) "Eusebius says in Hist., bk. 2, c. 23, that this Epistle has been corrupted." We respond. He says this not with regard to canonical authority but only with regard to the author because, according to Jerome in Catal., on James: "It gradually obtained authority as time passed." And from Eusebius himself one concludes that such a doubt was either of only a few people or a few churches.

Therefore we deem that this Epistle is both canonical and apostolic; that it was written at Jerusalem, inasmuch as it is likely that James was bishop of the church at Jerusalem; that he wrote it not long before his blessed death so that the faithful Jews might have the instruction of their apostle and bishop sealed in writing, with which they would be instructed even after his death.

It consists of five chapters in which the faithful who already for a long time have been established in the instruction of Christ (1) are dissuaded from various vices unbefitting their profession of faith and (2) are, on the other hand, exhorted to the virtues worthy of their profession. (E 1.279–282)

Bengel on James

Peter, John, and James were the apostles of circumcision; Gal. ii. James was especially employed at Jerusalem and in Palestine and Syria. . . . Of the twelve apostles, these and Jude have left us seven Epistles, which are called General Epistles, a title given to them all in ancient times, though not adapted to all alike, since some of them are addressed to individuals; they are also called the Seven Canonical Epistles, to distinguish them from the Canonical Epistles of St. Paul. . . . James wrote from Jerusalem to the twelve tribes scattered abroad. This James is an apostle: respecting him, see on Acts xv. 23. (Bengel 5:1)

Wesley on James

This is supposed to have been written by James the son of Alpheus the brother (or kinsman) of our Lord. It is called a General Epistle, because it was written not to a particular person or church, but to all the converted Israelites. Herein the apostle reproves that antinomian spirit, which had even then infected many, who had perverted the glorious doctrine of justification by faith into an occasion of licentiousness. He likewise comforts the true believers under their sufferings, and reminds them of the judgments that were approaching. (Wesley 572)

Challenges for Readers

Authorship and Context. Early tradition attributed the Epistle of James to the Lord's brother James, who became an important leader in the Jerusalem Church (cf. Mk 6:3; Ac 15:1–21; 21:18; 1Co 15:7; Gal 1:19). However, Eusebius notes that this authorship was disputed (*NPNF2* 1:128). "James" (Hebrew/Aramaic "Jacob") was a very common name among first-century Jews and Christians. Despite various proposals by modern scholars, the Lord's brother remains the most likely author. The character of the Letter fits well into the mid-first century as a general letter from a Jerusalem leader to congregations in the "Diaspora" (lands outside of Israel). The simplicity of the Letter, its emphasis on wisdom and OT ethics, and its reference to a Christian gathering as an "assembly" (Gk *synagoge*; 2:2) point to an early date.

Relationship of Faith and Works. See Luther's concerns above, the notes on Jas 2:14–26, and Melanchthon's careful study in the Apology of the Augsburg Confession (V 123–32). There is no evidence in the Letter that James was written to dispute Paul's teaching about justification and faith, as some scholars still maintain.

Parallels with Other NT Teachers. The Book of James shows numerous similarities to the teachings of Jesus, especially as recorded in Matthew (cf. Jas 1:27 with Mt 25:36; Jas 2:10 with Mt 5:19; Jas 2:15–16 with Mt 25:35–36; Jas 3:11–12 with Mt 7:15–19; Jas 3:18 with Mt 5:9; Jas 4:10 with Mt 23:12; Jas 5:2–3 with Mt 6:19; Jas 5:10 with Mt 5:12; 23:34; Jas 5:12 with Mt 5:34; Jas 5:19–20 with Mt 18:15). Luther and other scholars have noted similarities with points of doctrine from

Peter and Paul (see Luther's comments above). Luther viewed these as evidence that the writer depended on the works of Peter and Paul. However, the argument easily runs the other way, with James being written earlier, or they simply shared common expressions.

Legalism and Antinomianism. Two false views that have surrounded the Book of James come from overreactions to the Book's focus on "the law of liberty" (2:12) and other NT passages about the use of God's Law. On the one hand, some interpreters have taught that the Gospel is a new Law and that salvation is not by grace alone. Others have overreacted by asserting that the Law has no place in the Christian life and that good works done in view of the Law might be harmful to a Christian's faith (*antinomian* means "opposed to the law"). When read carefully, Jas 2:14–26 helpfully addresses these misunderstandings about faith, the Law, and good works.

Blessings for Readers

As you study the Epistle of James, pray for wisdom and the will to do what you know is right. Look for practical solutions to the issues that challenge your congregation. Yet realize that God's people are still sinners and will make mistakes. They will hurt one another, and they will need to confess their faults and forgive one another. When such troubles arise, abide in the love and patience of your heavenly Father, and rejoice in His good gifts and salvation, which can never be taken away.

Outline

I. Greeting (1:1)
II. Perfection through the Implanted Word (1:2–21)
    A. Trials Result in Blessing (1:2–12)
        1. Trials and testing (1:2–4)
        2. Endurance comes only from God (1:5–8)
        3. The crown of life (1:9–12)
    B. Being Saved from Death (1:13–21)
        1. The source of temptation (1:13–16)
        2. Birth by the implanted Word (1:17–21)
III. Works Done by Those in Whom the Word Has Been Planted (1:22–2:26)
    A. Consistency of Word and Deed (1:22–2:13)
        1. The cause of inconsistency (1:22–25)

PART 1

GREETING (1:1)

ESV	KJV

1 ¹James, a servant of God and of the Lord Jesus Christ,
    To the twelve tribes in the Dispersion:
    Greetings.
	1 ¹James, a servant of God and of the Lord Jesus Christ, to the twelve tribes which are scattered abroad, greeting.

1:1 The beginning of the Letter of James features an element of the standard pattern of ancient letter writing: a brief introduction in which the writer names himself, then his audience, and concludes with a brief greeting. The introduction reveals that this is not a private correspondence, however, but is intended for an audience of many, from one who considers himself God's servant, *James*. Because the author tells us nothing more than his name, readers of this Letter would assume he was a well-known figure, leading to the suggestion that he is a James known from the Gospels and the early Christian community. We know of James the son of Zebedee, brother of John (cf. Mk 1:19); James the son of Alphaeus (Mk 3:18), who may also be James the Younger (Mk 15:40); James the father of Judas (Lk 6:16); and James the brother of Jesus (Gal 1:19), a leader in the Early Church at Jerusalem (Ac 12:17; 15:13). James, John's brother and Zebedee's son, died early, as Luke records in Ac 12:2, and the other Jameses are rather more obscure than the leader of the Jerusalem Church, whose authority would lend credence to this Letter. It is therefore traditionally maintained that this Letter was written by James, the Lord's brother, a respected leader in of the Early Church in Jerusalem. *servant of God.* The word translated "servant" is a common word in the New Testament, *doulos*. It is often translated "slave" (e.g., Jn 8:34–35; Rm 6:16–20). It is also the word Paul uses to describe himself in the introduction to some of his letters (Rm 1:1;

17

Gal 1:10; Php 1:1; Ti 1:1) as do Peter (2Pt 1:1), Jude (Jude 1), and John (Rv 1:1). James is consistent here in identifying himself with the humble title, which also applies to Christians in general. *twelve tribes in the Dispersion.* The "twelve tribes" could indicate that James's audience was specifically Jewish, rather than Gentile, or on the other hand, that he intended to include all Christians, Jews and Gentiles alike, as a fulfillment of Israel in the promise of Christ. James later refers to the gathering of believers in the "assembly" (Gk *synagogue;* 2:2), and seems not to engage tensions between Gentiles and Jews in the Christian community. These facts suggest that his intended audience is probably predominantly a Jewish community and that the Letter is an early one (written around AD 50). In the centuries preceding the time of Christ, the Gk word *diaspora* referred to the scattering of Jewish people and communities who lived outside of Jerusalem after that city's fall in 586 BC. While 1Pt 1:1 uses the term "diaspora" (translated as dispersion in the ESV) with specific geographies in mind (Pontus, Galatia, Cappadocia, Asia, and Bithynia), James does not specify the location or locations of his intended audience. The term therefore suggests that the author intended the Letter to be distributed widely.

PART 2

PERFECTION THROUGH THE IMPLANTED WORD (1:2–21)

Trials Result in Blessing (1:2–12)

Trials and testing (1:2–4)

ESV	KJV
²Count it all joy, my brothers, when you meet trials of various kinds, ³for you know that the testing of your faith produces steadfastness. ⁴And let steadfastness have its full effect, that you may be perfect and complete, lacking in nothing.	²My brethren, count it all joy when ye fall into divers temptations; ³Knowing this, that the trying of your faith worketh patience. ⁴But let patience have her perfect work, that ye may be perfect and entire, wanting nothing.

Introduction to 1:2–12 The next seven verses of ch. 1 introduce a major theme of James's Letter: faith. Faith is introduced as something that undergoes trial. This experience of trial produces perseverance, or steadfastness, in the believer (1:3). James uses the word again to describe the manner in which one is to ask of wisdom from God (1:6), trusting in the giver of all good gifts instead of hesitating or doubting. The contrast the author offers between faith and doubt brings to the surface, rather early here in the first chapter, a primary focus of his Letter: the nature of faith. Trials are present for the Christian whether suffering the circumstance of wealth or poverty (1:9–11), but the believer who remains steadfast receives faith's reward: the crown of life, which God promises to those who love Him (1:12).

1:2 *all joy.* The confidence of the brothers James addresses is based on their hope in Christ. Paul uses the same formula in Rm 15:13, where he prays, "May the God of hope fill you with all joy and peace in believing, so that by the power of the Holy Spirit you may abound in hope." *brothers.* James employs the Gk *adelphoi* here and elsewhere through the Letter (cf. 1:16; 1:19), which can refer to siblings in a family, or as here, to fellow Christians. The masculine plural can refer to men or men and women collectively. Siblings in Christ, unrelated to each other by blood, are nevertheless adopted into the same family by virtue of their Baptism (cf. Gal 3:25–29). *trials.* The same Gk word, *peirasmos,* refers to both "testing" and "temptation" throughout the NT. Both of these senses appear in Jas 1. "Trials" is a better translation than "temptations" in vv. 2–12, as the context associates the experience not with something to be escaped or avoided (cf. Lk 22:46; 1Co 10:13), but rather with "testing." (Cf. 1Pt 4:12: "Beloved, do not be surprised at the fiery trial when it comes upon you to test you, as though something strange were happening to you"). James will go on in vv. 13–14 to distinguish the circumstances that befall Christians from temptations to sin.

1:3 *testing.* The "test" of faith is what the Christian suffers when facing trials, that is, circumstances that challenge trust in the Gospel. In the parable of the sower, Jesus compares those who fall under trial with those who bear fruit patiently (cf. Lk 8:13, 15). *steadfastness.* The endurance that trials produce in the Christian holds a promise: the crown of life. James points this out later in the chapter (1:12). Paul remarks on the same joy and confidence that Christians may have in the face of trials in Rm 5:3–5: "Not only that, but we rejoice in our sufferings, knowing that suffering produces endurance, and endurance produces character, and character produces hope, and hope does not put us to shame, because God's love has been poured into our hearts through the Holy Spirit who has been given to us." Calvin wrote:

> We certainly dread diseases, and want, and exile, and prison, and reproach, and death, because we regard them as evils; but when we understand that they are turned through God's kindness unto helps and aids to our salvation, it is ingratitude to murmur, and not willingly to submit to be thus paternally dealt with. (Calvin 280)

1:4 *perfect and complete.* In Gk, this verse has a play on the word *teleios,* an adjective describing both the "work" in the first clause and James's readers in the second clause. The sense of a purpose, a final end, is entailed in the word, and so the KJV chooses to translate both instances as "perfect." James is saying that endurance that comes from suffering trials results in being *complete*. This is a point worth noting early on, considering a prevailing theme of "need" or "lacking" throughout the Letter (cf. 1:4 "lacking in nothing"; 1:5 "lacking wisdom"; 2:15 "lacking in daily food" [and emphases on poverty in general]; 2:18, 26 [and elsewhere] "faith without deeds"; 3:2 "we all stumble" [and therefore are not perfect/complete]; 4:2 "you desire and do not have . . . cannot obtain . . . You do not have, because you do not ask"). From James's perspective, trials can lead to wholeness. This perspective seems to be shared by our Lord Jesus when He promises to His disciples: "Truly, I say to you, there is no one who has left house or brothers or sisters or mother or father or children or lands, for My sake and for the gospel, who will not receive a hundredfold now in this time, houses and brothers and sisters and mothers and children and lands, with persecutions, and in the age to come eternal life." (Mk 10.29–30). *lacking in nothing.* The author does not have material blessings in mind, but (as the next verses show) faith in the God who gives wisdom. This relates to the other thing James bids his readers become: "complete" (Gk *holoklēros*). This Gk word derives from *klēros*, which can denote an inheritance or apportioned lot. The connection of *holos* and *klēros* reminds the reader that when Jesus is doing the giving, He never leaves one with parts or fractions, but always gives "the whole lot!"

1:2–4 in Devotion and Prayer There is something precious about the gospel narratives in which Jesus restores people to health. He opens the eyes of the blind (Mk 8:22–26; 10:46–52; Jn 9:1–12). He cleanses lepers (Mk 1:40–45; Lk 17:11–19). He releases people from paralysis (Mt 9:1–8; Jn 5:1–18). He opens the ears of the deaf and mute (Mk 7:31–37). He restores a man with a withered hand (Mk 3:1–3). As these people stretch out their new limbs, blink with eyes adjusting to new light, perk up ears to hear the music of God's creation and the words of His salvation, they walk, skip, leap, and run. These are proofs of His compassion and pictures of His mission of restoration. Our God, Jesus, has come to restore what was lost in Adam's fall. The good news for a broken creation is that He delivers far more than temporary cures for life's maladies, be they physical, mental, sensory, social, or psychological. His mission of restoration goes beyond a tune up, a good scrub, and a fresh coat of paint. It involves, rather, complete transformation, complete change. He restores broken creation by becoming broken Himself. Power was removed from Him, dignity was taken away. He was robbed of His clothes, robbed of His freedom, and robbed of His blood. Abandoned by His disciples and by a world that shouted "Crucify!" Jesus completed His mission of restoration through His own ruination. But in transforming His life into death, He transforms our death into new life. He comes to complete us by drawing us to Him in the cross, by delivering wholeness in the brokenness of discipleship. "If anyone would come after Me . . . let him take up his cross," says this Jesus. And so we follow—walking, skipping, leaping, running to follow this Jesus, willingly engaging in sorrow, trial, and affliction—knowing that the Christ, who once restored palsied limbs to make them whole, came to do a whole lot more. He comes to you this day to give you more than sight, hearing, and healing. He comes to you this day to give you all that, and the cross. And the life that has been broken by the cross can be broken no further. He completes you, restores you, makes you whole by bidding you to come and die, and live compete in Him. • Plead for me, O Holy Spirit, as I struggle in the midst of my enemies the world and the devil. I am weak, but You are strong. I am small, but You are mighty. Hold me in Your powerful hand as I enter the trials of this day, knowing that You have hidden my life in Christ. Where I see pain, trouble, division, and ruination, You see healing, cheer, integrity, and restoration. Grant me faith in You that through trial I may be drawn to faith's goal, the salvation of my soul, through Jesus Christ. Amen.

Endurance comes only from God (1:5–8)

ESV	KJV
[5]If any of you lacks wisdom, let him ask God, who gives generously to all without reproach, and it will be given him. [6]But let him ask in faith, with no doubting, for the one who doubts is like a wave of the sea that is driven and tossed by the wind. [7]For that person must not suppose that he will receive anything from the Lord; [8]he is a double-minded man, unstable in all his ways.	[5]If any of you lack wisdom, let him ask of God, that giveth to all men liberally, and upbraideth not; and it shall be given him. [6]But let him ask in faith, nothing wavering. For he that wavereth is like a wave of the sea driven with the wind and tossed. [7]For let not that man think that he shall receive any thing of the Lord. [8]A double minded man is unstable in all his ways.

1:5 James picks up the idea of "lacking in nothing" from the previous verse with the same verb "lack" and the possibility that his readers may well be lacking in wisdom. If this is the case, James says, let him ask of God who gives "generously" (ESV), or "liberally" (KJV). These words translate the Gk word *haplōs*, an adverb derived from the word for "single" or "one." These English translations reflect an analogy with the related noun *haplotēs*, which can mean "generosity" as it does, for example, at 2Co 9:11: "You will be enriched in every way to be generous in every way, which through us will produce thanksgiving to God." It may be more helpful here to think of a God who gives "simply," or "in a straightforward way." James identifies God as the one who gives to all, to a degree that in this Epistle we might conceive of James's depiction of God as "giver-God." He describes this giver-God with confidence in His firm promise: when a Christian asks in faith, the gift will be given. God is reliable in His giving. *any of you.* Here and elsewhere in Jas (cf. v. 23; 2:18), the reader hears a call to come back to faith in the giver-God. *wisdom.* While there is a practical purpose for wisdom (especially in light of the aforementioned "trials" the faithful Christian endures, vv. 2–3), it is worth noting that "wisdom" colors the entire Letter. Generically, Jas most closely resembles the "wisdom" teaching of Christ in the parables, and is therefore coextensive with the wisdom literature of the OT, in which the distinction between "wise" and "foolish" denotes the distinction between "good" and "evil." While James is not explicitly Christological in this verse, it is yet worthwhile to recall how Paul connects wisdom and Christ in 1Co 1:22–24: "For Jews demand signs and Greeks seek wisdom, but we preach Christ crucified, a stumbling block to Jews and folly to Gentiles, but to those who are called, both Jews and Greeks, Christ the power of God and the wisdom of God" (cf. also Pr 8:22–31; Col 2:3). *without reproach.* The giver-God gives to all who ask in faith, because He is the generous one. Cf. the term "prodigal" in English, which we use to describe both the wasteful son and the generous father in Jesus' parable at Lk 15:11ff. Wesley wrote that wisdom means "To understand, whence and why temptations come, and how they are to be improved. Patience is in every pious man already. Let him exercise this, and ask for wisdom" (Wesley 597).

1:6 *doubting.* The Gk word for "hesitate," *diakrinō* (ESV "doubt"; KJV "waver") primarily means to make distinctions, judge, or discriminate. Its secondary, transferred meaning relates to the space of time necessary to make such distinctions, and so comes to mean hesitate or doubt in various contexts of the NT.

1:7 "Hesitation" in itself is not necessarily a sinful quality, but James's extrapolation of the point in vv. 7–8 hinges on the context of asking for gifts from the giver-God and relies on the manner in which he urges his reader to ask: "in faith." James's argument is essentially a dichotomy then between "faith" and "doubt" and brings the primary focus of his Letter, the nature of faith, to the surface rather early here in ch. 1.

1:8 *double-minded.* James uses both the words "person" (Gk *anthrōpos*; v. 7) and "man" (Gk *anēr*; v. 8). This sets up a parallelism: while the expectation, thought, and intention of the person is that a gift will be received, the double-minded person will not in fact receive from the giver-God because he does not ask in faith. Such asking is the way not of faith but of hesitation. This makes the proverbial statement, *in all his ways,* ring fresh with the image of the indecisive person at a crossroads of many ways, not being able to travel in any direction. The wishy-washy wavering of the wind-tossed waves (v. 6) is an appropriate image for such doubt when the object is the giver-God who gives, to all who ask, in a simple, straightforward way. We have every reason to be confident in the promises of God.

1:5–8 in Devotion and Prayer A sober reflection on James's warning about asking in faith preaches God's Law to the human heart of a person I see in the mirror on a daily basis. When we pray, do we pray according to faith or according to selfish desire? The "two-minded" man is in fact the description of all believers in Christ. The apostle Paul waxes eloquent on the subject in Rm 7:7–25, summarized at vv. 22–23: "For I delight in the law of God, in my inner being, but I see in my members another law waging war against the law of my mind and making me captive to the law of sin that dwells in my members." We are all two people: the old Adam, the new Adam; the dead and the living; the absolutely ruined and the absolutely perfect; the sinner and the saint. Both at the same time. James points out the distinction throughout this entire wisdom sermon, and Christians dare never forget the distinction throughout their entire lives. This *simul* ("at the same time") talk affects the way we ask God for anything and everything, the whole content of our prayer. The old sinner asks only to be allowed to live and to prove how faithful he is with his own works and righteousness. The new saint asks only this: that Your will be done in killing the old sinner, in forgiving my works, whatever they are, in lifting me up from the despair of my own unrighteousness, and in giving me confidence in Christ's righteousness alone. Such a prayer is no more, no less, than the prayer of faith. And such a prayer is indeed powerful and effective—it is the kind of prayer God has in fact promised to answer. Pray this way, and trust in the God who single-mindedly kills and makes alive, who single-mindedly laid down His own life only to take it up again, who single-mindedly does it all for you. • Dear Lord Jesus Christ, You are the Master of life and death. As You were buried, so draw me ever to my Baptism, where You buried me with You in Your death. As You were raised at Easter, so draw me ever to my Baptism, where You raise me up again to walk in newness of life. And as You give me Your promises, so grant me faith ever to live for You. Amen.

The crown of life (1:9–12)

ESV	KJV
[9]Let the lowly brother boast in his exaltation, [10]and the rich in his humiliation, because like a flower of the grass he will pass away. [11]For the sun rises with its scorching heat and withers the grass; its flower falls, and its beauty perishes. So also will the rich man fade away in the midst of his pursuits. [12]Blessed is the man who remains steadfast under trial, for when he has stood the test he will receive the crown of life, which God has promised to those who love him.	[9]Let the brother of low degree rejoice in that he is exalted: [10]But the rich, in that he is made low: because as the flower of the grass he shall pass away. [11]For the sun is no sooner risen with a burning heat, but it withereth the grass, and the flower thereof falleth, and the grace of the fashion of it perisheth: so also shall the rich man fade away in his ways. [12]Blessed is the man that endureth temptation: for when he is tried, he shall receive the crown of life, which the Lord hath promised to them that love him.

Introduction to 1:9–12 These verses suggest that James has in mind a congregation made up of people whose relationships may be particularly strained by their identification with possessions. The author does not decry an uneven distribution wealth, but rather flips human wisdom on its head by enjoining both the humble and the rich to exult in the gift of the giver-God (see commentary on v. 5ff.), who has given His kingdom to both. Even the rich man is invited to boast, but as one who is poor-in-spirit rather than in his wealth; cf. Mt 5:3: "Blessed are the poor in spirit, for theirs is the kingdom of heaven." When Jesus talks about the kingdom, He does so as James does here, contrasting the humble and the rich, who may feel as if their wealth is a sign of self-accomplishment. In contrast, Christ's kingdom exalts the humble and humbles the proud (cf. Mt 19:23–26; Lk 1:46–55).

1:9 *exaltation*. God exalts the humble and humbles the proud; James repeats this idea in 4:10 and describes it here as a matter of fact, reveling in the paradox of the poor being in an exalted condition and the rich being of low estate.

1:10 *like a flower of the grass*. As a wildflower looks beautiful one day but withers and dies the next, so outward appearances and circumstances are fleeting. Our worth is not to be found in our wealth or possessions.

1:11 *pursuits*. The Gk word means the "path" of a person's life. In the specific context of the wealthy, it may be intended to denote avenues chosen for the sake of gaining wealth. The imagery, picked up also at the beginning of 1Pt (1:23–24), is reminiscent of OT wisdom, probably most immediately recognizable in the evangelical prophecy of Is 40:6–8:

"A voice says, 'Cry!'
  And I said, 'What shall I cry?'

All flesh is grass,
  and all its beauty is like the flower of the field.
  The grass withers, the flower fades
  when the breath of the LORD blows on it;
  surely the people are grass.
  The grass withers, the flower fades,
  but the word of our God will stand forever."

1:12 The beginning of this verse echoes the invitation for poor and rich alike to exult. *Blessed is the man* recalls the wisdom-literature formula of the Beatitudes (Mt 5:2–12) as well as many OT wisdom passages, including Ps 1:1. Here, the beatitude is a fitting conclusion to the theme James introduced in v. 2: the circumstances of the faithful brother follow a natural progression from *trial* to endurance, and from endurance to its goal (*telos*), its perfect work, namely, the completion, the maturity, of the believer, lacking nothing. The *crown of life* is the prize at the end of this race, a symbol of eternal life with the giver-God, the perfection of the life to come (cf. Rv 2:10).

Being Saved from Death (1:13–21)

The source of temptation (1:13–16)

ESV	KJV
¹³Let no one say when he is tempted, "I am being tempted by God," for God cannot be tempted with evil, and he himself tempts no one. ¹⁴But each person is tempted when he is lured and enticed by his own desire. ¹⁵Then desire when it has conceived gives birth to sin, and sin when it is fully grown brings forth death. ¹⁶Do not be deceived, my beloved brothers.	¹³Let no man say when he is tempted, I am tempted of God: for God cannot be tempted with evil, neither tempteth he any man: ¹⁴But every man is tempted, when he is drawn away of his own lust, and enticed. ¹⁵Then when lust hath conceived, it bringeth forth sin: and sin, when it is finished, bringeth forth death. ¹⁶Do not err, my beloved brethren.

Introduction to 1:13–21 Circumstances external to the Christian are one thing; internal temptation is another. James warns that temptation comes not from God, but from being led astray by evil desire, which entraps the believer, leading the Christian into sin, followed by death (1:13–16). The giver-God, on the other hand, grants all good gifts through His creative power (1:17–18), above all His Word, which He implants in the believer, leading to righteousness and the salvation of souls (1:19–21).

1:13–14 *tempted.* Where in v. 2 "testing" was a better translation of the Gk *peirasmos* to indicate the external circumstances of the faithful in their interaction with the world, in this next section, James uses the cognate Gk verb *peirazō* to refer to the internal trial of temptation to sin. While the *peirasmoi* (testings) the believer undergoes externally in the world lead to endurance, the *peirasmoi* (temptations) of the Christian's other two enemies—the devil and the sinful flesh—lead to sin and ultimately death (v. 15). Consider what Luther wrote regarding the distinction between testing from God and temptations from Satan:

God's testing is a fatherly one, for James says in his letter (1:13): "God is not a tempter for evil"; that is, He does not test in order that we may fear and hate Him like a tyrant but to the end that He may exercise and stir up faith and love in us. Satan, however, tempts for evil, in order to draw you away from God and to make you distrust and blaspheme God. God sports with the children He loves and, as it seems to the flesh, shows Himself angry and dreadful. . . . But these are merely instances of sporting. God will not deceive or cheat you. Just hold fast to His infallible and unchanging promise. Even though you should lose honors, riches, and life itself, you should nevertheless not maintain that God is angry with you and therefore has cast you aside; but you should expect other far more excellent gifts, honor, and a better life from Him, as Job 13:15 states: "Even though He kills me, I will hope in Him." (LW 4:132)

Knox wrote:

The scribes and pharisees tempted Christ by divers means, questions, and subtleties. And of this matter, saith St. James, "God tempteth no man;" that is, by temptation proceeding immediately from him, he intends no man's destruction. And here you shall note, that although satan appear sometimes to prevail against God's elect, yet he is ever frustrated of his final purpose. By temptation he led Eve and David from the obedience of God, but he could not retain them for ever under his thraldom. Power was granted to him to spoil Job of his substance and children, and to strike his body with a plague and sickness most vile and fearful, but he could not compel his mouth to blaspheme God's majesty; and, therefore, although we are laid open sometimes, as it were, to tribulation for a time, it is that when he has poured forth the venom of his malice against God's elect, it may return to his own confusion, and that the deliverance of God's children may be more to his glory, and the comfort of the afflicted: knowing that his hand is so powerful, his mercy and goodwill so prompt, that he delivers his little ones from their cruel enemy, even as David did his sheep and lambs from the mouth of the lion. For a benefit received in extreme danger more moves us than the preservation from ten thousand perils, so that we fall not into them. And yet to preserve from dangers and perils so that we fall not into them, whether they are of body or spirit, is no less the work of God, than to deliver from them; but the weakness of our faith does not perceive it; this I leave at the present. (Knox 194)

1:15 *desire . . . gives birth to sin.* Natural progression was on display in the preceding section as it related to trial, endurance, and the wholeness of the work of God in the believer resulting in a crown of life. Parallel to the work of endurance and faith in James's argument here is the natural progression of temptation, delivered in terms of conception, birth, maturity, and its *telos*: death. The temptation of Adam and Eve involved a tree "to be desired to make one wise" (Gn 3:6), but such "wisdom" came as a result of desiring what God had forbidden, and therefore resulted in death. So James appeals to his reader, showing that temptation does not grow into true wisdom (which comes from asking of the giver-God, vv. 5–6), but rather progresses from generation to generation: temptation, sin, and death.

1:16 *Do not be deceived.* The verb recalls the passive participles in v. 14 ("lured and enticed"), and so the verse serves as a climax to the paragraph before James moves on to his new thought about the giver-God. The author pleads with his reader not to be led astray by the enticement of his own will or by the bait set to catch him in any other way.

1:13–16 in Devotion and Prayer Temptation. Sin. Death. James paints them all together in a picture of one big unhappy family. About 350 years ago, John Milton employed the image in his epic *Paradise Lost* (2.648–889), dramatically depicting the tragic, incestuous origin of sin and death in the world as a product of Satan himself. Satan at one point, shocked at the monsters Sin and Death, is ready to attack them as enemies, when Sin, personified as Satan's daughter, shouts: "O father, what intends thy hand, she cried, Against thy only son?" (2.727–728). The poetry tickles not only the imagination, but also invites the connection to the poet's own faith in a God who gave His only Son, who won the victory over death, over sin, and yes, even over temptation. Our God Jesus leads no one into temptation, as James reminds us. He resisted the temptations of the devil by God's Word, and He did it for all sinners who would be tempted. And with His strong Word, He now leads us sinners *out* of temptation, reminding us that we belong in His family, not the family of the devil. Indeed, the picture that faith gives us is one of God together with His one big happy family—which began with the birth of His only Son Jesus and continues into eternity with the new birth of you, His child, inheriting that identity through faith in Christ. • Lord God, I know that You tempt no one, but I pray that You would guard and keep me so that the devil, the world, and my flesh may not deceive me nor seduce me. Make me attentive to Your Word that I may rest in the knowledge that in Jesus Christ, Your Son, I have become Your dear child. Amen.

Birth by the implanted Word (1:17–21)

ESV	KJV
¹⁷Every good gift and every perfect gift is from above, coming down from the Father of lights with whom there is no variation or shadow due to change. ¹⁸Of his own will he brought us forth by the word of truth, that we should be a kind of firstfruits of his creatures. ¹⁹Know this, my beloved brothers: let every person be quick to hear, slow to speak, slow to anger; ²⁰for the anger of man does not produce the righteousness of God. ²¹Therefore put away all filthiness and rampant wickedness and receive with meekness the implanted word, which is able to save your souls.	¹⁷Every good gift and every perfect gift is from above, and cometh down from the Father of lights, with whom is no variableness, neither shadow of turning. ¹⁸Of his own will begat he us with the word of truth, that we should be a kind of firstfruits of his creatures. ¹⁹Wherefore, my beloved brethren, let every man be swift to hear, slow to speak, slow to wrath: ²⁰For the wrath of man worketh not the righteousness of God. ²¹Wherefore lay apart all filthiness and superfluity of naughtiness, and receive with meekness the engrafted word, which is able to save your souls.

1:17 *Every good gift and every perfect gift.* In this next section, the author once again plays on words he has brought up before. The giver-God gives gifts. James uses two Gk synonyms (*dosis* and *dōrēma*), which are translated by the same English word, gift. Both words derive ultimately from the Gk verb *didōmi*, "give"). The gifts God delivers have already been noted in v. 5 (wisdom), v. 9 (exaltation), and continue in this section in v. 18 (new birth as the firstfruits of His creatures). As a central theme of the work, it is fitting that the pattern of words in Gk for "every good and perfect gift" is set as poetry. The line very closely approximates a dactylic hexameter (easily recognizable by the ear, and the loftiest meter of Greek poetry), suggesting the author consciously intended to draw attention to the gifts given by this giver-God. *Father of lights.* God created light as the first of His creations (Gn 1:3–5, 14–19), and His creative work continues by His almighty Word, with *no variation or shadow due to change*. The author invites the reader to find comfort in the promise of God's unchangeable character, which He reveals as the Father of lights, who gives good gifts from above. Linking God's creative power in the image of light with the next verse's emphasis on this God bringing us forth as a kind of firstfruits argues for a baptismal image, a location for the Christian's comfort.

1:18 *brought us forth*. The verb is the same as that used in v. 15 to describe the death that sin brings forth. James's wordplay is on display once again in a parallelism. Here it is used as a means to reinforce how distinct the giver-God's work is in the believer, in comparison to the natural progression of temptation. The analogy to birth is in common with other references to new life in Christ through Baptism; indeed, vv. 17–18 encapsulate quite an image of a cosmic birth. James has introduced this as the work of the "Father of lights" (v. 17), the author of the first creation (Gn 1:3, 14–16), who in new creation gives gifts "from above." Jesus uses the same adverb (Gk *anōthen*) to describe new life to Nicodemus in Jn 3:3, 7; James will use the adverb again to describe the wisdom that comes from above in 3:15, 17. Joining the language of enlightenment with new birth in Baptism is common in Christian tradition. For example, in the sixth century, Cassiodorus Senator wrote, "By holy Baptism he declared us to be begotten, freely, not by meriting, so that by a new restoration we might be born into his family" (*Complexiones in epistulis Apostolorum* Jac 3, *MPL* 70, p. 1377). Bede, writing in the eighth century, said, "God has transformed us from being sons of darkness into sons of light, not by any of our own merits, but by the kindness of his own will, through the water of regeneration." (*De Jacobi Epistola, MPL* 93:15). Bengel wrote:

> In each word there is a metaphor taken from the stars, and used with singular propriety in this passage, where mention is made of lights. . . . [there is] a daily vicissitude of day and might, and has at one time a greater length of day, at another time a greater length of night; but there is nothing of this kind in God. He is pure, unsullied [nothing but] Light. (Bengel 9)

firstfruits. As the first and best of the harvest, these were offered to God in sacrifice (Ex 22:29; 23:19). In the NT, Christians are the "harvest" of the preaching of the Gospel: Paul talks about the first converts in Asia and Achaia as such (Rm 16:5; 1Co 16:15). Christ is the firstfruits of resurrection (1Co 15:20, 23), and through His creative power, God has recreated a people for Himself, restoring all creation in the risen Christ, beginning with "ourselves, who have the firstfruits of the Spirit" and "groan inwardly as we wait eagerly for adoption as sons, the redemption of our bodies. For in this hope we were saved" (Rm 8:23–24).

1:1–18 in Devotion and Prayer The last two verses of this Letter's opening section climax on a note that is key for understanding God's character: He is the God who gives, and His gifts are perfect. He is the giver-God. This "Father of lights" gives more than the sun and moon and stars, gifts of the created order. Unwavering in His promises, He gives Himself for people scattered throughout the world. Embracing Jew and Gentile, rich and poor alike, this is the God who gives salvation to those who lack, who need, who receive His gifts by faith. He brings forth Jesus as fulfillment of that character. His unchangeableness is good news for those who waver in faith. It is applied to believers in the unchangeable promise of Baptism, by which He brings forth children who live confidently in a changing world, because of God's grace. • "To all life Thou givest—to both great and small—in all life Thou livest, the true Life of all; we blossom and flourish as leaves on the tree And wither and perish—but naught changes Thee." Amen. (*LSB* 802:3; *H82* 423:3; *TPH* 263:3; *TUMH* 103:3)

1:19 The last three verses of this section conclude James's argument with a clarion call to wisdom: be in the know! And as true wisdom is the gift given by the giver-God (v. 5), the reader is directed to find this true wisdom in His Holy Word. In order to *hear* it, the believer must be *slow to speak*, a theme James will expand on in v. 26 and 3:1–12. The believer must also be *slow to anger*, having the very character of God who is described this way so many times in the OT, first in Ex 34:6–7: "The LORD passed before him and proclaimed, 'The LORD, the LORD, a God merciful and gracious, slow to anger, and abounding in steadfast love and faithfulness, keeping steadfast love for thousands, forgiving iniquity and transgression and sin, but who will by no means clear the guilty, visiting the iniquity of the fathers on the children and the children's children, to the third and the fourth generation." Because it is the character of God, being slow to anger is also a mark of the wisdom of man (cf. Pr 14:29; 15:18; 16:32; 19:11).

1:20 James parenthetically offers a reason to avoid anger: wisdom is to lead the believer to the *righteousness of God*. The Gk word for righteousness, *dikaiosynē*, is also translated as "justification" throughout the NT. What does James mean here? The answer can become confused because the word is used with a couple different senses in the NT. Moreover, "justification" and "righteousness" are watchwords in the Lutheran tradition, which boldly proclaims justification by grace alone, through faith alone. This fact may tempt a reader to stand on a false assumption of a monolithic English meaning and not to appreciate the nuances present in the language of the Bible. The NT talks about the "righteousness" of God as an attribute of God Himself—He is the just one, He is the righteous one—and the quality of being righteous is an expectation of holy people as well (e.g., in Mt 1:19, Joseph is described as "just" or "righteous," as are Zechariah and Elizabeth in Lk 1:6; Jesus warns His listeners that unless their "righteousness exceeds that of the scribes and Pharisees, you will never enter the kingdom of heaven," Mt 5:20). But the NT also talks about the "righteousness" of God as something that is credited to people: Abraham believed God, and it was credited to him as righteousness (Gn 15:6), an OT example Paul uses several times to underscore the sole means by which sinners are forensically declared righteous before God. This declaration of righteousness is most often rendered by the English translations "justify" and "justification." Cf. Paul's argument in Romans, where he introduces the theme of the Letter as the righteousness of God revealed in the Gospel that is by faith (Rm 1:17, 3:22) and then renders the same word to describe the sinner declared righteous by God as "justified by His grace as a gift, through the redemption that is in Christ Jesus" (Rm 3:24). God counts as "righteous" those who are found in Christ, those who trust in the sufficient death and glorious resurrection of Jesus for their salvation. God then calls and empowers them to live in His righteousness instead of the world's pattern. James and the Gospels typically use this meaning of "righteousness": the new condition in which Christians live as the result of being justified by faith, a use that is consistent in Paul as well (cf. Rm 6:13: "Do not present your members to sin as instruments for unrighteousness, but present yourselves to God as those who have been brought from death to life, and your members to God as instruments for righteousness." (Cf. also Ap IV 72; and FC Ep III 7–8.) A firm grasp of the nuances in this biblical word will also shape our understanding of 2:21, which out of context sounds as if Scripture affirms salvation by works. In fact, James's argument is that Abraham was shown to be righteous by the things he did—which followed his being declared righteous by faith! Sensitivity to context is the essential tool when making distinctions between possible meanings; James's argument in this section is not immediately interested in the nuance of forensic declaration, but rather what holy living looks like.

1:21 *meekness.* James reaches back to v. 12 to summarize the section with another beatitude word. Blessed is the man who endures trial, and blessed are the meek, not only because they will inherit the earth (Mt 5:5), but because it is the humble believer who can receive the alien, external, *implanted word* as a gift from the giver-God. "Implanted" recalls the rich tradition of agricultural motifs in Jesus' parables, of which the parable of the sower (Mt 13:3–9, 18–23) is particularly apt in this context. The Word sown, here "implanted," is the external Word of truth that James describes as giving the believer new birth in v. 18. The received Word is connected with salvation (cf. Eph 1:13: "In Him you also, when you heard the word of truth, the gospel of your salvation, and believed in Him, were sealed;" 1Co 15:1–2: "Now I would remind you, brothers, of the gospel I preached to you, which you received, in which you stand, and by which you are being saved, if you hold fast to the word I preached to you—unless you believed in vain"). The implanted Word not only declares the believer righteous, but also instructs in doing what believers do, as will be commanded in the following verse. As such, the Word is a Word of both Gospel and Law.

PART 3

WORKS DONE BY THOSE IN WHOM THE WORD HAS BEEN PLANTED (1:22–2:26)

Consistency of Word and Deed (1:22–2:13)

The cause of inconsistency (1:22–25)

ESV	KJV
22But be doers of the word, and not hearers only, deceiving yourselves. 23For if anyone is a hearer of the word and not a doer, he is like a man who looks intently at his natural face in a mirror. 24For he looks at himself and goes away and at once forgets what he was like. 25But the one who looks into the perfect law, the law of liberty, and perseveres, being no hearer who forgets but a doer who acts, he will be blessed in his doing.	22But be ye doers of the word, and not hearers only, deceiving your own selves. 23For if any be a hearer of the word, and not a doer, he is like unto a man beholding his natural face in a glass: 24For he beholdeth himself, and goeth his way, and straightway forgetteth what manner of man he was. 25But whoso looketh into the perfect law of liberty, and continueth therein, he being not a forgetful hearer, but a doer of the work, this man shall be blessed in his deed.

Introduction to 1:22–2:13 A philosopher friend of mine once regaled me with the following anecdote: "I was dining at a restaurant with a friend who happened to be an expert in the philosophical field of ethics. After our meal was done and we had paid the check, my friend slipped the silverware from the table into his attaché case, invisible to the waitstaff but in full sight of me. When he saw my shocked expression, he calmly replied, 'I only *teach* ethics.'"

Such a disconnect between knowledge and action seems to be at work in the congregation to whom James preaches in this Letter. The following verses argue that true religion receives God's Word as more than mere trivia, and faith as more than mere intellectual acknowledgement. Faith is rather a transformative gift that leads to application, demonstration of which constitutes true religion. One of the most striking images in James makes the point initially: no one forgets his own face after looking in a mirror, and likewise looking into the perfect Law of God transforms believers into doers of the word (1:23–25). Such transformation by God, who loves both the mind and the body, affects attitude as well as action, serving the body of Christ and realizing that the kingdom of God operates distinctly from the evil ways of the world (1:26–27). James offers a practical example for the congregation he has in mind: discrimination between the rich and the poor (2:1–7). The negative example he offers is far more than simple, practical advice of what to do or not do. Rather James uses it as a springboard to affirm the nature of the "royal law of scripture" (2:8)—the one who is guilty of breaking it in part is guilty of breaking it all. Therefore believers are called to show mercy rather than discrimination (2:9–13).

1:22–23 *Be doers . . . not hearers only.* One basic distinction between Law and Gospel is the subject of the action: Gospel refers uniquely to those things that God Himself moves and promises on behalf of His creation for their salvation, while Law implies a human subject who does the things God commands. To be a "doer" of the word, then, implies that James has the Law particularly in mind with this command.

1:23–24 *looks . . . in a mirror.* The analogy James uses to make his point taps into the root of the hearer's identity. Lutherans are used to thinking about the "mirror" as the "second use of the Law," reflecting our sins back at us and reducing us in contrition to acknowledge the accuracy of the Law's accusation. However, the reflection is not only damning because it points out violation of God's commands; the mirror also reflects back the new birth, reminding believers of their new identity in Christ, which is one of His implanted righteousness. This is precisely the illustration James employs to deliver his point: Christians' deeds are coextensive with their identity. One who has received the "implanted word . . . able to save" (v. 21) will do deeds of righteousness. Deeds of death are alien to the new life won in Christ and applied to the believer in Holy Baptism (Rm 6:1–4, 13), so someone who leaves the perfect image seen in the mirror of God's Word and does not live a righteous life as taught in the Word turns away from righteousness.

1:25 God's word is the *perfect . . . law of liberty*, not just perfect ("flawless") in itself, but energetic, creative, effective to make perfect as well. The Gk word translated "perfect" (*teleios*) recalls that God makes complete by this same word the one who *perseveres* (v. 4). In calling the Word a *law of liberty*, the author recalls once again the distinction between Law and Gospel. Here James reminds us that the Word is one, that the Law is also the counsel of God whose Law/Gospel Word works *liberty* (cf. Gal 5:1, 13). James uses the phrase once again at 2:12 (cf. note there). Wesley wrote regarding the perfect law of liberty that it is love established by faith:

> St. James here guards us against misunderstanding what St. Paul says concerning the "yoke and bondage of the law." He who keeps the law of love is free, John 8:31, &c. He that does not, is not free, but a slave to sin, and a criminal before God, James 2:10. (Wesley 599)

Examples of inconsistency (1:26–2:7)

ESV	KJV
²⁶If anyone thinks he is religious and does not bridle his tongue but deceives his heart, this person's religion is worthless. ²⁷Religion that is pure and undefiled before God, the Father, is this: to visit orphans and widows in their affliction, and to keep oneself unstained from the world. 2 ¹My brothers, show no partiality as you hold the faith in our Lord Jesus Christ, the Lord of glory. ²For if a man wearing a gold ring and fine clothing comes into your assembly, and a poor man in shabby clothing also comes in, ³and if you pay attention to the one who wears the fine clothing and say, "You sit here in a	²⁶If any man among you seem to be religious, and bridleth not his tongue, but deceiveth his own heart, this man's religion is vain. ²⁷Pure religion and undefiled before God and the Father is this, To visit the fatherless and widows in their affliction, and to keep himself unspotted from the world. 2 ¹My brethren, have not the faith of our Lord Jesus Christ, the Lord of glory, with respect of persons. ²For if there come unto your assembly a man with a gold ring, in goodly apparel, and there come in also a poor man in vile raiment; ³And ye have respect to him that

good place," while you say to the poor man, "You stand over there," or, "Sit down at my feet," [4]have you not then made distinctions among yourselves and become judges with evil thoughts? [5]Listen, my beloved brothers, has not God chosen those who are poor in the world to be rich in faith and heirs of the kingdom, which he has promised to those who love him? [6]But you have dishonored the poor man. Are not the rich the ones who oppress you, and the ones who drag you into court? [7]Are they not the ones who blaspheme the honorable name by which you were called?

weareth the gay clothing, and say unto him, Sit thou here in a good place; and say to the poor, Stand thou there, or sit here under my footstool:
[4]Are ye not then partial in yourselves, and are become judges of evil thoughts?
[5]Hearken, my beloved brethren, Hath not God chosen the poor of this world rich in faith, and heirs of the kingdom which he hath promised to them that love him?
[6]But ye have despised the poor. Do not rich men oppress you, and draw you before the judgment seats?
[7]Do not they blaspheme that worthy name by the which ye are called?

1:26 *religious . . . religion.* Haven't we all met someone who is full of pious platitudes, perhaps even impressive in the church with the holy speech that comes out of his or her lips? James is consistent with the lesson of the OT that God is not impressed with "talking the talk" but rather with "walking the walk" (cf. Is 29:13; Mt 15:7–9).

James personifies the seemingly religious person with a colorful image, one whose *tongue* is unbridled, that is, one whose tongue is allowed to run wild (we might think about the proverbial "bull in a china shop"). The caution here recalls his warning to be "slow to speak" (v. 19), and he devotes much more space to expand on this woe in 3:1–12. The one who does not control his tongue *deceives his heart*, that is, he deceives himself, since he considers himself to be righteous—this is self-righteousness, not righteousness given by the giver-God.

1:27 *Religion* (Gk *thrēskeia*) may be defined variously as a set of rites and ceremonies, a movement, a set of beliefs, or other things. But according to James, such things fail to confess what pure and undefiled religion actually is. In James, religion is rather the deeds a person does because of his beliefs. Such pure and undefiled religion is consistent with the character of God revealed in the OT ethic of taking care of the fatherless, the widow, and the alien in the midst of God's people (cf. Dt 10:18, 14:29, 16:11, 24:19; Hos 14:3; Lk 7:11–17).

As repeated in Luther's *Small Catechism*, the law James articulates in this verse is a call to fear and love God through avoiding certain actions as well as doing others. The world is noted here as an enemy of the Christian, from which God's people are to remain *unstained*, as its values oppose true religion; cf. 1Jn 2:15–17: "Do not love the world or the things in the world. If anyone loves the world, the love of the Father is not in him. For all that is in the world—the desires of the flesh and the desires of the eyes and pride of life—is not from the Father but is from the world. And the world is passing away along with its desires, but whoever does the will of God abides forever."

1:19–27 in Devotion and Prayer Slow to speak, quick to listen, and deliberate in service: these are the marks of saints who find their righteousness not in their own words, ideas, or wisdom, but in the Word. Righteousness delivered by that Word is righteousness received for holy action, particularly in Christian fellowship, a kingdom built by Christ of the forgotten, the disfranchised, the humble poor. Culminating in verse 27, James defines true religion in this kingdom. The English word "religion" is connected etymologically with other words like "ligature" and "obligation," which reveals something consistent with James's point here: religion "binds" us to God and one another. John Fawcett's English hymn "Blest Be the Tie That Binds" gets at the meaning in this verse well: • "We share our mutual woes, Our mutual burdens bear, And often for each other flows the sympathizing tear." Amen. (*LSB* 649:3; *TPH* 438:3; *TUMH* 557:3)

2:1 James commands the congregation not to show *partiality*, which means choosing between persons based on worldly criteria. God shows no partiality (Rm 2:9–11), or as we might say, "He is not a respecter of persons." God's people are to act similarly in reflection of His character. James front-loads this qualification for how God's people are called to hold on to the faith in our Lord Jesus and concludes the thought with a creedal statement: He is the *Lord of glory*. This glorious Lordship is demonstrated through His victorious resurrection and exaltation, as the Christ makes clear in the Emmaus narrative of Lk 24:26. *Glory* recalls also the nature of the "Father of lights" (1:17) and so associates the attributes of the unchanging Father with the Son. Since God shows no partiality, so ought the Christian not be easily shifted from righteous dealing to discrimination. Bengel wrote:

The Glory is Christ Himself. Thus James both declares Him to be the Son of God, and publishes His resurrection from the dead, as it becomes an apostle. Christ is Glory; and therefore faith in Him is glorious, and the faithful are glorious. This glory of the faithful is far above all worldly honour; no respecter of persons acknowledges it. (Bengel 13)

2:2–4 James continues with an example of a worldly criterion for discrimination and partiality: the treatment of the rich and the poor (cf. 1:9–10). If there is any truth to the proverbial "clothing makes the man," James capitalizes on it in his descriptions. The rich man in his example is clothed in *fine clothing* and wearing a *ring* on his finger (Gk *khrysodaktylios*, literally "gold-fingered"). The poor man, in contrast, is dressed in shabby clothing (echoed in v. 15 where "poorly clothed," translates the Gk word *gymnos*, literally "naked"; cf. note at 2:15). In the first-century synagogue James has in mind, as often in our own day, a person's appearance communicates his social status. Status is also reflected in basic customs of hospitality. To sit *at my feet* is to be accorded the lowest station, as opposed to the head of the table (cf. Lk 14:7–11). To make such *distinctions* based on social class is to become *judges with evil thoughts*. The root of the word in each case (Gk *krisis*, judgment) can also be rendered "discrimination," a telling play on words by James in this context. Such discrimination is evil, not because it is politically incorrect in our day and age, but because it is contrary to God's kingdom, in which He gives gifts to poor and rich alike, specifically the status they exult in: the humble state of the rich and the exaltation of the poor, which James has described in 1:9–10.

2:5 *has not God chosen those who are poor.* The initial beatitude of the Sermon on the Mount (Mt 5.3) is "Blessed are the poor in spirit, for theirs is the kingdom of heaven." The teaching is radically unique to the NT, expressing a view of God's kingdom, in contradistinction to the kingdom of the world, that still is seen today. It may be helpful to consider this teaching according to the opposites or paradoxes outlined in the words of Christ, e.g., Lk 1:51–53, 2Co 6:8–10. (Cf. Mt 19:30, "many who are first will be last, and the last first.") James introduces an extended comparison of rich and poor with this wisdom formula of the beatitude, and his rhetorical question frames a truth expressed so often in the Reformation church regarding the theology of the cross. In the *Heidelberg Disputation*, Luther said,

A theology of glory calls evil good and good evil. A theology of the cross calls the thing what it actually is. This is clear: He who does not know Christ does not know God hidden in suffering. Therefore he prefers works to suffering, glory to the cross, strength to weakness, wisdom to folly, and, in general, good to evil. These are the people whom the apostle calls "enemies of the cross of Christ" [Phil. 3:18], for they hate the cross and suffering and love works and the glory of works. Thus they call the good of the cross evil and the evil of a deed good. God can be found only in suffering and the cross, as has already been said. Therefore the friends of the cross say that the cross is good and works are evil, for through the cross works are dethroned and the old Adam, who is especially edified by works, is crucified. It is impossible for a person not to be puffed up by his good works unless he has first been deflated and destroyed by suffering and evil until he knows that he is worthless and that his works are not his but God's. (LW 31:53)

heirs. While an earthly heir would receive a family estate or plot of ground, the inheritance given here is nothing less than *the kingdom*, for the Father has established a relationship with His people through adoption (cf. Gal 4:1–7). The kingdom of God is therefore both a present reality and future hope, present on earth as God hides in the cross of Christ (Col 1:12–14, 3:3–4), and also the promised future inheritance of the Christian, where we will live with Him and receive the crown of life as James has stated earlier (1:12).

2:6–7 The three rhetorical questions that follow James's accusation of dishonoring the poor are intended to shame the whole community, and they build in a crescendo that climaxes with a reference to blasphemy. Discrimination that favors the rich is therefore not simply a matter of social ill; it is an idolatrous evil. James reminds the community that it is the *rich* who *oppress you*, who *drag you into court*, a word that recalls Paul's shame for the Corinthian church regarding lawsuits among believers (1Co 6:1–8).

2:7 *blaspheme the honorable name.* The climax of James's rhetorical questions focuses on the name of Christ, the Lord of glory invoked in v.1. Discrimination that honors the rich over the poor discredits the *name by which you were called.* The passive participle of this verb is used elsewhere in the NT only parenthetically in Acts (4:36, 10:18, 11:13, 12:12, 12:25) to identify the other name by which someone is known (e.g., Simon called Peter, John called Mark).

James uses the formula to remind his readers that Christ's name is the name that identifies them, the name that has been invoked over them. The significance of Christ's name being at issue, rather than a simple social distinction between rich and poor, extends the argument James employs regarding the baptismal identity of the believer (cf. notes at 1:17, 1:18, 1:23–24).

Inconsistency results in condemnation (2:8–13)

ESV	KJV
[8]If you really fulfill the royal law according to the Scripture, "You shall love your neighbor as yourself," you are doing well. [9]But if you show partiality, you are committing sin and are convicted by the law as transgressors. [10]For whoever keeps the whole law but fails in one point has become accountable for all of it. [11]For he who said, "Do not commit adultery," also said, "Do not murder." If you do not commit adultery but do murder, you have become a transgressor of the law. [12]So speak and so act as those who are to be judged under the law of liberty. [13]For judgment is without mercy to one who has shown no mercy. Mercy triumphs over judgment.	[8]If ye fulfil the royal law according to the scripture, Thou shalt love thy neighbour as thyself, ye do well: [9]But if ye have respect to persons, ye commit sin, and are convinced of the law as transgressors. [10]For whosoever shall keep the whole law, and yet offend in one point, he is guilty of all. [11]For he that said, Do not commit adultery, said also, Do not kill. Now if thou commit no adultery, yet if thou kill, thou art become a transgressor of the law. [12]So speak ye, and so do, as they that shall be judged by the law of liberty. [13]For he shall have judgment without mercy, that hath shewed no mercy; and mercy rejoiceth against judgment.

2:8–10 James moves in this section from the specific transgression of being a respecter of persons (discrimination that favored the rich over the poor, vv. 1–7) to the heart of the matter: the *royal law* or the "law of the kingdom" (cf. v. 5). Just as in Jesus' teaching about the kingdom of heaven, so here James magnifies the scope of the law to demonstrate its universality. *Partiality* is simply one example among many transgressions listed in Lv 19, and James argues that this is connected to the larger principle which summarizes that catalogue of transgressions as he quotes Lv 19:18: *you shall love your neighbor as yourself.* James sets up the sentence in these two verses with a parallelism of contrast: you fulfill the command to love your neighbor? Great! But you show partiality? Now you've broken the law—not just this one, but all of them! This is a hallmark of Jesus' teaching on the Law (cf. Mt 22:39, Lk 10:25–37), on the one hand magnifying the scope of God's Law to such a degree that man is shown utterly incapable of fulfilling it himself, and on the other hand demonstrating that Jesus alone is the fulfilment of the Law.

2:10–11 James's aim in these verses is to point out the sinner's inability to fulfill the law. The specific commandments considered here are intended to illustrate the principle of v. 10, that breaking one law renders one guilty of breaking all of it. While the teaching is consistent throughout the NT (cf. Mt 5:18–19, Rm 2:17–29, Rm 7:10–13, Gal 3:10, Gal 5:3), the examples James employs are the particular focus of Jesus at the beginning of the Sermon on the Mount as recorded in Mt 5:21–26 (murder) and Mt 5:27–32 (adultery). Just as Jesus magnifies the Law's scope with His "you have heard it said . . . but I say to you," so also James's audience is confronted with the sobering truth that while protesting fulfillment of one feature of the Law, other infractions are impossible to avoid (and they leave one with no excuse, cf. Rm 2:1–3). Calvin wrote:

> This sentence seems hard to some, as though the Apostle countenanced the paradox of the Stoics, which makes all sins equal, and as though he asserted that he who offends in one thing ought to be punished equally with him whose whole life has been sinful and wicked. But it is evident from the context that no such thing entered into his mind.

> For we must always observe the reason why anything is said. He denies that our neighbours are loved, when a part only of them is through ambition chosen, and the rest neglected. This he proves, because it is no obedience to God, when it is not rendered equally according to his command. Then as the rule of God is plain and complete or perfect, so we ought to regard completeness; so that none of us should presumptuously separate what he has joined together. Let there be, therefore, a uniformity, if we desire rightly to obey God. As, for instance, were a judge to punish ten thefts, and leave one man unpunished, he would betray the obliquity of his mind, for he would thus shew himself indignant against men rather than against crimes; because what he condemns in one he absolves in another. (Calvin 306)

2:12 At 1:25, James names the *law of liberty* "perfect" (Gk *teleios*, "completed"); the words here recall the earlier usage (the only other instance of the phrase in the NT), and the context of these last several verses likewise points to the completion, or fulfillment, of the Law in Christ. Forasmuch as the Law has been magnified in scope by James's argument in vv. 8–11, rendering it impossible for a sinner to fulfill, v. 12 exhorts the reader to *speak* and *act* not in light of guilt, shame, and threat, but rather as a response to the gift given by the giver-God. Here, as in 1:25, the law of liberty refers to the Gospel. *To be judged* according to this law is, as in Mt 25:34ff., to hear the King say "Come, you who are blessed by My Father, inherit the kingdom. . . . As you did it to one of the least of these My brothers you did it to Me."

2:13 James concludes the section with two final aphorisms relating to *judgment* and *mercy*. While "one who has shown no mercy" may recall the description of the rich over against the poor at the beginning of this chapter, taken together the thoughts are most reminiscent of Jesus' parable of the unmerciful servant (Mt 18:23–35). The final word on the matter for a Peter who would ask in Mt 18:21, "Lord, how often will my brother sin against me, and I forgive him? As many as seven times?" is the same as the final word on the matter in this section from James: *Mercy triumphs over judgment*, a mercy fulfilled in and distributed through Christ, giving the believer confidence at the final judgment.

2:1–13 in Devotion and Prayer Scriptures that emphasize the nature of the Law, and how God relates to sinners through it, can be read at least three ways. First, on the face of it, there is simply information: whoever would keep it whole, but trips in one part, is guilty of breaking it all! A second way would be a way of encouragement: perhaps James is encouraging, exhorting, or even expecting that his readers ought to be able to keep the Law whole and entire? On reflection, of course, faced with God's holy Law, the fallen human is incapable of fulfilling its demands. So the third way is the way of confession. "Reflection" in devotion and prayer is indeed first the "reflection" of the mirror that accuses sinners of being wholly unrighteous. But in Christ, sinners are at the same time saints, not trusting in how perfectly *we* keep the Law of God, but trusting rather in the One who did on our behalf. Trust that, in Christ, who took God's righteous judgment for your sin to His cross, you now receive from Him "mercy that triumphs over judgment." • Almighty God, whose compassion never fails and who invites us to call upon You in prayer, hear the heartfelt confession of our sins and receive our humble supplication for Your mercy. Spare us from the just punishment of sin, which our Lord Jesus Christ has borne for us, and enable us to serve You in holiness and purity of life; through Jesus Christ, our Lord, who lives and reigns with You and the Holy Spirit, one God, now and forever. Amen. (Collect for Day of Supplication and Prayer, *LSB Altar Book*, 992)

Living Faith (2:14–26)

Faith leads to action (2:14–19)

ESV	KJV
[14]What good is it, my brothers, if someone says he has faith but does not have works? Can that faith save him? [15]If a brother or sister is poorly clothed and lacking in daily food, [16]and one of you says to them, "Go in peace, be warmed and filled," without giving them the things needed for the body, what good is that? [17]So also faith by itself, if it does not have works, is dead. [18]But someone will say, "You have faith and I have works." Show me your faith apart from your works, and I will show you my faith by my works. [19]You believe that God is one; you do well. Even the demons believe—and shudder!	[14]What doth it profit, my brethren, though a man say he hath faith, and have not works? can faith save him? [15]If a brother or sister be naked, and destitute of daily food, [16]And one of you say unto them, Depart in peace, be ye warmed and filled; notwithstanding ye give them not those things which are needful to the body; what doth it profit? [17]Even so faith, if it hath not works, is dead, being alone. [18]Yea, a man may say, Thou hast faith, and I have works: shew me thy faith without thy works, and I will shew thee my faith by my works. [19]Thou believest that there is one God; thou doest well: the devils also believe, and tremble.

Introduction to 2:14–26 This bit of Scripture is sufficiently provocative for Reformation figures to have been given pause, indeed scandalous enough for critics to take Luther's "epistle of straw" assessment as a grounds for attack. (See Luther on James, p. 5.) Luther's opinions on James changed throughout his career, but his concerns about some of the particular weaknesses of the Epistle (e.g., the absence of Christ and the focus on OT ethics, culminating in the same example of Abraham brought up in Rm 4, seemingly employed in James to make the opposite point of Paul's letter) were not unwarranted, as controversies related to both legalism and antinomianism grew out of the Reformation in reaction to this section of the Epistle.

The equally extreme and equally incorrect views of the Law's role in the Christian life—the two poles of legalism and antinomianism—are not the only problems at issue in this section of James. The reformers also faced the challenge of demonstrating clearly how James was to be understood regarding monergism or synergism, that is, the relationship between salvation and works, whether God works alone or whether human agency cooperates in salvation. Justification hangs in the balance in the midst of the relationship between faith and works, though we've already seen that "righteousness/justification" (Gk *dikaiosynē*) is a word nuanced throughout the NT. So how do works and righteousness relate? Distinctly? Synergistically (that is, "working together")? On first glance, it may seem ironic that orthodox Christianity would fight so diligently against synergism in its history (e.g., Augustine versus Pelagius or the Lutheran synergistic controversy which led to the confession of FC II), only to have Jas 2:24 staring one in the face at the end of the day ("You see that a person is justified by works"), and also 2:22 which proudly and positively employs the Gk word *synergeō* (from which we get synergism) to relate Abraham's faith and works! But it is our contention that James is more sly than sinister in this passage—he is not attempting to undercut, compromise, or contradict the rest of apostolic teaching, but rather addresses a misunderstanding about faith from the beginning of this section (v. 14) and therefore employs words nuanced accordingly.

2:14 James's words regarding *faith* have so far demonstrated the centrality of the theme to the entire Letter. Furthermore, they have reinforced the understanding that faith is trust in God's saving work in Christ. In 1:3 and 1:6, the context of trial and endurance brought to the surface the contrast between faith and doubt. In 2:1 and 2:5, James located faith by zeroing in on its object (our Lord Jesus Christ, the Lord of glory) and its recipients (those who are considered poor according to the world's standards, but who in God's kingdom are the greatest—these He chose to have faith). James now explores a hypothetical question about faith and deeds, in which a hypothetical *someone says he has faith*. But the definition of this person's *faith* (Gk *pistis*, the word commonly used throughout the NT to describe trust in God's saving work), is artificially disconnected from actions. The situation James suggests nuances the word "faith" into something distinct from the definition of trust in God's saving work as normally understood in the NT; the meaning in James's hypothetical situation is shaded closer to "confidence" or "demonstrable proof," the sort of definition that we might distinguish with the synonyms "knowledge" or "rational assent" rather than "faith" or "trust." This is the simple distinction James makes regarding the word faith in this verse—it is as if he is saying, "Let's make certain you know what I mean by faith (*pistis*). Because demons (cf. v. 19) can say they have *pistis*, that is, "knowledge" or "confidence" that God is one. Is that what your "faith" is? Real faith isn't mere intellectual assent; rather it is trust in the giver-God who gives you something to trust in!"

Two other points are worthy of remark in this verse. The first is James's artificial separation, for the sake of argument, of faith and *works*. The divorce of faith and works is unnatural, as if one could exist without the other. James has already made this point clear (1:22–25: don't just be hearers, be doers too! Don't be like a guy who forgets his own face in the mirror!), and so has Jesus (e.g., in Mt 23:1–6 and elsewhere) when He points out the hypocrisy of those whose actions do not match their teachings. Cf. AC XX 27: "It is necessary to do good works. This does not mean that we merit grace by doing good works, but because it is God's will."

The second point is James's assumption that faith is indeed somehow connected with salvation, as he asks, *Can that faith save him?* To the chagrin of the legalist, however, the force of James's rhetorical question is not to deny that faith saves; he is questioning rather the distinction between saving faith that results in action (e.g., care of the needy, as he transitions to at vv. 15–16) and intellectual assent that is self-justifying. James refers elsewhere to salvation at 1:21, 4:12, 5:15, and 5:20. Wesley wrote:

> From James 1:22, the apostle has been enforcing Christian practice. He now applies to those who neglect this, under the pretence of faith. St. Paul had taught that "a man is justified by faith without the works of the law." This some began already to wrest to their own destruction. Wherefore St. James, purposely repeating (Jas 2:21, 23, 25) the same phrases, testimonies, and examples,

which St. Paul had used, Rom 4:3, Heb 11:17, 31, refutes not the doctrine of St. Paul, but the error of those who abused it. There is, therefore, no contradiction between the apostles: they both delivered the truth of God, but in a different manner, as having to do with different kinds of men. On another occasion St. James himself pleaded the cause of faith, Acts 15:13–21; and St. Paul himself strenuously pleads for works, particularly in his latter epistles. (Wesley 600)

2:15–16 Two verses earlier, James had brought up judgment and mercy (cf. note at v. 13). These verses recall again the judgment of the sheep and goats (Mt 25:35–36), as the *poorly clothed* are literally "naked." The parallel is significant, as Jesus' teaching shows that those who have lived according to the calling of the faith given them on the one hand are unaware that they fed, clothed, and visited Jesus, and on the other hand that they did so "as you did it to one of the least of these my brothers" (Mt 25:40). Those on the left hand, who protest their good works ("when didn't we do this to you, Lord?") strive rather to protest what in their mind was true religion, parallel to James's *be warmed and filled*. But James has already connected hypocrisy with the tongue (1:25–26), an echo of this warning against lip service here in 2:16, and thereby sets up a similar contrast between false and true religion (cf. 1:26).

It is interesting that Calvin spent less space on this passage and issue than did other reformers who commented on it. (See his comments in the introduction.) Cranmer wrote:

> St. James assimileth him, that hath this faith only in his mouth, unto a man that pitieth his naked or hungry brother, and biddeth him go warm him, or fill his belly; and yet will give him neither clothes nor meat, wherewith he may warm him or feed his hungriness. What availeth this mercy spoken only with the tongue, when he showeth no mercy in deed, in relieving his brother's necessity? But St. James saith, So say, so do; for he shall not receive mercy of God that speaketh mercifully, except he hath the same in his heart to do it in deed. For the mercy that is not in the heart, dieth even in the mouth, and he shall have judgment without mercy that showeth not mercy in deed, how mercifully that ever he speak. And as the body is but dead that lacketh a soul, even so is that faith but dead that is but in the mouth, and doth not enter effectuously into the heart, and work accordingly. (Cranmer 2:68)

2:17 James, with the diagnostic skill of a physician, declares death in the situation where *faith* is simply intellectual assent or self-justifying lip service. This kind of "faith," which is really false confidence, is what he uses Gk *pistis* to describe also at v. 14 and v. 19. As at v. 14, the issue is the unnatural separation of faith from the fruit it naturally produces (cf. vv. 18, 26).

2:18 "Deeds, not creeds!" says my neighbor, when challenged about what his "non-denominational" American evangelical church teaches, or when she reacts to the foreignness of sitting through a historic liturgy, critical of the recitation of the Nicene Creed or any other distinctive element. So facile a distinction is at play as James brings up the hypothetical in this verse with *someone will say, "You have faith and I have works."* It's the opposite of the previous verse, which we might imagine expressed just as crassly or ridiculously, "Creeds, not deeds!" In other words, James condemns equally both the attitude that says "so long as one's teaching, one's doctrine, the object of one's confidence is pure and in the right place, there is no need for charity"; and on the other hand the attitude that says something just as ridiculous: "so long as I do good, moral things, then it doesn't matter what I believe." James argues that one cannot have right faith without the response of right works, nor can one do good works without faith.

Note that "authenticity" or "genuineness" is not at issue here in ch. 2. The author is not after a definition of a "real Christian" or a "genuine brother" or an "authentic follower." Rather, he is after a definition of faith that is comprehensive and distinct from the nuance of antinomians who would say their deeds no longer matter in light of their "faith" (*pistis*). To this kind of hubris and self-justification the Lord has one answer: "Depart from me, you cursed, into the eternal fire prepared for the devil and his angels" (Mt 25:41; cf. note at 2:15–16). This, in fact, is the goal to which James drives in the following verse as he brings up the intellectual assent and confidence of demons—which may be called *pistis* because of that nuance, but is certainly not saving faith. The difference between a living faith and a dead faith is not the believing subject, but the object of faith, and the deliverer of the gift of faith: God who implants the word of truth (1:21) which bears fruit in action (cf. 1:22–27). Cranmer wrote:

> If these fruits do not follow, we do but mock with God, deceive ourselves, and also other men. Well may we bear the name of

Christian men, but we do lack the true faith that doth belong thereunto: for true faith doth ever bring forth good works, as St. James saith: Shew me thy faith by thy deeds. Thy deeds and works must be an open testimonial of thy faith: otherwise thy faith, being without good works, is but the devil's faith, the faith of the wicked, a phantasy of faith, and not a true Christian faith. And like as the devils and evil people be nothing the better for their counterfeit faith, but it is unto them the more cause of damnation: so they that be christened, and have received knowledge of God, and of Christ's merits, and yet of a set purpose do live idly, without good works, thinking the name of a naked faith to be either sufficient for them, or else setting their minds upon vain pleasures of this world, do live in sin without repentance, not uttering the fruits that do belong to such an high profession; upon such presumptuous persons, and wilful sinners, must needs remain the great vengeance of God, and eternal punishment in hell, prepared for the devil and wicked livers. (Cranmer 2:162)

2:19 "Hear, O Israel: The LORD our God, the LORD is one" (Dt 6:4). These words, known as the Shema, are the OT's basic confession of faith. James employs it here in order to connect to his audience, which is most likely an early Christian congregation that identifies with its OT roots (cf. note at 1:1). It also forms the basis of early Christian confession, as it is consistent with Jesus' teaching (cf. Mk 12:29), as well as Paul's (cf. 1Co 8:6; Eph 4:4–6). So is James mocking the repetition of a foundational confession of faith when he says *you believe that God is one*? He does add an ironic *you do well*—"congratulations!" "good for you!"—before stabbing his audience with the punchline. But James's argument is not anti-creedal. Rather he is underscoring the insufficiency of a definition of "faith" as anything that relies on a self-justifying or intellectual assent: believing certain facts to be true is not the same as believing certain facts to be true for the benefit of one's salvation! After all, *even the demons believe* according to that limited understanding of acknowledging the facts about God's nature. This is not a saving faith, which is received as Gospel (with its "for you" emphasis), as Luther contends:

It will profit you nothing to believe that Christ was delivered for the sins of other saints and to doubt that He was delivered for your sins. For both the ungodly and the demons believe this (James 2:19). No, you must take for granted in steadfast confidence that He was delivered for your sins too, and that you are one of those for whose sins He was delivered. This faith justifies you; it will cause Christ to dwell, live, and reign in you. (LW 27:172)

False and dead faith produces no fruit; living and true faith does, as Luther says:

> O it is a living, busy, active, mighty thing, this [true] faith. It is impossible for it not to be doing good works incessantly. It does not ask whether good works are to be done, but before the question is asked, it has already done them, and is constantly doing them. Whoever does not do such works, however, is an unbeliever. He gropes and looks around for faith and good works, but knows neither what faith is nor what good works are. Yet he talks and talks, with many words, about faith and good works. (LW 35:370)

Cranmer wrote:

> For the more large declaration of the pure Christian faith, it is to be considered, that there is a general faith, which all that be Christian, as well good as evil, have: as, to believe that God is, that he is the Maker and Creator of all things, and that Christ is the Saviour and Redeemer of the world, and for his sake all penitent sinners have remission of their sins; and that there shall be a general resurrection at the end of this mortal world, at the which Christ shall judge all the good to joy without end, and the evil to pain without end; with such other like things. Arid all these things even the devils also believe, and tremble, for fear and grievousness of God's indignation and torments, which they endure and ever shall do. But they have not the right Christian faith, that their own sins by Christ's redemption be pardoned and forgiven, that themselves by Christ be delivered from God's wrath, and be made his beloved children, and heirs of his kingdom to come. The other faith have all devils and wicked Christian people, that be his members; but this pure Christian faith have none, but those that truly belong to Christ, and be the very members of his body, and endeavour themselves to persevere in his precepts and laws: although many pretend to have the said pure faith, which nevertheless have it not, but only in their mouths. For as there is a love in the mouth, and a love in the heart, even so there is a faith in mouth and a faith in heart. Examine every man, if he trust in God and love God above all things; and in words, he will answer, yea; but examine every man's acts and deeds, and surely in a great number their acts and deeds condemn their words. (Cranmer 2:67)

51

Examples of faith (2:20–26)

ESV	KJV
²⁰Do you want to be shown, you foolish person, that faith apart from works is useless? ²¹Was not Abraham our father justified by works when he offered up his son Isaac on the altar? ²²You see that faith was active along with his works, and faith was completed by his works; ²³and the Scripture was fulfilled that says, "Abraham believed God, and it was counted to him as righteousness"—and he was called a friend of God. ²⁴You see that a person is justified by works and not by faith alone. ²⁵And in the same way was not also Rahab the prostitute justified by works when she received the messengers and sent them out by another way? ²⁶For as the body apart from the spirit is dead, so also faith apart from works is dead.	²⁰But wilt thou know, O vain man, that faith without works is dead? ²¹Was not Abraham our father justified by works, when he had offered Isaac his son upon the altar? ²²Seest thou how faith wrought with his works, and by works was faith made perfect? ²³And the scripture was fulfilled which saith, Abraham believed God, and it was imputed unto him for righteousness: and he was called the Friend of God. ²⁴Ye see then how that by works a man is justified, and not by faith only. ²⁵Likewise also was not Rahab the harlot justified by works, when she had received the messengers, and had sent them out another way? ²⁶For as the body without the spirit is dead, so faith without works is dead also.

2:20 James virtually repeats v. 17 here (cf. note), but the main differences include the use of the preposition *apart from*, which reminds the reader that his argument is not, "which one is better, works or faith?" Rather, he points out here, at the head of his examples, that the real problem in attempting to quantify or evaluate faith and works is the separation itself: you get them wrong if you pull them apart! One other main difference between v. 20 and v. 17 is the use here of the adjective "useless" instead of "dead" (in the ESV; the KJV repeats the word "dead"). As opposed to Gk *nekra* (dead) in v. 17 (which James will repeat at v. 26), the word in v. 20 is Gk *argē* (*a + ergon*, or "no-work," fruitless, useless), a word that puns on the point of his sentence: it is as if James is saying "Faith, without works, doesn't work!" On the separation of faith and works in his argument thus far, cf. notes at vv. 14 and 19.

2:21, 25 As in 1:20, so in this context James's argument is not focused on *justified* according to the nuance of forensic declaration. Nowhere in James's argument does he aim at proving that God's declaration of righteousness is based on human actions. He uses the word *justified* here and in 2:24 to describe rather what holy living looks like, and the word can mean "shown to be righteous," "recognized as righteous," or "to live as a righteous person" (see note on 1:20). Jesus uses it in this way in Mt 11:19: "The Son of Man came eating and drinking, and they say, 'Look at Him! A glutton and a drunkard, a friend of tax collectors and sinners!' Yet wisdom is justified by her deeds." He uses the word in the same way in Mt 12:36–37: "I tell you, on the day of judgment people will give account for every careless word they speak, for by your words you will be justified, and by your words you will be condemned." James is saying, in effect, "Was not Abraham our father shown to be a righteous person when he *offered up his son Isaac on the altar?*" The episode of the sacrifice is recorded in Gn 22, which transpires well after the declaration of righteousness connected to Abraham's faith in Gn 15:6 (which James quotes in 2:23).

The example James offers in Abraham is problematic on a different level than the one interested in the priority of faith versus works. Notice what is being considered righteous: filicide ought to provoke a different reaction than "yep, that proves it, he's a man after God's own heart." The example of Rahab (v. 25) is no better, really: she welcomed messengers (according to her chosen profession!) and betrayed her country. Murderous father on the one hand, sneaky Gentile whore on the other. The point is, had James wanted to argue about the necessity of moral actions and holy works as a precondition of God's declaration of righteousness, he could have argued with examples that paralleled better the moral commands he just summarized in the "mercy triumphs over discrimination" section at the beginning of ch. 2. After all, when commanding respect for the poor, the fatherless, the widow, the homeless, James could have mined the OT and come up with stories of kindness and piety less troublesome than the ones he chooses. The penitence of David, for example, or the humility of Jeremiah, the conviction of Joshua or the submission of Ruth all would have been sound, pious choices. Instead, he goes for examples that are arguably problematic: a matter as controversial as human sacrifice (of one's own child!) and the extraordinary tale of a duplicitous Gentile prostitute. Notice, however, where faith is located for each of these examples. Abraham's faith is not located in own abilities and efforts, but rather in God's words and power (Gn 15:6, trusting God's promise about his children being innumerable, leading him to trust that he would receive Isaac back from death; cf. Rm 4; Heb 11:17–19). Rahab's faith is not located in her own cleverness, but rather in the report of the miraculous salvation of the Israelites: "For we have heard how the LORD dried up the water of the Red Sea before you when you came out of Egypt, and what you did to the two kings of the Amorites who were beyond the Jordan, to Sihon and Og, whom you devoted to destruction. And as soon as we heard it, our hearts melted, and there was no spirit left in any man because of you, for the LORD your God, He is God in the heavens above and on the earth beneath" (Jsh 2:10–11). Abraham's faith and Rahab's faith are both located in the Word of God. Their actions are reactions to the saving work of God. They are, therefore, demonstrations or fruits of faith.

This may indeed be the point of this bit of Scripture: to draw two deliciously ridiculous illustrations of "deeds" of faith that demonstrate righteous living, in order to underscore the point that true faith is interested not in mere intellectual assent and satisfaction in worldly wisdom, but rather in a God whose worldview is topsy-turvy compared to the rest of the world. After all, this giver-God is the Father of lights, a Father of creative power, a God whose nature or characteristic is, as Luther avers in *Seven Penitential Psalms* (1517),

> to make something out of nothing. Hence God cannot make anything out of him who is not as yet nothing. . . . Therefore God receives none but the forsaken, heals none but the ill, gives sight to none but the blind, quickens none but the dead, makes pious none but the sinners, makes wise none but the ignorant—in short, He has mercy on none but the miserable, and gives grace to none but those who are in disgrace. Whoever therefore, is a proud saint, wise or just, cannot become God's material and receive God's work within himself, but remains in his own work and makes an imaginary, seeming, false, and painted saint of himself, i.e., a hypocrite. (LW 14:163)

Bengel wrote:

> Both St James and St Paul use this word . . . to justify, in one and the same sense, though St Paul in a more restricted, and St James

in a wider application; and for this reason, that St Paul is accustomed to speak of the act of justification, which chiefly consists in the remission of sins; whereas St James, which is especially to be observed, speaks of the state resulting from the same justification (which is incorrectly but frequently termed, a second justification), when a man continues in the righteousness which is of faith, and makes progress in that which is of works. (Bengel 20)

2:22 James essentially concludes the point with an assertion that faith and works, distinguished as they may be, in the end cannot be separated, as Abraham's *faith was completed* (Gk *eteleiōthē*), the verb form of the adjective James introduced at 1:4 ("perfect"; cf. note at 1:4). Final, perfect, complete—these are the description of the one who lacks nothing, who endures under trial; this is also the description of Abraham's faith, showing that it is more than simply intellectual assent. The goal or *telos* of faith is indeed service to God and neighbor, for righteousness received as declaration from God results in righteousness lived for others. Luther reflects on these two kinds of righteousness, saying, "When I have this [declared] righteousness within me, I descend from heaven like the rain that makes the earth fertile. That is, I come forth into another kingdom, and I perform good works whenever the opportunity arises" (LW 26:11).

2:23 Just as Abraham's faith was "completed" (v. 22), so the *Scripture was fulfilled*, another "completing" kind of word to demonstrate not just the goal of Abraham's faith, but the goal of God's declaring him righteous. This is seen in Gn 15:6 being the fulfillment of that promise from God in the sacrifice of a son. God had already credited righteousness to him on account of Abraham's faith (Gn 15:6). Now his faith had been demonstrated by his faithful work, just as Christ's active obedience in suffering perfects, completes, finalizes the work of "bringing many sons to glory" according to the author of Hebrews (cf. Heb 2:10). The completion of the Scripture, and the demonstration that Abraham's faith is complete, indicates an alliance. James points to it with the phrase *friend of God* (the opposite of a "friend of the world"; cf. 1:27 and 4:4). In the OT, Moses is spoken of as a friend of God (Ex 33:11), and Abraham also is called "beloved of God" or "friend of God" (ESV, cf. 2Ch 20:7; Is 41:8). Noncanonical Jewish literature also refers to Abraham this way.

2:24 James restates the general principle from the specific example of Abraham: just as he was shown to be righteous (cf. note at

v. 21), so also *you see that a person is justified* (the same verb as in v. 21). James is not negating or contradicting the *sola fide* principle of the Reformation by saying *not by faith alone*; rather he is affirming the impossibility of tearing faith away from its results, from its works. "Faith alone" in the context of this verse means rather faith that is mere intellectual assent or self-justifying confidence in facts (see notes, vv. 14, 18, 19). Cranmer wrote:

> St. James meant of justification in another sense, when he said, 'A man is justified by works and not by faith only.' For he spake of such a justification which is a declaration, continuation, and increase of that justification which St. Paul spake of before. (Cranmer 2:128)

2:25 *Rahab the prostitute* is mentioned in the NT in only three places: as an ancestor of Jesus (Mt 1:5), as a model of faith (Heb 11:31), and here. 1 Clement refers to both her faith and her active response: "On account of her faith and hospitality, Rahab the harlot was saved" (*ANF* 1:8). Faith precedes her demonstration of righteousness here as in the example of Abraham. (Cf. notes at vv. 21, 25.)

2:26 The concluding note of James's argument is "when in doubt, take a pulse." A body without *spirit*, that is, breath, is dead (Gk *pneuma* does not refer here to the Holy Spirit). And it is the same way with faith—the act of separating works from faith kills faith, makes it a breathless corpse (James repeats Gk *nekra* here; cf. v. 17). The opposite is also true; As Chrysostom said, "As faith without works is dead, so are works without faith dead" (*MPG* 53, p. 31). But rather than strive after or seek after works, the summary of James's argument leads the Christian to seek after a faith that has the integrity of deeds performed in loving service for God and neighbor. Luther said, "The works of faith . . . are those which are done out of the spirit of liberty and solely for the love of God" (LW 25:234).

2:14–26 in Devotion and Prayer A breathless body is simply a corpse. And deed-less faith is the same. Interesting, isn't it, that the parallelism of the analogy would argue for "body is to faith as breath is to deeds." But you can *see* a body, while we think of faith as invisible; on the other hand, we assume we can *see* deeds, but not breath. One would think James has got the analogy backwards. But the point about faith and deeds is much more than just the difference between visible and invisible, much different even than the distinction between physical and spiritual. In the end, James demands his reader look at the evidence of Scripture, of history, of experience, and realize faith is no mere acceptance of certain facts, but rather reception of gifts—a reception that changes everything about how they think, speak, and act. Faith is not a theology lesson; faith is a gospel "for you!" And the "for you" blesses you first and foremost by taking the spotlight off of you and rather putting it on the giver of the gift, our giver-God. It shifts the focus away from our faith and rather puts it on faith's object: the Christ. It moves the interest and scrutiny away from your works and rather invites trust in the works of Christ on your behalf, Christ's works in death and resurrection for you, Christ the object of faith, Christ the one who gives, Christ the giver-God. How can His gifts not inspire true faith and its response, an inseparable life of receiving and giving in turn, serving God and neighbor in reply to what has been received? God has given us a great gift. Through Christ Jesus, He has forgiven us and declared us righteous and holy. He now blesses us by calling us to serve Him in the lives of those around us. A living faith leads us gladly to share with others what we have freely received in Christ. • O Christ, giver of all good gifts, who calls us from friendship with the world to friendship with God, give us grace so to follow You in Your love and compassion for all who are in need, so that Your Church may be enabled to respond in loving kindness to all people, and to the end that they may receive their inheritance as children of God; for You live and reign with the Father and the Holy Spirit, ever one God, world without end. Amen.

PART 4

HUMBLING ONESELF IN LIGHT OF THE COMING JUDGMENT (3:1–5:6)

Call to Humility for the Sake of the Community (3:1–18)

Proper and improper speaking (3:1–12)

ESV	KJV
3 ¹Not many of you should become teachers, my brothers, for you know that we who teach will be judged with greater strictness. ²For we all stumble in many ways. And if anyone does not stumble in what he says, he is a perfect man, able also to bridle his whole body. ³If we put bits into the mouths of horses so that they obey us, we guide their whole bodies as well. ⁴Look at the ships also: though they are so large and are driven by strong winds, they are guided by a very small rudder wherever the will of the pilot directs. ⁵So also the tongue is a small member, yet it boasts of great things. How great a forest is set ablaze by such a small fire! ⁶And the tongue is a fire, a world of unrighteousness. The tongue is set among our members, staining the whole body, setting on fire the entire course of life, and set on fire by hell. ⁷For every kind of beast and bird, of reptile and sea creature, can be tamed and has been tamed by mankind, ⁸but no human being can tame the tongue. It is a	*3* ¹My brethren, be not many masters, knowing that we shall receive the greater condemnation. ²For in many things we offend all. If any man offend not in word, the same is a perfect man, and able also to bridle the whole body. ³Behold, we put bits in the horses' mouths, that they may obey us; and we turn about their whole body. ⁴Behold also the ships, which though they be so great, and are driven of fierce winds, yet are they turned about with a very small helm, whithersoever the governor listeth. ⁵Even so the tongue is a little member, and boasteth great things. Behold, how great a matter a little fire kindleth! ⁶And the tongue is a fire, a world of iniquity: so is the tongue among our members, that it defileth the whole body, and setteth on fire the course of nature; and it is set on fire of hell. ⁷For every kind of beasts, and of birds, and of serpents, and of things in the sea, is tamed, and hath been tamed of mankind:

restless evil, full of deadly poison. [9]With it we bless our Lord and Father, and with it we curse people who are made in the likeness of God. [10]From the same mouth come blessing and cursing. My brothers, these things ought not to be so. [11]Does a spring pour forth from the same opening both fresh and salt water? [12]Can a fig tree, my brothers, bear olives, or a grapevine produce figs? Neither can a salt pond yield fresh water.

[8]But the tongue can no man tame; it is an unruly evil, full of deadly poison. [9]Therewith bless we God, even the Father; and therewith curse we men, which are made after the similitude of God.

[10]Out of the same mouth proceedeth blessing and cursing. My brethren, these things ought not so to be.

[11]Doth a fountain send forth at the same place sweet water and bitter?

[12]Can the fig tree, my brethren, bear olive berries? either a vine, figs? so can no fountain both yield salt water and fresh.

Introduction to 3:1–18 The entirety of ch. 3 is an extended discussion on the distressing power of the tongue, followed by a call to use it for the teaching of the wisdom that comes from above. This section stands in the center of James's Letter as one of its more memorable selections, with its analogies to the horse's bridle, the ship's rudder, the ability to ignite a forest fire, and the inability to be tamed. The beginning of the section establishes the context of the discussion: the office of teaching, which entails a stricter judgment relative to those who hear instruction. Here we might pause a moment to reflect on the purpose of James's Letter, which itself indeed presumes to *instruct* in the idiom of wisdom literature. Here the teacher teaches (and warns) both fellow teachers and the taught, encompassing church and ministry together.

3:1 Because of the admonition attendant with the office, it is clear that James considers teachers to be an office in the Early Church distinct from others. The work of teaching makes the office of teacher (Gk *didaskalos*) a matter of function, not status, comparable to other functional offices (e.g., apostles and prophets), work eventually carried out by pastors (cf. Ac 13:1; 1Co 12:28–29; Eph 4:11). The admonition offered here nevertheless applies to all who claim to teach, as a stricter judgment waits for those who presume to speak on behalf of God (cf. Lk 11:45–46, 52; also Mt 18:5–6). James continues his exhortation to his audience by including the word that identifies their office of status, rather than function, as usual calling them *brothers* (cf. note at 1:2). Not all should presume to teach; those who do will be *judged*, because false teaching can destroy the faith of those being taught (cf. Gal 1:8–9; 2Tm 4:3; Mt 15:9). Notice that what is at issue is not "skill" in teaching or the presence of any other such human talent; the office is given to proclaim revealed truth and, as such, carries with it the burden of clearly delivering theological truth. James is not interested in peremptorily defining qualifications for filling the office, but admonishing his hearers about the gravity of the Second Commandment: that we not lie or deceive by God's name, which would include the teaching of false doctrine. This is why he notes the judgment will occur with more *strictness* than with other offices of service in the community: both a stricter standard of judgment and a harsher punishment (cf. Mt 18:5–6). Calvin wrote:

> The common and almost universal interpretation of this passage is, that the Apostle discourages the desire for the office of teaching, and for this reason, because it is dangerous, and exposes one to a heavier judgment, in case he transgresses: and they think that he said, Be not many masters, because there ought to have been some. But I take masters not to be those who performed a public duty in the Church, but such as took upon them the right of passing judgment upon others: for such reprovers sought to be accounted as masters of morals. And it was a mode of speaking usual among the Greeks as well as Latins, that they were called masters who superciliously animadverted on others.
>
> And that he forbade them to be many, it was done for this reason, because many everywhere did thrust in themselves; for it is, as it were, an innate disease in mankind to seek reputation by blaming others. And, in this respect, a twofold vice prevails,— though few excel in wisdom, yet all intrude indiscriminately into the office of masters; and then few are influenced by a right feeling, for hypocrisy and ambition stimulate them, and not a care for the salvation of their brethren. (Calvin 317–18)

3:2 *we all stumble.* None can avoid sin (cf. Rm 3:22–24), and James here underscores the impossibility of keeping the Law perfectly. This is a response to anyone who may have misinterpreted his message in ch. 2—works are not a quantifiable means towards attaining perfection, but rather a response to the gifts given by God and received by faith! The specific theme of ch. 3 is the tongue, however, and James brings it back to consider how a person stumbles in *what he says*. This reintroduces the issue of speech (1:19, 26) and serves as an overture to what he will expand on through the course of ch. 3. Because teachers speak often and authoritatively, they have both greater opportunity to teach falsely and temptation to speak wrongly for their own benefit (cf. 2Tm 4:3). As if to prove the matter with the extreme example, James offers the hypothetical *perfect man*: besides playing once again on the word "perfect" (Gk *teleios*, cf. note at 1:4), it is as if James is saying, "If anyone *could* do this without flaw (but of course we don't know anybody like that, do we?) . . . well, this guy would be perfect in every way, wouldn't he?" While not explicitly Christological, it is not difficult to think of James winking when he preaches this line, remarking on the *perfect man* who is the Christ. Rather than quantifiably striving after such perfection, all those called to serve in God's church receive His perfection by faith. Luther writes:

> Those who are truly righteous not only sigh and plead for the grace of God because they see that they have an evil inclination and thus are sinful before God, but also because they see that they can never understand fully how deep is the evil of their will and how far it extends, they believe that they are always sinners, as if the depth of their evil will were infinite. (LW 25:221)

The word for *man* used here may not only encourage a Christological interpretation, but also at least underscore James's understanding of the office: the word for "man" (Gk *anēr*) is specifically male as opposed to the generic word "person" (Gk *anthrōpos*), which might indicate either gender. The specificity of James's example in relation to this particular office shows that he assumes that such teachers (today we call them pastors) will be male.

3:3–5 Three colorful images impress James's audience: a very small bit directing a large horse; a very small rudder being even more effective than those "wind-tossed waves" (cf. 1:6); and the forest fire whose origin is just a small spark. The crescendo of images climaxes with the fire, which leads him to expand on the image in the subsequent verse.

3:6 While *world of unrighteousness* is certainly intended to be a hyperbolic climax to his colorful images, James's use of the word *world* (Gk *kosmos*) is also charged with opposition to God. James never uses the word in either the neutral or positive sense of God's good created order, but rather as the enemy of the Christian (cf. 1:27; 2:5). Our words are powerful. The children's rhyme claims, "Sticks and stones may break my bones, but words will never hurt me," but that rings untrue according to James's teaching, which is the same as Christ's (cf. Mk 7:14–23). Not only can the destructive tongue harm the individual, but also his *entire course of life:* This phrase compares life to a racecourse (alluding back to the bit and bridle image of 3:3). Bengel wrote:

> The metaphor is taken from a round wheel, and is very appropriate; for as a wheel is turned around with great velocity; so it is with the sphere of heaven, and the nature of man; and this being set on fire while it revolves, soon breaks out into a blaze in every part, so that the fire seems not only to be borne in a circle, but also to be a circle. (Bengel 25)

At the end of the race there is a reward for the tongue, not of a victor's crown (1:12), but a just reward, to be *set on fire by hell* (the Gk participle describes the tongue itself; this is more clearly seen in the KJV). Notice here how James unites the unholy trinity of the Christians' enemies that lead us to temptation (cf. 1:13–15): our own flesh (the tongue), the *world* of unrighteousness, and the *hell* of the devil.

3:7–8 James plays on the image of God (deliberately so, as seen in v. 9), given to man at creation, which involves dominion; Gn 1:26–28: "Let Us make man in Our image. . . . let them have dominion. . . . So God created man in His own image. . . . And God said . . . "Have dominion over . . . every living thing." Though all of creation can be controlled, no one is able to control the tongue (cf. Jas 3:9). It is more obstinate than a wild animal.

3:8 James extends the metaphors that have already shown how destructive the tongue is: if the tongue is a fire, it is also *full of deadly poison*, perhaps reminiscent of the sin of loose speech for which the Israelites were punished in Nu 21:4ff. Fiery serpents from the Lord put many to death until Moses, at God's command, fashioned such a snake from bronze and put it on a pole. Speaking falsely against God and against His prophet, grumbling against the provision of the Lord—the tongue is capable of harming not only others (vv. 5–6) but also oneself.

3:9 James uses the phrase *likeness of God* to extend the lesson on creation (cf. note at vv. 7–8); here it refers to the object of blessing—or cursing—by the same tongue. Identity is at stake in God's community, not just by virtue of creation but by a new creation, which delivers baptismal identity and which James has woven throughout his Letter to the point (cf. 1:2, 18, 23–24; 2:7). Indeed, people deserve respect because they are made in the image of God. Bengel wrote:

> We have lost the likeness of God: there remains however from that source a nobleness which cannot be destroyed, and this we ought to reverence both in ourselves and in others. Moreover, we have remained men, capable, by the Divine blessing, of being formed again after that likeness, to which the likeness of man ought to be conformed. They who curse, hinder that effect. (Bengel 27)

3:10–12 The final three verses of this section circle back to direct address of the *brothers* (cf. 3:1), which we do well to recall is inclusive of gender, highlighting once again the vocation of status given through faith in Christ: status before God and before one another. Hypocrisy has no place among such brothers and sisters. In his call for consistency, James expands the ridiculous bifurcation of two-faced-ness, which he introduced in 1:8 ("double-minded man") and followed up with the desperate impossibility of pulling apart the poles of faith and works (2:14–26). So at vv. 11–12, James once again argues using several examples that such a bifurcation is unnatural— indeed it is a perversion!—of the purpose and order for which God created the tongue. A *spring* is one thing or the other, either *salt* (the Gk word also means undrinkable, brackish) or sweet (v. 11). A *tree* or *vine* bears either one kind of fruit or the other (v. 12; cf. Mt 7:15– 19). A water source will be either salty (a different Gk word than used to describe the spring, this word means salty) or it will be fresh and drinkable (v. 12). So what is the nature of God's people? James has argued that we have received a new nature by virtue of the implanted Word (cf. 1:20–21), along with the command, therefore, to put away anger and to reflect rather what God has made us to be. The Word that recreated us is the Word that we say back to Him in service to God and neighbor. So we do well also to live securely and fully within the hedge of the Second Commandment: that we should not "curse, swear, use satanic arts, lie, or deceive by His name, but call upon it in every trouble, pray, praise, and give thanks."

God's wisdom produces right speaking (3:13–18)

ESV	KJV
¹³Who is wise and understanding among you? By his good conduct let him show his works in the meekness of wisdom. ¹⁴But if you have bitter jealousy and selfish ambition in your hearts, do not boast and be false to the truth. ¹⁵This is not the wisdom that comes down from above, but is earthly, unspiritual, demonic. ¹⁶For where jealousy and selfish ambition exist, there will be disorder and every vile practice. ¹⁷But the wisdom from above is first pure, then peaceable, gentle, open to reason, full of mercy and good fruits, impartial and sincere. ¹⁸And a harvest of righteousness is sown in peace by those who make peace.	¹³Who is a wise man and endued with knowledge among you? let him shew out of a good conversation his works with meekness of wisdom. ¹⁴But if ye have bitter envying and strife in your hearts, glory not, and lie not against the truth. ¹⁵This wisdom descendeth not from above, but is earthly, sensual, devilish. ¹⁶For where envying and strife is, there is confusion and every evil work. ¹⁷But the wisdom that is from above is first pure, then peaceable, gentle, and easy to be intreated, full of mercy and good fruits, without partiality, and without hypocrisy. ¹⁸And the fruit of righteousness is sown in peace of them that make peace.

3:13 As one can judge a tree by its fruits (cf. 3:12), so also the one who is *wise and understanding* will demonstrate this fact. James brings up this wise man in order to answer the need for those who teach (which he introduces at the beginning of ch. 3)—not one who is presumptive, but a leader whose works (cf. 2:14–26) prove his faithfulness. The encouragement for the wise teacher is not to lord it over others, but rather to show his understanding through *meekness of wisdom*, both attributes of a righteous person (cf. 1:5, Mt 5:5).

3:14, 16 *jealousy and selfish ambition* show up in several catalogues of sins in the NT (cf. Gal 5:20; Php 1:17, 2:3; Rm 13:13; 2Co 12:20). Notably, the factious context of the Corinthian church is furnished by the same sins, because they break down the unity and community God would establish (cf. 1Co 3:3), replacing it with *disorder and every vile practice* (v. 16). Such jealousy and ambition is the way of the kingdom of the world, not God's kingdom, where His citizens seek to be the least, the last, the lost that can be raised up by God. This is why James goes on in v. 14 to prohibit anyone's *boast*. "Boasting" in James is rather to be a confession of God's topsy-turvy kingdom where the lowly brother boasts in his exaltation and the rich man in his poverty (cf. 1:9; 4:16). Any other boasting is *false to the truth*. Denying one's sinfulness also denies God's Word. Very similar phrasing encourages honest confession before God and one another at 1Jo 1:6–10.

3:15 Evil boasting, lying against the truth, is certainly a kind of wisdom. James calls it *earthly, unspiritual, demonic*—a comparison he makes when talking about temptation giving birth to sin and eventually death in the natural progression laid out in 1:13–15. On the other hand, James identifies another kind of wisdom, the wisdom which the wise man ought both to understand (v. 13) and teach (v. 1): the *wisdom that comes down from above*. The author has already used the adverb "from above" (Gk *anōthen*) at 1:17–18 to describe the direction from which every good and perfect gift comes. The dynamic of sacramental gift and sacramental reception is reinforced here at the center of James. The theme of the Letter is generally wisdom. The genre of the Letter is largely wisdom literature; it can be considered the "Proverbs of the NT." The wisdom the author centers our attention on is not superficial human wisdom of success-aspiring morality or the devilish wisdom of secular humanism and selfish ambition, but rather an alien wisdom that must be received as given *from above*. This wisdom entails a catalogue of attributes James takes up in v. 17.

3:17 The catalogue of attributes describing the *wisdom from above* is ordered with priority (*first . . . then*), as James puts purity in the first place and from there lists works that follow. All the traits listed contrast with cursing and boasting (vv. 9–10, 14) and therefore are fruits that build up and unify. James closes the list with *mercy . . . impartial and sincere*, reinforcing the Letter's earlier teaching (ch. 2). It is significant that James closes his thoughts on the office of teacher in this kind of language. This quells ambition for selfish glory. It also reminds all Christians, both the teachers and the taught, that striving for praise of self or any other man is as foolish as defending one's own self-confidence and intellectual "faith" over against a living faith that blooms in service to God and neighbor (cf. 2:14–26). Luther highlighted this, saying,

It is certain that no man who is busy with commandments or righteousness performs this true service [true religion]. They cannot even comprehend it intellectually. For it is a teaching revealed from heaven which does not arise from the human heart or mind. The Holy Spirit must be the Teacher and Guide. Since He reaches men only through faith in Christ, whereas the work-righteous reject faith and retain the Law, it is impossible for them to perform this service. Therefore the Christian religion is easy, as I said, if you regard only the outward acts. But if you consider this spiritual service, it is most difficult, for you cannot perform this unless your heart is changed. (LW 12:87)

3:18 The beatitude, "blessed are the peacemakers" (Mt 5:9) rings here as a bright conclusion to a section encouraging wise leadership in teaching, putting down the venomous tongue, and putting away strife, jealousy, and ambition. James employs the thought also as a brilliant transition to the next major section of his Letter, which takes up the reason there are quarrels and fights in the community (4:1 ff.). Those who are peacemakers, however, who "sow in *peace*," sow *a harvest of righteousness*. In other words, they plant innumerable seeds of righteous actions and opportunities. The list in v. 17 is only representative; there is no limit to the benefits others receive from those who live by God's Word, fulfilling their calling by giving and receiving the gifts God freely gives from above.

Ch. 3 in Devotion and Prayer "You kiss your mother with that mouth?!" This sarcastic accusation, spoken by an elder relative who may or may not have intended to wash my mouth out with soap, is a humbling memory. God has plans for our body parts other than those uses we may choose. After all, He has given us reason and all our senses, eyes, ears, and ALL our members—including our mouths. God did not endow us with a mouth to have both blessings and curses flow from it. In fact, God gives us eyes, ears, and even our mouth to *receive* gifts from Him: the Word, read with eyes, heard with ears, even received under the bread and wine with the body and blood of our Lord Jesus. God calls us to use our mouths to respond in kind: to say back what He has said to us (the confession of faith!), and to proclaim the wisdom of God, Jesus Christ, to others. He came down from above to sow peace through the words of His people and to reap a harvest of righteousness: those who hear the Word from mouths sanctified for that purpose. • O Lord, "who can discern his errors? Declare me innocent from hidden faults. Keep back Your servant also from presumptuous sins; let them not have dominion over me! Then I shall be blameless, and innocent of great transgression. Let the words of my mouth and the meditation of my heart be acceptable in Your sight, O LORD, my rock and my redeemer." Amen. (Ps 19:12–14)

The Basis of God's Judgment (4:1–12)

Selfish behavior destroys the individual and community (4:1–4)

ESV	KJV
4 ¹What causes quarrels and what causes fights among you? Is it not this, that your passions are at war within you? ²You desire and do not have, so you murder. You covet and cannot obtain, so you fight and quarrel. You do not have, because you do not ask. ³You ask and do not receive, because you ask wrongly, to spend it on your passions. ⁴You adulterous people! Do you not know that friendship with the world is enmity with God? Therefore whoever wishes to be a friend of the world makes himself an enemy of God.	*4* ¹From whence come wars and fightings among you? come they not hence, even of your lusts that war in your members? ²Ye lust, and have not: ye kill, and desire to have, and cannot obtain: ye fight and war, yet ye have not, because ye ask not. ³Ye ask, and receive not, because ye ask amiss, that ye may consume it upon your lusts. ⁴Ye adulterers and adulteresses, know ye not that the friendship of the world is enmity with God? whosoever therefore will be a friend of the world is the enemy of God.

Introduction to 4:1–12 If I had a dime for every time I've heard 4:2 quoted out of context, as one among a panoply of "proof-texts" about divine secrets for godly financial freedom or biblical principles for budgeting or some other less savory "get-rich-quick the Jesus way!" scheme, well, such schemes probably wouldn't seem nearly so enticing! "You do not have because you do not ask" is not an invitation to build an empire of any sort with God's holy nod approving your worldly enterprise. In fact, the sum of these twelve verses promotes the exact opposite of a worldly empire. At play here is the distinction (and more than that, an absolutely adversarial enmity!) between the kingdom of the world and the kingdom of heaven come among us in Jesus Christ. The kingdom of heaven is where the world is enemy and God is friend (v. 4); where He opposes the proud and gives grace to the humble (v. 6); where the opposite of a noble standard of living is sought after (v. 9); and where God's citizens seek humility instead, only to see the transformation of sorrow and humility in the hands of God (v. 10). Citizenship in God's kingdom is not simply an individual membership between the citizen and God. It changes everything about how we relate to the neighbor as well (v. 11–12). "Godly finances"? On the contrary, James is arguing not for any superficial, human success system, but much rather an entirely topsy-turvy worldview that glories only in how, in God's kingdom, the first end up racing to last place and the last get promoted to first.

4:1 "Peace" is the final word of the previous sentence. Its exact opposite opens the next sentence, in language that clangs with the clash of combat: *quarrels* and *fights* (literally "wars" and "battles"). James magnifies the scope of the church's internal conflicts with militaristic language. This is not a call to pacifism, but rather an underscoring of the gravity of the unholy struggles of rich versus poor (ch. 1, 2), ambition versus God's calling (ch. 3). James poses the question about the source of conflicts in the church and in the world: *passions*. But James is no Buddhist. "Desire" (v. 2) is not the problem; rather the object of desire is. James employs the word *passions* (Gk *hēdonai*, "pleasures," from which we get the English word hedonism) to get at this idea. It encompasses more than simply the jealousy and ambition to which he refers at 3:14 and includes the whole catalogue of desire, murder, covetousness that he describes in the next two verses. This is a cycle that curves in upon itself and concludes with the same word *passions* at the end of v. 3.

4:2 As Jesus' words about *murder* (Mt 5:21–26) expand the scope of the Fifth Commandment to encompass the many transgressions against God's gift of life, so also James accuses the church of murder as the result of sinful desires and attitudes (cf. 1Jn 3:15). Actual murder is not an unthinkable exaggeration of what God's people are capable of, as envy (*you covet*) and a host of other sins, left unchecked and unconfessed (cf. 5:16), often lead to abominable behavior. Recall that jealousy led to violence in Gn 4:1–16; 37:1ff.; Mk 15:10; Ac 5:17–18. Cf. 1 Clem: "Envy and jealousy led to the murder of a brother [Abel]" (*ANF* 1:6). The continuation of James's catalogue of sins reminds the congregation that transgression in one part of the Law is a transgression of all of it. Such a snowball of sins begins as we forget that God is the giver-God, the source of all good gifts. *Desire* in v. 2 is rather neutral (Gk *epithumeite*), as is *you do not have*, explained after the parenthetical description of covetousness and murder with *you do not have, because you do not ask*. Desires of themselves are not evil, but desires that do not find satisfaction in the gifts that the Lord gives are sinful. Asking for the things that God has promised to give is key, as in Jas 1:5–8, where asking God for wisdom is encouraged (cf. v. 3).

4:3 James indicts his hearers with the full circle of his argument that begins in v. 1: When you finally DO ask, he says, *you ask wrongly* (Gk *kakōs*, "in a wicked way"). It's not as if James is advocating some kind of conjuring trick or pointing to a correct formula to get God to give gifts; rather, he is pointing out that the motive of sinners dissatisfied with the gifts given by the giver-God is evil, selfish, seeking only worldly treasures. James later shows what kind of asking is holy: instead of selfish prayer, intercessory prayer for others is encouraged (5:14–15). James's words here may usefully inform a theology of prayer, but they are not comprehensive. Popular misinterpretations, particularly in the twentieth and twenty-first centuries in the United States, use this verse to form a theology of material success (e.g., the "name it and claim it" preachers and other manifestations of a theology of glory instead of a theology of the cross). We do well to consider the larger context of James's logic when it has to do with the gifts God gives.

4:4 As James has brought the argument about passions full circle with the last word of the previous verse, he climaxes with the accusation *you adulterous people!* (in Gk, literally, "whores!"). Not only does the shocking accusation echo Yahweh's condemnation of Israel's covenant unfaithfulness (cf. Ezk 23:20–21; Hos 3:1), with its attendant puns connecting adultery/idolatry, but it is consistent also with Jesus' accusation "evil and adulterous generation" (Mt 12:39; 16:4). Cf. Mk 8:38: "whoever is ashamed of Me and of My words in this adulterous and sinful generation, of him will the Son of Man also be ashamed when He comes in the glory of His Father with the holy angels." James says the same thing in the words that follow his accusation: *friendship with the world is enmity with God*. James consistently uses "the world" to denote an enemy of Christianity (cf. 1:27; 2:5), and "friendship" with it here refers to sinful loyalty and sharing in all things with it. Wesley wrote, "Whosoever seeks either the happiness or favour of [the world], does thereby constitute himself an enemy of God; and can he expect to obtain anything of him" (Wesley 603).

Prophetic call to repentance (4:5–10)

ESV	KJV
[5] Or do you suppose it is to no purpose that the Scripture says, "He yearns jealously over the spirit that he has made to dwell in us"? [6] But he gives more grace. Therefore it says, "God opposes the proud, but gives grace to the humble." [7] Submit yourselves therefore to God. Resist the devil, and he will flee from you. [8] Draw near to God, and he will draw near to you. Cleanse your hands, you sinners, and purify your hearts, you double-minded. [9] Be wretched and mourn and weep. Let your laughter be turned to mourning and your joy to gloom. [10] Humble yourselves before the Lord, and he will exalt you.	[5] Do ye think that the scripture saith in vain, The spirit that dwelleth in us lusteth to envy? [6] But he giveth more grace. Wherefore he saith, God resisteth the proud, but giveth grace unto the humble. [7] Submit yourselves therefore to God. Resist the devil, and he will flee from you. [8] Draw nigh to God, and he will draw nigh to you. Cleanse your hands, ye sinners; and purify your hearts, ye double minded. [9] Be afflicted, and mourn, and weep: let your laughter be turned to mourning, and your joy to heaviness. [10] Humble yourselves in the sight of the Lord, and he shall lift you up.

4:5 This is a difficult verse to translate. Another possible meaning is "Do you think that the Scripture speaks uselessly? Does the spirit which He's caused to dwell in us crave jealously?" The difficulty begins with the word *Scripture* because there are no references in any surviving literature that indicate exactly what James might have in mind here, although the resonance with Gal 5:17 is striking ("For the desires of the flesh are against the Spirit, and the desires of the Spirit are against the flesh, for these are opposed to each other.") Since James is referring to some writing or other, it is probable that the people reading his Letter would get the reference and its connection with what he just said about envy—the word that the ESV renders as "*jealously*." The phrase need not mean "with jealousy" though; it could also mean "against jealousy." This *jealousy* (Gk *phthonon*) is, throughout the NT, an evil envy (cf. Rm 1:29; Gal 5:21; etc.), not the kind of jealousy God possesses for His people (He is described as Gk *zēlos*; cf. Ex 20:5). Perhaps it's best to look forward to James's description of God giving grace in v. 6 and assume that James wants to emphasize what God *has made to dwell in us*, and assume a lost bit of writing (that James's audience would be familiar with) that teaches something like "God's spirit—the one He's caused to dwell in us—longs against envy." Surely such a teaching would be no vain promise! Cf. Ps 42:1–2: "As a deer pants for flowing streams, so pants my soul for you, O God." This *spirit* need not be a reference to the Holy Spirit, but rather the breath of life that so yearns after its giver instead of the passions mentioned previously (vv. 1, 3).

4:6 Some wrongly consider *grace* to be a quantifiable thing to collect along with other quantifiable merits and good works. They speak as if it can be stored up and used to give confidence before God and the world. The NT offers a radically different idea. "Grace" is not so much a thing to be collected and quantified as it is an attitude of God, a lens through which He perceives humanity, the favor He confers upon us in view of the death and resurrection of Jesus Christ. Luther gets this distinction well:

> Those who say: Ah, but I have done as much as I possibly can; I have done enough, and I hope that God will give me grace—they set up an iron wall between themselves and the grace of God. But if you feel within yourself the urge to call upon God and pray and plead and knock, then grace is already there; then call upon it and thank God. (LW 51:43)

He gives more grace can also be translated "He gives a greater gift," that is, bigger, mightier, certainly worth more than individual merits could ever add up to. The gift given here repeats the emphasis from the beginning that this is a God who gives gifts and that we are on the receiving end of the gifts of this giver-God (cf. 1:5). Calvin wrote:

> Some think that the soul of man is meant, and therefore read the sentence affirmatively, and according to this meaning,—that the spirit of man, as it is malignant, is so infected with envy, that it has ever a mixture of it. They, however, think better who regard the Spirit of God as intended; for it is he that is given to dwell in us. I then take the Spirit as that of God, and read the sentence as a

question; for it was his object to prove, that because they envied they were not ruled by the Spirit of God; because he teaches the faithful otherwise; and this he confirms in the next verse, by adding that he giveth more grace. (Calvin 332)

4:7 James summarizes the preceding words on anger and envy being opposed to God and His gifts with an exhortation to friendship with God instead of with the world (cf. v. 4), an exhortation he expresses in the words *submit yourselves.* God's kingdom is diametrically opposed to the kingdom of the world, in which people scramble to the top, lording it over one another (cf. Mk 10:42–45). Citizenship in God's kingdom, on the other hand, races toward the bottom, to the least, the last, and the lost, hastening to serve the neighbor. This is why such submission to God's authority works itself out naturally in the submission of relationships: slaves to masters, workers to employers, wives to husbands, young to old, indeed all in the same way as, and because, the Church submits to Christ as head (cf. Eph 5:21ff.; 1Pt 2:13, 18; 3:1, 22; 5:5). Repentant citizens of God's kingdom are able to *resist the devil,* whose temptations are explained in the teaching and firm warning of 1:13ff. The devil is real. And the devil can be, and is to be, resisted—a glorious and comforting truth paralleled in 1Pt 5:8–9.

4:8–9 The repentance context introduced in v. 7 is filled out in the next three verses in one of James's crescendos, beginning here with a call to *draw near to God,* the only means by which to resist the devil (v. 7). Jesus resisted the devil with the Word of God (cf. Mt 4:1–11), and the promise for Christians is that God dwells in His Word, a truth James affirms with the promise that *He will draw near to you.* This is a parallelism of contrast with the devil's flight in v. 7.

Repentance (Gk *metanoia,* "change of mind" or "change of heart") is at work in resisting the devil and is matched with faith that trusts in God, drawing near to Him as He has drawn near to us. Such a life of repentance is the mark of the whole Christian life (cf. Luther, *95 Theses*), and James underscores that fact with more repentance language: *cleanse your hands . . . purify your hearts* (cf. Ps 24:3–4); *be wretched . . . mourn . . . weep* (cf. Mi 2:4; Jl 1:5); *let your laughter be turned to mourning . . . joy to gloom* (cf. Mi 1:8–9; Jl 1:12). The only cure for a double-minded man (cf. 1:8) is repentance and forgiveness.

4:10 James quotes Pr 3:34 at v. 6: God opposes the proud, but gives grace to the humble. The grand reversal James celebrates here is activated by the incarnation of Christ and continues to eternity as the topsy-turvy kingdom of God, in which God loves to pull this holy exchange, blinding the sighted and sighting the blind (Jn 9), filling the hungry and sending the rich empty away (Lk 1). This kingdom of God has come among us in Christ (Lk 17:21). This kingdom of God comes to you too, says James, as you *humble yourselves*, not protesting your own self-confidence, your own righteousness, justifying yourself, but being the lowly, repentant one, for this is the one whom God will *exalt*, even to a crown of life (1:12). This brief climax to a section on repentance is coextensive with Jesus' teaching that those who humble themselves before God will be exalted (Lk 18:14).

God alone is the Judge (4:11–12)

ESV	KJV
¹¹Do not speak evil against one another, brothers. The one who speaks against a brother or judges his brother, speaks evil against the law and judges the law. But if you judge the law, you are not a doer of the law but a judge. ¹²There is only one lawgiver and judge, he who is able to save and to destroy. But who are you to judge your neighbor?	¹¹Speak not evil one of another, brethren. He that speaketh evil of his brother, and judgeth his brother, speaketh evil of the law, and judgeth the law: but if thou judge the law, thou art not a doer of the law, but a judge. ¹²There is one lawgiver, who is able to save and to destroy: who art thou that judgest another?

4:11 The citizens of God's kingdom recognize their lowliness before God, and so also they recognize their lowliness before one another. This is precisely why they do not *speak evil* of one another (Gk *katalalei*, "talk down"). Slander, nitpicking, reviling—this is what the "Gentiles" do against the faithful according to 1Pt 2:12, and what the world does against believers on Christ's account (cf. Mt 5:11–12). That kind of talk has no place among fellow citizens in God's kingdom. And any such talk is not really against one's brother, says James, but *against the law* of God's kingdom, the "royal law" (Jas 2:8), over which there is only one judge: and it's not you! Your calling is not to be a *judge* of the law but to be a *doer of the law*, which James expands on comprehensively at 2:14–26.

4:12 The only *lawgiver and judge* is the One *who is able to save and to destroy*; cf. Mt 10:28: "Do not fear those who kill the body but cannot kill the soul. Rather fear Him who can destroy both soul and body in hell."

4:1–12 in Devotion and Prayer Repent, for the kingdom of heaven is near! The cry from the prophets of the OT is the same as the cry of John the Baptist, and it is a truth that persists to today. The kingdom of heaven is indeed near in Christ. In Him, God's kingdom has come among us, a new thing not like the old, a kingdom in which He heals the sick, mends the broken, lifts up the humble, raises the dead. To be naturalized as a citizen in this kingdom is to heed the call of the prophets, of John, and of Jesus Himself: Repent! We repent when we stop turning in upon ourselves and turn rather to the Christ who is turned to us: draw near to God and He will draw near to you! In Christ, we hear the call to repent in light of God's kingdom, not as a future event we need to get ready for, to clean up our act and show God how sorry we are before He comes in judgment. Rather, we repent because the kingdom of God *has drawn near*—the blessing of a God who has relented of sending upon us the destruction deserved for our sins and instead has delivered it upon His Son. No wonder that this kingdom of reversal would prove the location of the greatest reversal of all: His death means our life. Such kindness indeed leads us to live our entire life as a life of turning to Him, turning away from ourselves, turning our hearts and minds in constant repentance to the gift He gives in Christ. • "Create in me a clean heart, O God, and renew a right spirit within me. Cast me not away from Your presence, and take not Your Holy Spirit from me. Restore to me the joy of Your salvation, and uphold me with a willing spirit." Amen. (Ps 51:10–12)

Judgment on the Proud Person of Wealth (4:13–5:6)

Becoming proud in self-sufficiency condemned (4:13–17)

ESV	KJV
¹³Come now, you who say, "Today or tomorrow we will go into such and such a town and spend a year there and trade and make a profit"—¹⁴yet you do not know what tomorrow will bring. What is your life? For you are a mist that appears for a little time and then vanishes. ¹⁵Instead you ought to say, "If the Lord wills, we will live and do this or that." ¹⁶As it is, you boast in your arrogance. All such boasting is evil. ¹⁷So whoever knows the right thing to do and fails to do it, for him it is sin.	¹³Go to now, ye that say, To day or to morrow we will go into such a city, and continue there a year, and buy and sell, and get gain: ¹⁴Whereas ye know not what shall be on the morrow. For what is your life? It is even a vapour, that appeareth for a little time, and then vanisheth away. ¹⁵For that ye ought to say, If the Lord will, we shall live, and do this, or that. ¹⁶But now ye rejoice in your boastings: all such rejoicing is evil. ¹⁷Therefore to him that knoweth to do good, and doeth it not, to him it is sin.

Introduction to 4:13–5:6 James uses this section of his Letter to give two more warnings to rich people. The first has to do with making plans—particularly tuned to the traveling merchant—while being willfully oblivious to God. The author calls this arrogance. The second has to do with the injustice of actions against the poor, one final reminder of the theme James had expounded at 2:1–9. The balance of both warnings speaks a common message: "Do not lay up for yourselves treasures on earth, where moth and rust destroy and where thieves break in and steal, but lay up for yourselves treasures in heaven, where neither moth nor rust destroys and where thieves do not break in and steal. For where your treasure is, there your heart will be also" (Mt 6:19–21).

4:13 Human life and all our endeavors are conditional and contingent upon God's will. James plays out a hypothetical statement from one who rather thinks he is free to live the life he pleases, going so far as to tell the future, confident in the time, place, and duration of his business plans. The context shows that forethought and rational judgment are not being condemned in this part of the Letter (though notice that in Jesus' famous parables that put "planning" and "counting the cost" in a positive light, e.g., Lk 14:28–33, the point is to forsake all, worldly goods included, to follow Him). Rather, James reprimands the impious assumption of the one who, forgetting God's rule over all, thinks he can make all the money he wants, wherever and however he wants, and get away with it. (Cf. Jesus' parable of the rich fool, Lk 12:15–21.)

4:14 Here today, gone tomorrow. James's Gk words for *appears* and *vanishes* play on a common root that makes our *life* of *mist* sound like the stage performer doing a disappearing trick: "now you see it, now you don't." Confidence in a future that you yourself can create is confidence in a false idol, since only God is in control of time and history. (Cf. the "mist" image in Hos 13:1–3: "They sin more and more, and make for themselves metal images, idols skillfully made of their silver, all of them the work of craftsmen. It is said of them, 'Those who offer human sacrifice kiss calves!' Therefore they shall be like the morning mist or like the dew that goes early away, like the chaff that swirls from the threshing floor or like smoke from a window.")

4:15 Since the Lord is the one who upholds and controls the universe, accepting the condition of His approval is key to any human planning. While the context of a merchant's business is most immediately at play in this section, *if the Lord wills* is the humble attitude our Lord teaches us to have when we pray His own prayer: "Thy will be done." And what is His will? Luther explained:

> The good and gracious will of God is done . . . when God breaks and hinders every evil counsel and will that would not let us hallow the name of God nor let His kingdom come, such as the will of the devil, the world, and our flesh. Instead, He strengthens and keeps us steadfast in His Word and in faith until we die. This is His gracious and good will. (*Concordia*, SC, Third Petition)

4:16–17 Commission and omission are on display in the situation James condemns in this section. Active pursuit of riches upon riches without God's approval rises to the level of prideful *arrogance*, an attitude equivalent with self-deification (cf. Is 14:12–17; Lk 10:18). Failing to acknowledge God's sovereignty is a refusal to submit to God's will; it is to prefer the pursuit of what the world's kingdom says is best over what God's kingdom has promised (vv. 7, 10, 15).

4:13–17 in Devotion and Prayer Commenting on the parable of the rich fool (Lk 14:28ff.), St. Augustine cited Pr 13:8 as he preaches:

> For this reason, "the redemption of a man's soul is his riches." Vain and stupid, *that* man didn't have *these* riches—indeed, he was not redeeming his soul with alms, but was laying up fruits that would spoil. He was laying up, I say, fruits that would perish—this man who would himself soon perish, yielding nothing to the Lord, before whom he would soon appear. Oh, what shame will he have in that judgment, when he begins to hear, "I hungered, and you did not give me to eat?" He sought to sate his soul in fact with superabundant and excessive feasts, and in his excessive pride scorned so many empty bellies of the poor, giving no thought to the fact that the bellies of the poor were safer than his own storehouses. What he'd in fact laid up in those storehouses—perhaps even then it was being pilfered by robbers. If however he'd been laying it up in the bellies of the poor, though indeed it were divided up and distributed on the earth, it would nevertheless be preserved more safely in heaven. Therefore, "the redemption of a man's soul is his riches." (Sermon 36:9, *MPL* 38:219)

• O Lord Jesus Christ, You are the master of time and the author of my future. You know the plans You have for me and have promised never to leave me nor forsake me. Send me Your Holy Spirit that I may ever turn to You and the salvation You have won for Me, so that whatever my future may hold, I may hold fast only and ever to the gracious promise of eternal life with You, who reign with the Father and the Holy Spirit, one God, now and forever. Amen.

Becoming rich at the expense of others condemned (5:1–6)

ESV	KJV
5 ¹Come now, you rich, weep and howl for the miseries that are coming upon you. ²Your riches have rotted and your garments are moth-eaten. ³Your gold and silver have corroded, and their corrosion will be evidence against you and will eat your flesh like fire. You have laid up treasure in the last days. ⁴Behold, the wages of the laborers who mowed your fields, which you kept back by fraud, are crying out against you, and the cries of the harvesters have reached the ears of the Lord of hosts. ⁵You have lived on the earth in luxury and in self-indulgence. You have fattened your hearts in a day of slaughter. ⁶You have condemned and murdered the righteous person. He does not resist you.	5 ¹Go to now, ye rich men, weep and howl for your miseries that shall come upon you. ²Your riches are corrupted, and your garments are motheaten. ³Your gold and silver is cankered; and the rust of them shall be a witness against you, and shall eat your flesh as it were fire. Ye have heaped treasure together for the last days. ⁴Behold, the hire of the labourers who have reaped down your fields, which is of you kept back by fraud, crieth: and the cries of them which have reaped are entered into the ears of the Lord of sabaoth. ⁵Ye have lived in pleasure on the earth, and been wanton; ye have nourished your hearts, as in a day of slaughter. ⁶Ye have condemned and killed the just; and he doth not resist you.

5:1 The final sorrow for the self-reliant rich will be that they *weep and howl*, suffering because of God's judgment which comes not because of riches, but because of unfaithfulness (cf. Jl 1:5; Mal 2:13). Wesley suggested:

> This was written not long before the siege of Jerusalem; during which, as well as after it, huge calamities came on the Jewish nation, not only in Judea, but through distant countries. And as these were an awful prelude of that wrath which was to fall upon them in the world to come, so this may likewise refer to the final vengeance which will then be executed on the impenitent. (Wesley 604)

5:2–3 James puns here in v. 2 on *rotted* and *moth-eaten* (Gk *sesēpen* and *sētobrōta*), emphasizing how ephemeral possessions are with a Gk word that gives us the English word "sepsis." The exaggeration of wealth rotting or rusting (gold and silver do not actually naturally decompose to baser material) suggests more than simply the loss of wealth—there is judgment at work here. This echoes other biblical warnings, e.g., Jb 13:28: "Man wastes away like a rotten thing, like a garment that is moth-eaten" (cf. Mt 6:19–21; Lk 12:33–34). Interestingly, Jesus also associates the *last days* with a narrative about wealth, as He outlines the eschaton with parables in Mt 25 that include, besides the wise and foolish virgins and the sheep and the goats, the parable of the talents (Mt 25:14–30). The parable points out that the one who hoarded did so in fear, not putting anything given by God to any good use for His kingdom. This was a waste for the master and a punishable offense for the sinful steward. Riches, in this later chapter of James, testify to the greed of the rich, which in these last days (Heb 1:2; 1Pt 1:20) leading to the day of God's judgment (Am 8:9–10) will indeed *be evidence against* those who protest confidence in their own riches and works.

5:4 The prosecution is stacked against the rich in the Last Day: not only is the dross of their silver and gold exposed, but so is the wage that was never paid to the one who worked for it. As Abel's blood cried out against Cain (Ge 4; Heb 12, 13:), so also the injustice against God's poor cries out against those who have oppressed them (cf. Ex 22:21–27). In using the term *Lord of hosts*, James has in mind the OT references to the Lord who is the God of the heavenly armies, who in His military might and magnificent majesty is also the tender shepherd of His people. He defends the fatherless, the widow, the orphan, and the alien, the least, the last, the lost, the disfranchised, the citizens of His kingdom—including those oppressed by the rich (cf. Is 5:9; Zec 13:2).

5:5–6 Although James does not explicitly say "cow," his language evokes the image of cattle who are *fattened . . . in a day of slaughter*, who have in the meantime delighted themselves on dainty, delicate food and easy living. The underlying truth of such a comparison is that the dumb beasts, the rich, are largely unaware of the destruction awaiting them because of their injustice (cf. 2Pt 2:12). The injustice James has in mind is summarized in v. 6: *you have condemned and murdered*. Is it not the rich "who drag you to court?" asks James (2:6). He also reinforces here the idea of murder, which is brought up at 2:11 (cf. note at 4:2). While the remainder of the verse may

be translated "does [God] not resist you?"—evocative of God's resisting the proud in 4:6—the more immediate context argues for the
absolute victimization of the poor in the hands of the rich, blissfully
thoughtless of the wrong they commit in the name of their own self-
fattening.

5:1–6 in Devotion and Prayer Riches present a particular temptation to those who have them and to those who do not. For those
who strive after them at the expense of pursuits that provide more
lasting satisfaction, riches are an elusive mirage. Those who have
them find that it is difficult to be satisfied with any amount. To those
who lack them, riches symbolize a futile hope. For both the rich and
poor, then, Paul's words to Timothy ring true: "those who desire to
be rich fall into temptation, into a snare, into many senseless and
harmful desires that plunge people into ruin and destruction. For
the love of money is a root of all kinds of evils. It is through this
craving that some have wandered away from the faith and pierced
themselves with many pangs." (1Tm 6:9–10). The cure for such pain
is simply reception of the gifts our giver-God gives. After all, as Paul
also reminded Timothy, "godliness with contentment is great gain,
for we brought nothing into the world, and we cannot take anything
out of the world. But if we have food and clothing, with these we
will be content" (1Tm 6:6–8). • Gracious Lord, in Your infinite wisdom, You created moths and rust as part of a creation You call "very
good." Thank You for moths that wear away earthly clothing and for
rust that consumes earthly goods, so that I may be the more ready
and willing to rely on clothing that does not perish and on goods
that never fade away. Grant me a spirit that rejoices ever in being
clothed in Your righteousness alone, and preserve me in faith until it
is Your will to bring me to a new heaven and a new earth, that I may
receive the crown that rust will never touch. In Jesus' name. Amen.

PART 5

PROPER SPEAKING WHILE WAITING FOR THE LORD (5:7–20)

Patience in View of the Lord's Return (5:7–12)

ESV	KJV
[7]Be patient, therefore, brothers, until the coming of the Lord. See how the farmer waits for the precious fruit of the earth, being patient about it, until it receives the early and the late rains. [8]You also, be patient. Establish your hearts, for the coming of the Lord is at hand. [9]Do not grumble against one another, brothers, so that you may not be judged; behold, the Judge is standing at the door. [10]As an example of suffering and patience, brothers, take the prophets who spoke in the name of the Lord. [11]Behold, we consider those blessed who remained steadfast. You have heard of the steadfastness of Job, and you have seen the purpose of the Lord, how the Lord is compassionate and merciful. [12]But above all, my brothers, do not swear, either by heaven or by earth or by any other oath, but let your "yes" be yes and your "no" be no, so that you may not fall under condemnation.	[7]Be patient therefore, brethren, unto the coming of the Lord. Behold, the husbandman waiteth for the precious fruit of the earth, and hath long patience for it, until he receive the early and latter rain. [8]Be ye also patient; stablish your hearts: for the coming of the Lord draweth nigh. [9]Grudge not one against another, brethren, lest ye be condemned: behold, the judge standeth before the door. [10]Take, my brethren, the prophets, who have spoken in the name of the Lord, for an example of suffering affliction, and of patience. [11]Behold, we count them happy which endure. Ye have heard of the patience of Job, and have seen the end of the Lord; that the Lord is very pitiful, and of tender mercy. [12]But above all things, my brethren, swear not, neither by heaven, neither by the earth, neither by any other oath: but let your yea be yea; and your nay, nay; lest ye fall into condemnation.

Introduction 5:7–12 The following section coheres as a study in "patience." The Gk words sound like "big-souled-ness" (*makrothymia; makrothymeō*) and can also mean "courage" or "endurance." The final part of the Letter, then, is an exhortation to the congregation, once again addressed as *brothers* (v. 7), to endure in light of the Lord's appearance (v. 8), the impending judgment (v. 9), and the ultimate salvation for those who endure (for which Job serves as a model, v. 11). Thoughtless oaths (v. 12) do not honor the goal of the last days that Christians have in mind. Trusting in the Lord to deliver on His final promise, believers are called not to make any rash promises of our own.

5:7 Why does the righteous man not resist the unrighteous? Why does the poor man not resist the rich (cf. v. 6)? James's focus is no longer on the rich but the poor, who in the face of persecution are called to be *patient*. Believers have reason to "take courage," because the Lord keeps His promises (cf. 2Pt 2:9). James calls the believers *brothers*, an endearing and comforting term, including both men and women, that contrasts with the previous words of rebuke (and reiterates the address at the beginning of the Letter; cf. 1:2). The brothers have hope they can count on, a reason they can be encouraged, enduring, and patient: *the coming of the Lord* is imminent. They will not be victimized and discriminated against by the rich and powerful. The believer looks forward patiently for the appearance of Christ in glory (cf. 2Th 2:1), even as the *farmer waits*, not ignorant of the signs of His coming but observing the *early and the late rains*. This is an echo of vindication for the repentant, a gift delivered from the giver-God, e.g., at Jl 2:23: "Be glad, O children of Zion, and rejoice in the LORD your God, for he has given the early rain for your vindication; he has poured down for you abundant rain, the early and the latter rain, as before."

5:8 Ps 111:8 has in mind a similar idea to the one James commands when he says *establish your hearts*, that is, "make them strong" or "make them steady, make them firm." This, too, is a gift from the giver-God who grants the answer to the prayer of Ps 51:10, 12 (where the LXX employs the same Gk verb "uphold," with God as the subject): "Create in me a clean heart, O God, and renew a right spirit within me. . . . Restore to me the joy of Your salvation, and uphold me with a willing spirit." The comforting promise in light of steadfast endurance is the fact that the *coming of the Lord is at hand*, literally "has drawn near." There can be no doubt because Christ has died, Christ has risen, Christ will come again!

5:9 James has spent time at other places in his Letter playing on the word "judge"; he now recaps the emphasis of 4:11–12; 2:4 (cf. also 2:8 and 1:6). *Do not grumble*: unity is at issue here as it was throughout the middle of James (3:1–4:12), perhaps reflecting the same concern as Heb 13:17 of not just unity among the brethren, but unity with the leaders of the congregation (cf. 3:1–2, 13–18). Do not grumble lest you come under judgment—and *the Judge is standing at the door*. Jesus is the Judge whose return is imminent and to be welcomed by citizens of His kingdom who are ready and watching (cf. Mk 13:32–37).

5:10–11 Paradigms *of suffering and patience* include unspecified OT *prophets* as well as *the steadfastness of Job*. The emphasis on suffering recalls the beginning of James, which stresses enduring under trials (cf. 1:2–4, 12). The unspoken names remind the reader of the various trials outlined in the OT: the fate of Jonah, the desperation of Elijah, the lamentation of Jeremiah, just to name a few. The countless prophets whose tribulation goes unsung are included in this, all who defied the world and walked by faith in God's promise: "Some were tortured, refusing to accept release, so that they might rise again to a better life. Others suffered mocking and flogging, and even chains and imprisonment. They were stoned, they were sawn in two, they were killed with the sword. They went about in skins of sheep and goats, destitute, afflicted, mistreated—of whom the world was not worthy—wandering about in deserts and mountains, and in dens and caves of the earth" (Heb 11:35–38). The condemnations they spoke were not their own words but God's (cf. 2Ch 36:16). *Job* is offered as a paragon of *steadfastness* rather than "suffering," conjuring an image not of the OT hero scraping his skin on his dungheap and putting up with several friends who had done just fine by him until they opened their mouths, but rather the Job who said, "Naked I came from my mother's womb, and naked shall I return. The LORD gave, and the LORD has taken away; blessed be the name of the LORD" (Jb 1:21) and, though invited by his wife to "curse God and die," yet held fast with his retort: "Shall we receive good from God, and shall we not receive evil?" (Jb 2:10). In the same breath, James says you have heard about Job's endurance and you've seen the Lord's *purpose* (Gk *telos*, "goal"). Again, just as suffering and endurance were to have their final, mature, complete, and full effect, making the believer final, mature, complete, and full (1:4), so the echo here reminds us that the Lord is the one who carries things to the end He has in mind. This means that any suffering has a purpose (v. 10; cf. Rm 5:1–5: "Therefore, since we have been justified by faith, we have peace with God through our Lord Jesus Christ. Through Him we have also obtained access by faith into this grace in which we stand, and we rejoice in hope of the glory of God. Not only that, but we rejoice in our sufferings, knowing that suffering produces endurance, and endurance produces character, and character produces hope, and hope does not put us to shame, because God's love has been poured into our hearts through the Holy Spirit who has been given to us"). The Lord's goal is to give His believers a crown of life (1:12), to give us salvation, to fulfill our hope in His being *compassionate and merciful.*

5:12 Though this verse may well begin James's concluding remarks, as he says *above all* (or "as for everything else"), nevertheless it belongs here in a coherent picture of patience in light of the coming of the Lord. Vindication is not in the hands of people who make vain promises. Nor is final vindication for the believer to be found in the courtroom. In view of the coming judgment of the Lord, we trust in our final vindication to be delivered suddenly and swiftly by Him, a comfort that strengthens us to heed this encouragement not to *swear*, that is, to make an empty oath (cf. Mt 23:16–22). Wesley wrote:

> The apostle here particularly forbids these oaths, as well as all swearing in common conversation. . . . This abundantly demonstrates the horrible iniquity of the crime. But he does not forbid the taking a solemn oath before a magistrate. (Wesley 606)

5:7–12 in Devotion and Prayer Our Lord has promised to return. Soon. We do not know the day or the hour. Until the new heaven and new earth become manifest, we live in the world—a world James shows as the enemy of the Christian. Therefore suffering is to be expected. "In the world you will have tribulation," says Jesus, "but take heart; I have overcome the world" (Jn 16:33). This Jesus abides with us until the time He comes as the king of glory. He doesn't come as to orphans left to ourselves, but rather to soldiers on battle lines equipped with weapons of the Spirit where we simply endure, faithful to callings where He has posted us. Recall a great promise of God in the midst of our enemies, in the midst of a world of sin, a fleshly body of sin, and the one tempting us to sin, how the great general comes to equip His soldiers, Lk 21:15: "I will give you a mouth and wisdom, which none of your adversaries will be able to withstand or contradict." The harshness of life, the assault of the enemies we Christians have in this world, all is transformed ultimately by a Lord who has overcome the world, and whose purpose, compassion, and mercy in the final day give us reason to hope in Him. • Prepare me, Lord Jesus, to endure in the vocations to which You have called me this day, and prepare me to wait patiently for Your return, even as I hope in the new heaven and new earth that You have prepared for me. Amen.

Faithful Prayer in the Community (5:13–20)

ESV	KJV
¹³Is anyone among you suffering? Let him pray. Is anyone cheerful? Let him sing praise. ¹⁴Is anyone among you sick? Let him call for the elders of the church, and let them pray over him, anointing him with oil in the name of the Lord. ¹⁵And the prayer of faith will save the one who is sick, and the Lord will raise him up. And if he has committed sins, he will be forgiven. ¹⁶Therefore, confess your sins to one another and pray for one another, that you may be healed. The prayer of a righteous person has great power as it is working. ¹⁷Elijah was a man with a nature like ours, and he prayed fervently that it might not rain, and for three years and six months it did not rain on the earth. ¹⁸Then he prayed again, and heaven gave rain, and the earth bore its fruit. ¹⁹My brothers, if anyone among you wanders from the truth and someone brings him back, ²⁰let him know that whoever brings back a sinner from his wandering will save his soul from death and will cover a multitude of sins.	¹³Is any among you afflicted? let him pray. Is any merry? let him sing psalms. ¹⁴Is any sick among you? let him call for the elders of the church; and let them pray over him, anointing him with oil in the name of the Lord: ¹⁵And the prayer of faith shall save the sick, and the Lord shall raise him up; and if he have committed sins, they shall be forgiven him. ¹⁶Confess your faults one to another, and pray one for another, that ye may be healed. The effectual fervent prayer of a righteous man availeth much. ¹⁷Elias was a man subject to like passions as we are, and he prayed earnestly that it might not rain: and it rained not on the earth by the space of three years and six months. ¹⁸And he prayed again, and the heaven gave rain, and the earth brought forth her fruit. ¹⁹Brethren, if any of you do err from the truth, and one convert him; ²⁰Let him know, that he which converteth the sinner from the error of his way shall save a soul from death, and shall hide a multitude of sins.

Introduction to 5:13–20 Healing, prayer, Confession and Absolution—these are the topics in the final admonitions to James's readers. Though the Letter's closing thoughts fall along typical lines of warning and imperative command, nevertheless the balance of the final eight verses indicate the gifts received by those who have faith (cf. 1:6–8) in the promises of our giver-God (cf. note at 1:5).

5:13–14 After devoting many words to the misuse of the tongue (cf. 3:1–12), James offers a more productive alternative, a constructive use of the faculty of speech: use your words for prayer and praise. Whether *suffering . . . cheerful . . . sick*, the invitation to see that the Lord desires to hear His children call upon Him is a comfort. All circumstances, good or bad, are opportunities to rest secure in a God who knows and cares and continues to provide; cf. Php 4:11–13: "I have learned in whatever situation I am to be content. I know how to be brought low, and I know how to abound. In any and every circumstance, I have learned the secret of facing plenty and hunger, abundance and need. I can do all things through Him who strengthens me."

5:14 James is likely one of the earlier epistles in the NT, and this verse offers an important picture of early church leadership. There seems to be an assumption that there are *elders* to be called to serve people in need with their prayers, an extension of the OT office (cf. Ex 19:7; 24:1) reflected in the NT as well (Ac 11:30; cf. Ti 1:5). The terminology for offices in public service to God's people also includes overseer, pastor, and deacon. It is not surprising to see a plurality of elders in one location assumed by James and his hearers. As they serve the sick, elders are enjoined to *pray over him, anointing him with oil*, a physical sign accompanying prayer. No promise is referred to concerning the effect of the oil, as, for example, no particular property of incense determines the quality of prayer in Levitical worship (cf. Ex 30). The use of oil here is consistent with the use of oil in other holy activities, namely, consecration, that is, setting apart for particular use, identification, or care (cf. Mk 6:13; Ex 30:22–31), symbolizing the presence and power of the Holy Spirit. This is why it is important that James includes the injunction *in the name of the Lord*; the assumption is that oil in itself does not heal, but the Lord does! Calvin wrote, somewhat awkwardly, on the topic:

> It is, indeed, certain that they were not all healed; but the Lord granted this favour as often and as far as he knew it would be

expedient; nor is it probable that the oil was indiscriminately applied, but only when there was some hope of restoration. For, together with the power there was given also discretion to the ministers, lest they should by abuse profane the symbol. (Calvin 355)

Bengel wrote:

That which Christ had committed to the apostles, Mark vi. 13, was afterwards continued in the Church, even after the times of the apostles: and this very gift, remarkably simple, conspicuous, and serviceable, was of longer continuance than any other. . . . It even seems to have been given by God with this intent, that it might always remain in the Church, as a specimen of the other gifts: just as the portion of Manna laid up in the ark was a proof of the ancient miracle. It is clear that James assigns the administration of this oil to the presbyters, who were the ordinary ministers. (Bengel 39)

5:15 The *prayer of faith* is the right way to use the tongue (cf. 3:1–12); a fuller explanation is offered here for what he had earlier mentioned at v. 13, namely, that prayer is the proper response to all circumstances. Connecting prayer with *faith* recalls what James has earlier said about asking of the giver-God (cf. 1:5–8). Regarding prayer spoken from faith, cf. 1:6. *save.* While we often use this word in the context of our eternal salvation from sin, death, and the devil, the word itself has a broad range of meanings, including to rescue or deliver. The Gk word can also connote deliverance from illness and thus could rightly be translated as "heal," which is more appropriate here, though salvation is also in view in v. 16. *raise him up.* Make him better physically (Mk 2:9; Lk 7:14), but also with a view toward the ultimate goal of the resurrection of the dead in Christ. So in Ac 3:1–4:22, Peter raised up the lame man and announced that by the name of Jesus "whom God raised from the dead" (3:15; 4:10) the man was healed. *committed sins, he will be forgiven.* Illness is sometimes a consequence of specific sins (Dt 28:58–62; 1Co 11:29–30), but this is not always the case (Jn 9:1–3). Still, sickness and death are consequences of our general fallen condition. In Christ, God is able to heal our bodies, which He will raise up on the Last Day.

5:16 Combined with a picture of Christian community that includes spiritual care, medical care, and mutual consolation in prayer is the call to *confess your sins to one another.* Melanchthon wrote that this is not "confession made to priests, but is the reconciliation of brothers to each other. Confession should be mutual" (Ap XIIB 12). The Lord delivers the gift of Confession and Absolution to His people, an authority Jesus claims for Himself (cf. Mk 2:5–12) and gives to the Church that He chooses and commissions (Jn 20:21–23). The words of confession are none other than what the Lord has given us to say, as we speak back to Him the truth of our status before Him under the Law (we are sinful) and receive in faith the words He gives us to hear through His intermediary under the Gospel (we are justified for the sake of Christ). The cure for sin is not inward striving. The cure for sin is not outward repair of damage. The cure for sin is always Confession and Absolution. God directs us to confess our sins to others as to Him, to forgive sins in His name, and so to effect restoration of His community and fellowship in His kingdom, as He directs His disciples in Mt 18:15–16. This "same-saying," that is, confessing sins and confessing faith in the One who saves, is the lifeblood of the Christian community, as Luther notes: "Conduct yourselves in such a way that each humbles himself before the other and confesses his guilt, if he has offended someone" (LW 36:356). Jesus Himself prays for unity among His disciples (Jn 17:11–26) as the *righteous person* whose prayer *availeth much* (KJV). There is a great comfort in knowing that Jesus Christ the Righteous One is our advocate with the Father (1Jn 2:1–2). In light of His effectual mediation on our behalf, we are confident to follow His command to *pray for one another* as people who have been declared righteous by faith and so pray "in faith" (Jas 1:6; cf. 5:15). The *power* of a righteous person's prayer is not what our world most often refers to as it waves around an alliterative platitude in "the power of prayer," mostly aimed at some kind of emotional comfort or expectation of a miracle in the form of healing of physical, financial, or spiritual burdens. Rather, the "effectual" or "effective working" of prayer is God's work, in the life of the praying individual as much as the community for which he or she prays. Human will ought not be the aim of such prayer, as human will is shown over and over again to be at odds with God's will (4:1–5, 13–17; cf. 1Jo 2:17). But God invites us to pray for His will to be done, which "is done even without our prayer, but we pray . . . that it may be done among us also" (SC, Third Petition), whatever we may hear from God's response to prayer, which accomplishes what human will and strength cannot, as Luther taught:

"The prayer of a righteous man has great power in its effects if it is serious and persistent. ... God intends to test you to see whether you can hold on tight, and to teach you that your prayer is not displeasing to Him or unheard, simply because His answer is delayed and you are permitted to go on seeking and knocking. (LW 21:234–35)

Wesley wrote:

He does not say, to the elders: this may, or may not, be done; for it is nowhere commanded. We may confess them to any who can pray in faith: he will then know how to pray for us, and be more stirred up so to do. And pray one for another, that ye may be healed. (Wesley 606)

He concluded that the healing was about "spiritual diseases."

5:17–18 Elijah had a *nature like ours*, a human nature, a sinful nature, but there is another reason he is described this way (Gk *homoiopathēs*, "of similar feeling"). In a context in which James's admonitions have been playing on the sympathy the Christian community members have for one another, this word reinforces how sympathy leads us, just as it did Elijah, to pray. James is not saying simply, consider this anecdote, consider this OT figure, but rather more than that: consider this one who can sympathize with our humanity, with our feeling. As such, Elijah is a type of Christ, who also prayed and affected the weather ("who then is this, that even the wind and the sea obey him?" Mk 4:41) and who also prayed for His disciples, in His own and in later generations (including you!). Calvin wrote:

Many therefore think that James points out here the way of brotherly reconciliation, that is, by mutual acknowledgment of sins. But as it has been said, his object was different; for he connects mutual prayer with mutual confession; by which he intimates that confession avails for this end, that we may be helped as to God by the prayers of our brethren; for they who know our necessities, are stimulated to pray that they may assist us; but they to whom our diseases are unknown are more tardy to bring us help. (Calvin 358)

5:19–20 The final verses offer a fitting conclusion to a Letter that may have seemed to James, on the whole, rather heavily balanced towards the Law-end of the ledger. Notice how the author does not unravel the foundation he has constructed regarding the Law's demands, but rather applies the correct cure to the problem of sin, a salve that serves to cover sins and close his thoughts on this epistle of faith in God's gifts. It is as if he is expanded, throughout his Letter, on 1Jn 2:1, "My little children, I am writing these things to you so that you may not sin," and then at the end of his Letter, reminds his hearers of the conclusion of that same verse in John's Epistle: "But if anyone does sin, we have an advocate with the Father, Jesus Christ the righteous."

Since the person left in sin will die in sin (1:15; cf. 5:15), James's admonition is to be like the shepherd who searches for the lost sheep, to turn the wanderer back and so *cover a multitude of sins*. The Christian church can be conceived of as a big "cover-up" job—sinners are covered by the righteousness of Christ, and fellow Christians follow the Eighth Commandment, according to Luther's explanation in the SC, by "explaining everything in the kindest way." Notice how James's final exhortation does not say that the one turning a sinner from his wandering will "omit the possibility" of sins, saving his soul "from the possible roads he could wander," but rather that he will save his soul from death and cover over his sins. The exhortation is in the spirit of the great seeker parables of Lk 15. To the good shepherd, the one wandering sheep is the most to be sought after. To the loving father, the son is to be covered immediately with the robe and the ring, and the elder brother instructed: you are always with me, all I have is yours, but we must rejoice because this brother of yours was lost and now is found. Returning the wanderer from his way (v. 20) to the truth (v. 19), saving him from death, is no other than giving him Jesus, the giver-God in the flesh, who says, "I am the way and the truth and the life" (Jn 14:6).

5:12–20 in Devotion and Prayer When James says "confess your sins to each other," he is showing some assumptions about Christians in the first century. He assumes they are sinners, who need to confess. Not once, but all the time. And he assumes they are saints. Not once, but all the time. He assumes what God has shown to be true of the church of the first century and the Church all the time: that we are all saints and sinners simultaneously, and so are in constant need of the precious gift of Confession and Absolution that God gives to define our activity, corporately, individually, collectively, for today and tomorrow. "When I urge you to go to confession," says Luther in the Brief Exhortation of the LC (32), "I am simply urging you to be a Christian." The assumption of James's Christians is still true today. Sin is not simply an individual burden to bear, as if faith is something only between me and Jesus; no, just as we commune with the Lord and His people, so also we confess before God and His people—people who share that best gift of all, the Word of grace and forgiveness in Christ. The Word spoken on you in absolution is indeed the Word of God who forgives sin, and not the word of any other. It is this Word that inspires us also to join our individual voice with that of all our brothers as we confess together our common faith in the God who has given such gifts! • Thank You, dear Lord, for Your gift of Confession and Absolution. Direct me to Your Word, read, taught, heard, received, believed, Your Word for my life and salvation. Give me faith by that Word that I may praise You as a God who answers prayers and as a God who forgives. Amen.

Anointing with Oil (James 5:14–15)

The reformers gave significantly different evaluations of James's admonition to anoint the sick with oil. Luther rejected the idea that the practice was a sacrament as it was in the Medieval Church (extreme unction). He associated it with a practice of the twelve apostles in Mark 6:13, "They cast out many demons and anointed with oil many who were sick and healed them." Melanchthon mentioned unction as a rite "received from the Fathers" in the Apology of the Augsburg Confession (XIII 6). He provided further comment in his Loci, which Chemnitz repeated in his own edition of the Loci:

> At one time, anointing with oil was a medical concern. For God, in order to invest the fathers and the prophets with some authority, therefore equipped them from the beginning with the gift of healing, as in the case of Abraham, Isaac, Jacob, Isaiah, and men like them who were physicians by profession. . . . Christ revived this ancient custom when He sent the apostles, ordered them to heal the sick, and equipped [them] with the gift of healing. This gift remained in the church also later, and it is certain that many are still healed by the prayers of the church. It is useful to point these things out so that we may learn that a healthy body is a gift of God which He gives us so that we might serve others. He wants this to be sought and fostered with some diligence. But the rite of anointing as it now exists is only a superstitious ceremony. And invocation of the dead was added, which is ungodly. Therefore this rite of unction with its additions is to be rejected. (Melanchthon cited in Chemnitz 8:1360–61)

Calvin offered many similar comments and criticisms in his Institutes 4.19.18–21. In contrast, Cranmer provided extensive comment on and commendation of the practice of anointing as a sacrament. He wrote:

> Although it be not expressed in Scripture, that the said apostles had then any new commandment of Christ to anoint such as they had healed with oil; yet forasmuch as the holy apostle St. James, indued with the Holy Spirit of Christ, prescribed a certain rule or doctrine, and gave in manner a commandment, that whensoever any person should fortune to fall sick, he should call or send for the priests or ancients of the church, and cause them to pray over him, anointing him with oil in the name of our Lord; and further added hereunto, as an assured promise, that by the said prayer of the priests and the sick person, made in right faith and

confidence in God, the sick man should be restored unto his health, and God should set him then so on foot again, and if he were in sin, his sins should be forgiven him: it shall therefore be very necessary and expedient that all true Christian people do use and observe this manner of anointing of sick persons, with due reverence and honour, as it is prescribed by the holy apostle St. James.

And to the intent the same, should be had in more honour and veneration, the said holy fathers willed and taught, that all Christian men should repute and account the said manner of anointing among the other sacraments of the church, forasmuch as it is a visible sign of an invisible grace: whereof the visible sign is the anointing with oil in the name of God; which oil (for the natural properties belonging unto the same) is a very convenient thing to signify and figure the great mercy and grace of God, and the spiritual light, joy, comfort, and gladness which God poureth out upon all faithful people, calling upon him by the inward unction of the Holy Ghost. And the grace conferred in this sacrament is the relief and recovery of the disease and sickness wherewith the sick person is then diseased and troubled, and also the remission of his sins, if he be then in sin. This grace we be assured to obtain by the virtue and efficacy of the faithful and fervent prayer used in the ministration of this sacrament of anointing, according to the saying of St. James, before rehearsed, and also according to the sundry promises made by Christ unto the faithful prayer of his church; as when Christ saith, Whatsoever ye shall ask and pray my Father to give unto you in my name, it shall be granted unto you. For the better understanding whereof, two things be here specially to be noted. The first is, that St. James calleth here the prayer to be used in the time of this inunction, the prayer of faith: whereby he meaneth that this prayer ought to be made in that right faith, trust, and confidence, which we ought to have in God, to obtain the effect of our petitions made in the ministration of this sacrament and that it ought to contain nothing but that shall stand with the pleasure, the honour, and glory of God; and that when we direct our prayers unto God for any bodily health or relief, or for any other temporal commodity, we ought always to temper our said prayer with this condition, that is to say, if it shall so stand with God's will and his pleasure. And that we ought to say, as Christ said in his prayer unto his Father, Father, if it shall please thee, I am content to die and suffer this shameful and cruel death of the cross. Thy will be fulfilled herein: let not my will and desire be followed, but let thy will and disposition be fulfilled, whereunto I wholly commit myself. The second thing to be noted is, that to the attaining of the said grace, conferred in this sacrament of extreme unction, it is expedient also that the sick person himself shall knowledge his offences towards God and his neighbour, and ask forgiveness of them for the same; and likewise forgive all them that have offended him in word or deed: and so being in perfect love and charity, to pray himself (as he may) with faithful heart, and full hope and confidence in God, for the remission of his sins, and restoring unto his bodily health, if it shall so stand with God's pleasure. (Cranmer 2:46–47)

Not surprisingly, fellow Englishman John Wesley defended the practice of anointing with oil and praying for healing. He wrote:

This single conspicuous gift, which Christ committed to his apostles, Mark 6:13, remained in the church long after the other miraculous gifts were withdrawn. Indeed, it seems to have been designed to remain always; and St. James directs the elders, who were the most, if not the only, gifted men, to administer at. This was the whole process of physic in the Christian church, till it was lost through unbelief. That novel invention among the Romanists, extreme unction, practised not for cure, but where life is despaired of, bears no manner of resemblance to this. (Wesley 606)

1 PETER

INTRODUCTION TO
1 PETER

Overview

Author

Simon Peter the apostle

Date

Before AD 67

Places

Pontus; Galatia; Cappadocia; Asia; Bithynia

People

Peter; exiles of the Dispersion; unbelievers; Gentiles; governmental leaders; servants; wives and husbands; elders of the Church; younger believers; Silvanus; "she who is at Babylon"; Mark

Purpose

To instruct and encourage the Lord's people as they endure suffering for the sake of righteousness

Law and Sin Themes

Sin; ignorance of foolish people; perishable; disobeying God's Word; darkness; judgment; fiery trials

Grace and Gospel Themes

Christ bore our sins in His body; He suffered for us; He ransomed sinners; He is imperishable; Christ's death involved a righteous man dying for unrighteous people (the great exchange); marvelous light; stand firm in God's grace; God's Word is the living and abiding Word; good news; royal priesthood; holy nation; chosen race

Memory Verses

Ransomed by Christ's blood (1:17–19); the chosen people (2:9–10); healed by Christ (2:24–25); Baptism now saves you (3:18–22)

Luther on 1 Peter

This epistle St. Peter wrote to the converted heathen; he exhorts them to be steadfast in faith and to increase through all kinds of suffering and good works.

In chapter 1 he strengthens their faith through the divine promise and power of the salvation to come. He shows that this salvation has not been merited by us but was first proclaimed by the prophets. Therefore they ought now to live new and holy lives, and forget the old life, as those who have been born anew through the living and eternal Word of God.

In chapter 2 he teaches them to know Christ as the Head and the Cornerstone, and like true priests to sacrifice themselves to

God as Christ sacrificed himself. And he sets about giving instructions to the various estates. First he teaches in general subjection to temporal rulership; afterward he teaches in particular that servants are to be subordinate to their masters and [even] to suffer wrong from them, for the sake of Christ who also suffered wrong for us.

In chapter 3 he teaches wives to be obedient, even to unbelieving husbands, and to adorn themselves with holiness. Likewise, husbands are to be patient with their wives and bear with them. And finally, all in general are to be humble and patient and kind to one another, as Christ was because of our sins.

In chapter 4 he teaches us to subdue the flesh with sobriety, watchfulness, temperance, prayer, and to find comfort and strength through the sufferings of Christ. He instructs the spiritual rulers to inculcate the words and works of God alone, and each to serve the other with his gifts; and not to be surprised but to rejoice, if we have to suffer for the name of Christ.

In chapter 5 he exhorts the bishops and priests as to how they are to live and to tend the people. He warns us against the devil, who without ceasing pursues us everywhere. (LW 35:390–91)

For more of Luther's insights on this book, see *Sermons on the First Epistle of St. Peter* (LW 30:1–145).

Calvin on 1 Peter

The design of Peter in this Epistle is to exhort the faithful to a denial of the world and a contempt of it, so that being freed from carnal affections and all earthly hindrances, they might with their whole soul aspire after the celestial kingdom of Christ, that being elevated by hope, supported by patience, and fortified by courage and perseverance, they might overcome all kinds of temptations, and pursue this course and practice throughout life.

Hence at the very beginning he proclaims in express words the grace of God made known to us in Christ; and at the same time he adds, that it is received by faith and possessed by hope, so that the godly might raise up their minds and hearts above the world. Hence he exhorts them to holiness, lest they should render void the price by which they were redeemed, and lest they should suffer the incorruptible seed of the Word, by which they had been regenerated into eternal life, to be destroyed or to die. And as he had said, that they had been born again by God's Word, he makes mention of their spiritual infancy. Moreover, that their faith might not vacillate or stagger, because they saw that Christ was despised and rejected almost by the whole world, he reminds them that this was only the fulfillment of what had been written of him, that he would be the stone of stumbling. But he further teaches them that he would be a firm foundation to those who believe in him. Hence he again refers to the great honour to which God had raised them, that they might be animated by the contemplation of their former state, and by the perception of their present benefits, to devote themselves to a godly life.

He afterwards comes to particular exhortations—that they were to conduct themselves in humility and obedience under the government of princes, that servants were to be subject to their masters, that wives were to obey their husbands and to be modest and chaste, and that, on the other hand, husbands were to treat their wives with kindness. And then he commands them to observe what was just and right towards one another; and that they might do this the more willingly, he sets before them what would be the fruit—a peaceable and happy life.

As, however, it happened to Christians, that how much soever they sought peace, they were often harassed by many injuries, and had the world for no just cause inimical to them, he exhorts them calmly to bear their persecutions, which they knew would promote their salvation. For this purpose he brings forward the example of Christ. On the other hand, he reminds them what unhappy end awaits the ungodly, whilst in the meantime God wonderfully delivers his Church from death by death. He still further refers to the example of Christ to enforce the mortification of the flesh. To this exhortation he adds various and brief sentences; but shortly after he returns to the doctrine of patience, so that the faithful might mingle consolation with their evils, regarding it as good for them to be chastised by the paternal hand of God.

At the beginning of the fifth chapter he reminds the elders of their duty, that they were not to tyrannize over the Church, but to preside under Christ with moderation. He recommends to the young modesty and teachableness. At length, after a short exhortation, he closes the Epistle with a prayer.

As to the place from which he wrote, all do not agree. There is, however, no reason that I see why we should doubt that he was then at Babylon, as he expressly declares. But as the persuasion had prevailed, that he had moved from Antioch to Rome, and that he died at Rome, the ancients, led by this sole argument, imagined that Rome is here allegorically called Babylon. But as without any probable conjecture they rashly believed what they have said of the Roman episcopate of Peter, so also this allegorical figment ought to be regarded as nothing. It is indeed much more probable that Peter, according to the character of his apostleship, travelled over those parts in which most of the Jews resided; and we know that a great number of them were in Babylon and in the surrounding countries. (Calvin 22–23)

Gerhard on 1 Peter

In its inscription this Epistle is called "catholic" because it was written not to some one person—like Paul's Epistles to Timothy, Titus, and Philemon—nor to some one particular church—as Paul's to the Romans, Corinthians, etc.—but to converts from the Jews who were scattered here and there, as the inscription reveals. Yet certain matters in this Epistle occur that pertain chiefly to Gentiles (c. 2:5, 10; c. 4:3), namely, because converted Jews, along with those of the Gentiles who had been converted, were making up one Church and were embracing one another as brothers (1:14, 18). The apostle himself explains the aim of his writing toward the end of the Epistle. He says, "By Silvanus, a faithful brother as I regard him, I have written briefly to you, exhorting and declaring that this is the true grace of God in which you stand" (5:12). He had two purposes especially in this Epistle: (1) to bear witness to the converted Jews that the teaching regarding the grace of God through Christ, which they had embraced by faith and in the confession of which they were standing fast, is the one, indisputable way of salvation, heavenly truth, and immovable doctrine. (2) To exhort them both to persevere steadfastly in this faith and to live a life worthy of that confession and pleasing to God.

In 5:13 he greets those to whom he has written in the name of "the church that is gathered at Babylon," from which one concludes that Peter wrote this Epistle in the city of Babylon. The question arises, however, whether we should take the name "Babylon" properly for the city of Egypt or metaphorically for the city of Rome. Those who claim the former use the following arguments: (1) It fits with the apostleship of Peter, inasmuch as he was especially appointed for the Jews (Gal. 2:7), a great number of whom were living in those eastern regions and especially in Babylon.

(2) We should not abandon the literal sense unless necessity itself compels us, none of which appears here. . . . (3) No reason can be offered why the apostle would want to conceal the name of the city of Rome and hint at it with a degrading name if he had written this letter from Rome. (4) Some of the Papists—Erasmus (Annotat.) and Costerus (Enchir., c. 3)—acknowledge this: "It is not inappropriate to say that the first Epistle of Peter was written from Babylon of Egypt." . . .

Concerning this first Epistle of Peter, Eusebius witnesses (Histor. eccles., bk. 3, c. 3): "There never was in the Church any controversy about it as if it were not of Peter, who gives it his own name. For this reason it should be listed among the canonical books." For this reason we also place it among the canonical books of the first rank. . . .

In the theme that he placed at the beginning of his paraphrase of this Epistle, Erasmus suspects that "Peter had written to the same people still another letter before this first Epistle" because he says at the end of this Epistle: "By Silvanus . . . I have written briefly to you" (1 Pet. 5:12). However, the words of his second Epistle clearly refute this opinion: "This is now the second letter I have written to you, beloved" (2 Pet. 3:1). He ought not have said "second" but "third" had he already written them two. Therefore when he claims that he has written by Silvanus, he is speaking not about another but about this first Epistle. (Cf. Heb. 13:22; 2 John 12.) From the words of 1 Pet. 4:16—"But if as a Christian"—one gathers that this Epistle was written after the disciples already had begun to be called "Christians." Luke mentions when this happened (Acts 11:26).

It consists of five chapters and contains, besides the preface and conclusion, (1) a remembrance of the spiritual benefits of God and (2) an exhortation to the true use of those benefits and to the pursuit of piety that is worthy of Christians. (E 1.270–272)

Bengel on 1 Peter

There is a wonderful weightiness and liveliness in the style of Peter, which most agreeably arrests the attention of the reader. The design of each Epistle is, to stir up by way of remembrance the pure mind of the faithful, 2 Pet. iii. 1, and to guard them not only against error, but even against doubt, ch. v. 12. This he does by reminding them of that Gospel grace, by which believers, being anointed, are inflamed to bring forth the fruits of faith, hope, love, and patience, in every duty and affliction. (Bengel 43)

Wesley on 1 Peter

In this introductory note, one can see the dependence of Wesley on Bengel.

There is a wonderful weightiness, and yet liveliness and sweetness, in the epistles of St. Peter. His design in both is, to stir up the minds of those to whom he writes, by way of remembrance, 2Peter 3:1, and to guard them, not only against error, but also against doubting, 1Pet 5:12. This he does by reminding them of that glorious grace which God had vouchsafed them through the gospel, by which believers are inflamed to bring forth the fruits of faith, hope, love, and patience. (Wesley 582)

Challenges for Readers

Authorship. The excellent Greek style of this Letter and the use of the LXX has led some modern scholars to doubt whether Peter, known as a simple fisherman (Ac 4:13), could have written it. However, early Christian testimony unanimously attributes the work to Peter. The author acknowledges that he had help (1Pt 5:12). Silvanus, who was also a colleague of the apostle Paul (cf. Ac 15–17; 18:5; 2Co 1:19; 1Th 1:1; 2Th 1:1), likely acted as Peter's scribe and assistant.

Baptism. Though Baptism is mentioned directly only once (3:18–22), references to Baptism appear throughout the Letter (e.g., 1:3, 23; 2:2, 9–10). Some scholars have concluded that 1 Peter is actually based on an Eastertide liturgy or was originally presented as a sermon to newly baptized members of a congregation. However, it is not possible to prove these suggested occasions for the work.

Suffering. Peter writes about Jesus' suffering for our redemption (1:18–21; 2:21–25; 5:4) as a way of helping the congregation understand the deeper spiritual significance of the suffering they were experiencing. His focus on suffering is not meant to teach Christians that they must suffer or seek out suffering and persecution but to help them see they will never escape some suffering so long as they are living in a sinful world.

Use of the OT. Though the congregations of Asia Minor likely had more Gentile members than Jewish ones, Peter makes extensive use of OT imagery to describe them. For example, he calls them "elect exiles of the dispersion" (1:1), "a holy priesthood" (2:5), "a chosen race, a royal priesthood, a holy nation" (2:9). He calls the congregation children of Abraham and Sarah (3:6), writing as though they were naturally born Israelites. Peter illustrates that the OT truly functioned as the Holy Bible and fount of early Christian teaching. Also, he shows how God was uniting Jews and Gentiles in the Christian congregations.

Household Code. Peter begins ch. 3 with a "household code," a guideline for conduct. The apostle Paul also writes in this way, showing the importance of helping early Christians find their way in a society with very different beliefs and practices. See note, Eph 5:22–6:9.

Blessings for Readers

As you read 1 Peter, pray for your brothers and sisters who face suffering. Count it all joy that your Lord Jesus Christ suffered all pain and shame in order to redeem you (3:18) and all who call upon Him. As He gives you strength, rejoice in your sufferings, knowing that you share in the sufferings of Christ (4:13). As with Jesus, the sufferings you face must give way to the subsequent glories God will reveal in you (1:11; 5:10).

Outline

I. Apostolic Salutation (1:1–2)

II. Introductory Thanksgiving (1:3–12)
   A. God to Be Praised for New Life in Christ (1:3–5)
   B. Christians Are Strengthened and Sustained in Their Suffering by Joy and Hope (1:6–9)
   C. Salvation Was Foretold by the Prophets (1:10–12)

III. Christians Are to Lead Holy Lives (1:13–2:10)
   A. Newfound Status Demands That Christians Be Holy, as God Is (1:13–16)
   B. Believers Are Mindful of the Price of Their Redemption (1:17–21)
   C. Christians Turn Away from Malice as They Mature in Faith and Love (1:22–2:3)
   D. As Living Stones in God's Temple, His Royal Priesthood and Chosen People, Christians Proclaim His Excellencies (2:4–10)

IV. Specific Instruction and Encouragement for Holy Living (2:11–4:11)
   A. The Purpose of Holiness (2:11–12)
   B. Christians Submit to Civil Authorities (2:13–17)

PART 1

APOSTOLIC SALUTATION (1:1–2)

ESV	KJV
1 ¹Peter, an apostle of Jesus Christ, To those who are elect exiles of the dispersion in Pontus, Galatia, Cappadocia, Asia, and Bithynia, ²according to the foreknowledge of God the Father, in the sanctification of the Spirit, for obedience to Jesus Christ and for sprinkling with his blood: May grace and peace be multiplied to you.	*1* ¹Peter, an apostle of Jesus Christ, to the strangers scattered throughout Pontus, Galatia, Cappadocia, Asia, and Bithynia, ²Elect according to the foreknowledge of God the Father, through sanctification of the Spirit, unto obedience and sprinkling of the blood of Jesus Christ: Grace unto you, and peace, be multiplied.

Introduction to 1:1–2 The introductory greeting of the apostle follows the standard formula of ancient letters: he names himself, he names the Letter's recipients, and he greets them with a salutation of grace and peace. Peter identifies himself as an apostle. It is not certain why these particular churches are receiving this Letter, but since the specific districts are named, it is probable that the Letter was intended to make the rounds to the churches in these Roman provinces. The salutation also identifies God with a trinitarian description.

1:1 Peter identifies himself as an *apostle*, that is, one sent by Jesus Christ to proclaim His Word. Peter's career in the NT is a varied and detailed one. We see him as a fisherman being called by the Lord Jesus (Mt 4:18–20). We know he was married because the Lord heals Peter's mother-in-law (Mt 8:14–15). Peter is one of the "pillar disciples," an eyewitness to Jesus as a member of the inner circle of the Twelve (cf. Mt 16:17–19) as well as those who saw Him at the transfiguration (Mt 17:1–8). Peter was eyewitness not only to events surrounding Christ's Passion (Lk 22:54–62), but also to the resurrection of our Lord and His sending of the Eleven (cf. Lk 24:44–49; Jn 20:21).

Peter is writing to the *elect*, that is, those who are chosen by God's grace to belong to Him (consistent with the idea elsewhere in the NT; cf. Eph 1:4; Col 3:12; 2Th 2:13). The Christians receiving this Letter in their Asian churches would, just as Christians today, receive comfort knowing who is chosen (they themselves) and who does the choosing (God alone).

Peter does not leave the description at "election" however, but calls them *exiles* (ESV, or *strangers*, KJV). The Gk word *parepidēmois* means "sojourner," but can also denote "exile," as it refers to a person who is inhabiting or dwelling in a place but without being bound to make any investment or seek citizenship in that place, not putting down roots. Significantly, while Gk has a word for a resident alien (*metoikos*), Peter does not use that term here, but rather, the word for someone whose home is not yet here. These are people in the middle of journeying somewhere else, on unfamiliar ground. These are the kind of people described in Hebrews: "These all died in faith, not having received the things promised, but having seen them and greeted them from afar, and having acknowledged that they were strangers and exiles on the earth. For people who speak thus make it clear that they are seeking a homeland. If they had been thinking of that land from which they had gone out, they would have had opportunity to return. But as it is, they desire a better country, that is, a heavenly one. Therefore God is not ashamed to be called their God, for he has prepared for them a city" (Heb 11:13–16). They are the ones who know what it is to be in exile, for they are part of the *Dispersion* (Gk *diaspora*), which refers to Jews scattered beyond the land of Israel (cf. note at Jas 1:1). Not only are Jews and Christians in an earthly exile from a place they once inhabited, but Peter refers here to the dispersion of living away from their true home: heaven. Peter addresses both Jewish and Gentile Christians throughout Asia Minor (generally the northern areas, near the Black Sea), people who live in districts represented in the Pentecost narrative (Ac 2:9–11). This demonstrates Peter's own range of influence. Peter was himself the preacher on the occasion when the first Galatians, Cappadocians, Bithynians, and so on heard the good news of the outpouring of God's Holy Spirit in Jerusalem.

1:2 Peter's apostolic greeting includes works by the persons of the Trinity, particularly the *foreknowledge* of God, the *sanctification* of the Spirit, and the *sprinkling* of Christ.

In regard to God's *foreknowledge*, there is a comfort knowing that our God has us in mind from outside of time. We might think that we can pinpoint a specific moment in our lives when we became aware of God's grace for us in Christ. Perhaps we even assign a special memory to that moment, saying that this is "the moment God called me." But this verse is a comfort, not because it invites us to wait around for a special moment in our own human chronology, but rather because it indicates God's eternal election (cf. v. 1) of us and that He has always known us and known how He would bless us. Peter's apostleship is a fact brought about in time by an eternal—outside-of-time—foreknowledge. Likewise, the calling of God's elect is certain. It is brought about in time through the delivery of God's gifts of salvation. God not only knew us before we had any knowledge of Him, but He also chose us by His grace before the foundation of the world (Eph 1:4; 1Tm 2:4; 2Tm 1:9). God is interested in revealing a certain word about His gracious character when He delivers the truth about His divine foreknowledge. Here as elsewhere in the NT (e.g., Rm 8:29), the point is not so much a question of whether God knows everything before it happens (He does), but that God graciously knows us. Our salvation has always been all His doing, eternally from the beginning.

The sanctifying work referred to in v. 2 is the work of God the Holy Spirit—this is explicit in the syntax of the nouns Peter employs. This is a necessary teaching in light of the old Adam at work in us, which looks to wrest control of our lives from God with intentions born of our human nature. How often have we heard (or thought, assumed, or taught?) that "justification is God's work, and sanctification is our work in response to that"? Such a human-devised doctrine is patently false according to what God reveals in the NT. It is best to think of "justification" and "sanctification" as two sides of the same coin, the coin being what God works on behalf of the believer for the sake of Christ. On the one hand He effects our salvation, purchasing and winning salvation, not with gold or silver but with the precious blood and innocent suffering and death of Christ on the cross. On the other hand He effects our being made holy as well, by calling us by the Gospel, enlightening us with His gifts, sanctifying (that is, setting us aside for special use) and keeping us in the one true faith. Reformation Christians are used to thinking about sanctification being located in God's work of making saints in the ways He "applies" or "imputes" His gifts to us, e.g., Holy Baptism, Holy Absolution, the Lord's Supper. As Peter talks about *sanctification of the Spirit*, then, he is reminding us of God's calling us from sin to faith, holiness, and good works that He has prepared in advance, that we should walk in them (cf. Eph 2:10). He is the author of all our good works, which flow spontaneously from the gifts He has delivered.

Obedience and *sprinkling* are paired together in Gk, offering Peter's readers a picture of salvation that depends on Christ's active fulfillment of the Law on behalf of us sinners and passive, obedient, sacrificial death. These works of Christ match the works of God the Father ("foreknowledge") and of God the Holy Spirit ("sanctification") to effect our salvation. Jesus' obedience to death—sacrificial death, is completed in His *sprinkling*. Both ceremonial water and sacrificial blood are applied through sprinkling in the OT (cf. Ex 24:4–8; Lv, like Nu 19, also includes various sprinklings for various unclean situations). Christ's blood is similarly described in the NT (Heb 9:13–14, 21; 10:22). A bridge spanning these instances of "sprinkling" may be helpfully considered at Is 52:15 with its sacrificial, suffering-servant connotation (though there is some question whether the Hbr word should be translated "startle," as the LXX translates, rather than "sprinkle"). Based on context, Peter may be alluding to this sprinkling of the obedient suffering servant. Christ, the Suffering Servant's sprinkled blood covers the nations, all the dispersion of Jewish and Gentile Christians who wander the earth until they reach their home in heaven. It is this sprinkling—of Christ's sacrificial blood that gives us salvation, which salvation is further indelibly applied to Christians in the sprinkling of baptismal water—that makes us holy. Luther reflected on this sanctifying sprinkling saying,

> It would be the greatest slander and blasphemy of the name of Christ if we refused to honor Christ's blood for washing away our sin or refused to believe that this blood makes us holy. Hence you must believe and confess that you are holy, but by this blood and not by reason of your own piety. (LW 30:7)

Whether Peter intended this "sprinkling" language to be particularly tuned to Holy Baptism is a question not easily answered, but the trinitarian greeting beginning this Letter may reflect the use of an early creed. One aspect (among many) in the early development of Christian creeds is the relationship of trinitarian formulas to the confession of faith in the liturgy of Holy Baptism. It has been suggested that this Letter maybe based on an Easter liturgy or perhaps it served as a sermon for those about to be, or recently, baptized. The center of the Letter is arguably the comforting teaching of Baptism (cf. 3:18–22), and other references to Baptism rise to the surface at 1:3, 23; 2:2, 9–10, supporting such a conjecture. There is more to consider in 1 Peter than can be explained through simply one limited occasion or worship context, but it is a good reminder in any case that the whole of Christian life, centered as it is in Holy Baptism, does well to reflect on how the rest of the doctrine in 1 Peter flows from that center.

1:1–2 in Devotion and Prayer In our various vocations, we are called to live and behave as citizens of our local town or city, our state, our nation. We are called on to engage a world in a common humanity with decency and honor. But we are not citizens of the world as the NT conceives of "the world." Rather, by virtue of our God's baptizing us in His name, we are citizens of a new kingdom, the kingdom of heaven. This citizenship moves the Christian to serve God and neighbor responsibly by fulfilling our obligations in the societies we inhabit, but prompts us even more to look forward to our promised destination, where our true and eternal citizenship is waiting to be enjoyed. What a hope Peter's Christians had in the first century as they faced persecutions and other trials in the various districts of a Roman empire that demanded allegiance on the scale of idol worship of its citizens and noncitizens alike. And what a hope we have in our recent history as we await the return of Christ and look forward to the eternal privilege of sharing in heavenly citizenship with those Christians who first read this Epistle. • Grant patience, Lord Jesus, to Your Church, until Your return, that we may best serve the citizens of this world by pointing to our own citizenship in Your kingdom. Amen.

Election: From Calvin to Wesley

Calvin and Wesley's comments on 1 Peter 1:1–2 illustrate important differences that developed in the Reformed tradition from the sixteenth century to the eighteenth century. Because Calvin's doctrine was so thoroughly focused upon election by grace, any doubts and differences in that teaching were bound to have a profound effect on persons in that school of thought. First, read Calvin:

> It may be asked, how could this be found out, for the election of God is hid, and cannot be known without the special revelation of the Spirit; and as every one is made sure of his own election by the testimony of the Spirit, so he can know nothing certain of others. To this I answer, that we are not curiously to inquire about the election of our brethren, but ought on the contrary to regard their calling, so that all who are admitted by faith into the church, are to be counted as the elect; for God thus separates them from the world, which is a sign of election. It is no objection to say that many fall away, having nothing but the semblance; for it is the judgment of charity and not of faith, when we deem all those elect in whom appears the mark of God's adoption. And that he does not fetch their election from the hidden counsel of God, but gathers it from the effect, is evident from the context; for afterwards he connects it with the sanctification of the Spirit. As far then as they proved that they were regenerated by the Spirit of God, so far did he deem them to be the elect of God, for God does not sanctify any but those whom he has previously elected. (Calvin 24)

Calvin discouraged Christians from curiosities about other persons' election. He pointed to the usual, outward evidences of adoption as God's children (confession of faith, Baptism, sanctification of life) yet he also wrote that knowledge of election might be known by "the special revelation of the Spirit."

At the end of the sixteenth century, Jacob Arminius of Holland began to question Calvin's doctrine of election, concluding that Christ died for all people and that mankind had free will. The synod of Dort (1618–19) condemned Arminius's teaching and sent his supporters into exile. In 1635–37, a second controversy erupted in the Reformed churches of New England when Anne Hutchinson claimed for herself special revelation from the Spirit who allowed her to see who was elect and who was not. She was condemned for heresy.

Following these historical controversies, Wesley came to a different doctrine of election, one that relied not simply on God but also upon human works and perseverance, greatly influenced by Arminius. Wesley wrote:

Election, in the scripture sense, is God's doing anything that our merit or power have no part in. The true predestination, or fore-appointment of God is, 1. He that believeth shall be saved from the guilt and power of sin. 2. He that endureth to the end shall be saved eternally. They who receive the precious gift of faith, thereby become the sons of God; and, being sons, they shall receive the Spirit of holiness to walk as Christ also walked.

Throughout every part of this appointment of God, promise and duty go hand in hand. All is free gift; and yet such is the gift, that the final issue depends on our future obedience to the heavenly call. But other pre-destination than this, either to life or death eternal, the scripture knows not of. Moreover, it is, 1. Cruel respect of persons; an unjust regard of one, and an unjust disregard of another. It is mere creature partiality, and not infinite justice. 2. It is not plain scripture doctrine, if true; but rather, inconsistent with the express written word, that speaks of God's universal offers of grace; his invitations, promises, threatenings, being all general. 3. We are bid to choose life, and reprehended for not doing it. 4. It is inconsistent with a state of probation in those that must be saved or must be lost. 5. It is of fatal consequence; all men being ready, on very slight grounds, to fancy themselves of the elect number. But the doctrine of predestination is entirely changed from what it formerly was. (Wesley 608)

The differences on election have continued in the Reformed/Wesleyan tradi-tion to the present day.

PART 2

INTRODUCTORY THANKSGIVING (1:3–12)

God to Be Praised for New Life in Christ (1:3–5)

ESV	KJV
[3]Blessed be the God and Father of our Lord Jesus Christ! According to his great mercy, he has caused us to be born again to a living hope through the resurrection of Jesus Christ from the dead, [4]to an inheritance that is imperishable, undefiled, and unfading, kept in heaven for you, [5]who by God's power are being guarded through faith for a salvation ready to be revealed in the last time.	[3]Blessed be the God and Father of our Lord Jesus Christ, which according to his abundant mercy hath begotten us again unto a lively hope by the resurrection of Jesus Christ from the dead, [4]To an inheritance incorruptible, and undefiled, and that fadeth not away, reserved in heaven for you, [5]Who are kept by the power of God through faith unto salvation ready to be revealed in the last time.

Introduction to 1:3–12 Peter establishes the OT foundation of the salvation that he claims is certain for his reader. That salvation is an inheritance (v. 4), described in terms that argue for its certainty and permanence. In the meantime, in the face of persecutions while here on earth, we are guarded and our faith is tested (vv. 5–7), all in honor of the Jesus whom we do not see, and yet love (vv. 8–9). This is a reminder of Peter's privilege to be an eyewitness, and his holding in common with those who "have not seen and yet believe" (Jn 20:29) the hope in "the outcome of your faith, the salvation of your souls" (v. 9). The OT foundation of this faith is the prophets who saw that what was to be delivered was "grace" (v. 10), wrapped in the "sufferings of Christ" (v. 11), for a later generation, not their own (v. 12).

1:3 Praise is offered to God for giving us a new birth into a *living hope*, a promise that was begun in the resurrection of Christ, and continues on to its fulfillment in the new life of resurrection for us as well. Hope in such a life to come gives life in the "now" of our existence under God. Luther writes, "Peter . . . exhorts them to be steadfast in faith and to increase through all kinds of suffering and good works. . . . He strengthens their faith through the divine promise and power of the salvation to come" (LW 35:390). We have the firm assurance of our own life to come because of the *resurrection* of Christ from the dead: our redemption and eternal life are guaranteed by the resurrection of Jesus, the firstborn from the dead (Col 1:18).

1:4 The *inheritance* Peter names in v. 4 is described using both polysyndeton (a rhetorical device that draws attention to words by means of surplus conjunctions) and assonance (a succession of similar vowel sounds in this case). A literal rendering of the verse would sound like: "an inheritance that is UNcorrupted AND UNdefiled AND UNfading, kept in heaven for you. . . ."

The inheritance is *kept* for you. The word "kept" is a tender one, used in a variety of contexts to mean "keep safe" (as here). It is also the word used in the NT to mean "obey." We are directed to "keep" the laws of God, but this does not mean mindless, blind compliance with orders. This Gk word (*tērein*) is a translation of the Hbr *shamar*, the word used to describe what God does to His own covenants, and what He requires of His people with respect to the same covenants: to cherish, to hold dear, to consider precious, guard, observe, esteem, revere them. Perhaps the verb "treasure" gets at the idea best.

The "inheritance" we look forward to is kept in heaven for us. The Christian hope is a hope that is a present reality because of God's promise. Our present-day reality includes a yearning for the future because it is a "now" and "not-yet," a promise to be fulfilled at the Last Day. Rm 8:23–25 reflects this truth: "And not only the creation, but we ourselves, who have the firstfruits of the Spirit, groan inwardly as we wait eagerly for adoption as sons, the redemption of our bodies. For in this hope we were saved. Now hope that is seen is not hope. For who hopes for what he sees? But if we hope for what we do not see, we wait for it with patience." On the blessing of heaven, consider what Luther said:

> This blessing is ours forever and ever, even though we do not
> see it now. . . . On earth no pleasure is so great that it does not

become unpleasant as time goes on. We see that one becomes weary of everything. But this blessing is different. All this is ours in Christ, by God's mercy, if we believe. (LW 30:13)

1:5 The inheritance of salvation is being kept for people who are *guarded through faith;* God Himself is doing the guarding. God created faith in us. God keeps us in that faith He created. God saves us by that faith, a fact we do well to confess: "The knowledge of this faith is necessary to Christians, brings the most abundant comfort in all troubles, and shows us Christ's office" (Ap V 266). And the *salvation* that we trust in is *ready to be revealed in the last time*: God's promised salvation will be fully revealed on Judgment Day. The word "ready" in Gk has the sense of "inevitably." It will happen. The expectation and inevitability entailed with the phrase that is easy to miss if only the English "ready to be revealed" is relied on. Sure, our salvation is ready. But we're not hearing a short-order cook hit the bell and yell "order up," as if a meal is "ready" and just waiting to be served by someone who will get to it in his own sweet time. Analogies that get at the urgency, certainty, and inevitability of this last hour are frequent in the NT, and so we see the apostle in good company with James (cf. 5:7–8: just as plants grow, so the coming of the Lord will indeed happen), Paul (cf. Php 4:5: "the Lord is at hand"); and so on. Bengel wrote:

Peter considers the whole of the time, from the beginning of the New Testament to the coming of Christ in glory, as one time, and that short, in comparison with the times of the Old Testament. (Bengel 5:47)

Christians Are Strengthened and Sustained in Their Suffering by Joy and Hope (1:6–9)

ESV	KJV
⁶In this you rejoice, though now for a little while, if necessary, you have been grieved by various trials, ⁷so that the tested genuineness of your faith—more precious than gold that perishes though it is tested by fire—may be found to result in praise and glory and honor at the revelation of Jesus Christ. ⁸Though you have not seen him, you love him. Though you do not now see him, you believe in him and rejoice with joy that is inexpressible and filled with glory, ⁹obtaining the outcome of your faith, the salvation of your souls.	⁶Wherein ye greatly rejoice, though now for a season, if need be, ye are in heaviness through manifold temptations: ⁷That the trial of your faith, being much more precious than of gold that perisheth, though it be tried with fire, might be found unto praise and honour and glory at the appearing of Jesus Christ: ⁸Whom having not seen, ye love; in whom, though now ye see him not, yet believing, ye rejoice with joy unspeakable and full of glory: ⁹Receiving the end of your faith, even the salvation of your souls.

1:6–7 These verses form a complete thought in one sentence. Peter's readers *rejoice* in the fact of God's election and salvation for the same reason that Mary does when she announces her own exulting at the beginning of the Magnificat (Lk 1:47). When the Lord is running the show, the rich are brought low and sent empty away, but the humble are exalted and the poor are made rich, and those who have no claim to significance can all of a sudden rejoice in their cosmic significance. They have been called by God (v. 1), they have been sanctified by Him and sprinkled by His blood (v. 2), and given a salvific inheritance (v. 4). This is something to laugh happily about, something to rejoice in. The grand reversal of God's kingdom comes to bear in the life of a sinner, whose *trials* will yet be transformed into glorious good once all is revealed in Christ at the Last Day (cf. Rm 8:28–39). These "trials" are tests of faith (cf. Jas 1:2), which the Christian can face in faith with God's power. The apostle links the experience of "trials" with refining fire, here not so much a lesson in metallurgy (smelting metals to remove impurities) as consistent rather with the hyperbole of Jas 5:2–3: gold may perish! Indeed all earthly treasure *perishes*, but your *faith* is infinitely more valuable. It will certainly pass pure through the fire of tribulations until Christ's revealing, when we will live with our Savior forever. Luther wrote about the refiner's fire analogy thus:

> All Scripture compares temptation to fire. Thus here St. Peter also likens the gold that is tested by fire to the testing of faith by temptation and suffering. Fire does not impair the quality of gold, but it purifies it, so that all alloy is removed. Thus God has imposed the cross on all Christians to cleanse and to purge them well, in order that faith may remain pure, just as the Word is, so that one adheres to the Word alone and relies on nothing else. For we really need such purging and affliction every day because of the coarse old Adam. (LW 30:17)

1:8–9 These two verses also span one complete thought in one sentence, which plays on the human capacity of sight and expression. On the one hand faith in Christ is faith in what is unseen, and on the other hand, the object of our faith produces a joy that is ineffable. All the Christian communities of his day knew that Peter had seen Jesus, but his audience has *not seen Him*. Unlike Peter, we are not eyewitnesses of Jesus, but through faith, our love for the Lord is just as authentic. Cf. Jn 20:29: "Jesus said to [Thomas], 'Have you believed because you have seen Me? Blessed are those who have not seen and yet have believed.'" We see Christ in visible means applied to the Christian in the sacraments. The tangible Word kills and makes alive under water and God's name. To receive body and blood, under the elements of bread and wine, is to receive Christ Himself. Such gifts create faith, which leads to *joy that is inexpressible and filled with glory*. "Glory" again reminds us that Peter was an eyewitness of His glory in the transfiguration (2Pt 1:17–18). By faith we are filled with His glorious presence. And those who have this joy in salvation are *obtaining*, receiving, the *outcome* or goal of their faith. The present tense gets to the heart of the mystery of the "now" and "not-yet" hope of this salvation from God. While citizens of God's kingdom look forward to the new heaven and new earth of the Last Day, we press on in present hope, knowing that even now, we are receiving faith's goal. Salvation is both a present reality and an eternal promise, as the Lutheran reformers confessed: "It is clear from God's Word that faith is the proper and only means through which righteousness and salvation are not only received, but also preserved by God" (FC SD IV 35).

Salvation Was Foretold by the Prophets (1:10–12)

ESV	KJV
¹⁰Concerning this salvation, the prophets who prophesied about the grace that was to be yours searched and inquired carefully, ¹¹inquiring what person or time the Spirit of Christ in them was indicating when he predicted the sufferings of Christ and the subsequent glories. ¹²It was revealed to them that they were serving not themselves but you, in the things that have now been announced to you through those who preached the good news to you by the Holy Spirit sent from heaven, things into which angels long to look.	¹⁰Of which salvation the prophets have enquired and searched diligently, who prophesied of the grace that should come unto you: ¹¹Searching what, or what manner of time the Spirit of Christ which was in them did signify, when it testified beforehand the sufferings of Christ, and the glory that should follow. ¹²Unto whom it was revealed, that not unto themselves, but unto us they did minister the things, which are now reported unto you by them that have preached the gospel unto you with the Holy Ghost sent down from heaven; which things the angels desire to look into.

1:10–11 The central message of the OT foundation that Peter lays here for his reader is *grace*: he sums up all of what *the prophets . . . prophesied* by focusing solely on "grace" in Christ. The Christ concealed in the OT and revealed in the NT is a Christ whose *Spirit* moved the prophets (cf. 2Pt 1:19–21), a Christ whose *sufferings* were the subject of prophetic inquiry, suggesting that Peter has in mind specifically the messianic expectations of the OT prophets. That the *Spirit of Christ* is assumed interacting with OT prophets suggests further that Peter is establishing connections between OT faith and the identification of God as Trinity (cf. Nu 6:22–27, where the divine name "Yahweh" is put on the people three times during the Aaronic benediction). The prophets learned of Christ through the Holy Spirit. The Lutheran reformers wrote:

> The Spirit is and remains Christ's [1 Peter 1:11] and the Father's own Spirit to all eternity, not separated from God's Son. . . . The

entire fullness of the Spirit has been communicated by the personal union to Christ according to the flesh, which is personally united with God's Son. (FC SD VIII 73)

1:12 This verse is complex, but rich. This introductory section of Peter's Letter comes to a close by bringing together heaven and earth, angels and people, the past and the present, the prophecy and the fulfillment. The prophets were not *serving . . . themselves* in their oracles of old concerning the Messiah, they were serving *you*. And now others serve you too—the preachers appointed to proclaim the *good news to you*. And they do this, as did the prophets, through the *Holy Spirit*. Peter was there when the Holy Spirit was *sent from heaven*, as he had been with Jesus to hear Him promise to send the Comforter. Now preachers empowered by this same Spirit preach the mysteries foreseen by the OT prophets, yet not even revealed to the *angels* who also worship God! All this serves to put Peter's audience on quite a pedestal. We are privileged to be served as people who have been given cosmic significance, to hear a Word that comes by the Holy Spirit—not just by men—and to glimpse the incarnation and work of Christ, not on behalf of all the heavenly host, but on behalf of sinful humanity.

1:3–12 in Devotion and Prayer Faith is so much more than a feeling—it is a fact that has consequences. Whatever mood happens to color the surface of our character, whatever trial or circumstance happens to engage our attention, the faith we have been given in Christ is a matter of receiving the resurrection of Christ as a sure thing. And it has consequences: most remarkably your resurrection. This means that faith has a goal, and that goal is ultimately the salvation of our souls (v. 9). Our faith is a living hope in God's promise, that soon the trials will be over, but until then, we are guarded by Him until we inherit the kingdom. • Lord God, heavenly Father, You proclaimed Your grace to prophets of old and revealed that grace in Christ Jesus, Your Son. Grant grace to those who proclaim grace to me this day, and grant grace to me that I may hear it as a gift for me. Preserve me in the faith You give in Your Word, until the day You receive me in Your kingdom. Amen.

PART 3

CHRISTIANS ARE TO LEAD HOLY LIVES (1:13–2:10)

Newfound Status Demands That Christians Be Holy, as God Is (1:13–16)

ESV	KJV
¹³Therefore, preparing your minds for action, and being sober-minded, set your hope fully on the grace that will be brought to you at the revelation of Jesus Christ. ¹⁴As obedient children, do not be conformed to the passions of your former ignorance, ¹⁵but as he who called you is holy, you also be holy in all your conduct, ¹⁶since it is written, "You shall be holy, for I am holy."	¹³Wherefore gird up the loins of your mind, be sober, and hope to the end for the grace that is to be brought unto you at the revelation of Jesus Christ; ¹⁴As obedient children, not fashioning yourselves according to the former lusts in your ignorance: ¹⁵But as he which hath called you is holy, so be ye holy in all manner of conversation; ¹⁶ Because it is written, Be ye holy; for I am holy.

Introduction to 1:13–2:10 Peter describes the Christians he is talking to in words that proclaim their radically new identity in Christ. This is important to hear, as he has already granted their status as sojourners or exiles (1:1), that is, people without a home or a citizen status in the world. Who are they then? They are Gospel people, God's specially chosen nation. This language reminds the reader of the OT designations of God's chosen people Israel. Peter's words argue that God's election has been fulfilled in Christ. First, he exhorts them to deliberate self-identity and action based on the grace revealed in Christ (1:13) that calls them to obedience to a holy God in opposition to the world's way of doing things (1:14–16). After all, their identity is in Christ. They are a people bought at a price, and their conduct while in the world flows from this identity (1:17–21). There is great comfort in this identity, which translates into genuine and enduring love for one another, even as the source of their identity is the enduring and life-giving Word of God (1:22–25). This identity as God's chosen Gospel people is reflected in an analogy of a building, a spiritual house, in which all of God's people are living stones (2:1–8). Using OT imagery that describes the special status of God's beloved people, Peter concludes the section with an exhortation to remember who they are: sojourner-exiles still in relation to the world, but a people treasured by God, belonging to God (2:9–10).

1:13 Peter invites his readers to put their present hope in the future fulfillment of their "now" and "not-yet" salvation. Grace given by God motivates the attention of the Christian, who is encouraged in this verse to *gird up the loins of your mind,* as the KJV translates Peter's colorful Gk literally and vividly (the ESV paraphrases this as *preparing your minds for action*). Spiritual and mental preparation for what faces the Christian in the world begins with trust in Christ's salvation, and continues in fully hoping on the *grace that will be brought,* a confidence in the present reality of God's grace in Christ (the Gk participle more accurately means "is being brought") and the future manifestation of Christ (His *revelation*).

1:14 Like Paul at Rm 12:2 ("Do not be conformed to this world, but be transformed by the renewal of your mind, that by testing you may discern what is the will of God, what is good and acceptable and perfect"), Peter calls his "children of obedience" not to *be conformed to the passions of your former ignorance.* A mind renewed by the Holy Spirit who proclaims the mighty works of God (Ac 2:11), specifically the person and work of Jesus Christ for the Christian, is confronted with the Law that convicts sinners and the Gospel that gives them life, a new pattern (the root of the word translated "conformed") of Law-Gospel identity to replace the old pattern of the world with its passions. The pattern of the world is the only resort of sinners ignorant of Christ, as Luther noted: "Here you see how St. Peter traces all misfortune to ignorance. For where faith and the knowledge of Christ are lacking, nothing but error and blindness remain, so that one does not know what is right and what is wrong. Then people fall into vices of all kinds" (LW 30:31).

1:15–16 The pattern to which Christians are *called* is one established by a *holy* God. The saved sinner responds to God's holiness with a holy life. The nature of faith for the Christian is same-saying, same-doing, same-being; Peter says just as the one calling you to saving faith and a living hope *is holy*, that the Christian's calling is also to *be holy* in his conduct, that is, consecrated to God, set apart from the world, set apart for God's special use. Peter proves the teaching from Scripture, quoting Lv 11:44: *You shall be holy, for I am holy.* The Christian hears both a command in this and a description; less an encouragement to striving internally or externally to "do the right thing," this OT proof reminds Christians that our identity as holy is established by a holy God. Though we remain sinners, we are simultaneously saints, justified by Christ (in Latin theological shorthand, *simul iustus et peccator*, at the same time saint and sinner). The fact of our being *simul* in Christ empowers us to strive against the world and the devil.

Believers Are Mindful of the Price of Their Redemption (1:17–21)

ESV	KJV
[17]And if you call on him as Father who judges impartially according to each one's deeds, conduct yourselves with fear throughout the time of your exile, [18]knowing that you were ransomed from the futile ways inherited from your forefathers, not with perishable things such as silver or gold, [19]but with the precious blood of Christ, like that of a lamb without blemish or spot. [20]He was foreknown before the foundation of the world but was made manifest in the last times for the sake of you [21]who through him are believers in God, who raised him from the dead and gave him glory, so that your faith and hope are in God.	[17]And if ye call on the Father, who without respect of persons judgeth according to every man's work, pass the time of your sojourning here in fear: [18]Forasmuch as ye know that ye were not redeemed with corruptible things, as silver and gold, from your vain conversation received by tradition from your fathers; [19]But with the precious blood of Christ, as of a lamb without blemish and without spot: [20]Who verily was foreordained before the foundation of the world, but was manifest in these last times for you, [21]Who by him do believe in God, that raised him up from the dead, and gave him glory; that your faith and hope might be in God.

1:17 This verse begins a lengthy and complex Gk sentence that extends to the end of v. 21. Peter's central thought is expressed in this verse with the main idea *conduct yourselves with fear.* This is not a call to terror, but reverence (cf. Pr 1:7; 16:6), that is, awe and humility, acknowledging our place in view of God's holiness. Christians are identified as ones who conduct lives in such holy reverence *if you call on him as Father who judges impartially*, that is, without discrimination, based on each person's individual deeds. All who call on the name of the Lord (cf. Jl 2:32; Ac 2:21; Rm 10:13) have their deeds judged in Christ as the author of all good works (Mt 25:34–40), judgment based on the perfect holiness and righteousness of Christ. As Peter's sentence extends through this section, it is clear that the circumstances qualifying this encouragement to conduct lives of holy reverence rest on the identity of Christians as "sojourners," *throughout the time of your exile.* OT Israel sojourned in the desert, entering a promised land under the fear of God. This is a type of Christ, whose people also wander as exiles and are aiming at God's promise (cf. Ac 13:18ff.). Christians are people who move through life not simply waiting around for the Lord to be revealed on the Last Day, but in light of the gifts of God's grace, namely, salvation here and in eternity, faith, and new life in the resurrection. Christians deliberately live to God, until we enter our true, heavenly home (1:1).

1:18–19 "Conduct lives of holy reverence if you call upon the Father," Peter argues at the beginning of the sentence. He now continues, "Conduct lives of holy reverence" *knowing that you were ransomed.* Redemption ("buying back") has a price. Peter sums up the purchase price with a powerful parallelism. Luther echoed Peter's words in his explanation to the Apostles' Creed: Jesus Christ "has redeemed me, a lost and condemned person, purchased and won me from all sins, from death, and from the power of the devil; not with gold or silver, but with His holy, precious blood and with His innocent suffering and death, that I may be His own" (SC, Second Article; cf. Mt 20:28; Eph 1:7; Rv 5:9). Peter links Christ's blood with the blood of OT sacrifice in v. 19, comparing Christ to *a lamb without blemish or spot.* In the OT, a sacrifice had to be perfect. This foreshadowed Christ the perfect sacrifice, free from all sin and worthy of saving all people (cf. Ap XIII 8). God's righteousness is satisfied with substitutionary blood. OT Israel did not sacrifice animals because they merited forgiveness, but because God's righteous Law provided a means for His people to be in community with God and with one another, until such time as the One Holy and Perfect Sacrifice would be delivered to death, to deliver His people. The perfection of Christ's innocent blood satisfies God's righteousness fully, as Luther commented:

> Just one drop of this innocent blood would have been more than enough for the sin of the whole world. Yet the Father wanted to pour out His grace on us so abundantly and to spend so much that He let His Son Christ shed all His blood and gave us the entire treasure. Therefore He does not want us to make light of and think little of such great grace; but He wants us to be moved to conduct ourselves with fear, lest this treasure be taken away from us. (LW 30:36)

The ransom of Christ buys back from *the futile ways inherited from your forefathers*. Which forefathers does Peter have in mind? Some have thought this verse indicates that Peter is talking variously to either Jews or Gentiles as a specific audience (cf. v. 1), but it is difficult to imagine Peter, who quotes the OT frequently, broadly condemning Jewish Christians with such a general accusation. It is probably simpler to consider Gentile Christians as a specific audience, thought we need not be so specific: Peter's point throughout the Letter is that Christians are elect, called, sojourners "in the world and not of the world." Whether Gentile or Jewish Christians, then, the OT identity of "God's people" has been transferred to those who receive faith and are in Christ. Whether Jew or Gentile, "futile ways of our forefathers" include various ways of living apart from God's will, such as pursuing evil desires, following other religions, or relying on ritualism or laws to save. There is no redemption apart from Christ's work.

1:20–21 "Conduct your lives in holy reverence" because you are end-times people! Be faithful because you are the ones who receive the gift of faith in Christ's resurrection! Your faith and hope are in God! Peter's extended thought concludes with a confession of Christ, who was *foreknown before the foundation of the world* as well as *made manifest* now to us in these *last times*. The focus here is not the eternal election of the faithful, but rather the eternal plan of salvation, whose subject is Christ. Even before creation, God determined the plan of salvation and chose to send His Son to be our Redeemer, a plan that has been *made manifest* in human time, at

Christ's incarnation, and will culminate in His glorious return. All this has been revealed for the sake of God's people, who *through Him* are believers, as Christ is the only way to the Father. Christ and the Father are inextricably connected; Peter concludes the thought doxologically, reinforcing the relationship between the Father and the Son by identifying *God, who raised him.* Christ's resurrection is attributed to the Holy Trinity (cf. Rm 8:11). The *glory* of Christ's resurrection completes the glory He claims through His death (cf. Jn 12:23–32).

Christians Turn Away from Malice as They Mature in Faith and Love (1:22–2:3)

ESV	KJV

22Having purified your souls by your obedience to the truth for a sincere brotherly love, love one another earnestly from a pure heart, 23since you have been born again, not of perishable seed but of imperishable, through the living and abiding word of God; 24for
 	
"All flesh is like grass
   and all its glory like the flower
     of grass.
The grass withers,
   and the flower falls,
25but the word of the Lord
   remains forever."
 	
And this word is the good news that was preached to you.
 	
2 1So put away all malice and all deceit and hypocrisy and envy and all slander. 2Like newborn infants, long for the pure spiritual milk, that by it you may grow up into salvation—3if indeed you have tasted that the Lord is good.
	22Seeing ye have purified your souls in obeying the truth through the Spirit unto unfeigned love of the brethren, see that ye love one another with a pure heart fervently:
	23Being born again, not of corruptible seed, but of incorruptible, by the word of God, which liveth and abideth for ever.
	24For all flesh is as grass, and all the glory of man as the flower of grass. The grass withereth, and the flower thereof falleth away:
	25But the word of the Lord endureth for ever. And this is the word which by the gospel is preached unto you.
	2 1Wherefore laying aside all malice, and all guile, and hypocrisies, and envies, and all evil speakings,
	2As newborn babes, desire the sincere milk of the word, that ye may grow thereby:
	3If so be ye have tasted that the Lord is gracious.

1:22–23 When Peter describes his readers as having *purified* themselves, he uses a word that does not mean simply "cleanse," like taking a bath, but rather "consecrate," that is, make pure for a ritual function (the same Gk word is used at Jas 4:8 and 1Jn 3:3). As such, it is consistent with the work of God the Holy Spirit in "sanctifying" the believer (setting aside for holy use; cf. v. 1). *Obedience to the truth* is what consecrates God's people for holy action, because it depends on its object, the truth. Peter calls forgiven Christians to do what God's Word teaches: actions that flow from the life we have in Christ's resurrection (v. 21). The holy action to which God calls those who have been thus consecrated is *sincere brotherly love*. God does not need our good works, but our neighbor does. Our sanctification, our consecration, is located in the space in which God makes His people holy, and our communion with Him is at the same time a communion with *one another*, a pure and eager ("sincere, genuine") brotherly love. Peter uses two different words for love in v. 22: the un-hypocritical brotherly love (Gk *philadelphia*) that results from obedience to the truth, and the love (Gk *agapē*) marked by self-sacrifice from a *pure heart* (Cf. Ps 51:10). The source of the loving community of Christ's Church is that we are in fact brothers (cf. Jas 1:2) because we share a common birth, a birth from above. We are *born again* in Christ's resurrection. This is not a rebirth that leads to another death, because the source, the *seed* of this new life, is not *perishable* but *imperishable*. This life has its source in the *word of God, which liveth and abideth forever* (KJV). Cf. Jn 1:12–14: "to all who did receive Him, who believed in His name, He gave the right to become children of God, who were born, not of blood nor of the will of the flesh nor of the will of man, but of God. And the Word became flesh and dwelt among us, and we have seen his glory, glory as of the only Son from the Father, full of grace and truth."

1:23–25 What does Peter mean when he says *word*? As an eye-witness to the ministry of Jesus, Peter had a front-row seat to His person and work, and also the words of Jesus Himself. As a witness to the resurrection, Peter knows that the promise of Christ's words about new life is confirmed by His glorious resurrection from the dead. The Word of God makes alive! And this same Word of God is what is sown in the hearts of hearers, guaranteeing their resurrection as well. But the Word of God is also the OT promise that is fulfilled in Christ (Jn 5:39; Mt 5:17). The content of the apostles' preaching is the fulfillment of the OT promise in Christ (cf. Ac 2:14–42); the re-cord of apostolic teaching is indeed also the Word of God that Peter is concerned with as he and his contemporaries are involved in the emerging NT documents. The Word of God is tangible—not just ink on paper, not just a "what," but a "Who": Jesus Christ, the Word made flesh (Jn 1:14).

1:24–25 Peter underlines the truth of God's enduring and living Word being the imperishable seed that makes Christians enduring and living too, by offering the proof-text of Is 40:6 and 8 (cf. Jas 1:10–11). This *word* was proclaimed as good news to Peter's hearers—the good news here being that the Word of the Lord endures *forever* (lit., "unto the age"). This is Gospel talk after the Law. The Law kills (*all flesh is like grass . . . grass withers . . . the flower falls*), but the Gospel makes alive, with a permanent, enduring, and living Word of God that lasts forever. Those raised by the Word, who grow as God's living members from this living, imperishable seed, also have the living hope that they will live forever. O death, where is thy sting? (1 Cor 15:55).

1:13–25 in Devotion and Prayer A commonplace of Lutheran teaching is the emphatic predominance of Gospel in our proclamation of Christ. This is more than simply making sure not to leave a Sunday morning congregation on the edge of a cliff with the demands of God's Law by tying up a sermon with "Oh, and don't forget, Jesus died for you and rose again." Rather, the Gospel predominates preaching, teaching, and indeed the whole life of the Christian because the Gospel is the center of God's revelation of Himself and therefore becomes the center of our identity in Christ. Peter affirms the centrality of Christians' "Gospel identity" by contextualizing his exhortation to Christian living in an appeal to the historic acts that define us sojourners as we travel in this world, aiming always at our goal of life forever with God. What do we do, and why do we do it? Peter's answer is this: we are Christ's. He won us. He paid for us with His blood. He rose! He gave us faith. He places Himself in our midst with His gifts; He places us in community with one another through those same gifts. So love! Because He so loved us. The Gospel has changed us into people with Gospel identity. We no longer walk in conformity with the pattern of this world. Raised to new life, transformed, God renewing our minds, we walk in God's will, confident in nothing other than the grace of God in Jesus Christ. • Lord Jesus Christ, in Holy Baptism You applied Your death to me that the body of sin may be drowned, and You applied Your resurrection life to me that a new Adam may arise and walk in newness of life. Make me ever mindful of Your resurrection from the dead, applied to me in Holy Baptism, that I may walk as a sojourner here and anticipate joyfully the life to come. Amen.

2:1–2 The Christian is called to *put away* all manner of sinful behavior. Peter punctuates the catalogue of sins with *hypocrisy*, recalling the adjective sincere (KJV *unfeigned*, lit., "un-hypocritical") in 1:22 to describe the love we have for one another. "Putting away" such sins is a calling to daily contrition and repentance, in light of the constant state of grace that defines a Christian life. Christians repent of *deceit* (Gk *dolon*). The remedy for such sin is the *pure* (Gk *adolon*, the opposite of the word for deceit, literally "un-tricky," that is, unadulterated; cf. the Luther quotation below) *milk* which Peter calls his reader to *long for*. The image Peter offers is a tender one. Just as he has encouraged his readers with "brotherly love" (1:22) and called them "children" (1:14), so here he compares them to newborns who crave the best nourishment for newborns: mother's milk. Christians crave what's best for them in Christ: the Word of God that nourishes them (cf. 1Tm 4:6).

It is interesting that Peter would include this phrase *grow up into salvation*, because taken out of context, it might leave the impression that salvation is a quantifiable activity. How much do you have? Do I have less than her? I've got 78% salvation, but I hope to get up to 81% by Maundy Thursday? Such quantifications are neither implied nor encouraged by this verse. *Salvation,* in this phrase, is not an unattained goal to acquire by collecting the right amount of tokens; it is the already-attained goal of Christ that provides the habitation of those growing up. Peter is rather extending the metaphor of babies being nourished by milk who grow up into strong children and adults; so also Christians are called to be nourished on the rudimentary, nourishing principles of salvation, which result in a mature faith, as Luther noted:

> The milk is nothing but the Gospel, which is also the very seed by which we were conceived and born, as we heard above. This is also the food that nourishes us when we grow up; it is the armor which we put on and with which we equip ourselves. Yes, it is everything put together. But the admixture is the human doctrines with which the Word of God is adulterated. (LW 30:48–49)

The author of Hebrews refers to Christian learning under the same figure: "For though by this time you ought to be teachers, you need someone to teach you again the basic principles of the oracles of God. You need milk, not solid food. . . . But solid food is for the mature, for those who have their powers of discernment trained by constant practice to distinguish good from evil" (5:12, 14).

2:3 Ever reinforcing his teaching with the "living and abiding word of God" (1:23), Peter underscores the milk metaphor with the reminder that his readers have *tasted that the Lord is good*, a reference to Ps 34:8. It is probable that the Psalter was employed not only as a teaching text in Peter's Christian community, but was also (as still today) the substance of recited and sung worship. Peter may be suggesting more than just the climax of his metaphor here. Perhaps he assumes his readers know the other stanzas of this hymn: "Oh, taste and see that the LORD is good! Blessed is the man who takes refuge in him! Oh, fear the LORD, you His saints, for those who fear Him have no lack! The young lions suffer want and hunger; but those who seek the LORD lack no good thing" (Ps 34:8–10). "Tasting and seeing" God's goodness is receiving His Word. What extraordinarily palpable, tactile, material language to use for receiving the Word of God! Naturally so, for Christians receive the Word in the water of Baptism, who likewise receive the Word in the bread and wine, in the body and blood of the Lord.

As Living Stones in God's Temple, His Royal Priesthood and Chosen People, Christians Proclaim His Excellencies (2:4–10)

ESV	KJV
⁴As you come to him, a living stone rejected by men but in the sight of God chosen and precious, ⁵you yourselves like living stones are being built up as a spiritual house, to be a holy priesthood, to offer spiritual sacrifices acceptable to God through Jesus Christ. ⁶For it stands in Scripture: "Behold, I am laying in Zion a stone, a cornerstone chosen and precious, and whoever believes in him will not be put to shame."	⁴To whom coming, as unto a living stone, disallowed indeed of men, but chosen of God, and precious, ⁵Ye also, as lively stones, are built up a spiritual house, an holy priesthood, to offer up spiritual sacrifices, acceptable to God by Jesus Christ. ⁶Wherefore also it is contained in the scripture, Behold, I lay in Sion a chief corner stone, elect, precious: and he that believeth on him shall not be confounded.

⁷So the honor is for you who believe,
but for those who do not believe,
"The stone that the builders
rejected
has become the cornerstone,"
⁸and
"A stone of stumbling,
and a rock of offense."

They stumble because they disobey the word, as they were destined to do. ⁹But you are a chosen race, a royal priesthood, a holy nation, a people for his own possession, that you may proclaim the excellencies of him who called you out of darkness into his marvelous light. ¹⁰Once you were not a people, but now you are God's people; once you had not received mercy, but now you have received mercy.

⁷Unto you therefore which believe he is precious: but unto them which be disobedient, the stone which the builders disallowed, the same is made the head of the corner, ⁸And a stone of stumbling, and a rock of offence, even to them which stumble at the word, being disobedient: whereunto also they were appointed. ⁹But ye are a chosen generation, a royal priesthood, an holy nation, a peculiar people; that ye should shew forth the praises of him who hath called you out of darkness into his marvellous light; ¹⁰Which in time past were not a people, but are now the people of God: which had not obtained mercy, but now have obtained mercy.

2:4–5 Peter proceeds with another metaphor drawn from the OT, this one being particularly significant to the apostle himself. God's people come to a *living stone* and are built up as *living stones* in Him. Who better to deliver a picture of *stones* than the one who got his named changed by Jesus, from "Simon" to "Rocky"?: "Jesus answered him, "Blessed are you, Simon Bar-Jonah! For flesh and blood has not revealed this to you, but My Father who is in heaven. And I tell you, you are Peter [Gk *Petros*], and on this rock [Gk *petra*] I will build My church, and the gates of hell shall not prevail against it" (Mt 16:17–18).

The sentence extending over vv. 4–5 has an interesting interplay of singular and plural nouns. The subject of the sentence is everyone Peter is addressing: the many who *come to Him*, the One Living Stone: Jesus. He was rejected by men, but chosen of God and honored. They are being built together as living stones also, not into multiple holy dwelling places, but as one singular *spiritual house*, that is, the temple where the Holy Spirit dwells; cf. 1Co 3:16–17 (where the "you" is also notably plural, and the "temple" notably singular): "Do you not know that you are God's temple and that God's Spirit dwells in you? If anyone destroys God's temple, God will destroy him. For

God's temple is holy, and you are that temple." The single building has a single purpose: a single *holy priesthood to offer spiritual sacrifices*, namely prayer, praise, and thanksgiving. Cranmer wrote:

> Another kind of sacrifice there is, which doth not reconcile us to God, but is made of them that be reconciled by Christ, to testify our duties unto God, and to show ourselves thankful unto him; and therefore they be called sacrifices of laud, praise, and thanksgiving. The first kind of sacrifice Christ offered to God for us; the second kind we ourselves offer to God by Christ. And by the first kind of sacrifice Christ offered also us unto his Father; and by the second we offer ourselves and all that we have, unto him and his Father. And this sacrifice generally is our whole obedience unto God, in keeping his laws and commandments. Of which manner of sacrifice speaketh the prophet David, saying, A sacrifice to God is a contrite heart. And St. Peter saith of all Christian people, that they be an holy priesthood to offer spiritual sacrifices, acceptable to God by Jesu Christ. And St. Paul saith, that alway we offer unto God a sacrifice of laud and praise by Jesus Christ. (Cranmer 2:449)

The people of God collectively are the temple in which He dwells. Their works are *acceptable* because they are in Christ, the *chosen and precious* cornerstone of the temple. Wesley wrote:

> There is a wonderful beauty and energy in these expressions, which describe Christ as a spiritual foundation, solid, firm, durable; and believers as a building erected upon it, in preference to that temple which the Jews accounted their highest glory. And St. Peter speaking of him thus, shows he did not judge himself, but Christ, to be the rock on which the church was built. (Wesley 611)

The *priesthood* that serves God's purpose is a calling enjoyed by God's people, a single status regardless of specific vocation. This means that Christians, variously called to particular roles as parents or children; employees or employers; citizens, subjects, rulers; neighbors, relatives, friends; all nevertheless share a common identity as "priests." This does not mean that each and every Christian in the church is a minister or temple-priest by specific vocation, but rather that we share in a priest*hood* by virtue of God calling us His own. It is helpful to consider this "priesthood" as a status, in distinction to any particular priestly function. Peter is employing OT imagery. Not every Israelite was called, for example, to be a Levite in charge of the temple or regulate animal sacrifice, or called to the Aaronic priest-hood, but all Israel was a holy priesthood to God (Ex 19:5–6; cf. v. 9 below). What is described here by the apostle is a special identity, one that expresses collectively our role before God in Christ, much as the image of the "Bride of Christ" is to be understood collectively; the benefits of that collective identity are no less than God's imputed righteousness, as Luther noted: "Since Christ is the Groom and we are the bride, the bride has everything that the Groom has, even His own body. When He gives Himself to the bride, He gives Himself entirely as what He is; and the bride, in turn, also gives herself to Him" (LW 30:53).

2:6 Peter moves through the OT in the next several verses to fill out his "stone" analogy. The first text he quotes, Is 28:16, is the beginning of an alarm ringing from Is 28–33 in response to the twi-light and impending doom of Israel's Northern Kingdom. Jerusalem's leaders sought security in an alliance with Egypt as her northern neighbors were succumbing to Assyrian destruction. Isaiah proph-esies similar devastation for Jerusalem, but assures the remnant of Israel that in spite of Jerusalem's coming destruction, God would build a new Jerusalem that could not be destroyed. Paul uses the prophecy of Isaiah as he considers the faith of the remnant (Rm 9:33; 10:11); Peter would have his readers see that the Christian Church is that remnant of Israel, because the *cornerstone* of Isaiah's prophecy is Christ. The OT language of *Zion* extends past simply the Temple Mount of Jerusalem, to encompass wherever God dwells. As Peter notes at v. 5, this dwelling place is now the "spiritual house" built of the "living stones" who have approached "The Living Stone," Christ.

2:7 Peter quotes Ps 118:22. He distinguishes those who receive *honor from God, who exalts those* trusting in Him. The leaders of the world and those wise in the way of the world rejected Christ, just as the world thought nothing of God's Israel in the OT. In such a way those who are nothing to the world are of great worth to God, who grants citizenship in a new Jerusalem as a free gift to be received by those who *believe*. Calvin wrote about the cornerstone:

> Therefore the Prophet not only calls him a corner-stone, which connects the whole edifice, but also a stone of trial, according to which the building is to be measured and regulated; and farther, he calls him a solid foundation, which sustains the whole edi-fice. He is thus, then, a corner-stone, that he might be the rule of

the building, as well as the only foundation. But Peter took from the words of the Prophet what was especially suitable to his argument, even that he was a chosen stone, and in the highest degree valuable and excellent, and also that on him we ought to build. This honour is ascribed to Christ, that how much soever he may be despised by the world, he may not be despised by us; for by God he is regarded as very precious. But when he calls him a cornerstone, he intimates that those have no concern for their salvation who do not recumb on Christ. What some have refined on the word "corner," as though it meant that Christ joins together Jews and Gentiles, as two distinct walls, is not well founded. Let us, then, be content with a simple explanation, that he is so called, because the weight of the building rests on him. (Calvin 67–68)

2:8 Is 8:14 serves as a counterpoint to the distinction introduced in v. 7. "Honor" is given by God to those who trust in Christ the cornerstone, who was to be a sanctuary for Judah and Israel. But those who rejected Him would find another kind of stone: not a "cornerstone" but a "stumbling block": *a stone of stumbling and a rock of offense.* "Offense" (Gk *skandalon*, lit., a "trap" or "snare," cf. Mt 18:7) here indicates the umbrage or outrage God's wisdom causes the rulers of the world. The image is powerful: either you will have the Christ who is the cornerstone, or you will have the other Christ, the one at whom you take offense, the Judge to whom Jesus refers at Lk 20:17–18: "What then is this that is written: 'The stone that the builders rejected has become the cornerstone'? Everyone who falls on that stone will be broken to pieces, and when it falls on anyone, it will crush him" (cf. Ps 2). All who do not repent and come to faith in Christ the cornerstone are *destined* so to stumble, which Peter indicates means ultimate destruction.

2:9 Ex 19 records the words the Lord commanded Moses to speak to the people when He first brought Israel to the Sinai wilderness. Peter paraphrases this speech for his "sojourners" in the wilderness of this world, highlighting God's actions as no less miraculous than—indeed the fulfillment of!—that OT salvation event. The LORD commanded Moses to say, "You yourselves have seen what I did to the Egyptians, and how I bore you on eagles' wings and brought you to Myself. Now therefore, if you will indeed obey My voice and keep My covenant, you shall be My treasured possession among all peoples, for all the earth is Mine; and you shall be to Me a kingdom of priests and a holy nation" (Ex 19:4–6). Peter identifies Christians in similar terms, beginning with four brief phrases that crescendo, describing the miracle of an insignificant people being given cosmic significance.

Peter calls Christians a *chosen race*. Just as the Israelites were once the chosen people of God, now Christians are the new Israel, chosen by God. The election of Christ as the Lord's chosen and precious stone (vv. 4, 6) is matched by the election of the Lord's people (1:1). In light of Ex 19:6, Peter modifies the phrase he just used, "holy priesthood," to *royal priesthood*. Not "kingly priests," but rather a priesthood in the kingdom of the King: God Himself. God's election is what effects this general priesthood (again to be understood as status rather than function, cf. note at v. 5), an identity that is established through faith that receives God's gifts. As such every member of the kingdom of God is considered His royal priest, from the greatest to the least, slave, free, child, man, woman. The only "office" to point to in this priesthood is that which receives our status: faith, as Luther points out: "Each and all are . . . equally spiritual priests before God. . . . Faith alone is the true priestly office. . . . Therefore all Christian men are priests, all women priestesses, be they young or old, master or servant, mistress or maid, learned or unlearned" (LW 35:101). Peter continues with the description of the Christian Church as a *holy nation*, again a direct quotation of Ex 19:6 (LXX). The people of God's calling are holy because He is holy; cf. note at 1:15–16. Finally Peter includes the description *a people for His own possession*. This translates the Hbr word *segulah*, which means "treasured possession"; the keepsake, the precious, cherished, beloved prize that God holds dear. This tender description was applied to Israel first at Ex 19:5 and continues through Dt 7:6; 14:2; 26:18; Ps 135:4; Mal 3:17. God's people, individually and collectively, are set apart to do His will, because God's people are valued by Him more than any other thing.

Being thus chosen and consecrated, God's Gospel people respond in proclamation of His *excellencies* (Gk *aretas*). Better than "virtue," or even *praises* (KJV), the object of Christian proclamation is the superlative action that won our salvation, the perfect life, death, and resurrection of the Son of God (cf. Php 4:8). He is the One who *called you out of darkness into his marvelous light*, because He is the light of the world (cf. Jn 1:4–13; 3:19–21). The ones He has called priests proclaim this light of the world, and so are lights to the world, as Luther noted:

> We must recognize in our hearts and believe that we receive everything from Him and that He is our God. Then out with it, and freely and openly confess this before the world—preach, praise, glorify, and give thanks! This is the real and only worship of God, the true office of the priest, and the finest, most acceptable offering. (LW 14:32)

2:10 In saying *not a people . . . not received mercy*, Peter concludes the section identifying the Christian Church in terms of OT Israel with a parallelism reminiscent of Hos 1:6–9; 2:1, 23. The grand reversal God effects in showing mercy to No Mercy, in saying to Not My People, "You are My people," results in the same-saying confession of faith: "You are my God" (Hos 2:23). The relationship Christians enjoy with God are the result of God establishing our identity. Having received God's blessings, He places us in His Body, the Church. Now we belong; we *are God's people.*

2:4–10 in Devotion and Prayer You've got keepsakes. You know how special they are. The toy that once upon a time was painted brightly but has been worn with use, time, and love. The ornament that has hung on the tree in a special place for years before you were born and is cared for so that it will continue to hang on other trees long after you are gone. For all the baubles in the jewelry box, the one piece that is the most special, that was given to your ancient grandmother before she was ancient, that you are going to entrust to your daughter someday. These things are kept close in our families because they are close to our heart. They are well-loved tokens that render immeasurable value, not in money, but in memories, not in cold, countable capital, but in a fortune of feeling and affection. Dear Christian, this is how our God has called you. Peter names you: "a people for His own possession" (1Pt 2:9), just as God had called Israel His *segulah*, His "treasured possession," His keepsake. God's people are valued by Him more than any other thing. You are cherished by Him because He is reminded of Christ's love for you, dying to take away your death, living to give you new life. Rejoice that you are kept—far more than silly sentiment and of far greater value than anything else in all creation, our Lord treasures you. • Holy Spirit, You are our Comforter of priceless worth. Abide with Your Church, and raise us from seeking treasures on earth to acknowledging that You have called us Your treasure, kept for heaven with You. Move us to faith in You, that we may be found worthy on the Last Day. Amen.

PART 4

SPECIFIC INSTRUCTION AND ENCOURAGEMENT FOR HOLY LIVING (2:11–4:11)

The Purpose of Holiness (2:11–12)

ESV	KJV
[11]Beloved, I urge you as sojourners and exiles to abstain from the passions of the flesh, which wage war against your soul. [12]Keep your conduct among the Gentiles honorable, so that when they speak against you as evildoers, they may see your good deeds and glorify God on the day of visitation.	[11]Dearly beloved, I beseech you as strangers and pilgrims, abstain from fleshly lusts, which war against the soul; [12]Having your conversation honest among the Gentiles: that, whereas they speak against you as evildoers, they may by your good works, which they shall behold, glorify God in the day of visitation.

Introduction to 2:11–3:12 This part of Peter's Letter covers a great many instructions intended for specific groups in the congregation, according to the estates God establishes for society (family and work, church, and citizenship in a state). The apostle contextualizes his instructions in the reminder that Christians are alien sojourners, but their conduct should be a matter of positive remark among others (2:11–12). The realm of the state is God's gift, and we are called to live as responsible people who do good, submitting to the leader God has placed in society (2:13–17). The realm of marriage and family includes the command for house-slaves to submit to their masters, so as not to deserve punishment (2:18–20). Unjust punishment is a cause to rejoice, however, because it unites the sufferer with the unjust treatment of Christ (2:21–25). God's gift of the realm of the home invites the submission of wives to husbands, disdain for luxurious excess, and a beauty from within instead of external beauty

(3:1–6). Husbands are addressed as well, being admonished to love their wives (3:7). Peter summarizes the section with an exhortation to unity and a call to return goodness in exchange for the abuse of the world (3:8–12). Submission to God's order in the realms He has established, the orders of preservation or creation, is the prevailing theme through this section, which is exemplified by the submission of Christ in the following part of the Letter.

2:11 The tender designation of God's people as loving in "brotherly love" and as "children" continues as Peter calls his congregation members *beloved*. A fellow member with them in the family of God, Peter is also a fellow among the *sojourners and exiles*, that is, citizens of heaven whose citizenship is not here on this earth, but instead are waiting for the new heaven and the new earth (cf. 1:1, 17). This distinction marks differences in actions as well, as the citizens of the world indulge in *passions of the flesh*, that is, sinful desires, from which God's Gospel people are to abstain. "Fleshly" (Gk *sarkikos*) denotes more than simply "of the human body." Peter uses the word as a synonym for "sinful" (as Paul does in Rm 7:5, 18, etc.). Such sinful passions *wage war* (Gk *strateuontai*, "advance with an army") against the soul. The military metaphor is reminiscent of Jas 4:1–3 and of Paul's exhortation to protect oneself like a soldier at Eph 6:10–20.

2:12 *Gentiles* (Gk *ethnē*, "nations") is a reference not to non-Jews as distinct from Jewish believers, but rather the citizens of the world that surround God's Gospel people, the sojourners and exiles. Though our citizenship is different, even unbelievers pay attention to their neighbors, so Peter exhorts his readers to *good deeds*. Such actions may in fact inspire the abuse of those who do not care for God's kingdom or His citizens right now (as they certainly did for Christians of the first century who faced the imperial regime of Rome), but will, in the future, have a surprising reversal. God will be glorified when the true source of those good works is revealed (Mt 5:16). The *day of visitation* of the Lord can mean different things in the Scriptures. One meaning is His visitation in the OT to reveal a blessing. This sense was fulfilled in Christ's birth, as Zechariah prophesies: "Blessed be the Lord God of Israel, for He has visited and redeemed His people" (Lk 1:68). Another meaning is a visitation of punishment, as in Ex 20:5: "I the LORD your God am a jealous God, visiting the iniquity of the fathers on the children to the third and the fourth generation of those who hate Me." The "day of visitation" that

Peter refers to, then, could be a matter of either a blessing or a curse. Indeed, this is one way Christians should look at Judgment Day, the great and terrible day of the Lord: it will be either one or the other— a time of punishment or a time of salvation. It is in either case the time when God reveals Himself: He is the judge, leading Christians to do good works in the "now," not for their own praise and glorification, but in light of a "not yet" in which such fine conduct will in fact give the "Gentiles" a reason to glorify God. Bengel wrote:

> There is an allusion to the divine visitation, when God brings to light the innocence of the righteous, which has long been hidden: and He often brings about this result by means of even hostile magistrates, during the process of inquiry, and He often converts adversaries themselves. . . . Until such a day arrives, there is need of patience. (Bengel 5:58)

2:1–12 in Devotion and Prayer "Not of this world"—you've probably seen the bumper stickers and other Christian paraphernalia that proclaim the radical identity of God's people in 1Pt 2. An identity as God's child throws into question how best to deal with the world around us. Like those in the Early Church who fled cities because of persecution, we might flee from cultural engagement with the world too. We have other options for dealing with the culture around us as well. We can succumb, become subsumed within the darker aspects of the sinful world in which we live, and excuse ourselves with the thought that we can't help but be in the world, and "if you can't beat 'em, join 'em." We might act like the desert hermits, who thought Christianity had become too secularized after it was first tolerated and then made an arm of the imperial administration. They martyred themselves in spirit, countering secular culture with alternatives. We might do this by creating our own monasticism by attempting to show the world how much better life can be as a Christian. You probably have some idea of what plastic Christianity looks like: smiling people, happy families, no more problems, not too real or ordinary, but rather ashamed if you're not *extra*ordinary. Or we can live authentically within the culture in which we find ourselves and be a Christian in spite of it. The life that is driven by the Spirit of God is one that sees that we dare not escape the world. There is a mission field and a purpose for which God sent us here. It may not be a purpose that is filled with many blessings that we can see. The Christian life isn't a life that looks perfect, not a "Better Homes and

Gardens" picture of American life. It looked like the cross for Jesus, and it looks like the cross for us. In the end, that's all we have to offer the world. On the other hand, the Spirit-driven life cannot be one that succumbs to culture either, but must instead meet it, facing it head-on with the same cross. It's not easy to be a Christian. But the desert monastery is a vocation—and a vacation—for the coward. We're called to a real faith and a real life among a real people right here. Really. Those words from 1Pt 2 that urge us to be "strangers and aliens in the world" are significant here. *In* the world. Not out of the world. Not escaped from the world. And of course not of the world. But *in* the world we have a job to do. Be real, Christian. And you will find that you're being a real Christian too. • Lord Jesus, as the cornerstone, You make us living stones in Your house and servants of Your Gospel. Bless us with a heart for the lost, that they may come to saving faith in You. Amen.

Christians Submit to Civil Authorities (2:13–17)

ESV	KJV
¹³Be subject for the Lord's sake to every human institution, whether it be to the emperor as supreme, ¹⁴or to governors as sent by him to punish those who do evil and to praise those who do good. ¹⁵For this is the will of God, that by doing good you should put to silence the ignorance of foolish people. ¹⁶Live as people who are free, not using your freedom as a cover-up for evil, but living as servants of God. ¹⁷Honor everyone. Love the brotherhood. Fear God. Honor the emperor.	¹³Submit yourselves to every ordinance of man for the Lord's sake: whether it be to the king, as supreme; ¹⁴Or unto governors, as unto them that are sent by him for the punishment of evildoers, and for the praise of them that do well. ¹⁵For so is the will of God, that with well doing ye may put to silence the ignorance of foolish men: ¹⁶As free, and not using your liberty for a cloke of maliciousness, but as the servants of God. ¹⁷Honour all men. Love the brotherhood. Fear God. Honour the king.

2:13–14 *every human institution* refers to those things that have been founded or established by God, things He has ordained for our living in society. They are not "human institutions" because they were created by humans, but rather because they have to do with our existence as humans in community. These are God-given "holy orders"—orders of creation, orders of preservation, orders divinely ordained, such as the institution of the Church (the ecclesiastical estate), the home (the institution of marriage or the economic estate), and the state (the institution of the sword). Civic virtue (righteous conduct with our neighbor in the various estates) is as much God's concern for His people as their righteousness before Him. He is the ruler of not only the Church but also of the other estates, and His Gospel people are His subjects in whatever realm He rules. Reformation Christians are used to thinking about living in "two kingdoms," both His kingdom of power and His kingdom of grace. God established the Church to bless His people. But He has also established secular government for good order and a harmonious life. Christians are subjects of both kingdoms. *King* (KJV) refers, for Peter's first-century audience, to the *emperor* (ESV), that is, the supreme authority. Christians are to *be subject* to not only the human authority of state that God has ordained, but also the lieutenants of that authority, as he continues in v. 14, who *punish* and *praise* according to their vocation. Evildoers invite the full justice of the civil law; the obedient are given wide latitude to use their freedom. As Luther notes, God does not rule in this estate to "make people righteous before God, nevertheless [worldly government] is instituted in order to accomplish at least this much, that the good may have outward peace and protection and the bad may not be free to do evil in peace and quietness, and without fear" (AE 35:379).

2:15 Peter claims that God's will is to shut the mouths of the ignorant, identified here with those who slander the Christian (cf. vv. 11–12). The evidence of a Christian life, one that shuns the "fleshly passions" mentioned in v. 11, renders silent the accusations of the world.

2:16 In this verse, Peter calls Christians both *free* and *servants* (Gk *douloi*, lit. "slaves"): slaves to God, lest we use our "freedom" as an excuse for wickedness, a *cover-up for evil*. Peter is striving to get at a point that eludes those who think God's Gospel is a license to indulge the sinful nature. In this context Peter wants his readers not so much to consider what they have been freed FROM, as much as what they have been freed FOR: namely, service to God and neighbor. Recall the point Luther made in *The Freedom of the Christian*: "To make the way smoother for the unlearned—for only them do I serve—I shall set down the following two propositions concerning the freedom and the bondage of the spirit: A Christian is a perfectly free lord of all, subject to none. A Christian is a perfectly dutiful servant of all, subject to all" (LW 31:344). Living in this way before God and man is what God calls us all to if we are *living as servants of God*, actions motivated not by any Law but by love of God.

2:17 A series of imperative clauses sums up Peter's section here: *Honor everyone* rightfully in authority, whether in the Church or the state. Cf. Rm 13:7: "Pay to all what is owed to them: taxes to whom taxes are owed, revenue to whom revenue is owed, respect to whom respect is owed, honor to whom honor is owed." The congregation that loves one another with "brotherly love" (cf. 1:22–23), Peter here calls the *brotherhood*, that is, the Church, where God rules with Law and Gospel. In the threefold rule of church, home, and state, the Church is itself the top rule for all, in its jurisdiction (the Keys that open heaven and retain sins), and in its administration (of the Sacraments), leading us to see God as source of all rule in every estate. God's people are therefore ultimately called to *fear God*—but that is not all. Once again, Peter repeats the command *honor the emperor* (cf. v. 13). One might wonder how Peter would answer the question of what happens when the two are in conflict; Peter's answer in Ac 5:29, "We must obey God rather than men," is worth putting to practice and to memory.

Household Slaves Submit to the Authority of Their Masters (2:18–25)

ESV	KJV
[18]Servants, be subject to your masters with all respect, not only to the good and gentle but also to the unjust. [19]For this is a gracious thing, when, mindful of God, one endures sorrows while suffering unjustly. [20]For what credit is it if, when you sin and are beaten for it, you endure? But if when you do good and suffer for it you endure, this is a gracious thing in the sight of God. [21]For to this you have been called, because Christ also suffered for you, leaving you an	[18]Servants, be subject to your masters with all fear; not only to the good and gentle, but also to the froward. [19]For this is thankworthy, if a man for conscience toward God endure grief, suffering wrongfully. [20]For what glory is it, if, when ye be buffeted for your faults, ye shall take it patiently? but if, when ye do well, and suffer for it, ye take it patiently, this is acceptable with God. [21]For even hereunto were ye called: because Christ also suffered for us,

example, so that you might follow in his steps. ²²He committed no sin, neither was deceit found in his mouth. ²³When he was reviled, he did not revile in return; when he suffered, he did not threaten, but continued entrusting himself to him who judges justly. ²⁴He himself bore our sins in his body on the tree, that we might die to sin and live to righteousness. By his wounds you have been healed. ²⁵For you were straying like sheep, but have now returned to the Shepherd and Overseer of your souls.

leaving us an example, that ye should follow his steps: ²²Who did no sin, neither was guile found in his mouth: ²³Who, when he was reviled, reviled not again; when he suffered, he threatened not; but committed himself to him that judgeth righteously: ²⁴Who his own self bare our sins in his own body on the tree, that we, being dead to sins, should live unto righteousness: by whose stripes ye were healed. ²⁵For ye were as sheep going astray; but are now returned unto the Shepherd and Bishop of your souls.

2:18 The Gk word translated *servants* here (*oiketai*) refers specifically to house slaves. In Peter's time slavery was ubiquitous; in fact much of the Church was made up of the extremely poor, among whom slaves would be the poorest. We do well to consider the difference, however, between our more modern conception of New World nineteenth-century chattel slavery and the slavery of Peter's day. Slaves most commonly entered the empire as a result of foreign conquest or being born of people already enslaved; rarely did anyone end up as a bondslave in the first century because of debt. Slaves with domestic skills, artisans, craftsmen, or with good education could most often expect to work in the city, perhaps in houses as one of a staff of household servants (like the ones Peter's addresses here). On the other hand, those who because of military prowess could be expected to give a good show in the amphitheater might find themselves outfitted as a gladiator. Those considered fit for difficult manual labor or needing to pay a punishment might find themselves on the large farming estates of the rich, or worst of all, in the mines (where a long survival was not anticipated). Instead of an image of masses of field hands or a chain gang responding to the master's whip, the context of this verse offers exhortation more apropos to a present-day working relationship between employers and employees, not a matter of chattel-ownership and human trafficking. Slaves and masters, particularly in homes, could develop very close

145

relationships. Manumission (freeing one's slaves) was frequent in the Roman Empire, and many slaves could in fact purchase their own freedom from willing masters if they were able to save enough money. Indeed slaves are considered part of the Roman *familia*, which includes children, animals, and so on.

Even a place in the family does not preclude the possibility of corporal punishment, however, especially in the ever-violent Roman world. *Patria potestas*, the legal authority possessed by the eldest living male in a household over all members of his family, gave the "paterfamilias" the power of life and death of his slaves as well. Beatings could be expected from good and bad masters alike (cf. v. 20), which is why Peter exhorts reverent submission to *good and gentle* masters as well as to *unjust* (Gk *skolios*, lit., "crooked"). Not only is it a holy thing to obey those called to be in authority over you, but also vocational, holy submission was in Peter's day, as still today, a means of witnessing to the Gospel (cf. 3:1). Cranmer wrote:

> With what conscience can you, being but subjects, do to your King that thing which you would condemn in your servants towards yourselves? But answer me this, Be you subjects or no? . . . God's will is, that you should be ruled by your princes. But whether is this to be ruled by your King, or to rule your King, to say, "Thus we will have the realm governed?" Your servants be by the Scripture commanded, as they fear God, to be obedient to their masters, whether their masters be good or evil. And can you think it meet or lawful for you to disobey your undoubted King, being a prince most innocent, most godly, and most careful for your surety and wealth? If any thing can declare disobedience, what can declare it more, than subjects to come with force of arms to their natural King and Prince, and say, "This we will have"? (Cranmer 2:205)

2:19–20 Strangers and sojourners all, God's Gospel people can expect to be treated badly in the world in which they do not claim citizenship as they await the kingdom of God (cf. "trials," 1:6; Jn 16:33). It is a favorable thing to be persecuted for righteousness (cf. Mt 5:10–12), and righteous living in the face of injustice demonstrates reliance on God's grace. Christians who suffer for the sake of the Gospel find favor with God and witness to His power: this is *a gracious thing in the sight of God*, as opposed to the shame entailed in receiving deserved beatings.

2:21 Christians are *called*, not just to imitate Christ, but to receive what He gives as all good, including suffering. Peter frames the suffering of Christ in a hymn (vv. 21–25), woven with poetic language with allusion to the Suffering Servant hymn of Is 53. In light of Christ's suffering for us, God calls Christians to live out their faith in the midst of suffering, as Luther noted: "You cannot escape the smoke when compelled to live in the inn where the devil is host and the whole house is filled with it. Again, if you would have fire, you must have smoke as a consequence; if you would be a Christian and a child of God, you must endure the resultant evils that befall you" (Lenker, *Sermons of Martin Luther* 7:248–71). Receiving Christ's suffering for us is receiving not only the benefits of His cross but also suffering in kind. This imitation of Christ is a blessing for the Christian: we know that because He suffered, He is near us when we suffer too (cf. Rm 8:18–39). Peter's devotional reflection on Christ's death at this point of his Letter is appropriate to his immediate, specific addressee, the slave who submits to his master, because Christ's execution is the sort of death reserved only for slaves and criminals (persons of status were not disgraced with such a horrible manner of public execution). The "you" in the phrase *Christ also suffered for you* extends beyond the slaves mentioned in v. 18, however, to encompass the universal scope of those on whose behalf Christ died. We may be tempted to think that what we face as suffering is in some way comparable or worse than the suffering of people of an earlier, gladder age. It is more honest to remember the history of our Christian forefathers who suffered not only hatred and abuse but also government-sanctioned pogroms and capital punishment for their confession of faith. And lest we think that such tribulation is the zenith of suffering, Peter reminds his readers of an honest memory still fresh in his and their own minds: the suffering of Christ on the executioner's gibbet. Do not be shocked, Christian, whether in the first or twenty-first century, when Christ sees fit to hand you a cross and to say "Follow Me." He has given you a model, an *example*, in order *that you might follow in His steps*! Cf. Lk 9:23–27; Mt 10:38–39.

2:22–23 In Christ we have a high priest "who in every respect has been tempted as we are, yet without sin" (Heb 4:15), and "because He Himself has suffered when tempted, He is able to help those who are being tempted" (Heb 2:18). Christians rejoice in tribulation because of a shared intimacy with Christ, who suffered yet knew no sin. Christ remained faithful to His Father through every trial and was faithful to save us! The loyalty Christ showed in His suffering is a reference to Is 53:9, and is in contradistinction to the *deceit* in the mouth of his accusers; Peter's diction connects Christ's purity with the sincerity he exhorts in his readers (cf. 1:22; 2:1; 3:10). This connection highlights the substitutionary role of Christ's suffering for us, a key point of the Servant Song of Is 53, which Peter employs freely in these verses.

2:24 Peter exploits the dynamic of personal pronouns in this verse, moving between "him" and "us" to underscore the substitutionary purpose of Christ's atoning death. Christ *bore our sins* to death, not because He deserved to die, but because we do (cf. Rm 6:23: "the wages of sin is death"). He carried our sins to the *tree* (cf. Ac 5:30; 10:39; 13:29; Gal 3:13), in order *that we might die to sin and live to righteousness.* Christians identify with Christ's death. The death He died is a real death, and as it is applied to us it becomes a real death for us as well, a dynamic that bears fruit in new life through Christ's resurrection, a new life in the "now" and the "not-yet" of Christians (the tree of death for us has become a tree of life; cf. Rv 2:7; 22:2, 14). A theology of the cross glories in such reversals: the terrible executioner's cross that means shame, humiliation, suffering, and death becomes for the Christian pride, glory, confidence, life, and healing: *by His wounds you have been healed*, as Peter quotes Is 53:5. Luther expanded on this theology of the cross:

> We crucified Him with our sins. We are still far from suffering what He suffered. Therefore if you are a pious Christian, you should tread in the footsteps of the Lord and have compassion on those who harm you. You should also pray for them and ask God not to punish them. For they do far more harm to their souls than they do to your body. If you take this to heart, you will surely forget about your own sorrow and suffer gladly. Here we should be mindful of the fact that formerly we, too, led the kind of unchristian life that they lead, but that we have now been converted through Christ. (LW 30:86)

2:25 Peter's hymn quotes Is 53 freely; the final verse paraphrases Is 53:6 ("All we like sheep have gone astray; we have turned—every one—to his own way; and the LORD has laid on Him the iniquity of us all") and identifies his readers as the ones who were *straying* into sin *but have now returned to the Shepherd and Overseer of your* *souls.* The pastoral care of the Lord for his flock is a frequent image through the Scriptures, one Peter owns through his own calling from the Lord Jesus (Jn 21:15–17) and one that underscores the reversals of the theology of the cross once again. The Lord almighty is Lamb and Shepherd, the one who is mighty and the one who is tender, cf. Is 40:10–11: "Behold, the Lord GOD comes with might, and His arm rules for Him; behold, His reward is with Him, and His recompense before Him. He will tend His flock like a shepherd; He will gather the lambs in His arms; He will carry them in His bosom, and gently lead those that are with young."

2:13–25 in Devotion and Prayer What should we expect to suffer as Christians? We come before holy God with no sense of entitlement, knowing that we justly deserve present and eternal punishment, for sins of commission and omission, for sins of thought, word, and deed. We know also that our God does not treat us as our sins deserve, for in Christ, our sins have been exchanged for His righteousness, and we have His new life in place of sins. The benefits of His cross, namely, life and salvation, bring with them a living hope that does not disappoint us, a confidence that we shall not suffer punishment from God for our sins: those sins have been punished in Christ, and a new life has been given. So what should we expect to suffer as Christians? The devastating consequences of human sinfulness are yet inescapable in this life. Whether they be consequences of our own actual sins or those of others, or more generally the effects of human sinfulness that affect us all since the fall—sickness, disease, death—our suffering is wrapped up in knowing the reality of a new life as a hope that has not been fully revealed yet. The promise of citizenship brings with it an assurance that our utter dependence on Jesus Christ may bring with it persecutions, but the goal is life eternal: "Truly, I say to you, there is no one who has left house or brothers or sisters or mother or father or children or lands, for my sake and for the gospel, who will not receive a hundredfold now in this time, houses and brothers and sisters and mothers and children and lands, with persecutions, and in the age to come eternal life. But many who are first will be last, and the last first" (Mk 10:29–31). So what should we expect to suffer as Christians? We should expect that Jesus, who suffered for us, will invite us so to find our comfort in Him, that we become intimate with His wounds, His suffering, His cross. And where His strength is made perfect in weakness, He will help us bear up under whatever we suffer, even as He bore His cross for us. • Dear Jesus, You promise that Your grace is sufficient for me, that Your power is made perfect in weakness. As You became weak to win a strong victory over my death, so look on me mercifully in my time of trial, save me, and lead me to rejoice in the cross You have given, that I may see my own wounds reflected in Yours, which purchased my salvation. Amen.

A Wife Yields to Her Husband's Authority as Head of the Household (3:1–6)

ESV	KJV
3 ¹Likewise, wives, be subject to your own husbands, so that even if some do not obey the word, they may be won without a word by the conduct of their wives, ²when they see your respectful and pure conduct. ³Do not let your adorning be external—the braiding of hair and the putting on of gold jewelry, or the clothing you wear—⁴but let your adorning be the hidden person of the heart with the imperishable beauty of a gentle and quiet spirit, which in God's sight is very precious. ⁵For this is how the holy women who hoped in God used to adorn themselves, by submitting to their own husbands, ⁶as Sarah obeyed Abraham, calling him lord. And you are her children, if you do good and do not fear anything that is frightening.	*3* ¹Likewise, ye wives, be in subjection to your own husbands; that, if any obey not the word, they also may without the word be won by the conversation of the wives; ²While they behold your chaste conversation coupled with fear. ³Whose adorning let it not be that outward adorning of plaiting the hair, and of wearing of gold, or of putting on of apparel; ⁴But let it be the hidden man of the heart, in that which is not corruptible, even the ornament of a meek and quiet spirit, which is in the sight of God of great price. ⁵For after this manner in the old time the holy women also, who trusted in God, adorned themselves, being in subjection unto their own husbands: ⁶Even as Sara obeyed Abraham, calling him lord: whose daughters ye are, as long as ye do well, and are not afraid with any amazement.

3:1–2 Peter moves forward in his argument about the conduct of Christians in the estates God has established (see 2:13–14) by exhorting husbands and wives to holy living in the institution of the family. The operating paradigm for life with one's spouse depends on the assumption that God has called us to live together in estates He has established, which is why Peter continues with the word *likewise*: as believers submit to civil authorities (2:13–17) and servants submit to masters (2:18–25), *wives* are to *be subject to your own husbands*. What God has established for marriage, as for all His created order, is "very good" (cf. Gn 1:27–31), and the submission Peter calls for is in no way a matter of burden or affliction, but rather delight in God's order. The Gospel provides the cure for sin's corruption of God's order of creation, so that in Christ there is sanctity and forgiveness in marriage. Peter encourages submission especially as it promotes the sake of the Gospel: men's and women's disruption of the order of creation, not conducting themselves in a manner consistent to the holy office to which they are called (husband and wife), breaks down that order. But conduct consistent with calling can even cause unbelieving husbands to *be won without a word*. Proclamation of the Gospel certainly may be verbal, but it takes on many other forms as well. When Peter is talking about our behavior in the estates God has provided for us, we do well to remember that actions speak louder than words! The sanctified life of such wives is what Peter calls *pure conduct*, purity of the same sort he has exhorted his readers to at 1:22–23. Such behavior is born of "obedience to the truth," that is, receiving God's Word and responding in faith.

3:3–4 "Beauty is only skin deep" may summarize the idea Peter has in mind as he outlines what the true beauty of a wife ought to be. The first-century church was remarkable in its egalitarian reach; different social classes, various races, rich and poor, men and women—all were welcome to a community marked by the Gospel (cf. Gal 3:26–29). But as with all groups of varied people, distinctions could be (and still may be!) distracting. Peter is not forbidding outward adornment because there is something inherently sinful about *braiding of hair, gold jewelry*, or *clothing*. He is not laying down austerity measures for the Christian community; nor does this command simply reflect Jewish culture or Peter's opinion. Cranmer provided repeated treatment of this passage. He wrote:

> The same manner of speech used also St. Peter in his first Epistle, saying, That the apparel of women should not be outwardly with braided hair and setting on of gold, nor in putting on of gorgeous apparel, but that the inward man of the heart should be without corruption.

In which manner of speech he intended not utterly to forbid all braiding of hair, all gold and costly apparel to all women; for every one must be apparelled according to their condition, state, and degree; but he meant hereby clearly to condemn all pride and excess in apparel, and to move all women that they should study to deck their souls inwardly with all virtues, and not to be curious outwardly to deck and adorn their bodies with sumptuous apparel. (Cranmer 2:344)

Wesley wrote:

[God] looks at the heart. All superfluity of dress contributes more to pride and anger than is generally supposed. The apostle seems to have his eye to this by substituting meekness and quietness in the room of the ornaments he forbids. "I do not regard these things," is often said by those whose hearts are wrapped up in them: but offer to take them away, and you touch the very idol of their soul. Some, indeed only dress elegantly that they may be looked on; that is, they squander away their Lord's talent to gain applause: thus making sin to beget sin, and then plead one in excuse of the other. (Wesley 613–14)

Peter points to the woman's vocation, what she is called to in the estate of marriage: not flashy external display for attraction (which distracts) but *the imperishable beauty of a gentle and quiet spirit*. Beauty like this is far deeper than skin-deep: it is born of that "imperishable" seed, the Word of God and our response to it in service to Him. This is a theology of the cross once again: this kind of beauty, hidden from the world's eyes, is to Him *very precious*: God values the hidden things (cf. Mt 6:5–6).

3:5–6 The children's song says, "Father Abraham had many sons." According to Peter, we could just as well sing "Sarah the matriarch had many daughters, and I am one of them, and so are you," because the key to this example is the faith of the OT figures. Peter offers the example of Sarah and other *holy women who hoped in God* to give authority to his point. Submission and a quiet spirit are not the key to a woman's place in the Christian community, but the fact that they "hope in God." God's Gospel people of the OT all the way to today are identified solely by this chief virtue: faith in Christ. Sarah's relationship with Abraham was one of faithful response as she *obeyed Abraham*. The Gk word translated *obeyed* (*hupakouō*, "listen, respond to") is the same word used of Abraham "obeying" the Lord at Heb 11:8. Sarah becomes a special example for all women (Peter even calls such women *her children*). Sarah called Abraham *lord*, that is, "master" or "sir"; the word is a title of respect, again confessing the holy order, the estate God has established. Those who live according to their callings in the estates God has established have no reason to fear, even in spite of unjust persecution (cf. 2:20); in the same way Peter exhorts wives (who may not have believing husbands): *do not fear*, for God will be their hope.

A Husband Demonstrates Godliness by Respecting His Wife (3:7)

ESV	KJV
[7]Likewise, husbands, live with your wives in an understanding way, showing honor to the woman as the weaker vessel, since they are heirs with you of the grace of life, so that your prayers may not be hindered.	[7]Likewise, ye husbands, dwell with them according to knowledge, giving honour unto the wife, as unto the weaker vessel, and as being heirs together of the grace of life; that your prayers be not hindered.

3:7 Peter's words for wives are matched by an appeal to husbands, who also have a unique vocation in the estate of marriage that God has established. They are to *live* "according to knowledge" (Gk *gnosis*), that is, in an *understanding way*. Peter is not talking about "tolerance" or "gentleness," but really understanding God's will for marriage. This understanding begins by showing *honor* to his wife as a gift given by God, who is of one flesh with her husband (cf. Gn 2:24; Eph 5:28–29; 1Co 7:3). This honor extends to the things we consider most precious. Think of the special vase that sits in an honored position in the house: fragile, very expensive—certainly more fragile than the everyday utensils of the house, and certainly more expensive! Such is Peter's argument when he uses the phrase *weaker vessel*. This is not a matter of disrespect, but a carefully chosen expression to get at the care that husbands are called to in respect of their wives. Peter exhorts husbands to protect and to cherish their partners who, vulnerable to abuse, typify the "least, last, lost" of God's kingdom—those most precious to God. In a first-century Roman world in which *patria potestas* gave men the right of life and death over all family members, Peter's admonition to husbands not to exploit their size and strength in unkind ways could in fact be considered countercultural. This reinforces Peter's emphasis on Christians' identity as "sojourners and aliens." They are all are to inherit a heavenly crown; Peter calls Christian wives *heirs with you*, for all are saved in the same way: by grace. Rendering honor to wives in this way fulfills a holy calling of the husband and results in the great benefit that *your prayers may not be hindered*. Praying together as spouses is like praying in community worship: reconciliation and mutual love and forgiveness are essential (cf. Mt 5:23–24; 6:14–15). How much more so when in the intimacy of the home that God has established! Luther notes further that a deliberate attitude regarding our vocations as husband and wife leads to what can be called a Christian marriage: "A husband must bear in mind that his wife is a Christian too and is God's work or vessel. Both should conduct themselves in such a way that the wife holds her husband in honor and that the husband, in turn, gives his wife the honor that is her due. If this were observed, peace and love would reign. Otherwise, where this understanding is lacking, there is nothing but aversion in marriage. For this reason it happens that if a man and a woman take each other solely for the purpose of sensual pleasure and are intent on having happy days and sensual pleasure, they find nothing but heartache. But if you have regard for God's work and will, you can lead a Christian life in matrimony. Then you will not live as the heathen live" (LW 30:92).

3:1–7 in Devotion and Prayer St. Paul wrote: "God has so composed the body, giving greater honor to the part that lacked it, that there may be no division in the body, but that the members may have the same care for one another. If one member suffers, all suffer together; if one member is honored, all rejoice together" (1Co 12:24–25). He was talking about the Church, particularly a congregation whose dysfunction led them to thinking one person was better than another because of how God had gifted them. But this is the attitude often taken in any group. Honor goes to what's flashy and attractive, to leadership, to power, to what seems desirable based on human lust or invention. We have a tendency to buck against authority, particularly divine authority. So when God has a word about marriage, using words like "submit" and "honor," we tend to think such things old-fashioned, stuffy, perhaps outdated or good for a certain people of a certain time—but certainly *we* can figure things out without God wagging His finger and saying, "Order! Order!" But "order" is what it's all about: God has ordered creation, down to the members of our

own individual body. And He arranged its parts for health and life. So also does He arrange human marital society: we are parts, one of another, the two become one flesh. God has given us an order, a holy order, where husband and wife can live according to their callings. Men are called to love their wives, giving them honor, giving their lives for them! Women are called to love their husbands, being subject to them even for the sake of their salvation! Rather than giving us these callings to burden His children, God calls us to serious business: salvation is at stake, and only those particularly called to such high office are prepared for what God's holy order requires.
• Gracious Lord, fit me for my calling as neighbor, as Christian, as spouse. Help me to love, and help me so to live, that I may honor and serve as You have called me to, in the name of Him who honored and served all Your children with His sacrificial love. Amen.

Humility, Unity, a Tender Heart, and Brotherly Love Characterize Christian Brotherhood (3:8–12)

ESV	KJV

[8]Finally, all of you, have unity of mind, sympathy, brotherly love, a tender heart, and a humble mind. [9]Do not repay evil for evil or reviling for reviling, but on the contrary, bless, for to this you were called, that you may obtain a blessing. [10]For
 	
"Whoever desires to love life
  and see good days,
let him keep his tongue from evil
  and his lips from speaking
    deceit;
[11]let him turn away from evil and
  do good;
let him seek peace and pursue it.
[12]For the eyes of the Lord are on
  the righteous,
  and his ears are open to their
    prayer.
But the face of the Lord is against
  those who do evil."
	[8]Finally, be ye all of one mind, having compassion one of another, love as brethren, be pitiful, be courteous: [9]Not rendering evil for evil, or railing for railing: but contrariwise blessing; knowing that ye are thereunto called, that ye should inherit a blessing.
	[10]For he that will love life, and see good days, let him refrain his tongue from evil, and his lips that they speak no guile: [11]Let him eschew evil, and do good; let him seek peace, and ensue it. [12]For the eyes of the Lord are over the righteous, and his ears are open unto their prayers: but the face of the Lord is against them that do evil.

3:8 Peter wraps up his section on the obligations of Christians in the estates established by God, summarizing his thoughts in a catalog reminiscent of Paul's exhortation in Php 2:1–4. He calls the Christian congregation to *unity of mind*, a oneness of intention and purpose that flows from a oneness of faith. Even as the Father and the Son are one, so Jesus has prayed for and effected a unity among believers (Jn 17:11). Such unity produces "like feeling," a literal rendering of the word translated as *sympathy* (ESV) or *compassion* (KJV). This "like feeling" is shared by people who love one another with *brotherly love* (cf. 1:22–23). *Tender heart* sounds so much nicer to our ears than Gk *eusplangkhnoi*, which literally translates "good-gutted." This visceral word emphasizes compassion for others. As Paul's catalog in Php 2:1–4 was answered in the example of Christ's humility (Php 2:6–8), so also Peter here finishes the list of exhortations in this verse with a call to have a *humble mind*, not exalting oneself in pride but considering others as Christ did. Such an attitude flows from a relationship defined by brotherly love, as Luther noted:

> Here you see what true brothers are. They cling together much more closely than any friends do. We Christians should also do this, for we are all brothers through Baptism. After Baptism even my father and my mother are my brother and my sister, for through faith I have the very same blessing and inheritance from Christ that they have. (LW 30:96)

3:9 The grand reversals that operate under a theology of the cross translate to reversals of action in believers. So as Christ has transformed death to life, suffering to healing, calls the first last and the least the greatest, so also believers are called to do what the world would never consider sane: to answer cursing with a blessing. Retaliation is not the way of God's Gospel people who are called to *bless* in response to wrongs; once again Christ is not only the example of such a response in His innocent death, but the teacher as well; cf. Mt 5:39: "I say to you, Do not resist the one who is evil. But if anyone slaps you on the right cheek, turn to him the other also."

3:10–12 This is the second overt reference to Ps 34 in 1Pt, the first being "taste and see" quoted at 2:3. Here Ps 34:12–16 serves Peter as a conclusion to this section. David wrote these words while fleeing for his life from Saul, a comparable context to the trials that Peter assumes his readers suffer.

Christian Virtue Sends a Powerful Message to Outsiders and Gives Opportunity for Witnessing (3:13–17)

ESV	KJV
[13]Now who is there to harm you if you are zealous for what is good? [14]But even if you should suffer for righteousness' sake, you will be blessed. Have no fear of them, nor be troubled, [15]but in your hearts honor Christ the Lord as holy, always being prepared to make a defense to anyone who asks you for a reason for the hope that is in you; yet do it with gentleness and respect, [16]having a good conscience, so that, when you are slandered, those who revile your good behavior in Christ may be put to shame. [17]For it is better to suffer for doing good, if that should be God's will, than for doing evil.	[13]And who is he that will harm you, if ye be followers of that which is good? [14]But and if ye suffer for righteousness' sake, happy are ye: and be not afraid of their terror, neither be troubled; [15]But sanctify the Lord God in your hearts: and be ready always to give an answer to every man that asketh you a reason of the hope that is in you with meekness and fear: [16]Having a good conscience; that, whereas they speak evil of you, as of evildoers, they may be ashamed that falsely accuse your good conversation in Christ. [17]For it is better, if the will of God be so, that ye suffer for well doing, than for evil doing.

Introduction to 3:13–4:11 Peter matches the previous section's emphasis on submission in Christian vocations according to the various estates with a study of Christ's submission to God's will. This submission leads Jesus to suffering, death, and exaltation. His identity becomes ours through Baptism, and this changed identity leads to a new life in the here and now. Suffering for righteousness is a blessing (3:13–14), but Christians can be confident in the midst of persecution when they have a ready defense for their hope in Christ (3:15–17). Our defense rests on the death, resurrection, and exaltation of Christ (3:18–20); the work of Jesus Christ is applied to us in Holy Baptism (3:21–22), leading to a new life of service for the baptized (4:1–2). The old life and its practitioners present an enemy for the Christian (4:3–4), but they will receive their just reward: judgment (4:5–6). Instead of the catalog of sins that defines the world, the Christian is called to live in the light of the world to come by leading a holy life (4:7–9) and using God's gifts to serve one another, edifying God's Church to His glory (4:10–11).

3:13–14 Suffering for righteousness has been something of a watchword for Peter throughout this Letter. It is a constant reminder that the readers are indeed "sojourner-exiles," whose citizenship is not of this world. Christians are called not to fear what the world around them fears, and Peter punctuates this call with another nod to Is 8, which he had already quoted at 2:8: "For the LORD spoke thus to me with His strong hand upon me, and warned me not to walk in the way of this people, saying: 'Do not call conspiracy all that this people calls conspiracy, and do not fear what they fear, nor be in dread. But the LORD of hosts, Him you shall honor as holy. Let Him be your fear, and let Him be your dread. And He will become a sanctuary and a stone of offense and a rock of stumbling to both houses of Israel, a trap and a snare to the inhabitants of Jerusalem. And many shall stumble on it. They shall fall and be broken; they shall be snared and taken'" (Is 8:11–15). Christians face trials, confident that Christ, the stone of offense to the world, is in fact the cornerstone of their faith, a strong building that the gates of hell will not overcome.

3:15 Peter moves from his emphasis in prior verses of outward behavior to an emphasis on the location in time and space of Christian faith: on the one hand trust in the person and work of Jesus Christ in his death, resurrection, and exaltation (which Peter was eyewitness to), and on the other, confession of that faith as a ready defense in the face of the world's reactions to Christian living. That faith and its confession begin with the exhortation: *in your hearts honor Christ the Lord.* The source of Christian witness is not righteous behavior or even a feeling, but a fact: Jesus Christ is Lord! More than a confession that Jesus is the "Lord of my life," Peter is offering a radical creed: Jesus Christ is God. This is an objective fact: Jesus Christ is named the Lord of all by His glorious exaltation by the Father (Php 2:9–11). It is a subjective fact as well, as the believer comes to faith in Christ. Luther wrote:

> If now you are asked, What do you believe in the Second Article of Jesus Christ? answer briefly: I believe that Jesus Christ, true Son of God, has become my Lord. But what is it to become Lord? It is this, that He has redeemed me from sin, from the devil, from death, and all evil. For before I had no Lord nor King, but was captive under the power of the devil, condemned to death, enmeshed in sin and blindness. (LC 27)

The substance of faith in this good news, the historic death and resurrection of Jesus Christ on behalf of sinners, is the content with which Christians are *prepared to make a defense* (Gk *apologia*). The historic death and resurrection of Christ is verified by reliable testimony of historic documents, which is why Christianity stands up to scrutiny and investigation and has done so for two millennia. Peter's exhortation to a confident apologetic is not based on being able nimbly to win arguments, to demonstrate agility with rhetoric or philosophy, or convince with human logic regarding matters of open debate. Rather, the apologetic of Christians is a matter of responding to verifiable historical record to which human people, including Peter himself, were eyewitness; cf. 1Co 15:3–8: "For I delivered to you as of first importance what I also received: that Christ died for our sins in accordance with the Scriptures, that He was buried, that He was raised on the third day in accordance with the Scriptures, and that He appeared to Cephas, then to the twelve. Then He appeared to more than five hundred brothers at one time, most of whom are still alive, though some have fallen asleep. Then He appeared to James, then to all the apostles. Last of all, as to one untimely born, He appeared also to me." The defense of this Gospel, the historic death and resurrection of Jesus Christ, is the center of God's mission, as the Spirit enables the apostles and other defenders of the faith through Acts and the rest of the NT period, up to our own day. The historic death and resurrection is the source of Christian *hope*, which is distinctive in a world where all face the same kinds of adversity. Christians respond not in despair, but in the confidence of God's care and imminent transformation of all tribulation to a new heaven and new earth, the life of resurrection toward which God's Gospel people, sojourner-exiles, are journeying. "I don't worry," says the Christian in face of adversity. "I don't worry, because my God is Jesus Christ." Such "hope" is itself a witness to people in the world who may respond to adversity by seeking the reason for such hope and thus hear the center of the Christian apologetic: the Gospel, the historic death and resurrection of Christ on behalf of sinners. Peter knows human nature, though, and follows up his exhortation to a ready defense of the Gospel by reminding his readers to be winsome, to defend the Gospel with *gentleness and respect* rather than with arrogance or militance. God calls for a gentle witness to the truth before all people, both unbelievers and believers alike (cf. Jas 1:21; 3:13).

3:16 A ready defense is the product of a *good conscience* which is given to the Christian at Baptism (v. 21). A "good conscience" is the source of confidence in the face of the Christian's enemies, our own sinful flesh, death, and the devil. Such confidence does not rest in things we have done: Peter is not referring to assurance that we have done our part, so we can be satisfied with God doing the rest, and so face trials innocently because after all, we have done our best. Rather, in Baptism, God has delivered to us an awareness of Himself: that He has become our Father, that Christ has become our God, that the Spirit operates within us, confirming our election and status before Him as sanctified. This awareness is the conscience, a firm assurance in our standing before Him as the baptized. This baptized status is not the last resort for Christians faced with trials, but is the very Word of God, "a trusty shield and weapon," the "one little Word that fells" the enemies the Christian faces: "I am baptized!" Anyone who would *revile* one of God's baptized children will indeed *be put to shame*, because they revile not just a fellow sinner, but the Word of God that identifies him or her as an heir of God's kingdom. Ambassadors of foreign nations have diplomatic immunity when they travel abroad into states not their own. It is as if they are clothed with a foreign citizenship. The ground they walk on, the cars they travel in, are set apart as a sacrosanct embassy. They speak on behalf of their own nation, not the nation they happen to inhabit at present. So it is with Christians, God's Gospel people: they have every reason to believe they are foreign ambassadors with diplomatic immunity. They invite public conversation, invite the non-Christian to examine the factual grounding of the hope within them. Such ambassadors do so with a good conscience. It is their calling, after all, a vocation sealed on them by the Lord of their nation Himself, signed with His name, applied to them in Holy Baptism.

3:17 Peter lived in a time we may be tempted to think was unique: the Neronian Roman empire. Near the end of Nero's reign, following the great fire of Rome in AD 64, Christians were subjected to systematic persecution. While Peter does not have this historic persecution in mind (his Letter is written earlier; cf. introduction), nevertheless the Roman world of the first century was a difficult one in which to live as a monotheist, particularly with the exclusive confession of Christians that their one God had been revealed in Jesus Christ. Torture, public humiliation, and death notwithstanding, persecution was, and is, a reality for Christians all over the world. The difficult situations we face in our own lives may or may not compare to the experiences of our Christian forebears, but whatever the situation, Peter's words ring true: God's plans for the situations He puts us in are to chastise, strengthen, draw us back into His fold, or to benefit others. Christians have confidence in God's promise that whatever He leads us to suffer, He will never give us more than we can bear (cf. 1Co 10:13; Heb 12:3–11). On Peter's point about suffering for righteousness, Luther stated:

> Here St. Peter again presents the Lord Christ to us as an example and always refers to the suffering of Christ. . . . Christ was righteous. For doing right He also suffered for us, who were unrighteous. But He did not seek the cross. No, He waited until it was God's will that He should drink the cup. He should be the model for us to imitate. (LW 30:110)

Jesus Was Treated Unjustly and Then Gloriously Vindicated (3:18–22)

ESV	KJV
[18]For Christ also suffered once for sins, the righteous for the unrighteous, that he might bring us to God, being put to death in the flesh but made alive in the spirit, [19]in which he went and proclaimed to the spirits in prison, [20]because they formerly did not obey, when God's patience waited in the days of Noah, while the ark was being prepared, in which a few, that is, eight persons, were brought safely through water. [21]Baptism, which corresponds to this, now saves you, not as a removal of dirt from the body but as an appeal to God for a good conscience, through the resurrection of Jesus Christ, [22]who has gone into heaven and is at the right hand of God, with angels, authorities, and powers having been subjected to him.	[18]For Christ also hath once suffered for sins, the just for the unjust, that he might bring us to God, being put to death in the flesh, but quickened by the Spirit: [19]By which also he went and preached unto the spirits in prison; [20]Which sometime were disobedient, when once the longsuffering of God waited in the days of Noah, while the ark was a preparing, wherein few, that is, eight souls were saved by water. [21]The like figure whereunto even baptism doth also now save us (not the putting away of the filth of the flesh, but the answer of a good conscience toward God,) by the resurrection of Jesus Christ: [22]Who is gone into heaven, and is on the right hand of God; angels and authorities and powers being made subject unto him.

3:18 Peter's exposition of Christ's actions at the cross and the tomb echoes the trinitarian greeting of 1:2, as God the Father, Son, and Holy Spirit are mentioned together in this verse working together in the cause of our redemption. Peter argues that the "suffering" he mentioned in vv. 16–17 must be understood in comparison to Christ, who *suffered once for sins.* Our own sufferings do not atone for our sin, but Christ's sufferings do. Death and resurrection go together in this verse. So also do our atonement and our confidence: Christ made atonement for us by His cross, and His resurrection gives absolute certainty that His sacrifice was effective—eternally so, since when Peter says "once," he doesn't mean "once upon a time," but rather "one time and one time only." This is consistent with Heb 7:27: "He has no need, like those high priests, to offer sacrifices daily, first for His own sins and then for those of the people, since He did this once for all when He offered up Himself." *alive in the spirit.* The death and resurrection of Christ are applied to the sinner in Holy Baptism, and so His death and life become our death and life, as St. Paul teaches (Rm 6:1–4) and as Luther comments: "We are one sacrifice with Him. As He dies, so we, too, die according to the flesh; as He lives in the spirit, so we, too, live in the spirit" (LW 30:111).

3:19–20 These two verses serve as an interesting transition from Peter's teaching about Christ's suffering, death, and resurrection (v. 18) to the application of the benefits of that work of Christ in Holy Baptism (v. 21). The transition centers on Noah and salvation by water on the one hand, and on the other, the judgment on those who *did not obey* in those days. Cf. Heb 11:7: "By faith Noah, being warned by God concerning events as yet unseen, in reverent fear constructed an ark for the saving of his household. By this he condemned the world and became an heir of the righteousness that comes by faith." The tricky bit here is the teaching on Christ's descent into hell, a matter of Christian confession. There are things we can say for sure, and there are things that are more unclear. Bengel wrote:

> In a subject full of mystery, we ought not to dismiss from it the proper signification of the language employed, because it has no parallel passages. For they, to whom each mystery has first been revealed, have most nobly believed the word of God even without parallel passages. (Bengel 5:69)

It is evident from the fact that the risen Lord Jesus *went and proclaimed to the spirits in prison* that the descent is not a point of Christ's suffering and humiliation, but rather exaltation. Christ descended into hell to declare His victory over death and all evil forces. His power surpasses all others. But who are these "spirits" and what is the content of Christ's "proclamation"? Scripture does not teach that He offered these spirits a second chance for salvation, nor does it exactly identify these spirits other than the fact that they disobeyed. As the Lutheran reformers noted:

> It is enough if we know that Christ descended into hell, destroyed hell for all believers, and delivered them from the power of death and of the devil, from eternal condemnation and the jaws of hell. We will save our questions ‹and not curiously investigate› about how this happened until the other world. Then not only this ‹mystery›, but others also will be revealed that we simply believe here and cannot grasp with our blind reason. (FC Ep IX 4)

Since, however, this passage focuses on the many who did not believe and the few saved in the ark, we may have confidence that the substance of Christ's preaching is his exaltation, even as Noah was preaching to these spirits (unbelievers) about the exaltation of God, and that the spirits are those who failed to hear and believe God's Word. Thus they perished and remain in hell until the final judgment.

3:21 Noah's flood killed and it made alive. It judged the unbeliever and gave new life to Noah and his family. The is a typological reflection, that is, a figure, consistent in its teaching, of *Baptism, which . . . now saves you.* In the case of Noah, and in the case of Baptism, water kills and makes alive. The world was cleansed when Noah and his family were lifted up by the flood. Baptism cleanses and raises us to new life. By grace, Baptism is a means of salvation through which the Holy Spirit produces faith (cf. Eph 5:25–27). This Baptism is not a simple bath, but a fulfillment of the earlier Noaic figure. It is, as Luther wrote, "by far a greater flood than was that of Noah. . . . Baptism drowns all sorts of men throughout the world, from the birth of Christ even till the day of judgment. . . . [Noah's flood] was a flood of wrath, this is a flood of grace" (LW 35:32). Peter defines Baptism as what saves *through the resurrection of Jesus Christ* (cf. Rm 6:4). He also takes the opportunity to say what Baptism is not and what it is. It is not *a removal of dirt from the body* but, as the next words are more literally translated, "a good conscience's question to God." This sounds close to the words of Heb 10:22, but there are a couple of difficulties that hinder absolute certainty regarding what Peter might mean by the phrase. One question that arises is whether to understand this phrase closer to how KJV translates it: *the answer of a good conscience towards God*, or as ESV does: *an appeal to God for a good conscience*. Since the "good conscience" has been mentioned already in the immediate context (v. 16), it seems that Peter considers it to be in the possession of the believer. This speaks in favor of the KJV rendering "of" over the ESV "for." The preferred reading is one that takes the "good conscience" as possessing a "question" or "answer" rather than being the object of what one might "appeal" to God for. This leaves one other difficult question to answer, namely how best to understand the Gk *eperōtēma*: as meaning "question," "answer," or "appeal" (all of which are legitimate meanings)? The noun is derived from the verb in Gk for "asking," making "question" or "appeal" seem appealing. The word occurs only once in the NT, adding to the confusion. We are content to let the difficulties of this verse rest in the surer light that Baptism saves through the resurrection of Christ, that it is not a bath to wash soiled flesh, and that the good conscience, already in possession of the believer by virtue of that Baptism, has a question to put to God. The "appeal" of confident prayer, as dear children would ask their dear Father, is perhaps most appealing.

3:22 The *right hand of God* is not a physical place but a description of supreme authority, explained by the rule He has over *angels, authorities, and powers*. The sovereign reign of Christ at God's right hand is creedal and confessional: "Now He has ascended to heaven, not merely as any other saint, but as the apostle testifies [Ephesians 4:10], above all heavens. He also truly fills all things, being present everywhere, not only as God, but also as man. He rules from sea to sea and to the ends of the earth, as the prophets predict [Psalm 8:1, 6; 93:1–4; Zechariah 9:10] and the apostles testify [Mark 16:20]. He did this everywhere with them and confirmed their word with signs. This did not happen in an earthly way. As Dr. Luther explained, this happened according to the way things are done at God's right hand. . . . 'God's right hand' is no set place in heaven, as the Sacramentarians assert without any ground in the Holy Scriptures. It is nothing other than God's almighty power, which fills heaven and earth" (FC SD VIII 27–28).

3:8–22 in Devotion and Prayer The corporeal reality of Christ's work for us is revealed in the simplest way possible. God does not make His fallen creatures jump through philosophical hoops, require a system of special codes and symbols, or spend a lifetime of research in science or theology to gain knowledge of Him. God rather addresses our limitations by using cheap and readily available tools we understand: human flesh, understandable language, plain water. God becomes one of us. Jesus is God in the flesh, the baby in swaddling clothes, the dusty-road-walking rabbi who raises widows' sons from the dead, the falsely-accused innocent whose connective tissue was broken with Roman nails as He suffered for our sins. God wraps this miracle in something we live in every day: human flesh. He delivers the witness of Jesus into human eyes like Peter's, human ears like ours, in language that invites us to investigate the facts of history. He paints this miraculous revelation on poor, limited, corporeal, and real people: babies, people who walk dusty roads today, and all who suffer the adversity of living in this country yet a while longer. A miracle is hidden in history, the history of a God who died and a man who rose again, and the history of a you who dies and rises in that same way as He applies Himself to you in Word and water, in the simple miracle of an identity with God in Baptism.
• "Almighty eternal God, according to Your righteous judgment You condemned the unbelieving world through the flood. In Your great mercy You preserved believing Noah and his family. You drowned hard-hearted Pharaoh with all his host in the Red Sea and led Your people Israel through the same on dry ground. By these events You prefigured this bath of Your Baptism. And through the Baptism of Your dear Child, our Lord Jesus Christ, You consecrated and set apart the Jordan and all water as a salutary flood and rich and full washing away of sins. We pray through Christ for Your boundless mercy that You will graciously behold us and bless us with true faith in the Spirit. Then, by means of this saving flood, all that has been born in us from Adam and which we ourselves have added thereto may be drowned in us and engulfed. May we be separated from the number of the unbelieving, preserved dry and secure in the holy ark of Christendom, and serve Your name at all times fervent in spirit and joyful in hope. With all believers may we be made worthy to attain

eternal life according to Your promise; through Jesus Christ our Lord. Amen" (*TLWA*, p. 364).

Jesus' Example Inspires His People to Overcome Surrounding Evil (4:1–6)

ESV	KJV
4 ¹Since therefore Christ suffered in the flesh, arm yourselves with the same way of thinking, for whoever has suffered in the flesh has ceased from sin, ²so as to live for the rest of the time in the flesh no longer for human passions but for the will of God. ³For the time that is past suffices for doing what the Gentiles want to do, living in sensuality, passions, drunkenness, orgies, drinking parties, and lawless idolatry. ⁴With respect to this they are surprised when you do not join them in the same flood of debauchery, and they malign you; ⁵but they will give account to him who is ready to judge the living and the dead. ⁶For this is why the gospel was preached even to those who are dead, that though judged in the flesh the way people are, they might live in the spirit the way God does.	4 ¹Forasmuch then as Christ hath suffered for us in the flesh, arm yourselves likewise with the same mind: for he that hath suffered in the flesh hath ceased from sin; ²That he no longer should live the rest of his time in the flesh to the lusts of men, but to the will of God. ³For the time past of our life may suffice us to have wrought the will of the Gentiles, when we walked in lasciviousness, lusts, excess of wine, revellings, banquetings, and abominable idolatries: ⁴Wherein they think it strange that ye run not with them to the same excess of riot, speaking evil of you: ⁵Who shall give account to him that is ready to judge the quick and the dead. ⁶For for this cause was the gospel preached also to them that are dead, that they might be judged according to men in the flesh, but live according to God in the spirit.

4:1–2 Christ's submission to God's will led Him to suffer, die, and be exalted by the Father. Christ's identity has become ours through Baptism, and this changed identity leads to a new life in the here and now. That *Christ suffered in the flesh* leads Christians to a new life of service. Truly man (Jn 1:14), Christ suffered just as other humans do, so Christian hope has its source in the humanity God shared in common with us in Christ (cf. Heb 2:18). We also share in Christ's suffering and death, as Luther commented: "He [became] a man like us, so that it could be called God's dying, God's martyrdom, God's blood, and God's death. For God in his own nature cannot die; but now that God and man are united in one person, it is called God's death when the man dies who is one substance or one person with God" (LW 41:104). Peter exhorts Christians as a general would exhort his troops, saying *arm yourselves* (Gk *hoplisasthe*, related to "hoplite," the Greek soldier outfitted with heavy armor, shield, and weapons; cf. Eph 6:10–17). Christians are to be equipped with the *same way of thinking*: Christ's compassion and grace in suffering, delivered through His Word, is "a trusty shield and weapon." Because we have been united with Christ in His sacrificial death, we now have *ceased from sin*. Such death to sin makes way for a new focus that is not occupied with personal pleasure. Though we continue to be sinners, we are also declared righteous and saints before God. The new life of forgiveness in Christ transforms believers into those who serve God and neighbor. The life we live as Christians does not seem perfect from our perspective, because we are always *simul*: at the same time sinner and saint, as Luther reminds us: "We never become perfectly pure while we are living on earth, and everyone still finds evil lust in his body. To be sure, faith begins to slay sin and to bestow heaven; but it has not yet become perfect and really strong" (LW 30:118). Cf. Rm 7.

4:3 The catalog of sins Peter offers here is a reflection on the life of death in the world from which Christ's death has saved us. "Are we to continue in sin that grace may abound?" asks Paul in Rm 6:1. He answers in 6:2: "By no means! How can we who died to sin still live in it?" Peter's answer is the same: the *time that is past suffices*—it is time to put away the things of death. Those belong in the grave, not outside the grave in the risen life of the new Adam. Those sins are dead! They have been buried! They are in the grave! Why would you want to crawl back in that stinking bed? In Baptism God has exchanged paradise for the grave. The life of the baptized no longer seek out new sins to commit (all of which are ultimately *lawless idolatry*; cf. LC I 319–29). Rather, baptized children, forgiven in Christ, seek opportunities to point to the hope that is within us (3:15).

4:4–5 The suffering Christians face in the world, even if not persecution on the level of shedding blood, is ever the trial of engaging with a world that is *surprised when you do not join them in the same*

167

flood of debauchery. Temptations to sin are always around us, and sometimes temptation is great because, frankly, sin is fun. Sometimes the temptation is great because sin seems to be what everyone else is doing. Peer pressure does not stop in high school. The new life of the baptized must be one equipped to defend the truth (3:15), defend oneself with spiritual armor (4:1), and defend the neighbor who is in danger of perishing in sin, for sinners will *give account* to God for their sins as the one who is going to *judge the living and the dead*. Cf. Mt 18:15–17; Mt 25:31–46.

4:6 Peter points forward to a final judgment as he says *the gospel was preached even to those who are dead*. Christ's exaltation led Him to proclaim victory over sin and death in His glorious sacrifice for sins, all on behalf of those who trust in God's promises. This judgment is not just for Christians of the NT period (including us), but for all people who are living and dead. Bengel wrote:

> Peter calls those dead who lived through the whole period of the New Testament. . . . The Gospel is preached also to the living; but he mentions the dead, because the saying, that they might be judged, etc., is especially accomplished in death. And from this very thing it is plain that the preaching of the Gospel which is meant, is before that death, and not subsequent to it. When the body is put off in death, the condition of the soul is altogether fixed, either for evil or for good. The gospel is preached to no one after death. (Bengel 5:75)

Life and death is not only a physical reality, what we may think of immediately from our limited and linear perspective, but includes a spiritual dimension: God slays and makes alive through His Law and His Gospel. Before the Gospel enlivened us with a saving faith in Christ, we were spiritually dead in our sins; the Gospel makes alive those who are dead (cf. Ezk 37:1–14).

Nearness of the End Stimulates Christians to Faithfulness (4:7–11)

ESV	KJV
⁷The end of all things is at hand; therefore be self-controlled and sober-minded for the sake of your prayers. ⁸Above all, keep loving one another earnestly, since love covers a multitude of sins. ⁹Show hospitality to one another without grumbling. ¹⁰As each has received a gift, use it to serve one another, as good stewards of God's varied grace: ¹¹whoever speaks, as one who speaks oracles of God; whoever serves, as one who serves by the strength that God supplies—in order that in everything God may be glorified through Jesus Christ. To him belong glory and dominion forever and ever. Amen.	⁷But the end of all things is at hand: be ye therefore sober, and watch unto prayer. ⁸And above all things have fervent charity among yourselves: for charity shall cover the multitude of sins. ⁹Use hospitality one to another without grudging. ¹⁰As every man hath received the gift, even so minister the same one to another, as good stewards of the manifold grace of God. ¹¹If any man speak, let him speak as the oracles of God; if any man minister, let him do it as of the ability which God giveth: that God in all things may be glorified through Jesus Christ, to whom be praise and dominion for ever and ever. Amen.

4:7 Peter pointed forward to a final judgment in the last verse. He closes this section by calling Christians to a behavior different than the catalog of sins he lists in vv. 3–4. That behavior is ordered by the firm promise that the *end* of human, linear, chronological history *is at hand*. Christians live in expectation of the return of Christ, which could be anytime. Whether by His return or by our death, we should always be prepared to meet Him with a kind of vigilance Peter had encouraged at 3:15. This vigilance is characterized by being *self-controlled and sober-minded*. Such vigilance isn't simply inward reflection; it is also outward action. Sin in fact turns us in upon ourselves. Christian vigilance is important *for the sake of your prayers*, as sin hinders prayer by turning our attention from God to ourselves (cf. v. 3).

4:8–9 Living in light of the world to come means living the life that is "hidden with Christ in God" (Col 3:3). In fact the life in God's Church is the job of covering over the life of death. Just as Christ covers us in Baptism (Gal 3:27), so we cover the sins of others, seeing in them the risen life of Christ rather than seeing their sins which have been forgiven in Christ. This is the practical effect of Christian community, that Peter expresses as *love covers a multitude of sins*. (See note at Jas 5:19–20.) In Christ, we love others and freely forgive them. Of itself, our love has no power to forgive, but the love of Christ moves us to forgive and restore to God's kingdom (Mt 18:15–17). Melanchthon wrote: "No apostle would have imagined (a) our love overcomes sin and death, (b) love satisfies God's wrath and reconciles us to God, while excluding Christ as Mediator, and (c) love in and of itself is righteousness before God without Christ as Mediator" (Ap V 117); Luther wrote: "Let everyone use his tongue and make it serve for the best of everyone else, to cover up his neighbor's sins and infirmities [1 Peter 4:8], excuse them, conceal and garnish them with his own reputation" (LC I 285). Such love reveals itself in the classic virtue of *hospitality* (literally, "love of a stranger"), which Christians are commanded to exercise in welcome to all people, not just fellow believers (cf. Heb 13:2).

4:10–11 God the Holy Spirit gives gifts to His Church in order for it to edify the neighbor, to *serve one another*. It is a *varied grace*: different gifts for different people, called to different kinds of service in the Church (cf. Rm 12:3–8; 1Co 12; Eph 4:7–16). The gifts are the Lord's, and so rely on the Lord's provision, the Lord's *oracles* (that is, His own words), and the Lord's strength. Calvin wrote:

> We learn from these words of Peter, that it is not lawful for those who are engaged in teaching to do anything else, but faithfully to deliver to others, as from hand to hand, the doctrine received from God; for he forbids any one to go forth, except he who is instructed in God's word, and who proclaims infallible oracles as it were from his mouth. He, therefore, leaves no room for human inventions; for he briefly defines the doctrine which ought to be taught in the Church. (Calvin 131)

Welsey wrote:

> Let all [the preacher's] words be according to this pattern [the oracles of God], both as to matter and manner, more especially in public. By this mark we may always know who are, so far, the true or false prophets. The oracles of God teach that men should repent, believe, obey. He that treats of faith and leaves out repentance, or does not enjoin practical holiness to believers, does not

speak as the oracles of God: he does not preach Christ, let him think as highly of himself as he will. (Wesley 616)

While the end or goal of using gifts on behalf of the neighbor is the edifying of the Lord's Church, the end for the Lord is His *glory forever and ever. Amen* (cf. Dn 7:14). Peter is not just giving a lesson in doctrine; he is actually worshiping the Lord with this doxology, one of many creedal elements that have surfaced in chs. 3–4.

4:1–11 in Devotion and Prayer This section of Peter's Letter closes the apostle's thoughts on what the incarnate Christ's sufferings should inspire in the way of Christian response to a fallen world. Peter's point is that you have received a gift. Use it wisely. Use it in service. Use it, don't lose it. Protect it. Cherish it. Share it with a world that will be judged. The sufferings of Christ are a gift applied to you, and that gift is as varied as the Body of Christ—as He suffered in His body, so now He has placed you in that Body, His Church! And here, too, you have been given gifts, and like the chief financial officer (Gk *oikonomos*, v. 10) of God's treasury, you have been made His steward, His manager. You have access to the full storehouse of His grace; you have the key to sharing the gifts of this generous God with all, believers and unbelievers alike. You have received a gift, none other than the love of Christ that covers over all your sins. Now share that love, that gift, that grace that was won for you in the sufferings of Christ and applied to you in Holy Baptism. Who needs to have that kind of love shared with them today? • Grant, Lord Jesus, that as Your steward, I may be found faithful to using the gifts You have given, both as a witness against the ways of the enemy and this world, and as a bold witness to Your love and compassion for me and all Your creation. Empower me with Your strength, equip me with Your words, and help me to love with Your heart, that Your love may cover a multitude of sins. Amen.

PART 5

Joy amid Suffering and Further Clarifications about What Is Expected of the Community (4:12–5:11)

Suffering for the Sake of Christ Is a Sharing in Him (4:12–19)

ESV	KJV
¹²Beloved, do not be surprised at the fiery trial when it comes upon you to test you, as though something strange were happening to you. ¹³But rejoice insofar as you share Christ's sufferings, that you may also rejoice and be glad when his glory is revealed. ¹⁴If you are insulted for the name of Christ, you are blessed, because the Spirit of glory and of God rests upon you. ¹⁵But let none of you suffer as a murderer or a thief or an evildoer or as a meddler. ¹⁶Yet if anyone suffers as a Christian, let him not be ashamed, but let him glorify God in that name. ¹⁷For it is time for judgment to begin at the household of God; and if it begins with us, what will be the outcome for those who do not obey the gospel of God?	¹²Beloved, think it not strange concerning the fiery trial which is to try you, as though some strange thing happened unto you: ¹³But rejoice, inasmuch as ye are partakers of Christ's sufferings; that, when his glory shall be revealed, ye may be glad also with exceeding joy. ¹⁴If ye be reproached for the name of Christ, happy are ye; for the spirit of glory and of God resteth upon you: on their part he is evil spoken of, but on your part he is glorified. ¹⁵But let none of you suffer as a murderer, or as a thief, or as an evildoer, or as a busybody in other men's matters. ¹⁶Yet if any man suffer as a Christian, let him not be ashamed; but let him glorify God on this behalf. ¹⁷For the time is come that judgment must begin at the house of God: and if it first begin at us, what shall the end be of them that obey not the gospel of God?

¹⁸And "If the righteous is scarcely saved, what will become of the ungodly and the sinner?" ¹⁹Therefore let those who suffer according to God's will entrust their souls to a faithful Creator while doing good.	¹⁸And if the righteous scarcely be saved, where shall the ungodly and the sinner appear? ¹⁹Wherefore let them that suffer according to the will of God commit the keeping of their souls to him in well doing, as unto a faithful Creator.

Introduction to 4:12–5:11 When we suffer, we share something intimate with Christ, who also suffered. Peter expounds the theme at the end of ch. 4 and beginning of ch. 5. Far from being something strange, Christians should expect such suffering before Christ's glory is revealed (4:12–13). That glory is revealed already in suffering for righteousness, even as Christ revealed His own glory in the cross, a reversal of what the world would consider glory (4:14–17). This theology of the cross distinguishes believers from the world and confirms Christians in God's will (4:18–19). As a sharer in Christ's sufferings, Peter exhorts his fellow elders to shepherd God's flock in such a way as to receive a crown of glory (5:1–4). He encourages youth to submit to elders, with the invitation to cast all anxiety on God in humility (5:5–7). The sufferings experienced by the churches Peter addresses are common to believers all over the world, and he enjoins them to resist the devil (5:8–9) with a strength that comes from the God of grace, who will restore and strengthen believers who suffer (5:10–11).

4:12–13 Once again Peter tenderly addresses his fellow believers as *beloved* (cf. 2:11–12), as he encourages them to see the *fiery trial* they are bound to experience as a *test*: an opportunity in their calling. A major theme in the Letter, Peter's encouragement further unpacks his exhortations on testing and endurance at 1:6–7 and 2:20–21. Suffering persecution as Christians is a way to bear the cross of Christ, and the promise of God is that He strengthens them through affliction. Luther reminds his readers of this same thing: "God lays a cross on all believers in order that they may taste and prove the power of God—the power which they have taken hold of through faith" (LW 30:127). Seeing suffering as an opportunity to bear Christ's cross reminds Christians that in doing so, we *share Christ's sufferings*—an honor for Christians, who know that their Savior suffered to save them (cf. Php 3:10; Rm 5:3–5). Before His death, Christ called

His cross the moment of His glory (Jn 12:23–33), and Peter unites the "not-yet" glory of His return with the "now" glory of sharing in His cross, which results in joy *when His glory is revealed*, not only at the end of time, but in the present moment, as the Gospel's effects are seen in the life and witness of those who suffer for His name.

4:14 Suffering for Christ's name is a particular sharing in His cross, the location in time and space of the insults He endured. Therefore when Christians *are insulted* for His name, they are *blessed* by God in the grand reversal of the theology of the cross. Christ transforms the world's taunts into His blessing. Peter is speaking from personal experience (cf. Ac 5:41). Christ also shares His glory as He shares His cross; when Christians are persecuted for His name, they are never alone, but empowered and blessed with the *Spirit of glory and of God.*

4:15–16 "Bearing the cross" is not suffering the effects of our own sin (cf. 2:19–21). Reformation Christians talk often about "cheap grace," that is, a self-justifying concept of a tolerant God, without a respect for the actual cost of God's favor in the innocent blood of Christ (Dietrich Bonhoeffer coined the term in *The Cost of Discipleship*). But we seldom talk about the other side of that coin, "cheap Law," again a self-justifying concept of a God who is always on the side of believers who feel they have free reign to act as offensively as they please, and chalk up everything they suffer as a result of the persecution of a world that is out to get them because they happen to be Christians. We must remember: sin has consequences! Christians are *simul iustus et peccator*—at the same time saint and sinner. And as sinners, breaking the Law of God still brings with it temporal consequences! Such suffering is not identity with Christ's wounds; rather it puts us on the inflicting side of those wounds! This is not limited to gross sins such as murder and theft, but even things we might more easily justify in ourselves, even in the communion of the Church, such as being a *meddler*—one who wants to supervise the affairs of others. Suffering "with" Christ means being subject to both the very costly Law and very costly Gospel that unites us with His death and life. Suffering as a Christian brings an honor distinct from suffering for wrongdoing, and the proper response to such suffering is to *glorify God* by confessing Christ, even if it means death or adversity.

4:17 Peter echoes Paul's call to *judgment* among ourselves *at the household of God*: both God's judgment and our own: "For anyone who eats and drinks without discerning the body eats and drinks judgment on himself. That is why many of you are weak and ill, and some have died. But if we judged ourselves truly, we would not be judged. But when we are judged by the Lord, we are disciplined so that we may not be condemned along with the world" (1Co 11:29–32). Calvin wrote:

> Hence the complaints of the godly, that the wicked pass their life in continual pleasures, and delight themselves with wine and the harp, and at length descend without pains in an instant into the grave—that fatness covers their eyes—that they are exempt from troubles—that they securely and joyfully spend their life, looking down with contempt on others, so that they dare to set their mouth against heaven. (Job xxi. 13; Ps. lxxiii. 3–9.) In short, God so regulates his judgments in this world, that he fattens the wicked for the day of slaughter. He therefore passes by their many sins, and, as it were, connives at them. 'In the meantime, he restores by corrections his own children, for whom he has a care, to the right way, whenever they depart from it. (Calvin 139)

Repentance is the goal of such judgment, as we see the effects of our own sin (v. 15), and even as God allows us to face consequences. Christians believe in the Gospel that saves. Without faith in Christ, there is no hope, which is what Peter preaches for the sake of all, for those who believe and *for those who do not obey the gospel.* Luther commented on this verse: "The time of judgment, foretold by the prophets, is at hand [Jer 25:29; Ezk 9:6]. When the Gospel is preached, God begins to punish sin, in order that He may kill and make alive" (LW 30:130).

4:18–19 Peter concludes his meditation on sharing in Christ's sufferings by quoting Pr 11:31, reminding Christians that they may suffer the effect of their sins. The difference between them and unbelievers is that Christians face such suffering in faith, trusting in God's deliverance. We are called therefore to *suffer according to God's will*: not for sins (Christ has suffered for sins already—once!, for all time— cf. 3:18), but for the sake of the Gospel. Luther reminds us of this truth: "[Peter] teaches us to subdue the flesh with sobriety, watchfulness, temperance, prayer, and to find comfort and strength through the sufferings of Christ" (LW 35:391). Christians therefore *entrust their souls* to a God who preserves them, a *faithful Creator*, as Luther confessed: "I believe that God has made me and all creatures; that He has given me my body and soul, eyes, ears, and all my members, my reason and all my senses, and still takes care of them" (SC, explanation of the First Article of the Apostles' Creed).

4:12–19 in Devotion and Prayer The consequences of sins are not "crosses" that the Christian bears. On the other hand, suffering for the name of Christ is indeed a sharing in the sufferings of Christ. But what about other kinds of suffering? For example, when faced with a crippling illness, some faithful Christians may say, "It's just a cross I bear." When natural disaster hits, is this a sharing in the cross of Christ? Does illness or other affliction rise to the level of what Peter has in mind here? It's helpful to think in terms of two distinct truths: (1) the enemies Christians face, and (2) the honor to which Christians are called. As Christians we face an unholy trinity of enemies: the world, the devil, and our own sinful flesh that leads us to death. When the world has us in its crosshairs, the Christian finds that the target on his back is shaped the same way, and receives whatever the world slings at him as a union with Christ on His cross, "for so they persecuted the prophets who were before you" (Mt 5:12). Where the Gospel is preached in its purity, there will be Christ's cross, for the devil hates it (as Peter warns in the next few verses, 5:8–9). This, too, is a cross Christians bear. And while "sinful flesh" does not bear honor for suffering in the name of "sin," Christians can yet bear the honor of suffering in "flesh," for so Christ suffered (4:1). Suffering in the flesh can be sickness and any other affliction that weakens us in the eyes of the world or ourselves. Suffering in the flesh because of the evil or accidents of others, while a result of sin generally, is still suffering that God cares about, and He calls His children to bear up under such suffering patiently, waiting on Him for ultimate healing, in the "now" and the "not-yet" (Rm 12:12). Not every affliction seems like a gift from God at the time, especially the initial shock of debilitating or terminal illness. But for those who can bear to hear it, even the sufferings we bear in this corruptible flesh can be an opportunity to honor God as the One who will, soon and very soon, vindicate the saints who bear His name, by completing what was sown in corruption by raising it to His imperishable honor. "For I consider that the sufferings of this present time are not worth comparing with the glory that is to be revealed to us. For the creation waits with eager longing for the revealing of the sons of God. For the creation was subjected to futility, not willingly, but because of Him who subjected it, in hope that the creation itself will be set free from its bondage to corruption and obtain the freedom of the glory of the children of God. For we know that the whole creation has been groaning together in the pains of childbirth until now. And not only the creation, but we ourselves, who have the firstfruits of the Spirit, groan inwardly as we wait eagerly for adoption as sons, the redemption of our bodies. For in this hope we were saved. Now hope that is seen is not hope. For who hopes for what he sees? But if we hope for what we do not see, we wait for it with patience" (Rm 8:18–25). • Lord, as I pray this day "Thy will be done," I ask that You honor me with the power to accept Your will. Honor me with strength to endure the onslaught of insult and abuse the world heaps on Your name. Honor me with Your divine grace to resist the temptations and lies of the devil. Honor me with sure forgiveness of sins, and honor me with a sharing in Your flesh, that I may live this day remembering that You came not to redeem me from my flesh, but that You came in the flesh to redeem me from my sins. Raise this flesh as You have promised, that I may join all believers at the resurrection and give You the honor that You have merited through Your glorious resurrection. Amen.

Elders Have Special Responsibilities and Promises (5:1–4)

ESV	KJV
5 ¹So I exhort the elders among you, as a fellow elder and a witness of the sufferings of Christ, as well as a partaker in the glory that is going to be revealed: ²shepherd the flock of God that is among you, exercising oversight, not under compulsion, but willingly, as God would have you; not for shameful gain, but eagerly; ³not domineering over those in your charge, but being examples to the flock. ⁴And when the chief Shepherd appears, you will receive the unfading crown of glory.	5 ¹The elders which are among you I exhort, who am also an elder, and a witness of the sufferings of Christ, and also a partaker of the glory that shall be revealed: ²Feed the flock of God which is among you, taking the oversight thereof, not by constraint, but willingly; not for filthy lucre, but of a ready mind; ³Neither as being lords over God's heritage, but being examples to the flock. ⁴And when the chief Shepherd shall appear, ye shall receive a crown of glory that fadeth not away.

5:1–2 Peter addresses leaders of the Christian congregations he writes to, encouraging them *as a fellow elder.* Already in the earliest Christian Church, the structure of public service in the congregation is confessed as one of gifts being given, proceeding from apostolic ministry (cf. Ac 2:42); Peter holds this ministry in common with others who teach and distribute the gifts of the Lord. The terms *elders . . . shepherd . . . oversight* are words used in the NT to describe the pastoral office (cf. Ti 1:5, 7; Ac 20:17; Php 1:1; 1Tm 3:2) that extend to the NT Church of our own day: "All who preside over churches are both bishops and elders" (Tr 62). Peter is in a special position to exhort the undershepherds of the Good Shepherd, because he is a *witness* to Christ's earthly ministry, being with Jesus from the beginning. He was an eyewitness of all of its phases, including the climactic events of His *sufferings* and resurrection. Witnessing the transfiguration (Mk 9:2–8) was particularly moving for Peter, who has this event in mind as he identifies himself as a *partaker in the glory* (cf. also 2Pt 1:16–18). Peter's exhortation to his fellow elders to *shepherd the flock of God* recall his words about the Good Shepherd who has restored his wandering sheep (2:25). Shepherds of God's flock are to do their work *not under compulsion, but willingly,* as God's children are called to exercise their vocations in all realms. As the Lutheran reformers confessed: "Truly good works should be done willingly, or from a voluntary spirit, by those whom God's Son has made free" (FC SD IV 18). Cf. Luther's commentary on Peter's words:

> A pastor must not only lead to pasture by teaching the sheep how to be true Christians: but, in addition to this, he must also repel the wolves, lest they attack the sheep and lead them astray with false doctrine and error. For the devil does not rest. Now today one finds many people who can let the Gospel be preached, provided that one does not cry out against the wolves and preach against the prelates. But even if I preach in the right way and tend and teach the sheep, this protecting and guarding does not suffice to keep the wolves from coming and leading the sheep astray. For what is built if I lay stones and watch someone else knock them down? (LW 30:135)

5:3 What are pastors called to do? This verse is essential to the vocation of shepherd: elders of God's Church are to serve His people in a way that is *not domineering,* because pastors are servants of the Church, not taskmasters (Mk 10:42–45; cf. Php 2:6–11). On the other hand, they are to be *examples.* A Latin proverb states, *vita clericorum liber laicorum*: the life of the clergy is the book of the laypeople. Shepherds are called to model the faith as well as to teach it. Bengel wrote:

The congregation is not the peculiar property of the elder, but [the elder] who lords it, treats it as though it were his lot or property. . . . The purest obedience is obtained by example. Such frank intercourse subdues the itching desire for rule. (Bengel 5:81)

5:4 Christ is the *chief Shepherd* (cf. 2:25), the head of the Church (Eph 5:23); all pastors serve under His authority and ministry. *crown.* There are several "crowns" mentioned throughout the NT, the crown of life (Jas 1:12; Rv 2:10), the crown of righteousness (2Tm 4:8), even the athlete's prize (1Co 9:25; 2Tm 2:5), and of course the crown of thorns (Mk 15:17). Christ alone is described as "crowned with glory and honor because of the suffering of death" (Heb 2:9). Peter here points to the goal of faithful undershepherds of the Chief Shepherd, a *crown of glory* that is *unfading*, a symbol of salvation that reaches back to the inheritance with which he began the Letter (1:4).

Younger Men Are to Submit Humbly to the Community's Elders (5:5)

ESV	KJV
[5]Likewise, you who are younger, be subject to the elders. Clothe yourselves, all of you, with humility toward one another, for "God opposes the proud but gives grace to the humble."	[5]Likewise, ye younger, submit yourselves unto the elder. Yea, all of you be subject one to another, and be clothed with humility: for God resisteth the proud, and giveth grace to the humble.

5:5 Young men are mentioned here not simply as the opposite of "elders" (vv. 1–4), but because those who are young in faith are especially in need of the pastor's spiritual care. Those who are younger are called to *be subject* (ESV) or *submit* (KJV); as with submission in the other estates (2:13–3:7), such deferral to God's holy order is a blessing, not a burden. Submission requires God's people to *clothe yourselves . . . with humility*. In the grand reversal of God's work with His people through the cross, He raises up the humble and sends the proud away empty. God *gives grace*: true honor comes from the Lord; He knows what we need and provides it.

Concluding Exhortation to Humility and Trust (5:6–11)

ESV	KJV
⁶Humble yourselves, therefore, under the mighty hand of God so that at the proper time he may exalt you, ⁷casting all your anxieties on him, because he cares for you. ⁸Be sober-minded; be watchful. Your adversary the devil prowls around like a roaring lion, seeking someone to devour. ⁹Resist him, firm in your faith, knowing that the same kinds of suffering are being experienced by your brotherhood throughout the world. ¹⁰And after you have suffered a little while, the God of all grace, who has called you to his eternal glory in Christ, will himself restore, confirm, strengthen, and establish you. ¹¹To him be the dominion forever and ever. Amen.	⁶Humble yourselves therefore under the mighty hand of God, that he may exalt you in due time: ⁷Casting all your care upon him; for he careth for you. ⁸Be sober, be vigilant; because your adversary the devil, as a roaring lion, walketh about, seeking whom he may devour: ⁹Whom resist stedfast in the faith, knowing that the same afflictions are accomplished in your brethren that are in the world. ¹⁰But the God of all grace, who hath called us unto his eternal glory by Christ Jesus, after that ye have suffered a while, make you perfect, stablish, strengthen, settle you. ¹¹To him be glory and dominion for ever and ever. Amen.

5:6 Peter moves from a focus on youth to a general exhortation to all who are under the care of the Good Shepherd, calling on all believers to *humble yourselves* (cf. Jas 4:10). God is not bound by our chronological limitations and expectations, but operates according to His *proper time*; the exaltation of the humble will therefore occur in the "now" and "not-yet" of God's purpose, for the benefit of others or ourselves, and to His glory.

5:7 Peter was among the disciples who, seeing the wind and waves, cried out to their Master asleep on the sea, "Teacher, do you not care that we are perishing?" only to learn that even the wind and sea obeyed Jesus (Mk 4:38–41). Now he uses the same construction to convey the comforting truth that *He cares for you*. There is no doubt of His perfect love and care. Melanchthon wrote: "The person who knows that he has a Father who is gracious to him through Christ truly knows God" (AC XX 24).

5:8 In view of the return of Christ, Peter calls all to *be sober-minded* and *watchful* as we pray for Christ's return (cf. 1Th 5:6, 8). Christian vigilance is necessary because *the devil prowls around like a roaring lion*. Peter alludes to the messianic Ps 22:21, reminding those under the devil's attack that the enemy succumbed to certain defeat in the death of Christ. Satan however still seeks to harm Christians in any way possible, a tool subject to the Lord's will until His final judgment. The image was palpable for first-century Christians, for under Nero, some literally faced death by lions in the Roman arena. The devil "tries every trick and does not stop until he finally wears us out, so that we either renounce our faith or throw up our hands and put up our feet, becoming indifferent or impatient" (LC V 26). Rather than fearing the devil who seeks *to devour*, Christians fear and trust the Lord, who has promised to swallow up death in victory (1 Cor 15:54, 2Co 5:4).

5:9 As James exhorts Christians ("resist the devil, and he will flee from you," Jas 4:7), so Peter reminds Christians that the enemy can be, and is to be, resisted. Christians *resist him* by God's Word, which gives us strength and guidance to face temptations (Eph 6:11–18; cf. Mt 4:4, 7, 10). Peter echoes Paul at 1Co 10:13 ("No temptation has overtaken you that is not common to man") as he reminds his readers that temptation and persecution are the universal lot of Christians in all times and places. The *suffering . . . brotherhood throughout the world* is called to hope in the strength of God's care for His people, as Luther comments: "You must be sober and vigilant, but in order that the body may be ready. But this does not yet vanquish the devil. It is done only in order that you may give the body less reason to sin. The true sword is your strong and firm faith. If you take hold of God's Word in your heart and cling to it with faith, the devil cannot win but must flee" (LW 30:142).

5:10 We do not suffer alone: Christ Himself suffered in the flesh (4:1). And we certainly do not rely on our own strength and will for care and restoration. Rather, God will care for all our needs, even in persecution. Peter affirms that He is *the God of all grace*; the verbs are in His control to *restore, confirm, strengthen, and establish you.* The Lutheran reformers confessed: "God has kindled in their hearts this beginning of true godliness. He will further strengthen and help them in their great weakness to persevere in true faith unto the end" (FC SD II 14); "Through the Word, by which He calls us, the Holy

Spirit bestows grace, power, and ability for this purpose" (FC SD XI 33). This is surely reason to glorify Him with the doxological conclusion of 5:11: words of praise are a fitting response to God's blessings (cf. 4:11).

5:1–11 in Devotion and Prayer Servants in care industries know the particular joy of concern over people who will never be able to reward them in kind. The NICU nurse, the social worker, the firefighter—people faithful to these vocations do not work for accolades, but to help those who are not able to help themselves. Just so do people serve whom one might not immediately consider as life-savers: the elementary school teacher, the parent, the pastor. "Shepherd" is such a fitting analogy, for sheep cannot survive without them: "When He saw the crowds, He had compassion for them, because they were harassed and helpless, like sheep without a shepherd" (Mt 9:36). Compassion drives the Christian community to serve the neighbor, faithful to their callings, because Christ first showed compassion to us. And better than the care that promises one more day of survival in this world is the kind of pasture to which Christ the Good Shepherd would lead His lambs: His Word that promises eternal life. He feeds His lambs with the living bread from heaven, He waters them with His Baptism, He nourishes them with His body and blood. He leads His faithful undershepherds to care for His lambs. Even as He enjoined Peter: "Tend My sheep" (Jn 21:16), so He calls His pastors to the pulpit, to the bedside, to the home, to the graveside, to wherever His children need care. • Gracious heavenly Father, thank You for faithful ministers of Your Word who feed, clothe, nourish, and tend Your lambs. Lead Your shepherds always only to Your cross so that Your sheep may be fed constantly with Your Word. Amen.

PART 6

FINAL GREETINGS (5:12–14)

Silvanus's Help (5:12)

ESV	KJV
[12]By Silvanus, a faithful brother as I regard him, I have written briefly to you, exhorting and declaring that this is the true grace of God. Stand firm in it.	[12]By Silvanus, a faithful brother unto you, as I suppose, I have written briefly, exhorting, and testifying that this is the true grace of God wherein ye stand.

Introduction to 5:12–14 The last three verses of the Letter form Peter's final salutation, comprised of a recommendation for Silvanus and his teaching (v. 12), a greeting from the Church at Rome (v. 13), and an invitation to love and peace (v. 14).

5:12 Here Peter acknowledges the one who helped him in ministry and also helped in the formation or delivery of the Letter, as he states that he has *written briefly, by* (that is, with the help of) *Silvanus,* also known as "Silas." Silvanus was also a colleague of the apostle Paul (cf. Ac 15–17; 18:5; 2Co 1:19; 1Th 1:1; 2Th 1:1). Peter concludes his Letter by summarizing his teaching as *the true grace of God* in which believers are to *stand firm.* With the constant emphasis throughout the Letter of God's people experiencing persecution, Peter reminds Christians that strength is to be found in the teaching of God's grace alone (cf. 2Th 2:15).

Other Brothers from the Church in "Babylon" (Rome) Send Greetings (5:13)

ESV	KJV
[13]She who is at Babylon, who is likewise chosen, sends you greetings, and so does Mark, my son.	[13]The church that is at Babylon, elected together with you, saluteth you; and so doth Marcus my son.

5:13 It was common for elders to share greetings from other churches. Here, Peter forwards a greeting from the Church at Rome, coded under the name *She who is at Babylon*, symbolizing Rome's persecution of believers (cf. Rv 14:8; 17:5, 18; 18:2, 10). Particular sensitivity to persecution throughout the Letter contextualizes this final reminder that the Christians of the Asian churches are not alone in their struggles against the world. Peter forwards a personal greeting here as well, from *Mark, my son*. This is probably not a biological son, but refers rather to a son in the faith, the evangelist Mark (cf. Ac 12:12; Col 4:10).

The Holy Kiss and the Peace of Christ (5:14)

ESV	KJV
[14]Greet one another with the kiss of love. Peace to all of you who are in Christ.	[14]Greet ye one another with a kiss of charity. Peace be with you all that are in Christ Jesus. Amen.

5:14 The *kiss of love*, or brotherly kiss, was a common greeting of friends and family; cf. 1Co 16:20; 2Co 13:12; 1Th 5:26; Rm 16:16. Here it reminds the reader of Peter's exhortation in 4:8–9 to love and to show hospitality, as the kiss was a common cultural feature of ancient Mediterranean hospitality (cf. Lk 7:45). Peter finishes the Letter with the word "shalom": *peace to all . . . in Christ*. True peace is ours because of Christ's work.

5:12–14 in Devotion and Prayer The tramping feet of soldiers. The crashing of waves and the scream of the wind around a little boat in the Galilee. The shouting of riots fired up by authorities in

Jerusalem. The pointing fingers and accusations in the wee hours of a Friday morning outside the temple courts. So much noise, din, and danger in Peter's memories of Christ's ministry and the early days of the Church! And more recently, the shouts of the crowd, the dust of the amphitheater, the jeering of citizens, and the roar of wild animals. The little flock Peter had been mandated to feed was growing up in the midst of a world growing wilder around them every week. What word to leave these sojourner-exiles with, what word of comfort, what word of warning, what word would do? The Lord's Word. That's the only one that will ever do. So the Lord's Word it is. Shalom. Peace. Be still. And the waves die down. For in Christ, shalom, true peace, is a completed fact. In spite of a world grown wild and wooly around us, the risen Christ comes, for Peter, for His disciples, for His Church, for you. • O Lord Jesus Christ, You promise that You keep him in perfect peace whose mind is stayed on You, because he trusts in You (Is 26:3). Keep my mind stayed on You, that in the midst of a world seeking after nothing more than constant hostility and superficial cease-fire, I may know a perfect peace in You. Deliver me to my last day from this belligerent world, that I may enjoy citizenship in Your heavenly kingdom forever. And strengthen me to work as You have called me, yet this little while, in harmony and peace, that Your Word may bring Your sheep to Your perfect peace. Amen.

2 PETER

INTRODUCTION TO
2 PETER

Overview

Author
Simon [Simeon] Peter the apostle

Date
c. AD 68

Places
Mount of Transfiguration; Sodom and Gomorrah

People
Simeon Peter; Jesus; false prophets/teachers; the unrighteous; the apostles; Paul

Purpose
To warn against false teachers who promoted sinful lifestyles and questioned whether Jesus would return in judgment

Law and Sin Themes
Exhortations to virtue; warnings against false prophets; ignorance; nearsightedness; forgetfulness; fiery judgment; destruction of the ungodly

Grace and Gospel Themes
God's sure Word; the Spirit's work; Christ cleansed us from our former sins; eternal kingdom; God promises new heavens and a new earth; God does not wish any to perish

Memory Verses
A sure prophetic word (1:19–21); new heavens and a new earth (3:13)

Luther on 2 Peter

This epistle is written against those who think that Christian faith can be without works. Therefore he exhorts them to test themselves by good works and become sure of their faith, just as one knows trees by their fruits [Matt. 7:20].

He begins accordingly by praising the gospel over against the doctrines of men. He says that people ought to hear the gospel alone and not the doctrines of men. For, as he says, "No prophecy ever came by the impulse of men" [II Pet. 1:21].

For this reason he warns in chapter 2 against the false teachers who are to come. They are preoccupied with works and thereby deny Christ. He threatens these men severely with three terrible illustrations and depicts them so clearly with their avarice, pride, wickedness, fornication, and hypocrisy that one must plainly see he means the clergy of today. For these have swallowed the whole world in their greed and are wickedly leading an irresponsible, fleshly, worldly life.

In chapter 3 he shows that the Last Day will come soon; and though in the sight of [*fur*] men it may seem a thousand years, yet in the sight of [*fur*] God it is as one day. He describes what will happen at the Last Day, how everything shall be consumed by fire. However, he also prophesies that at that time people will be scornful and, like the Epicureans, will think nothing of faith.

In summary, chapter 1 shows what Christendom was to be like at the time of the pure gospel. Chapter 2 shows how it was to be in the time of the pope and the doctrines of men. Chapter 3 shows how, after this, people will despise both the gospel and all doctrine, and will believe nothing—and this is now in full swing—until Christ comes. (LW 35:391–92)

For more of Luther's insights on this Book, see *Sermons on the Second Epistle of St. Peter* (LW 30:147–99).

Calvin on 2 Peter

The doubts respecting this Epistle mentioned by Eusebius, ought not to keep us from reading it. For if the doubts rested on the authority of men, whose names he does not give, we ought to pay no more regard to it than to that of unknown men. And he afterwards adds, that it was everywhere received without any dispute. What Jerome writes influences me somewhat more, that some, induced by a difference in the style, did not think that Peter was the author. For though some affinity may be traced, yet I confess that there is that manifest difference which distinguishes different writers. There are also other probable conjectures by which we may conclude that it was written by another rather than by Peter. At the same time, according to the consent of all, it has nothing unworthy of Peter, as it shews everywhere the power and the grace of an apostolic spirit. If it be received as canonical, we must allow Peter to be the author, since it has his name inscribed, and he also testifies that he had lived with Christ: and it would have been a fiction unworthy of a minister of Christ, to have personated another individual. So then I conclude, that if the Epistle be deemed worthy of credit, it must have proceeded from Peter; not that he himself wrote it, but that some one of his disciples set forth in writings by his command, those things which the necessity of the times required. For it is probable that he was now in extreme old age, for he says, that he was near his end. And it may have been that at the request of the godly, he allowed this testimony of his mind to be recorded shortly before his death, because it might have somewhat availed, when he was dead, to support the good, and to repress the wicked. Doubtless, as in every part of the Epistle the majesty of the Spirit of Christ appears, to repudiate it is what I dread, though I do not here recognise the language of Peter. But since it is not quite evident as to the author, I shall allow myself the liberty of using the word Peter or Apostle indiscriminately.

I shall now come to the argument, which may be briefly stated.

The design is to shew, that those who have once professed the true faith of Christ, ought to respond to their calling to the last. After having then extolled, in high terms, the grace of God, he recommends to them holiness of life, because God usually punishes in hypocrites a false profession of his name, with dreadful blindness, and on the other hand he increases his gifts to those who truly and from the heart embrace the doctrine of religion. He, therefore, exhorts them to prove their calling by a holy life. And, to give a greater weight to his admonitions, he says that he is already near his end, and at the same time, excuses himself that he so often repeated the same things, his object being that they who should remain alive on the earth after his death, might have what he, when alive, wrote, more deeply fixed in their minds.

And as the foundation of true religion is the certainty or the truth of the gospel, he shews, first, how indubitable is its truth by this fact,—that he himself had been an eyewitness of all things which it contains, and especially that he had heard Christ proclaimed from heaven to be the Son of God; and, in the second place, it was God's will that it should be borne witness to, and approved by the oracles of the prophets.

He, however, predicts, at the same time, that danger was approaching from false teachers, who would spread impious inventions, as well as from the despisers of God, who would mock all religion; and he did this, that the faithful might learn to be watchful, and that they might be fortified. And he seems to have spoken thus designedly, lest they expected that the course of truth in the kingdom of Christ would be tranquil and peaceable, and free from all contention. He afterwards, as on a tablet, describes the character and manners of those who would, by their corruptions, pollute Christianity. But the description which he presents, especially suits the present age, as it will be more evident by a comparison. For he especially draws his pen against Lucianic men, who abandon themselves to every wickedness, and take a profane license to shew contempt to God, yea, and treat with ridicule the hope of a better life; and at this day we see that the world is everywhere full of such rabble.

He further exhorts the faithful, not only to look always for the coming of Christ with suspended and expectant minds, but also to regard that day as present before their eyes, and in the meantime to keep themselves unpolluted for the Lord: in which doctrine he makes Paul as his associate and approver; and to defend his writings from the calumnies of the ungodly, he severely reproves all those who pervert them. (Calvin 363–65)

Gerhard on 2 Peter

In the early Church some people had doubts about the latter Epistle of Peter as well. Consequently, we place it also among the canonical books of the second rank. Eusebius, Hist., bk. 3, c. 3: "One Epistle of Peter, which is called 'the Former,' was accepted without controversy. The old presbyters used it in their writings without any hesitation. But we have accepted that the one which is called 'the Latter' is not legitimate and canonical. Yet because it seems useful to many, it is used along with other Scriptures." And later: "Regarding those letters that are attributed to Peter, of which I realize that only one of them was held to be truly an epistle of that man in the estimation of the ancient presbyters, let this still be said." In the same book, c. 22, after enumerating the canonical books of the first rank, he adds: "Those that are spoken against, though they are well-known to many, are these: the Epistle attributed to James, the Epistle of Jude, 2 Peter, and 2 and 3 John." [Gerhard cites other Fathers who questioned whether Peter wrote the second letter.]

There are ready arguments, however, to persuade that this is an apostolic Epistle and that Peter wrote it. (1) Its author in clear words calls himself "Simon Peter, servant and apostle of Jesus Christ." (2) It was entitled as written to the same people as was the first, namely, to the Jews scattered throughout the Roman Empire who had been converted to Christ and whose apostle Peter was. (3) The spirit in it is apostolic. (4) Its style and composition are in conformity with those of the first Epistle. . . . (5) The author of this letter says that "the putting off of his tabernacle had been declared

by Christ" (2 Pet. 1:14). With these words he is undoubtedly looking to Christ's prediction in John 21:18. (6) He says that he was
an eyewitness of the transfiguration on the mountain (2 Pet. 1:16).
But now, Peter was there along with James and John. (7) He mentions a prior Epistle (2 Pet. 3:1). (8) He calls Paul his "beloved
brother" (2 Pet. 3:15). (9) It is placed in the canon under Peter's
name by the Council of Laodicea (canon 59), the third Council of
Carthage. . . . [Gerhard cites numerous other Fathers.]

To that which some argue to the contrary, that is, the diversity in
style from the first Epistle, we respond with a denial. Even if there
were a diversity of style here, the same things also occur in the
Pauline Epistles. . . .

It was written to the same people as was the first, namely, to
the converted Jews (3:1), which is also concluded from 1:19. It
consists of three chapters in which are added to the apostolic
introduction (1) an exhortation to a zeal for continuing and per-
severing in the faith; and (2) a warning to watch out for both
seducers as well as mockers and scorners who deny the final
coming of Christ. The whole Epistle concludes with a doxology
worthy of the apostle. (E 1.283–84)

Bengel on 2 Peter

At the beginning of his former Epistle he had only placed his sur-
name: here he adds his name also; at the close of his life reminding
himself of his former condition, before he had received his sur-
name. The character of this Epistle agrees in a remarkable manner
with the former Epistle of Peter, and with the speeches of the same
apostle in the Acts. (Bengel 84)

Wesley on 2 Peter

The parts of this epistle, written not long before St. Peter's death,
and the destruction of Jerusalem, with the same design as the former, are likewise three: The inscription, . . . A farther stirring up
of the minds of true believers, . . . The conclusion. (Wesley 593)

Challenges for Readers

Authorship. Many modern scholars have concluded that Peter
could not have written this Letter for the following reasons: (1) the
style differs from 1 Peter and is not that of a Galilean fisherman; (2)
the writer's opponents could be Gnostics, who appeared after Peter's

time; (3) the Letter likely depends on Jude, so the work is not original; and (4) after Peter's death, his students may have written the work to address issues of their own time. In contrast, other scholars have noted the following: (1) the style of the Letter is different from 1 Peter and demonstrates training in Greek rhetoric; however, Peter is reputed to have written through a scribe (1Pt 5:12; see "Authorship," p. 104) and may have done the same for this Letter; (2) the false teachers are not described as Gnostics but behave like Epicurean Greeks, who were contemporary with Peter (see below); (3) Jude's Letter may depend on 2 Peter (see below); (4) the modern notion of "schools" aligned with different apostles is not readily described in early Christian literature, which typically emphasizes the unity of the apostles (cf. 2Pt 3:15); and (5) during the first and second centuries, early Jewish and Christian texts written under pseudonyms did not commonly include letters. Although Peter's authorship of the Letter was questioned by some early Christians, the Letter was still commonly attributed to Peter and not to other authors. Peter, working with a scribe, remains the most likely author.

Relationship to Jude. 2Pt 2 and the Book of Jude demonstrate a strong literary relationship (note the many cross-references to Jude in the center column for 2Pt 2; the entries largely follow the same order as the passages in Jude). However, it cannot be determined whether Peter borrowed from Jude, Jude borrowed from Peter, or they both borrowed from a common work. Research on Greek letters has demonstrated that form letters were common. Early Jewish writers also adapted letters and copied them to different Jewish communities. That one writer should borrow from the good content of another should not be a surprise. In fact, Jude may state that he has done just that when he cites "the predictions of the apostles" (Jude 17), which could refer to 2 Peter.

Identifying the False Teachers. A century ago, scholars commonly read early Christian references to "knowledge" as responses to Gnostic heretics (from Greek *ginosko*, "to know"), who claimed special knowledge and revelation and taught a complex system of heavenly mediators between God and the physical world. After the discovery of the Gnostic Nag Hammadi Manuscripts in 1945, the understanding of Gnostics changed significantly. Scholars realized that, although Gnostic ideas were developing in the first century AD, the Gnostics did not develop into a strong movement until the second century, when they began to infiltrate Christian congregations and Neo-platonic groups. False teachers, such as those described in 2 Peter, could have shared some ideas with later Gnostics but could not truly be called Gnostics (sometimes scholars speak of "proto-gnostics"). There are many uses of Greek terms for knowledge in 2 Peter (cf. 1:2–3, 5–6, 16, 20; 2:20–21; 3:3, 17–18), but these should not be viewed as evidence of debate with Gnostics. As noted above, it is more likely that the false teachers described in 2 Peter were influenced by common Greek teachings such as those of the Epicureans.

Testament Style. Some scholars see 2Pt 1:12–15 adapting the Jewish "testament" style, which first became popular in the second century BC. This style of literature follows the example of Gn 49, where a patriarch gathers his family for instruction before he dies. Such Jewish testaments were attributed to the patriarchs and were therefore pseudonymous. In contrast, 2 Peter is plainly in the form of a letter. The writer clearly anticipates his death, but this hardly makes it an example of testament literature. The setting of a teacher wishing to provide instructions for his flock before he dies is completely natural (cf. Ac 20:17–38).

Blessings for Readers

Peter addresses four key areas of Christian teaching: (1) knowledge of the Lord and the problem of forgetfulness; (2) true godliness and piety; (3) God's gifts (faith, promises, Holy Scripture); and (4) the end times. He guides readers to resist the appeals of false teachers, since everyone will face the Lord as judge when He returns.

As you read 2 Peter, consider the state of your faith and the character of your life. Commit your ways to the Lord by practicing daily repentance and praying for Christ's return. Through this sure prophetic Word, you will grow in the grace and knowledge of your Lord and Savior Jesus Christ.

Outline

I. The Apostolic Salutation (1:1–2)

II. Exhortation to Godliness (1:3–21)

    A. Content of This Exhortation (1:3–11)

    B. Necessity of This Reminder (1:12–15)

    C. Certain Basis of the Exhortation in the Revelation of Christ and Scripture (1:16–21)

III. Warning against False Teachers (ch. 2)

    A. Anticipation of False Teachers (2:1–3)

    B. God Delivers the Righteous and Punishes the Ungodly (2:4–10a)

    C. Denunciation of the Motives, Character, and Message of the False Teachers (2:10b–22)

IV. Answers to Skepticism regarding the End of This World (3:1–10)

V. Final Exhortation on the Basis of Christian Expectation and Hope (3:11–18)

PART 1

THE APOSTOLIC SALUTATION (1:1–2)

ESV	KJV
1 ¹Simeon Peter, a servant and apostle of Jesus Christ, To those who have obtained a faith of equal standing with ours by the righteousness of our God and Savior Jesus Christ: ²May grace and peace be multiplied to you in the knowledge of God and of Jesus our Lord.	*1* ¹Simon Peter, a servant and an apostle of Jesus Christ, to them that have obtained like precious faith with us through the righteousness of God and our Saviour Jesus Christ: ²Grace and peace be multiplied unto you through the knowledge of God, and of Jesus our Lord,

Introduction to 1:1–2 Peter wrote this Letter to fellow Christians, with an emphasis on the "fellow." The common faith to which we have all been called is the one to which he was called as apostle and slave, to which all are called in equal honor (v. 1). He offers a standard epistolary greeting, saluting his readers with grace and peace that comes from knowing God in Christ (v. 2).

1:1 Peter introduces himself in this Letter as *Simeon*. His name is spelled this way also at Ac 15:14. The use of this Aramaic or Hbr spelling of his name may indicate a Jewish audience, which is otherwise not distinguished beyond the general greeting he offers in this verse. Calling himself a *servant* (or "slave," Gk *doulos*) emphasizes his belonging to Jesus, who had purchased him (1Pt 1:18–19; cf. also Jas 1:1). Peter also calls himself *apostle*; on Peter's apostleship and NT career, cf. note at 1Pt 1:1. Peter addresses people who possess *a faith of equal standing with ours.* On the one hand, this might sound like a challenge; after all, Peter was an eyewitness to Christ's earthly ministry! But Peter is not here making distinctions between "those who have not seen and yet have believed" (Jn 20:29) as much as he is indicating the key to equal honor before God: *righteousness.* Faith that rests on Christ's righteousness is faith that God honors (cf.

1Pt 4:12–13). Such righteousness is a gift from Christ, who is *our God and Savior.* There is no distinction here between God and Jesus; indeed the confession of Christ as God is the substance of the apologetic Peter encourages at 1Pt 3:15 (see note there).

1:2 Peter prays that his hearers possess *knowledge of God and of Jesus our Lord* in this greeting, a combination of the common Gk greeting ("*grace*") and common Hbr greeting ("*peace*"), brought together here by the apostle. Throughout this Letter, *knowledge* indicates both knowing God relationally and also knowing about God (i.e. content or doctrine). The content of Peter's doctrine, the grace of Jesus Christ, is "knowledge" that saves.

This emphasis on knowledge is also an early apologetic against false teachers whose philosophical systems stressed secret knowledge. Their false teachings often included notions of otherworldly mediators between God and the world. In the coming century, such heresies would be codified in Gnostic frameworks. Peter's reference to "knowledge" (Gk *epignosis*) here already offers a defense against philosophies that seek to displace knowing Christ as God. The true relationship with God (knowing Him) comes to us through God's Word alone, preparing us for a godly life on earth and for an eternity in heaven to come.

1:1–2 in Devotion and Prayer We may think to ourselves, "that person has more faith than I have" or "I could never have the kind of faith that other person has." Our own subjective evaluation of the "quantity" or "quality" of our faith, however, is largely a waste of energy and time. After all, faith is an objective reality: our God, Jesus Christ, has called us to trust in Him. We don't get a piece of Jesus when we trust in Him. We get Him—all of Him. When Peter speaks of "a faith of equal standing" (v. 1), we should not doubt that he speaks of us. Anytime we hear faith talk, we are invited to look outside of ourselves to discover not "how big" or "what kind" our faith is, but "in whom" and "in what" our faith is. We find that when we look at Christ, our faith is honored, equally with all who have trusted in Christ's promise. We are credited with Christ's righteousness. Here is the glorious objective fact: God creates faith (Rm 10:17), God preserves faith (Heb 10:39), God heaps on gifts in accordance with that faith (Eph 2:8–9). You have nothing to do with it; Christ—the whole Christ—has everything to do with it! • Preserve your faithful, dear Lord Jesus, in the faith that You have created by the delivery of Your Word. Grant grace and peace to those who trust in Your Word, and send me this day to share that Word, that others too may be brought to the same faith in You. Amen.

PART 2

EXHORTATION TO GODLINESS (1:3–21)

Content of This Exhortation (1:3–11)

ESV	KJV
³His divine power has granted to us all things that pertain to life and godliness, through the knowledge of him who called us to his own glory and excellence, ⁴by which he has granted to us his precious and very great promises, so that through them you may become partakers of the divine nature, having escaped from the corruption that is in the world because of sinful desire. ⁵For this very reason, make every effort to supplement your faith with virtue, and virtue with knowledge, ⁶and knowledge with self-control, and self-control with steadfastness, and steadfastness with godliness, ⁷and godliness with brotherly affection, and brotherly affection with love. ⁸For if these qualities are yours and are increasing, they keep you from being ineffective or unfruitful in the knowledge of our Lord Jesus Christ. ⁹For whoever lacks these qualities is so nearsighted that he is blind, having forgotten that he was cleansed from his former sins. ¹⁰Therefore, brothers, be all the more diligent to confirm your calling and election, for if you practice these qualities you will never fall. ¹¹For in this way there will be richly provided for you an	³According as his divine power hath given unto us all things that pertain unto life and godliness, through the knowledge of him that hath called us to glory and virtue: ⁴Whereby are given unto us exceeding great and precious promises: that by these ye might be partakers of the divine nature, having escaped the corruption that is in the world through lust. ⁵And beside this, giving all diligence, add to your faith virtue; and to virtue knowledge; ⁶And to knowledge temperance; and to temperance patience; and to patience godliness; ⁷And to godliness brotherly kindness; and to brotherly kindness charity. ⁸For if these things be in you, and abound, they make you that ye shall neither be barren nor unfruitful in the knowledge of our Lord Jesus Christ. ⁹But he that lacketh these things is blind, and cannot see afar off, and hath forgotten that he was purged from his old sins. ¹⁰Wherefore the rather, brethren, give diligence to make your calling and election sure: for if ye do these things, ye shall never fall:

entrance into the eternal kingdom of our Lord and Savior Jesus Christ.	¹¹For so an entrance shall be ministered unto you abundantly into the everlasting kingdom of our Lord and Saviour Jesus Christ.

Introduction to 1:3–11 Peter begins the Letter proper by identifying God as the one who has established our knowledge of Him, our relationship with Him, through His promises. We partake of the divine now and the world is our enemy (vv. 3–4). A catalogue of Christian virtue follows (vv. 5–7) which describes the fruit God bears in the Christian (v. 8). Election is linked with Baptism (v. 9), and consideration of how God's promises produce fruit prepares the believer for a triumphant entrance into Christ's enduring kingdom (vv. 10–11).

1:3–4 The sentence spanning these verses acts like a nuanced footnote to the apostolic salutation's emphasis on "knowledge of God" (v. 2). It is a complex sentence, a feature common to introductory material when an author wants to draw special attention to important literary work. While not as ambitious as a history like Luke's NT volumes (cf. Lk 1:1–4), Peter's Letter is worthy of attention as its theme is a matter of life or death: the knowledge of God (cf. 3:17–18). The style is distinct from Peter's other Letter, suggesting scribal difference (Peter was assisted by Silas in writing 1Pt, and may have been assisted in the writing of this Letter as well).

The circumstances of believers receiving what the apostle prays for have everything to do with God's *divine power* which has given *all things that pertain to life and godliness*. Bengel wrote, "The flame is that which is imparted to us by God and from God, without any labour on our part: but the oil is that which man ought to add by his own diligence and faithfulness, that the flame may be fed and increased" (Bengel 5:85). This is what the *knowledge* of God grants: life and salvation, a life that is holy. Such life begins when God the Holy Spirit works through the Word to call us to faith. The "divine power" (Gk *dynamis*) at work is the power of the Gospel, which is delivered by the Holy Spirit's declaration of righteousness through faith (cf. Rm 1:16–17), giving us the knowledge that results in eternal life and that fosters our life and conduct in Christ. It is the power of God for salvation, and so gives *all things* that are needed to live the Christian life, as Luther affirmed:

St. Peter does not want this divine power in us to be understood in such a way that we also have the ability to create heaven and earth and should work miracles, as God does. . . . No, we have divine power with us to the degree that it is useful and necessary for us. . . . That is, we have the kind of divine power with which we are abundantly blessed to do good and to live eternally. (LW 30:153)

Knowledge of Him results in eternal life, and has come because He has *called us* (Gk *kaleō*), recalling the "election." Peter also reminds believers of this at 1Pt 1:1–2. Salvation is not a human decision but a divine call that comes to us through God's Word (cf. Rm 10:17; 1Co 1:9; Gal 1:6, 5:8; Eph 4:1, 4). He has called us to *His own glory and excellence*, a reminder of what God has shown glory to be in Christ. While Peter and others were partakers of Christ's glory in various ways, witnessing the miracles (Jn 2:11) and the transfiguration (as Peter will mention at vv. 16–18), Jesus connects His glory always with the cross (cf. Jn 12:23–33). In fulfilling His mission at the cross and the tomb, Jesus attained the goal of our salvation, truly a victory over sin and death (cf. 1Co 15:54–56). Like an athletic victor whose goal is "excellence" (Gk *arētē*), so our Victor calls us to His own point of pride and glory: His glorious victory over death. "Virtue" may have been a good English translation in 1611 when the translators chose this word for the KJV, but over the last half millennium, the word has adopted a sense closer to "chastity." The word really means "manly excellence" here, connecting us to the perfect Man and pointing forward to a perfection to come in the resurrection body.

1:4 By his own glory and excellence, overcoming sin and death, our God Jesus grants us *very great promises*, by which He invites and enables us to participate in His divine nature. Peter is eyewitness to Jesus' revelation as God of glory (Mt 17:2), but refers here to His second coming (cf. 3:4, 9), the Last Day when He will establish "new heavens and a new earth in which righteousness dwells" (3:13). "Promises" is Gospel-talk, reminding readers that a holy life has its source ever and only in the God who delivers and keeps His promises, both in the "not-yet" and in the "now," drawing us to faith through the means of grace. Being *partakers of the divine nature* depends wholly on God's perspective of the sinner-made-saint. Believers have been born again in Baptism, which is a death to the old sinner and a new birth of a new saint, raised to live to God (Rm 6:1–4). The new life is lived as

203

Christ lives in the believer (Gal 2:20–21). It means having the mind of Christ (1Co 2:16). Peter is not arguing that "partaking of the divine nature" means that we become part of the Godhead, but rather that God dwells in us through His Holy Spirit. Cranmer wrote:

> And when I said that Christ is in us naturally by his Godhead, I forgat not what I said, as you say of me; for I plainly expounded what I meant by "naturally," that is to say, not by natural substance to make us gods, but by natural condition giving unto us immortality and everlasting life, which he had of his Father, and so making us partakers of his godly nature, and uniting us to his Father. And if we attain to the unity of his Father, why not unto the unity of the Godhead, not by natural substance, but by natural propriety? As Cyrill saith that we be made the children of God and heavenly men by participation of the divine nature, as St. Peter also teacheth. And so be we one in the Father, in the Son, and in the Holy Ghost. (Cranmer 3:257–58)

Certain philosophies, including the Stoicism of Peter's own day, emphasized man's role in theosis ("becoming like God"; cf. Ac 17:28–29). Peter and other NT writers turn the table on this notion, pointing solely to God's ability to make us holy. Our calling has made us sojourner-exiles (cf. 1Pt 1:1) who have *escaped from the corruption that is in the world*. The world is now set in enmity to the Christian (cf. 1Jn 2:15–17). The world is seen in the NT as an enemy of Christians, having been corrupted *because of sinful desire*, from which Christ has set us free. The Lutheran reformers confessed: "We also, in whom Christ dwells only by grace, on account of that great mystery, are 'partakers of the divine nature' in Christ" (FC SD VIII 34). Luther commented on the verse:

> We shall also have all that God has, and in Him we shall have all that is necessary for us: wisdom, righteousness, strength, and life. All this we now believe. We grasp it only with our ears and have it in the Word of God. But then the Word will cease. Then our soul will open and behold and feel that all this is actually there. (LW 30:164)

1:5–7 Peter catalogues particular Christian virtues that come about as a response to God's work in the believer. They are the fruits of the Spirit (cf. Gal 5:17–26). The qualities selected for emphasis are all in contrast to the characteristics of the false teachers, who pervert the way of truth (ch. 2) and deny the heart of the Christian hope (3:3–4).

We do well to guard against reading this catalogue as a progression in holiness, some sort of ladder to Christian perfection. The structure of the catalogue achieves rhetorical effect by adding these together as a whole, not as rungs of holiness by which to judge one's own (or anyone else's!) relative standing before God and neighbor. The whole, so described by Peter, results in a Christian life that is effective and fruitful (v. 8).

1:5 In ancient Greece, a "khorēgos" was the producer who got top billing in putting together a tragedy, a very expensive affair, that could only be accomplished by a wealthy citizen. Individuals would compete for this role so as to receive credit for doing a good work in the community. Peter uses a verb that comes from this idea; just as a khorēgos would "supply, furnish" all the money and other resources for actors, playwright, chorus, etc., so Christians have the unique calling to *supplement*, that is, to "supply, or furnish" a variety of fruits for the Christian life, from the vast treasury available to them in the Gospel promises of God. The image is worthy of remark: God has taken poor sinners and made them rich beyond their wildest imagination! What to do with all this treasure? Use it to serve God's community. God perceives such service with eyes of gratitude and honor (cf. Mt 25:40). God's free and all-sufficient giving motivates and makes possible the wholehearted response of the believer to *make every effort* to bring these gifts out of their storehouse: we give because He gave (cf. Php 2:12–13). It is as if God is saying, "I have given you everything. Now hurry up and give it away, for My sake!" *Faith* holds first place in Peter's catalogue because it is the work of God that is the source of all holy living. Faith receives the promises delivered by the Holy Spirit (v. 4), and faith alone produces true good works (Heb 11:6). Certainly people can act "virtuously" without faith, certainly a godless world can recognize self-control or brotherly affection. But Peter's point here is that without faith, all works are empty (cf. Mt 25:44–45). Wesley wrote:

> In this most beautiful connection, each preceding grace leads to the following; each following, tempers and perfects the preceding. They are set down in the order of nature, rather than the order of time. For though every grace bears a relation to every other, yet here they are so nicely ranged, that those which have the closest dependence on each other are placed together. (Wesley 621)

Virtue and *knowledge* are the first fruits Peter mentions as out-growths of Christian faith. As in v. 3, so here *virtue* means far more than "chastity" or some such; it is instead a call to the kind of manly excellence that describes the Olympic victor in competition or the honorable soldier in time of battle (cf. 1Co 14:12; 2Co 8:7; Php 4:8). *Knowledge* also reaches back to Peter's first words to his readers (v. 2), indicating that growth in Christian living is God's work. God calls them and establishes them in His own excellent death and res-urrection to give them an identity. God reveals Himself to them in a relationship by which they gain knowledge of Him, a knowledge only revealed in Christ.

1:6 *Self-control* is "mastery over oneself," referring to one's emo-tions, impulses, and desires. Self-mastery is a reflection of the real-ity that we are not masters, but slaves (cf. v. 1), to Christ and His righteousness, to which authority believers willingly submit. Wesley wrote:

> Christian temperance implies the voluntary abstaining from all pleasure which does not lead to God. It extends to all things inward and outward: the due government of every thought, as well as affection. "It is using the world," so to use all outward, and so to restrain all inward things, that they may become a means of what is spiritual; a scaling ladder to ascend to what is above. Intemperance is to abuse the world. He that uses anything below, looking no higher, and getting no farther, is intemperate. He that uses the creature only so as to attain to more of the Creator, is alone temperate, and walks as Christ himself walked. (Wesley 621)

Steadfastness is patient endurance. Christians live in steadfastness because God is a "God of endurance and encouragement" (Rm 15:5; cf. also Rm 5:3–5). We are called to "run with endurance the race that is set before us" (Heb 12:1). This is, again, a response to what God has first done in Christ, who is the founder and perfecter of our faith: consider Him who endured (Heb 12:2–3)! *Godliness* reaches back once again to v. 3: the Holy Spirit has given all things needful for a life of reverence, respect, and devotion owed to God and His Word. As Luther noted:

> This means that in our whole outward life, in what we do or suf-fer, we should conduct ourselves in such a way that we serve God and do not seek our own glory and advantage. It means that God alone must be praised by what we do and that we must act

in such a way that one can see that we do everything for God's sake. (LW 30:156–57)

"Godliness" is also one of Paul's most frequent exhortations to Timothy in 1Tm, e.g., 4:7: "Have nothing to do with irreverent, silly myths. Rather train yourself for godliness." Peter echoes this point at v. 16.

1:7 Peter encourages *brotherly affection* (Gk *philadelphia*) in 1 Peter as well (1:22; 3:8; cf. 2:17; 5:9), a kindness that is to characterize how Christians relate to one another as "brothers" (cf. v. 10). The climax of the catalogue is *love* (Gk *agapē*), the selfless, sacrificial giving of self for the sake of the one loved, even as God in Christ has loved us.

1:8 Jesus, the True Vine, said to Peter and His other disciples: "Every branch in Me that does not bear fruit He takes away, and every branch that does bear fruit He prunes, that it may bear more fruit. Already you are clean because of the word that I have spoken to you. Abide in Me, and I in you. As the branch cannot bear fruit by itself, unless it abides in the vine, neither can you, unless you abide in Me. I am the vine; you are the branches. Whoever abides in Me and I in him, he it is that bears much fruit, for apart from Me you can do nothing" (Jn 15:2–5). So also the fruits that Peter lists in this catalogue *are increasing* all the time, as we are in Christ and Christ causes us to grow (1Co 3:6–7). Such fruit makes it so that we are "not-*ineffective*," and "not-*unfruitful*." The force of these Gk double-negatives is a rhetorical device to convince Peter's readers that a holy life is in fact very fruitful.

1:9 This sentence characterizes the one who is fruitless, lacking these virtues. In considering this, we do well to focus on the head of Peter's catalogue which is the search of all the others: "faith" (v. 5). The one without faith, and therefore without its attendant results, obliterates the cleansing of his sins in forgetfulness. Combined with the descriptions *nearsighted* and *blind* (literally, blind and squinting), Peter locates the identity of the Christian in the cleansing waters of Baptism (cf. 1Jn 2:9–11; Jn 9:39–41). Baptism is enlightenment, giving sight to blinded sinners. To forget the location of God's promises given at Baptism is to become willingly blind. Spiritual blindness looks only at the self, and so lives a life of sin; spiritual sightedness looks only to the works of God in Christ done on behalf of the sinner. The tree does not look to its own abilities to produce fruit; rather the branches produce fruit as they depend on the True Vine.

1:10 Peter can call his readers *brothers* because they have brotherly love towards one another (v. 7), and because in Christ not only are we related to Him through the knowledge of God (v. 2), but a common inheritance of His grace has made us fellow heirs with Him. (See note, Jas 1:2.) The encouragement of v. 5 ("hurry up and furnish the holy life with these fruits") is matched here with a similar "hurry up and confirm your election," that is, *confirm your calling and election*. God is the One who calls, who elects. Before the world's creation, God chose us to be His own. The Christian life is one of same-saying and same-doing: saying back to God what He has said to us in Christ, and living a life of holiness as God is holy. This is not a life that has its source in the personal efforts or inward striving of the sinner, but in Christ's power and preservation, as Luther noted:

> I have already been preaching Christ and fighting against the devil in his false teachers for a number of years; but I have experienced how much difficulty this business has caused me. For I cannot repel Satan as I would like. Nor can I finally grasp Christ as Scripture propounds Him to me, but the devil often suggests a false Christ to me. Thanks be to God, however, for preserving us in the Word, in faith, and in prayer! We know that one should walk in humility and fear in the sight of God and not presume upon our own wisdom, righteousness, doctrine, and courage. One should rely on the power of Christ. When we are weak, He is strong; and through us weaklings He always conquers and triumphs. To Him be glory forever. Amen. (LW 26:196)

The promise Peter holds out here is that the one who lives a life full of these Christians fruits *will never fall*. He does not promise that believers do not sin (we are always "*simul*": at the same time sinner and saint). He speaks of redeemed sinners who do in fact stumble for "we all stumble in many ways" (Jas 3:2). We rely on Christ's work, the Gospel, for our salvation, and not on the Law (cf. Jas 2:10). God has established our holy life to draw us always back to Him, and Peter exhorts that we cultivate these virtues so as not to fall away from the path that leads to Christ's kingdom. Salvation depends utterly on Christ's work. Our good works follow in faith. Melanchthon wrote:

> Peter speaks of works following the forgiveness of sins and teaches why they should be done. . . . Do good works in order that you

may persevere in your calling, in order that you do not lose the gifts of your calling. They were given to you before, and not because of works that follow, and which now are kept through faith. (Ap XX 90)

Cranmer wrote:

Therefore let us do good works, and thereby declare our faith to be the lively Christian faith. Let us, by such virtues as ought to spring out of faith, show our election to be sure and stable, as St. Peter teacheth. Endeavour yourselves to make your calling and election certain by good works. And also he saith, Minister or declare in your faith virtue, in virtue knowledge, in knowledge temperance, in temperance patience, again in patience godliness, in godliness brotherly charity, in brotherly charity love. So shall we shew indeed that we have the very lively Christian faith, and may so both certify our conscience the better that we be in the right faith, and also by these means confirm other men. (Cranmer 2:161–62)

1:11 Peter employs the same word "furnish, supply" as in v. 5. God is the one who provides the benefit of salvation and *an entrance into the eternal kingdom*. He is the rich man, who brings out of His own storehouse the abundant wealth of an inheritance with Him forever; He freely distributes this wealth among those who gladly enter His kingdom as stewards of the gifts He has given; cf. Mt 25:21, 23, 29. The image answers Peter's rhetorical figure at 1Pt 4:17–19: in the midst of suffering, this life doesn't look too abundant. "What, Lord? You call me to be a 'khorēgos,' a 'producer'? You call me to live lavishly, as if my storehouse is full and I can produce such virtues out of an unending treasury?" "Yes, My child," says God, "for I am the One whose storehouse it is. Not as you see it, not as the world sees it, but as I see it, as I equip you, as I promise you. Trust only in Me. I will provide everything needed." Our assurance is not in our good works, but in God's Word, which guarantees us a victorious, triumphal entry into His *kingdom*, which is *eternal*: both in the sense that it is never ending and in that its Ruler is the Eternal One, Jesus Christ our God.

Necessity of This Reminder (1:12–15)

ESV	KJV
¹²Therefore I intend always to remind you of these qualities, though you know them and are established in the truth that you have. ¹³I think it right, as long as I am in this body, to stir you up by way of reminder, ¹⁴since I know that the putting off of my body will be soon, as our Lord Jesus Christ made clear to me. ¹⁵And I will make every effort so that after my departure you may be able at any time to recall these things.	¹²Wherefore I will not be negligent to put you always in remembrance of these things, though ye know them, and be established in the present truth. ¹³Yea, I think it meet, as long as I am in this tabernacle, to stir you up by putting you in remembrance; ¹⁴Knowing that shortly I must put off this my tabernacle, even as our Lord Jesus Christ hath shewed me. ¹⁵Moreover I will endeavour that ye may be able after my decease to have these things always in remembrance.

1:12–21 In the last half of ch. 1, Peter emphasizes the reliability of God's Word in contrast to the deceptions preached by false teachers (ch. 2). God's Word is the basis of faith and fellowship for the community of believers. He begins with a reflection that he is close to the end of his life (vv. 12–15); it is as if Peter wants to leave his readers with his final instructions, or final blessings (as Paul had at Ac 20:17–38). The source of Peter's doctrine is Christ Himself, to whom he was eyewitness (v. 16), and Peter references the transfiguration (vv. 17–18). Far better than myths (v. 16), and even better than the OT word of prophecy, Christ's bodily fulfillment of God's promise has established His Word as promise, to which believers are to listen until the end of time (vv. 19–21).

1:12 Peter's Letter is a reminder and an encouragement to remain and grow in the Word of Christ, that the work of Christ may be manifested in the believer's life. This was beneficial to his first readers and beneficial for the Church of our time as well. Pure doctrine has its source in trusting in the historic death, resurrection, and exaltation of Christ (cf. 1Pt 3:15), and recollection of that is matched with the reminder to live holy lives. Peter does not assume his audience is ignorant of either fact, the work of Christ at Calvary or the work of Christ in them, but knows that they are *established in the truth*. After all, they had been catechized with apostolic teaching (Ac 2:42), even as the Church is still today. Consider Luther's Small Catechism, Sixth Petition:

> We pray in this petition that God would guard and keep us so that the devil, the world, and our sinful nature may not deceive us or mislead us into false belief, despair, and other great shame and vice. Although we are attacked by these things, we pray that we may finally overcome them and win the victory.

1:13 Peter refers to his *body* (Gk *skēnōma*) as something ephemeral. The word he chooses literally means "tent," a vivid reminder of the fact that life in this world is temporary. On the one hand, it reminds his readers that the sojourn-exile (cf. 1Pt 1:1) is nearing its end: a permanent home is what Christians long for, where they have a citizenship established for them by God's work in Christ. On the other hand, this reminder is intended *to stir . . . up* Peter's readers, that is, to awaken them, to arouse them to action. It is interesting that the same verb is used once of a storm blowing up around a little boat in the Galilee (Jn 6:18). On a similar occasion, Jesus was in the boat with the disciples and heard them say, "Teacher, do you not care that we are perishing?" (Mk 4:38). Jesus then awoke (literally, "was stirred," the same Gk verb) and calmed the storm (Mk 4:39). Jesus does care—even at the end of Peter's life, He still cares. In that boat, Jesus woke to give faith to the disciples; Peter's reminders in this Letter are intended to keep that faith vigilant as well.

1:14–15 Peter knows that his death is close at hand, because the *Lord Jesus Christ made clear* to him that it would happen soon. What Peter has in mind specifically is not known, but John made generally known what Peter would face in the future: "Jesus told Peter, 'Truly, truly, I say to you, when you were young, you used to dress yourself and walk wherever you wanted, but when you are old, you will stretch out your hands, and another will dress you and carry you where you do not want to go.' (This He said to show by what kind of death he was to glorify God.) And after saying this He said to him, 'Follow Me'" (Jn 21:18–19). Peter promises that he will *make every effort* that his readers *may be able at any time to recall* what he teaches them. Peter is not promising some sort of esoteric spiritual presence, but rather concretizes what is important about his role in their life: his teaching. Peter's readers will not go on like sheep without a shepherd; he was called to feed Christ's sheep (Jn 21:17), and Peter's

211

written words ensure a continual pasture for God's people on God's Word, until they too join Peter in a *departure* (Gk *exodos*, "exodus"). This word choice connects the believer's death with the single most significant salvation event of the OT: the delivery of God's people to the Promised Land.

1:3–15 in Devotion and Prayer Peter was about to enter the promised land, for Christ has called him to an exodus, a departure from this world of suffering and sin, and an entrance to an enduring and eternal kingdom. In such a way, God calls you out of this world with its sinful desires and to a new identity, a new citizenship, a new life with a new goal: to put off this tent and inherit a home that endures. Tents might be fun to vacation in for a day or two, but they're uncomfortable. They're sufficient for temporary survival, but they are not intended to be a permanent dwelling. Thank God we move ever closer to the day when we put the tent away, wash off the dust of our journey, and rest in a permanent place where we breathe the sigh of relief: There's no place like home! • Dear Heavenly Father, You called Your people out of the land of sin to a place You had chosen for them. You deigned to dwell in a tabernacle for the good of Your wandering people. When the time had fully come, You sent Your Son to make His dwelling among us, in the tent of our human flesh, sanctifying our bodies. Grant me grace, Father, so to live the days You have appointed me in the tent of this corruptible flesh, because You have appointed a day for my own exodus from this land of sin and suffering. Lead me to the promised land of the new heavens and the new earth, O Lord, for the sake of Your Son who raises incorruptible that which is sown in corruption, in a lasting, eternal inheritance. Amen.

Certain Basis of the Exhortation in the Revelation of Christ and Scripture (1:16–21)

ESV	KJV
[16]For we did not follow cleverly devised myths when we made known to you the power and coming of our Lord Jesus Christ, but we were eyewitnesses of his majesty. [17]For when he received honor and glory from God the Father, and the voice was borne to him by the Majestic Glory, "This is my beloved Son, with whom I am well pleased," [18]we ourselves heard this very voice borne from heaven, for we were with him on the holy mountain. [19]And we have something more sure, the prophetic word, to which you will do well to pay attention as to a lamp shining in a dark place, until the day dawns and the morning star rises in your hearts, [20]knowing this first of all, that no prophecy of Scripture comes from someone's own interpretation. [21]For no prophecy was ever produced by the will of man, but men spoke from God as they were carried along by the Holy Spirit.	[16]For we have not followed cunningly devised fables, when we made known unto you the power and coming of our Lord Jesus Christ, but were eyewitnesses of his majesty. [17]For he received from God the Father honour and glory, when there came such a voice to him from the excellent glory, This is my beloved Son, in whom I am well pleased. [18]And this voice which came from heaven we heard, when we were with him in the holy mount. [19]We have also a more sure word of prophecy; whereunto ye do well that ye take heed, as unto a light that shineth in a dark place, until the day dawn, and the day star arise in your hearts: [20]Knowing this first, that no prophecy of the scripture is of any private interpretation. [21]For the prophecy came not in old time by the will of man: but holy men of God spake as they were moved by the Holy Ghost.

1:16–17 Peter introduces an apologetic here for the deity of Christ that rests on *eyewitnesses of his majesty*. Peter calls Jesus God (cf. vv. 1–2; 1Pt 3:15). His proof, unique to this argument, is the divine *voice . . . "This is my beloved Son."* Such historic recollection, confirmed by other eyewitnesses, is far different than *cleverly devised myths.* The Mediterranean world of the first century was culturally fluent in innumerable stories set against a complex mythological backdrop that could reach back to literature and oral accounts, some almost a thousand years old. The idea that people could become gods, or that gods could take on the form of humans or any other created thing, would not bother most people in Peter's time. The apostle wants to make certain that his readers acknowledge the distinctive characteristic of the Christian message, however. Christ is not one among many gods; He is God almighty, who will return gloriously in *power*, subduing all His enemies and consummating His kingdom. Christ's exaltation is a historic event, verifiable by more than just Peter. He and other eyewitnesses heard the voice that spoke when Christ *received honor and glory*. God the Father is referred to here as *the Majestic Glory*, a Hbr manner of referring to God the Father indirectly so as to piously defer to God's holy name.

1:18 *We ourselves heard* the event, which occurred on *the holy mountain* (the Mount of Transfiguration; cf. Lk 9:28–32). Peter does not have to say "we" because Gk verbs include their subjects in the verb endings. In this case, he includes the unnecessary plural pronoun to emphasize and support his apologetic point. When you have multiple witnesses to an event, testimony to its occurrence can be verified. If a group of people attempts to lie about something, it becomes difficult, even to the point of impossibility, for individuals in the group to keep the story straight (as any interrogator or cross-examiner will tell you).

1:19 Peter here encourages his readers to consider what a great gift they have in the treasury of the OT prophets, who pointed to Christ like a light in the darkness. As in v. 1, the faith that the Word of God creates is the same for Peter and for his readers, even though they were not on the mountain with the other disciples. What can we trust in, since we were not "eyewitnesses of His majesty"? We have *the prophetic word*, the OT Scriptures, which confirm the entire apostolic witness of Christ. This is not a new and surer prophetic word from God, but the prophetic word that is made surer, more certain, confirmed (cf. v. 10), by its fulfillment in Christ's death, resurrection, and exaltation. Calvin wrote:

> The sense also is a forced one, when it is said to be "more sure," because God really completed what he had promised concerning his Son. For the truth of the gospel is here simply proved by a twofold testimony,—that Christ had been highly approved by the solemn declaration of God, and, then, that all the prophecies of the prophets confirmed the same thing. But it appears at first sight strange, that the word of the prophets should be said to be more

sure or firmer than the voice which came from the holy mouth of God himself; for, first, the authority of God's word is the same from the beginning; and, secondly, it was more confirmed than previously by the coming of Christ. But the solution of this knot is not difficult: for here the Apostle had a regard to his own nation, who were acquainted with the prophets, and their doctrine was received without any dispute. As, then, it was not doubted by the Jews but that all the things which the prophets had taught, came from the Lord, it is no wonder that Peter said that their word was more sure. Antiquity also gains some reverence. There are, besides, some other circumstances which ought to be noticed; particularly, that no suspicion could be entertained as to those prophecies in which the kingdom of Christ had so long before been predicted. (Calvin 385)

Peter is not handing over to his readers a new Gospel, but the Gospel as it has always been: the promises of God in Christ. Peter's own eyewitness is not an anomaly, or some other path to certainty, but the same certainty because it is grounded on the Word of God. Because God continues to speak through His prophets in the OT and the NT witness of Christ, we do well to perk up our ears, to *pay attention* to the teaching of God's Word. This, in fact, was the practice of the NT Church as it is in our own day (cf. Ac 2:42). It should continue as a light in the darkness *until* a new light *dawns*: a poetic picture of Christ's return (cf. Rv 22:16). Luther commented: "We must have the light [of the Word] and cling to it until the Last Day. Then we shall no longer need the Word, just as artificial light is extinguished when the day dawns" (LW 30:166). We require such light to make our way in a world darkened by suffering. It doesn't lead us blindly in any direction, but shines on those elements that give us sure footing on the journey of our Christian life, as Luther noted:

He bids us fix our eyes and keenness of mind on the Word alone, on Baptism, on the Lord's Supper, and on absolution, and to regard everything else as darkness. I do not understand, or care about, what is done in this world by the sons of this age; for they crucify me. I cannot escape or draw away that horrible mask which hides the face of God, but I must stay in darkness and in exceedingly dark mist until a new light shines forth. (LW 8:33)

1:20 Peter is not talking about "how to interpret" Scripture in this verse, but rather getting at how it was produced. He says it was not produced according to *someone's own interpretation* of what was going on in his own time and place, as if an attempt to leave some kind of historical or cultural legacy. Rather, people wrote what God inspired them to write (cf. 2Co 3:16–17). This verse should be read in light of 1Pt 1:10–12, where Peter quite clearly acknowledges the human element in the writing: human biblical authors knew how to express things in perspicuous language, but that does not mean they knew exactly why God had them write what they wrote. He had a different plan in mind: not just to serve their own time and place, but to serve those who would be shown Christ in the words He had them write.

1:21 False prophecy is the subject of the next chapter. It was experienced by the infant Christian Church on occasion as confirmed in the NT (cf. 1Co 13:8; 14:32, 37) and other early Christian documents (e.g., the *Didache*). *The will of man* produces false doctrine (cf. 2:1; Dt 18:18, 22), but genuine prophecy is never of human design, desire, or origin; rather *men spoke . . . by the Holy Spirit*. The Scriptures are of divine origin as the Holy Spirit inspired the words of each of the authors, in accord with their own style. They wrote only the words that God had given them, as Luther confessed: "They were holy, says he, since the Holy Spirit spoke through them" (SA III VIII 13). That God inspired the words of Holy Scripture gives us confidence in the truth of the incarnation, as Luther attested:

> We do not let ourselves be troubled by the blasphemies which the devil, through the mouths of his lying servants, speaks against Christ the Lord—now against His divinity, now against His humanity—and by the attacks which he then makes against Christ's office and work. But we cling to the Scriptures of the prophets and apostles, who spoke as they were moved by the Holy Spirit (2 Peter 1:21). Their testimony about Christ is clear. He is our Brother; we are members of His body, flesh and bone of His flesh and bone. (LW 22:23)

1:16–21 in Devotion and Prayer A century after Peter wrote these words, a man named Marcion decided he didn't like the mean old God of the OT and thought he saw in Jesus a kinder, gentler God to whom he could relate. Taking up a metaphorical eraser, he decided God was speaking only through the Scriptures that he thought consistent with the god he formed in his mind. This led him to erase the OT, and a lot of the NT as well. We might think of modern examples of the same kind of cutting and pasting, the same kind of picking and choosing which verses God *really* speaks through and which are just suggestions. But Peter is firm here: all of God's counsel invites us to (or rather demands that we!) perk up our ears and listen to what God shows in His Word. And what does God show? No more, no less than this: His Word shows us our sin, and it shows us our savior. This is all God says we need to hear from Him. Rather than being a history book or a rule book or a business manual or "life's little instruction" book, God speaks these words to point you to your need for a Savior, and to point out that Savior to you. So go ahead, rip out any page you like—so long as it doesn't point you to these things. You will find that what you are left with is exactly the Bible that was in front of you when you started, from Genesis to Revelation. • Save me, Lord, from the error of hearing Your Word with little zeal, little love, little joy. Create in me a trust that longs to hear Your Word aright, hold it sacred, and gladly hear and learn it, that the old man may be slain and the new man rise to live to You. Help me this day to read, mark, learn, and inwardly digest the Word of Life, that I may honor You as the God who sustains me by Your Word. Amen.

PART 3

WARNING AGAINST FALSE TEACHERS (CH. 2)

Anticipation of False Teachers (2:1–3)

ESV	KJV
2 ¹But false prophets also arose among the people, just as there will be false teachers among you, who will secretly bring in destructive heresies, even denying the Master who bought them, bringing upon themselves swift destruction. ²And many will follow their sensuality, and because of them the way of truth will be blasphemed. ³And in their greed they will exploit you with false words. Their condemnation from long ago is not idle, and their destruction is not asleep.	**2** ¹But there were false prophets also among the people, even as there shall be false teachers among you, who privily shall bring in damnable heresies, even denying the Lord that bought them, and bring upon themselves swift destruction. ²And many shall follow their pernicious ways; by reason of whom the way of truth shall be evil spoken of. ³And through covetousness shall they with feigned words make merchandise of you: whose judgment now of a long time lingereth not, and their damnation slumbereth not.

Introduction to 2:1–3 Peter introduces a section that extends through the rest of ch. 2, which is a warning against false teachers. It bears close resemblance in many places to the Book of Jude, both in its concerns and the words used. While the identity of the false teachers is not explicit in this chapter, Peter connects their impending presence with the fact that OT Israel also had to deal with false prophets (v. 1). Teaching false doctrine is a damnable sin, matched by following false doctrine, which is blasphemy (v. 2). God is yet vigilant; their destruction will come, so Christians are to be aware that the words of such teachers are false (v. 3). The Lutheran reformers confessed: "When they have heard God's Word, they make light of it again and ignore it. But their wickedness is responsible for this ‹that they perish›, not God or His election" (FC Ep XI 12).

2:1 From his previous words regarding OT prophecy, Peter moves to the history of *false prophets* Israel faced. This sad history serves as a backdrop for his warnings about *false teachers* yet to come. Moses was instructed by God about true and false prophets, and Israel could take comfort in the fact that false prophets were nothing to fear (Dt 18:21–22). *False teachers*, on the other hand, are occasion for great alarm, because they take the inspired Scriptures and twist or isolate selected passages out of the context of salvation by grace alone through faith in Christ and reshape them purely for their own personal gain and glory. These are people who have known redemption, as is evident in their rejection of *the Master who bought them* and in that they know enough secretly to introduce *heresies*, false teachings that may resemble apostolic teaching to a certain degree, but are altered to promote personal rights or immorality. If believed, heresy destroys faith in Christ alone. Jesus has false prophets and false teachers in mind at Mt 7:19–23. Though they protest that what they do is in the name of the Lord, Jesus declares "I never knew you; depart from me, you workers of lawlessness" (Mt 7:23). Peter states that such teachers are headed for *swift destruction*. Luther pointed out that true and false prophets exist side by side to the end of time:

> Just as all prophecy has emanated from the Holy Spirit since the beginning of the world, so this must be true until the end of the world, in order that nothing but God's Word may be preached. Yet it has always happened that there have been false teachers alongside the true prophets and God's Word. And so it will remain. Therefore since you now have God's Word, you must expect to have false teachers too. . . . They will retain the terms "God," "Christ," "faith," "church," "Baptism," "Sacrament" and let them remain. Under these terms, however, they will proceed to establish something different. (LW 30:168, 170)

Calvin wrote:

> Many imagined that the Church would enjoy tranquillity under the reign of Christ; for as the prophets had promised that at his coming there would be real peace, the highest degree of heavenly wisdom, and the full restoration of all things, they thought that the Church would be no more exposed to any contests. Let us then remember that the Spirit of God hath once for all declared, that

the Church shall never be free from this intestine evil; and let this likeness be always borne in mind, that the trial of our faith is to be similar to that of the fathers, and for the same reason—that in this way it may be made evident, whether we really love God, as we find it written in Deut. xiii. 3. (Calvin 392)

2:2 Blasphemy, the misuse of God's name (cf. Lv 24:10–23), includes false doctrine. Luther wrote: "But, the greatest abuse occurs in spiritual matters, which pertain to the conscience, when false preachers rise up and offer their lying vanities as God's Word" (LC, Second Commandment, 54). Here the result of hearers being persuaded by false doctrine is that the *way of truth* is *blasphemed*, that is, slandered; Christianity itself gets a bad name when wolves lead sheep to their destruction.

2:3 False teachers try to buy and sell people with fictitious arguments; Peter points to the source of this destructive activity: *their greed*. Charlatans that seem to be able to get away with such merchandizing of God's people will be judged, however. God's patience is intended to magnify such sin to the point that those who commit it are utter unable to justify themselves or expect mercy from God (cf. Rm 1:24–2:5).

God Delivers the Righteous and Punishes the Ungodly (2:4–10a)

ESV	KJV
[4]For if God did not spare angels when they sinned, but cast them into hell and committed them to chains of gloomy darkness to be kept until the judgment; [5]if he did not spare the ancient world, but preserved Noah, a herald of righteousness, with seven others, when he brought a flood upon the world of the ungodly; [6]if by turning the cities of Sodom and Gomorrah to ashes he condemned them to extinction, making them an example of what is going to happen to the ungodly; [7]and if he rescued righteous Lot, greatly distressed by	[4]For if God spared not the angels that sinned, but cast them down to hell, and delivered them into chains of darkness, to be reserved unto judgment; [5]And spared not the old world, but saved Noah the eighth person, a preacher of righteousness, bringing in the flood upon the world of the ungodly; [6]And turning the cities of Sodom and Gomorrha into ashes condemned them with an overthrow, making them an ensample unto those that after should live ungodly;

the sensual conduct of the wicked 8(for as that righteous man lived among them day after day, he was tormenting his righteous soul over their lawless deeds that he saw and heard); 9then the Lord knows how to rescue the godly from trials, and to keep the unrighteous under punishment until the day of judgment, 10aand especially those who indulge in the lust of defiling passion and despise authority.

7And delivered just Lot, vexed with the filthy conversation of the wicked: 8(For that righteous man dwelling among them, in seeing and hearing, vexed his righteous soul from day to day with their unlawful deeds;) 9The Lord knoweth how to deliver the godly out of temptations, and to reserve the unjust unto the day of judgment to be punished: 10But chiefly them that walk after the flesh in the lust of uncleanness, and despise government.

Introduction to 2:4–10a With three examples from OT history, Peter demonstrates the Lord's righteous judgment on the wicked and indicates that the godly will be rescued: evil angels were cast into hell to await judgment (v. 4); the flood punished the ungodly while Noah and his family were saved (v. 5); God destroyed Sodom and Gomorrah (v. 6); at the same time, He rescued Lot while he lived among the ungodly (vv. 7–8). This is how we know that God not only rescues the godly, but judges the ungodly (vv. 9–10).

2:4 Nowhere in Scripture is there a single extended account of the fall of *angels when they sinned*, but there are fallen angels, a matter of history to which the NT alludes, e.g., Eph 6:12: "For we do not wrestle against flesh and blood, but against the rulers, against the authorities, against the cosmic powers over this present darkness, against the spiritual forces of evil in the heavenly places"; cf. 1Co 6:3; 1Jn 3:8; and Rv 12:7–9, which describes John's vision of the battle in heaven. The judgment of evil angels who forsake their proper office before God is certain (cf. Jude 6). He has condemned them to *chains of gloomy darkness*, demonstrating that God is yet in control of His creation, even of the wicked, powerful, rebellious devils. He has a divine purpose for them: a damnation at Judgment Day, which is to come, as Luther pointed out: "God cast them [the angels who sinned] into hell. There they don't suffer punishment as yet, although they are condemned. For if they were already punished, the devils wouldn't engage in so much knavery" (LW 54:447). In other words, the fact that the devil is chained by God does not mean his final judgment has occurred. It might rather be more helpful to think of the chain as a leash. The devil is chained like a vicious dog is chained: the Master is in control of him, but it may yet be best not to get too close. Devils know their judgment is at hand (Mt 8:29; Jas 2:19) and that any time they have in which they work wickedness on the earth is temporary; cf. Lk 8:31; Eph 2:2.

2:5 A picture of divine judgment on *the ancient world* is matched by picture of salvation for *Noah, a herald of righteousness*. Peter's central figure of Baptism in 1Pt 3:20–21, Noah is noted here as a prophet, announcing God's judgment, as Heb 11:7 also maintains: "By faith Noah, being warned by God concerning events as yet unseen, in reverent fear constructed an ark for the saving of his household. By this he condemned the world and became an heir of the righteousness that comes by faith." Noah walked with God obediently (Gn 6:9, 22) and so was shown to be righteous, while the rest of his *ungodly* generation was only evil all the time (Gn 6:5). Noah was saved *with seven others* (literally "the eighth man"), underscoring the minute number of God's remnant for salvation in comparison with the rest of the world.

2:6–8 Gn 18–19 record the destruction of Sodom and Gomorrah by fire (cf. Gn 19:24). Jesus refers to Sodom and Gomorrah in a similar way when teaching about Judgment Day in Lk 17:20–37, indicating that the end will come with fire. Sodom and Gomorrah therefore serve as a type of God's judgment (*an example of what is going to happen to the ungodly*), to be fulfilled when Christ returns in judgment over all, including the false teachers who will suffer punishment for blasphemy. The illustration of Sodom and Gomorrah, like that of Noah, is also a picture of remnant theology. Just as Noah, "the eighth man" (v. 5), reflects the smallness of Christ's "little flock" (Lk 12:32), so also does the preservation of *righteous Lot* recall how few were the number of those shown to be righteous in his day: not even ten could be found (cf. Gn 18:22–33). Lot was *distressed by the sensual conduct of the wicked*, leading him to defend angelic visitors (Gn 19:1–11). His disapproval of the Sodomites' conduct results in him being considered a *righteous man*. Like Peter's audience, Lot was a sojourner in a foreign land. His struggle was with a world that may have seemed like a paradise when he first chose the Jordan Valley for his flocks' pasture (Gn 13:8–12), but only too soon showed its true colors (Gn 13:13; Gn 19:4–5). Even Lot's family succumbed to the wickedness of the world around them. His wife looked back at the destruction and was judged for it (Gn 19:26). His daughters resorted to incest with their father rather than trust God's plans (Gn 19:30–38). Living in the midst of a world set against God's Law can cause God's Gospel people distress. It can also result in painful temporal consequences. God promises delivery to the faithful and is not slow in fulfilling His threats to destroy the wicked. The OT examples here serve as a reminder to later generations that unrighteousness, false teaching, immorality, and evil (be they in Lot's day, Peter's day, or today) will eventually result in the carrying out of God's judgment.

2:9 If God knows how to punish evil angels, evil generations, and evil cities, then He can take care of false teachers. Do not worry; their end is at hand—they are already bound to judgment. They are *under punishment* (cf. v. 4), awaiting their final sentence and execution. And if God knows how to rescue Lot and Noah, then He *knows how to rescue the godly from trials*, a truth we affirm every time we pray "Deliver us from evil." Luther wrote: "We pray in this petition, in summary, that our Father in heaven would rescue us from every evil of body and soul, possessions and reputation, and finally, when our last hour comes, give us a blessed end, and graciously take us from this valley of sorrow to Himself in heaven." (SC, Seventh Petition).

2:10a Peter closes his thoughts in the middle of v. 10 by concluding with a footnote about those who, being under judgment now, are awaiting their final sentence (v. 9). Such judgment awaits *especially those who indulge in the lust of defiling passion*, literally "those going after the flesh in lust of defilement." The sense is that to go after the world is to bring pollution on oneself, that believers are to be separate, unpolluted, undefiled, perfect, and holy. "Defilement" (stain, pollution) is general enough to describe a state of being that would require purification through ceremonial washing and pronouncement by the priest. This included anything from touching ceremonially unclean things to voluntary or involuntary homicide. Lust "of" or "for" such defilement is what the world is accused of (cf. 1Jn 2:15–17). Trying to nail down one particular actual sin Peter has in mind here is probably not fruitful. Unbridled lust might be the likeliest candidate, since this is mentioned in the Sodom and Gomorrah illustration (Gn 19:4–5, 9). Luther seems to rest on this general idea as well: "To 'indulge in the lust of defiling passion' is to live like an irrational beast according to one's own notion and all lust" (LW 30:180).

There are some who have attempted to make much of the word translated "defiling passion" (Gk *miasmos*), since this word occurs only in 2 Peter. We do well to be cautious of our own cultural biases that might color the reading of Scripture in a light unfaithful to the original intention. In our day of partisan politics considering the respect of persons and an alarmingly licentious view of human sexuality, willfully ignorant of natural law as understood for millennia, the sin of Sodom and Gomorrah may present as just such an opportunity to polarize opinions about the Bible. If sexual relations between people of the same sex happened at Sodom, one might argue that this becomes a picture by which to condemn the sin of Sodom as the sin of homosexuality. The fact is, the depravity of Sodom and Gomorrah, indeed, of the world of Peter's day and our own day, reaches far deeper than can be encompassed by the label of "homosexuality," which in our day in the West has become a matter of cultural identification in a way unknown in Peter's day and age. Sexuality in the Mediterranean world of the NT involved not so much a cultural identification of one's sexual choices on the basis of a moment or a lifetime, nor less one's preference or genetic inclination. For men, it involved the much more basic action of penetrating things with sexual organs: other sexual organs or bodily orifices, belonging to free people, slaves, men, women, children, and other things. Boys have boy parts; girls have girl parts; the rest was often seen as being up to chance, or worse, up to the strength and violence of the male or female who desired sex any way they might choose. "Homosexuality" doesn't quite scratch the surface of such an ignorant, or aberrant, view of the natural activity God created for natural purpose and pleasure between man and woman (Gn 2:24; Mt 19:4–6).

The violent will to power shown by the rapists in the Sodom and Gomorrah narrative is more generally the nucleus of human sin that characterizes the world in its fallen state. It is this violence and domination in all its facets (seen in the Sodomites' rejection of natural law in forsaking various boundaries of sexuality, among which gender is one, and also in forsaking the natural bonds of human friendship in godless inhospitality) that God's kingdom comes, in Christ, to rival. Sinful men's, and evil angels', inclination to arrogate themselves over the will of God is particularly set against His sovereignty (cf. Ps 2:1–3). Such arrogance results in those who *despise authority* (v. 10a), no longer fearing God, not trembling at blasphemy, bold and arrogant

(v. 10b). The picture Peter gives us is similar therefore to Jude, who indicates that the problem with the sin of the angels (and by extension, of the false teachers) is one of abrogation of office (Jude 6): they "did not stay within their own position of authority, but left their proper dwelling." Vocation, obligation, office—these are matters of the created order that have as much to do with hospitality and sex as they do with obeying rulers and living in peace with your fellow human (cf. Jude 8–10). The breakdown of vocation, obligation, and office is the result of sin. It is the description of our fallen world. And it is a spiral in that it also produces sin after sin—all of which is driving towards a final judgment. Blessed is the one who flees to the only One who can save from such judgment: Christ our God, who declares righteous those who have faith in Him.

Denunciation of the Motives, Character, and Message of the False Teachers (2:10b–22)

ESV	KJV
10bBold and willful, they do not tremble as they blaspheme the glorious ones, 11whereas angels, though greater in might and power, do not pronounce a blasphemous judgment against them before the Lord. 12But these, like irrational animals, creatures of instinct, born to be caught and destroyed, blaspheming about matters of which they are ignorant, will also be destroyed in their destruction, 13suffering wrong as the wage for their wrongdoing. They count it pleasure to revel in the daytime. They are blots and blemishes, reveling in their deceptions, while they feast with you. 14They have eyes full of adultery, insatiable for sin. They entice unsteady souls. They have hearts trained in greed. Accursed children! 15Forsaking the right way, they have gone astray. They have followed the way of Balaam, the son of Beor,	10bPresumptuous are they, self-willed, they are not afraid to speak evil of dignities. 11Whereas angels, which are greater in power and might, bring not railing accusation against them before the Lord. 12But these, as natural brute beasts, made to be taken and destroyed, speak evil of the things that they understand not; and shall utterly perish in their own corruption; 13And shall receive the reward of unrighteousness, as they that count it pleasure to riot in the day time. Spots they are and blemishes, sporting themselves with their own deceivings while they feast with you; 14Having eyes full of adultery, and that cannot cease from sin; beguiling unstable souls: an heart they have exercised with covetous practices; cursed children:

who loved gain from wrongdoing, [16]but was rebuked for his own transgression; a speechless donkey spoke with human voice and restrained the prophet's madness.

[17]These are waterless springs and mists driven by a storm. For them the gloom of utter darkness has been reserved. [18]For, speaking loud boasts of folly, they entice by sensual passions of the flesh those who are barely escaping from those who live in error. [19]They promise them freedom, but they themselves are slaves of corruption. For whatever overcomes a person, to that he is enslaved. [20]For if, after they have escaped the defilements of the world through the knowledge of our Lord and Savior Jesus Christ, they are again entangled in them and overcome, the last state has become worse for them than the first. [21]For it would have been better for them never to have known the way of righteousness than after knowing it to turn back from the holy commandment delivered to them. [22]What the true proverb says has happened to them: "The dog returns to its own vomit, and the sow, after washing herself, returns to wallow in the mire."

[15]Which have forsaken the right way, and are gone astray, following the way of Balaam the son of Bosor, who loved the wages of unrighteousness;

[16]But was rebuked for his iniquity: the dumb ass speaking with man's voice forbad the madness of the prophet.

[17]These are wells without water, clouds that are carried with a tempest; to whom the mist of darkness is reserved for ever.

[18]For when they speak great swelling words of vanity, they allure through the lusts of the flesh, through much wantonness, those that were clean escaped from them who live in error.

[19]While they promise them liberty, they themselves are the servants of corruption: for of whom a man is overcome, of the same is he brought in bondage.

[20]For if after they have escaped the pollutions of the world through the knowledge of the Lord and Saviour Jesus Christ, they are again entangled therein, and overcome, the latter end is worse with them than the beginning.

[21]For it had been better for them not to have known the way of righteousness, than, after they have known it, to turn from the holy commandment delivered unto them.

[22]But it is happened unto them according to the true proverb, The dog is turned to his own vomit again; and the sow that was washed to her wallowing in the mire.

Introduction to 2:10b–22 Blasphemous arrogance is the common characteristic of false teachers destined to suffer judgment from the Lord (vv. 10–13). Peter catalogues their sins, including revelry, adultery, and greed (vv. 13–14), embodied in the OT example of Balaam (vv. 15–16). Peter describes such teachers as puffed up but powerless and their teaching as enticing to lust (vv. 17–18). Such enticements enslave false teachers to corruption (v. 19); and though knowledge of Christ frees from such slavery, false teachers are in danger of a judgment compounded by having been saved by God's grace in Christ and willingly turning away from it to teach falsely (vv. 20–22).

2:10b–12 In their arrogance, false teachers *blaspheme the glorious ones*, that is, they speak against God's angels. To speak against anything of God is to speak against God Himself. Peter points up the irony of the false teachers' blasphemy, in that the angels of the Lord do not dare to speak *judgment against them before the Lord*. Such teachers however are wholly ignorant of the Lord's, or His angels', attitude towards them, because they are *irrational animals, creatures of instinct* (Gk *physika*, that is, completely tuned to the natural world and ignorant of spiritual matters). That they are *born to be caught and destroyed* is an illustration consistent with the context. Their irrational actions make them like animals that are hunted. We must be careful not to misapply this phrase by reading it out of context to make it appear to support the erroneous theology of God's election of some to damnation (cf. 1Tm 2:4–6). Destruction of false teachers begins with the self-destruction brought about by their defiling passions and culminates with their eternal destruction in hell, explicated by Peter in the intensive language he uses at the end of this phrase: *destroyed in their destruction*.

2:13 Sins have consequences. The eternal consequence of our sinfulness and our actual sins was the unfathomable price of the death of the Lord Jesus Christ (cf. Rm 6:23). Sins continue to bear temporal consequences, and the unrepentant sinner will suffer not only temporally, but also eternally for sins that Christ died to forgive. Peter illustrates this as the end of the false teachers in their judgment as well, *suffering wrong as the wage for their wrongdoing*. Peter plays on the merchandizing metaphor from earlier in the chapter (cf. v. 3): although false teachers expect to profit from evil deeds, God will strip them of any gain they hope to realize. They will be paid back with

harm for the harm they have done. Peter proceeds with a brief catalogue of the false teachers' sins, which begins with the description
that they *revel in the daytime*, which indicates their shamelessness;
cf. Rm 13:13; Jn 3:19–21; Jer 6:15; 8:12). Peter associates this reveling
with the feast shared by the Christian community, where such false
teachers *feast with you*. Evidently they had worked their way into the
Christian community to the point that they even attended the Lord's
Supper, at which they caroused (cf. 1Co 11:17–22). Deeper than the
error at Corinth, Peter is addressing the role of false teachers, which
continues to our own day. Melanchthon wrote: "Peter predicted that
there would be godless bishops who would abuse the alms of the
Church for luxury and neglect the ministry. . . . Therefore, let those
who defraud the Church know that they will pay God the penalty
for this crime" (Tr 82). False teachers are *blots and blemishes*, a poor
picture of Christianity, and a cause of bad repute to the unbeliever.
They are, like blemishes on the face or the body, symptomatic of a
deeper problem in the body itself; thus Peter's warning is not just
addressed to the teachers themselves, but the congregation that may
fall victim to such teachers.

2:14 Peter's catalogue of sins continues by describing their *eyes
full of adultery* and their *hearts trained in greed*. The *unsteady* ("unstable," 3:16) *souls* of those who are seduced by false teachers are
lured by them because they are not grounded in the whole testimony
of the Scriptures; this makes it easy for false teachers to "twist" apostolic teaching "to their own destruction" (3:16). James describes the
victim of false teaching as the "one who doubts . . . like a wave of
the sea that is driven and tossed by the wind" (Jas 1:6). The cure for
instability and enticement to false teaching is the certainty of faith in
God's sure and certain Word.

2:15–16 The sin of greed mentioned by Peter in the previous
verse is illustrated from the OT by *Balaam*, a diviner who, when
God would not let him curse the people of Israel (cf. Nu 22–24), proceeded to corrupt the people by promoting immorality and idolatry
(cf. Nu 25; 31:16). God did not need to employ His holy angels to
deliver His message clearly to such a wickedly-motivated prophet,
however. One of the "bold and willful" (v. 10), Balaam was brought
down to size by God who spoke to him by opening the mouth of his
donkey. By having him rebuked by a donkey, God showed what He
thought of proud Balaam (Nu 22:21–41).

2:17–18 Peter highlights the futility of the false teachers and their doctrine by referring to the impotence of their teaching: they fail to deliver anything worthwhile. Like James' argument about the tongue in Jas 3:11–12, Peter calls the false teachers *waterless springs*, filled up, swollen, but only full of bluster, *speaking loud boasts of folly*, but nothing fertile for any productive teaching. False teachers possess no ability to give life and satisfy spiritual thirst. Like threatening clouds, such teachers are *mists*, lacking substance, and transitory (cf. v. 15). They are already under judgment, living under the cloud of the *gloom of utter darkness*, which will be their final destination as well (recall that this is properly the punishment of the evil angels; cf. 2:4; Jude 12–13). Though they are now arrogant enough to teach falsely their error in broad daylight, they will come to darkness for eternity, as Luther commented: "To be sure, they [false teachers] live well now and fare as they themselves desire; but an eternal darkness will come upon them, even though they do not believe or feel this" (LW 30:188).

2:18 Orthodoxy, like pregnancy, is not something that can be enjoyed in moderation. One either is or is not—there is no in between. This is why a smorgasbord of religious teaching is such a subtly dangerous thing: a little bit of this and a little bit of that is a rapid path to destroying the truth of Christianity, which rests on exclusive claims of Christ's deity, His person and work, and the application of His person and work to the believer. False teachers add to what God has revealed in His Word as they include heterodox teaching, heretical teaching, personal opinion, and their own personality or charisma to the Christian message. They subtract from it as well as they fail to confess the whole Word of God in Law and Gospel, properly distinguished. A little of this and a little of that especially hurts *those who are barely escaping*. This refers to a new convert to whom the Holy Spirit has proclaimed the Word, but who may fall victim to having that Word choked by false teaching—a little of this, a little of that—some thorns to grow up along with the seed sown by the Sower in Christ's parable (Mt 13: 5–7, 19–23). Knowledge of God that rests on the Word of God purely and rightly taught is the only preservative for life and salvation. The devil and his false teachers are indeed the enemy of the Christian, seeking to snatch away a faith that saves.

2:19 False teachers mix enough Christian philosophy with their own ideas to convince their hearers and *promise them freedom*. But false teachers lure people away from the faith by perverting the freedom of the Gospel into an excuse for indulgence. "Freedom" is the state of being that has been promised to Christians in opposition to "slavery": bondage to the principles of the world in enmity to the Christian (Gal 5:13), bondage to human traditions wrought by even well-meaning religious leaders (Jn 8:31–38), and slavery to God's Law and its demands (Gal 4:21–5:1; Rm 7:23–8:4). Such freedom is good news! But such freedom is confused with sin if identified with a liberty to indulge the sinful nature that has been put to death in Christ's death and the death of the sinner who has been washed in Holy Baptism. Peter attacks the libertine doctrine of false teachers, whose teaching was coextensive with philosophies of their own and later epochs that distinguished between spiritual and fleshly levels of existence. If one wishes to be truly spiritual, they might say, then deny the body!; on the other hand, if the body counts for nothing, it doesn't matter what you do with the body, so go ahead and do whatever feels good! Both paths to error are consistent with the later Gnostic heresy, which Peter's false teachers anticipate. Such "freedom" leads right back to slavery (cf. Rm 6:16), but God's "perfect Law of liberty" (Jas 1:25) is equivalent to the knowledge of God, that relationship with Christ that is the primary theme of Peter's Letter.

2:20–21 What is better, dying in ignorance, or dying with full knowledge that you did not have to die? What is worse, an accidental homicide, a stupid accident, or a willful, deliberate, premeditated murder? This is the context in which Peter considers the willful rebellion of the fallen human against God's *holy commandment* that was *delivered to them* according to apostolic teaching and tradition. Peter is saying that it is one thing to be a natural fallen man; it is quite another to be a regenerated Christian who decides to self-exclude himself through heresy. So did Christ describe at Lk 11:24–26: "When the unclean spirit has gone out of a person, it passes through waterless places seeking rest, and finding none it says, 'I will return to my house from which I came.' And when it comes, it finds the house swept and put in order. Then it goes and brings seven other spirits more evil than itself, and they enter and dwell there. And the last state of that person is worse than the first." Such sin, the deliberate choice to self-exclude from the truth of Christianity, is called apostasy. Though the Holy Spirit is ever the "hound of heaven," always calling out with the Word of God that saves, those who harden their hearts against this Word face unforeseeable consequences. The one who hardens his heart will eventually get his wish: God knows how to act the gentleman and give the heart what it desires, even in final judgment, by confirming the hardness of the heart, going so far as to harden it Himself (cf. Ex 8:15, 32; 9:12; 10:1). Such a one is caught like a fish in one of Peter's old nets, *again entangled . . . and overcome*, and so are his students, who escaped the world (vv. 18–19) and are now caught in a new kind of slavery to false doctrine—out of the frying pan and into the fire of their own defiling passions (v. 10).

2:22 On this aphoristic conclusion to Peter's warning against false teachers, Luther commented:

> Through Baptism these people threw out unbelief, had their unclean way of life washed away, and entered into a pure life of faith and love. Now they fall away into unbelief and their own works, and they soil themselves again in filth. . . . But if you want to become pious, you must ask God to give you a genuine faith, and you must begin to desist from unbelief. When you receive faith, then good works will come automatically, and you will lead a pure and chaste life. Otherwise you will preserve yourself by no other means. And even if you are able to conceal the knave in your heart for a while, yet he will finally emerge. (LW 30:190–91)

The first proverb with which Peter closes his warnings is from Pr 26:11, a palpable reflection on the slavery to which false teachers subject their students, and to which they cannot help but be enslaved themselves. The second, extrabiblical aphorism reinforces the bestial description Peter employs earlier in the chapter, calling such false teachers irrational, instinctive animals (v. 12). Both animals are unclean according to Jewish dietary law, underscoring the invective of Peter: these are people who reject God's Word.

2:1–22 in Devotion and Prayer You do not have to get caught in a cult to hear false doctrine. We do well to speak up against the more popular and attractive heresies of our day, like Mormonism and Jehovah's Witnesses; we ought constantly to be on guard against anyone who attempts to get into our wallet "in the name of God"; and we should be rightly alarmed by both libertine fads and oddball fanaticism, whether violent or not. But false teaching is at the root of any word that compromises the truth of God's Gospel. All such teaching is of the devil, who seeks primarily to question God's Word ("did God *really* say?"). And you do not have to join a cult to hear the Word of God taught falsely. Wolves in sheep's clothing pop up in the Christian Church and can be identified easily in a couple of ways. They do not rely on the Bible as the source of God's counsel, but rather rely on their own creative stories. They push Jesus to the margins of their message and replace Him with their own ideas at the center. Devote time and energy in considering what your teachers teach you. And when you teach, take heed of Paul's advice to young Timothy: "Do your best to present yourself to God as one approved, a worker who has no need to be ashamed, rightly handling the word of truth. But avoid irreverent babble, for it will lead people into more and more ungodliness, and their talk will spread like gangrene. Among them are Hymenaeus and Philetus, who have swerved from the truth, saying that the resurrection has already happened. They are upsetting the faith of some. But God's firm foundation stands, bearing this seal: 'The Lord knows those who are His,' and, 'Let everyone who names the name of the Lord depart from iniquity.'" (2Tm 2:15–19). • Lord Jesus Christ, You are the Way, the Truth, and the Life. Thank You for teachers who divide Your Word of truth responsibly. Continue to grant Your Church faithful teachers, that Your flock may be preserved in truth. Bless all who teach, that Your truth may be the center of their message. Amen.

PART 4

ANSWERS TO SKEPTICISM REGARDING THE END OF THIS WORLD (3:1–10)

ESV	KJV
3 ¹This is now the second letter that I am writing to you, beloved. In both of them I am stirring up your sincere mind by way of reminder, ²that you should remember the predictions of the holy prophets and the commandment of the Lord and Savior through your apostles, ³knowing this first of all, that scoffers will come in the last days with scoffing, following their own sinful desires. ⁴They will say, "Where is the promise of his coming? For ever since the fathers fell asleep, all things are continuing as they were from the beginning of creation." ⁵For they deliberately overlook this fact, that the heavens existed long ago, and the earth was formed out of water and through water by the word of God, ⁶and that by means of these the world that then existed was deluged with water and perished. ⁷But by the same word the heavens and earth that now exist are stored up for fire, being kept until the day of judgment and destruction of the ungodly. ⁸But do not overlook this one fact, beloved, that with the Lord one day is as a thousand years, and a thousand years as one day. ⁹The Lord is not slow to fulfill his promise as	*3* ¹This second epistle, beloved, I now write unto you; in both which I stir up your pure minds by way of remembrance: ²That ye may be mindful of the words which were spoken before by the holy prophets, and of the commandment of us the apostles of the Lord and Saviour: ³Knowing this first, that there shall come in the last days scoffers, walking after their own lusts, ⁴And saying, Where is the promise of his coming? for since the fathers fell asleep, all things continue as they were from the beginning of the creation. ⁵For this they willingly are ignorant of, that by the word of God the heavens were of old, and the earth standing out of the water and in the water: ⁶Whereby the world that then was, being overflowed with water, perished: ⁷But the heavens and the earth, which are now, by the same word are kept in store, reserved unto fire against the day of judgment and perdition of ungodly men. ⁸But, beloved, be not ignorant of

some count slowness, but is patient toward you, not wishing that any should perish, but that all should reach repentance. ¹⁰But the day of the Lord will come like a thief, and then the heavens will pass away with a roar, and the heavenly bodies will be burned up and dissolved, and the earth and the works that are done on it will be exposed.

this one thing, that one day is with the Lord as a thousand years, and a thousand years as one day.

⁹The Lord is not slack concerning his promise, as some men count slackness; but is longsuffering to us-ward, not willing that any should perish, but that all should come to repentance.

¹⁰But the day of the Lord will come as a thief in the night; in the which the heavens shall pass away with a great noise, and the elements shall melt with fervent heat, the earth also and the works that are therein shall be burned up.

Introduction to 3:1–10 Peter knew that he was approaching the end of his own earthly life, as he had said at the end of ch. 1. He has this in mind as he reminds his readers that it may be the end of earthly existence for them too, any day, any time, for the day of judgment is near. The final chapter of this Letter deals with Judgment Day, which is not a new invention of the Christian Church, but is a truth proclaimed by both OT prophets and NT apostles, as Peter reminds his readers (vv. 1–2). The world disbelieves the end is near, to the point of mocking such doomsday preaching (vv. 3–4), but they misread history, forgetting the example of the flood (vv. 5–6). God will destroy the world again, through fire (v. 7). Christians can find comfort knowing that the Lord's moments do not depend on our sense of human chronology or dispensations, but that the time of His appearance in judgment is being delayed for the purpose of waiting for the unbeliever to come to repentance (vv. 8–9). The destruction of this present world concludes Peter's picture of Judgment Day (v. 10), striking a tone of Law and judgment on the unbeliever, and hope in new heavens and a new earth for the believer in the conclusion of the Letter (v. 13).

3:1 As at 1Pt 2:11 and 4:12, Peter refers to his readers here as *beloved*, showing Peter's close relationship with and concern for them. He repeats the sentiments he had shared at 1:12–15, including the striking verb "stir up"; Peter's purpose is to arouse the people to vigilance in light of not only false teaching, but also the judgment to come, which forms the emphasis of this chapter.

3:2 In spite of those who do not share Christian faith, along with its attendant belief in Christ's imminent return (vv. 3–5; cf. 1Pt 3:14–17), Peter exhorts his readers to *remember the predictions* of the OT Scriptures (cf. 1:19), which are matched by apostolic teaching, referring to Peter's own words, but also to the words of Paul, as he mentions near the end of the Letter (vv. 15–16). The preaching and teaching of the Day of the Lord is nothing new; Peter points his readers back to the OT Scriptures and the tradition of the apostles. Cf. 1Co 11:23: "For I received from the Lord what I also delivered to you. . . ."

3:3 Interpretations of this verse have made guesses regarding the identity of the *scoffers* Peter refers to. Are these people known to Peter? Are they to be understood as the false teachers he dealt with in ch. 2? The distinguish mark of those who come *in the last days with scoffing* is that they follow *their own sinful desires.*

3:4 The content of the mockers' scoffing is that Christ's return has not come, which would vindicate His messiahship. *Where is the promise of His coming?*, that is, Where is the Lord's promised return for the final judgment? After all, if the Messiah comes to restore God's kingdom on earth, where is the fulfillment of the promise that was given to *the fathers* who *fell asleep*? While some believe "fathers" refers to the first Christian generation, some of whom (e.g., Stephen, James the son of Zebedee, James the Just) had already suffered martyrdom by the time this Letter was written, it is more likely that Peter here refers to the forefathers of Judaism, the patriarchs and the OT prophets who pointed forward to the Day of the Lord, especially as the "scoffers" reach back to OT history. The criticism is that there has been no change to ordinary events. Instead, *all things are continuing as they were from the beginning of creation.* Calvin wrote:

> It was a dangerous scoff when they insinuated a doubt as to the last resurrection; for when that is taken away, there is no gospel any longer, the power of Christ is brought to nothing, the whole of religion is gone. Then Satan aims directly at the throat of the Church, when he destroys faith in the coming of Christ. For why did Christ die and rise again, except that he may some time gather to himself the redeemed from death, and give them eternal life? All religion is wholly subverted, except faith in the resurrection

remains firm and immovable. Hence, on this point Satan assails us most fiercely. (Calvin 415)

3:5–6 Peter's analysis of his opponents' arguments regarding God's OT salvation history reveals that *they deliberately overlook* facts about creation, including its coming into being by God's almighty Word. He refers to creation *out of water and through water* (cf. Gn 1:2: "The earth was without form and void, and darkness was over the face of the deep. And the Spirit of God was hovering over the face of the waters") in order to match the beginning with the end, creation with judgment. Thus he highlights God's judgment when *the world that then existed was deluged with water and perished.* Though God is eternal, that is, outside of time, He breaks into time and space, making His presence known to human history as He intervenes in time. The great flood was one example; the Day of the Lord will be the concluding note of human history, after which we will know Him in eternity (cf. 1Co 13:12).

3:7 The same Word that created the world, the same Word that judged the world in the flood, is the same Word that preserves the world, and *by the same Word the heavens and earth . . . are stored up for fire.* Peter refers here to a day of judgment the way OT prophets do (cf. Zep 1:18; 3:8; Mal 4:1). The Word is God's counsel of Law and Gospel; at the day of judgment, that Word of Law will be the *destruction of the ungodly,* just as the wicked were destroyed in the flood. The Word of promise, the Gospel, is salvation for a remnant, just as Noah was saved (cf. 2:5; 1Pt 3:20–21). Luther's commentary on this verse richly confessed the trustworthiness of God's promises:

> When the Last Day breaks all of a sudden, in one moment there will be nothing but fire. Everything in heaven and on earth will be reduced to powder and ashes. Everything must be changed by fire, just as the water changed everything at the time of the Flood. Because God let what took place at that time be a sign, therefore the fire shall be the sign that He will not lie. (LW 30:195)

3:8–9 When Peter refers to Ps 90:4, saying *one day is as a thousand years,* he is confessing the eternal nature of God, indicating a level of perception distinct from humans in time. This is much different than saying that a thousand years and a day are the same thing. Peter does not write this as an invitation to calculate estimated calendars for the return of Christ or identify distinct dispensations of God's grace through millennia. Rather he is referring to the Psalm in the way Moses intended when he wrote the ancient prayer: as a comfort in the face of our own very brief human lifespan. Contrary to God's eternity, this life is a flash in the pan, so do not get hung up feeling frustrated about the slowness of Judgment Day's arrival—it will be here soon enough! In the meantime, live in the "now" of God's patience, knowing that He is holding back that day of destruction in order to fulfill His will *that all should reach repentance*. Faith and salvation wrought by repentance is what the Lord cares about. He is not bound to a system of man's devising or human mathematics. Rather, He binds Himself to His promise of salvation in Christ, leading sinners to sorrow over their sins and trust in God's forgiveness. Luther wrote: "Confession has two parts. First that we confess our sins, and second, that we receive absolution, that is, forgiveness, from the pastor as from God Himself, not doubting, but firmly believing that by it our sins are forgiven before God in heaven" (SC, Confession, I). Bengel wrote:

> No delay happens which is long to God. As to a man of excessive wealth, a thousand guineas are as a single penny; so to the Eternal God a thousand years are as one day. . . . He gives us space for repentance without any annoyance to Himself. (Bengel 5:106)

3:10 As Jesus had taught Peter (Mt 24:43–44), so the apostle repeats: *the day of the Lord will come like a thief*. The "day of the Lord" is the Last Day, Judgment Day, when the Lord returns to judge the ungodly and to redeem the faithful, as taught in the OT (cf. Is 13:9; Jer 46:10; Ezk 30:3; etc.) and the NT (1Th 5:2; 2Th 2:2). As Jesus and Paul emphasized, so Peter also points out, using the image of an unexpected "thief," that the Day will be sudden and a surprise (cf. Mk 13:36; Lk 21:34), precluding any attempt to calculate when it will happen (cf. Mt 24:36; 1Th 5:2; Rv 3:3; 16:15). Peter offers quite a vivid illustration of what will transpire: sound (*with a roar*, or closer to the whistling sound of an arrow, indicating the speed and force with which the heavens will pass away) and sight, as the *heavenly bodies* (sun, moon, and stars) are *burned up and dissolved* (cf. Rm 8:21). A textual problem at the end of the verse renders the final verb uncertain: will Judgment Day result in the works on the earth being *exposed* (that is, "found" or "discovered," as ESV relates) or *burned up* as KJV renders it? Either reading is consistent with what is reported elsewhere in the Scriptures of the Last Day, and if the *works* of humans on the earth are to be *exposed* (cf. Jn 3:20–21), then they will be exposed to the fire of God's judgment, acting to refine and purify them as the "new heavens and a new earth" (v. 13). This Judgment Day is an anticipation of eternity for the Christian; Luther's comment on the verse reminds us that Christians already are invited to consider their life in view of eternity:

> This life amounts to eating, drinking, sleeping, digesting, begetting children, etc. Here everything goes by number: hours, days, and years in succession. Now when you want to look at the life to come, you must erase the course of this life from your mind. You dare not think that you can measure it as this life is measured. There everything will be one day, one hour, one moment. (LW 30:196)

PART 5

FINAL EXHORTATION ON THE BASIS OF CHRISTIAN EXPECTATION AND HOPE (3:11–18)

ESV	KJV
[11]Since all these things are thus to be dissolved, what sort of people ought you to be in lives of holiness and godliness, [12]waiting for and hastening the coming of the day of God, because of which the heavens will be set on fire and dissolved, and the heavenly bodies will melt as they burn! [13]But according to his promise we are waiting for new heavens and a new earth in which righteousness dwells.	[11]Seeing then that all these things shall be dissolved, what manner of persons ought ye to be in all holy conversation and godliness,
	[12]Looking for and hasting unto the coming of the day of God, wherein the heavens being on fire shall be dissolved, and the elements shall melt with fervent heat?
[14]Therefore, beloved, since you are waiting for these, be diligent to be found by him without spot or blemish, and at peace. [15]And count the patience of our Lord as salvation, just as our beloved brother Paul also wrote to you according to the wisdom given him, [16]as he does in all his letters when he speaks in them of these matters. There are some things in them that are hard to understand, which the ignorant and unstable twist to their own destruction, as they do the other Scriptures. [17]You therefore, beloved, knowing this beforehand, take care that you are not carried away with the error of lawless peo-	[13]Nevertheless we, according to his promise, look for new heavens and a new earth, wherein dwelleth righteousness.
	[14]Wherefore, beloved, seeing that ye look for such things, be diligent that ye may be found of him in peace, without spot, and blameless.
	[15]And account that the longsuffering of our Lord is salvation; even as our beloved brother Paul also according to the wisdom given unto him hath written unto you;
	[16]As also in all his epistles, speaking in them of these things; in which are some things hard to be understood, which they that are unlearned and unstable wrest, as they do also the other scriptures, unto their own destruction.

ple and lose your own stability. [18]But grow in the grace and knowledge of our Lord and Savior Jesus Christ. To him be the glory both now and to the day of eternity. Amen.

[17]Ye therefore, beloved, seeing ye know these things before, beware lest ye also, being led away with the error of the wicked, fall from your own stedfastness.

[18]But grow in grace, and in the knowledge of our Lord and Saviour Jesus Christ. To him be glory both now and for ever. Amen.

Introduction to 3:11–18 The Lord's delay in returning is actually a matter of urgency for the Church, which He has called to spread the Gospel of repentance and salvation. The tone of Law that is struck by the impending Day of the Lord leads God's people to live not in fear of the Law, but in the fear of the Lord, living holy lives as they anticipate the day of their judgment coming at any time (vv. 11–12). We do not depend on the fear that the world knows, but on God's promise for a new heavens and a new earth (v. 13). It is the Gospel promise of a world to come that motivates the Christian to live as God's saint (v. 14) and to preach repentance to a world that is dying without Him. It is a call from the apostle not to grow impatient or unfaithful, but rather to chalk up our sojourner-exile status in this world as God's patience, an opportunity for salvation of the unbeliever, consistent with apostolic teaching from Paul, whose teachings are, like Peter's, subject to distortion (vv. 15–16). The final call to Peter's readers is therefore to keep the faith pure and to hold strictly to the tradition of the apostles, and not to false teachers, as the only way to "grow in the grace and knowledge of our Lord and Savior Jesus Christ" (vv. 17–18).

3:11–12 Luther paraphrases these verses in the following way: "Since you know that everything must pass away, both heaven and earth, consider how completely you must be prepared with a saintly and godly life and conduct to meet this Day" (LW 30:197). One's conduct (translated in ESV in this instance under the phrase *lives of holiness*) is an oft-repeated emphasis of Peter: cf. 1Pt 1:15, 18; 2:12; 3:1–2, 16; 2Pt 2:7. As God is patient with the world before Christ's return, so Christians are called also to a life of patience, *waiting for* His coming and *hastening* it as we pray "Your kingdom come" and

"Come, Lord Jesus!" (Mt 6:10; Rv 22:20). The vivid destruction of the old world matches the prediction of Peter in v. 10.

3:13 The most succinct and comforting description of what awaits believers in the life to come is the biblical phrase *new heavens and a new earth*. Rather than leave things wrapped in mystery and obscurity, the Holy Spirit has delivered words that comfort and give confidence regarding the reward of the faithful: when Christ returns, all things will be made new. Better than the paradise Adam and Eve knew, not to mention the world corrupted by their (and our sin), God has a new and better good world for us to inhabit with Him forever (cf. Rm 8:19–22; Rv 21:1–4). Luther compared the Paradise lost through our sin and the Paradise "regained" at Christ's appearance:

> That will be a broad and beautiful heaven and a joyful earth, much more beautiful and joyful than Paradise was. There were no stinging nettles or prickly thorns and thistles or noxious creatures, worms, or vermin in Paradise, but lovely and noble roses and aromatic creatures. All the trees in the garden were lovely to behold and good to eat. . . . Then no sin or unrighteousness will dwell on earth, no homicide or murder, no hate or envy, but perfect righteousness, love, and friendship. Now unrighteousness and infidelity dwell on earth; from this we should realize what we have lost through Adam's fall and our sin and learn to long and yearn for the restoration and renewal of the creation and for the liberty of the children of God. (LW 12:121)

3:1–13 in Devotion and Prayer Christians too often fall into the world's habits and ways of thinking when it comes to matters undeniably difficult to talk about with certainty. The end of life is one such matter. Of no less difficulty is the end of time itself. We get caught up trying to soften the blow of death by employing the term "passed away," when the Bible knows of no such euphemism, preferring the terms "death" and "falling asleep"—both anticipating something: a waking, a resurrection, a new life. So also Christians tend to think of this world as the first part of our life and heaven as another place we go when we die, complete with a cloud to reside on, a harp, a halo, and wings a-waiting, glossing over what God has actually revealed. Even the heavens we think of in our fallen, earthly imagination right now will be burned up in judgment along with this old earth. But just as death anticipates resurrection, so the judgment in fire on this world anticipates God who makes "all things new" (Rv

21:5). You get to anticipate a new heavens and a new earth because Christ our God, who lives anew in His resurrection, has also made you new (2Co 5:17) and has prepared a place for you in His Father's house (Jn 14:1–7). • Patient Lord, You waited in the days of Noah and preserved Your remnant, eight souls in all, saving them through water. You draw Your Church through water too, lifting her up in Baptism to salvation, saving her, cleansing her, making her new, preparing her as a bride adorned for her Husband. In Your patience, do not quickly destroy the wicked, but draw them to repentance, even as You have shown patience to Your bride, the Church. And in Your perfect timing, come quickly, O Lord, that the dwelling place of God may be with man, and that You may wipe away every tear from our eyes. In the name of the Church's Bridegroom. Amen.

3:14 In direct contrast to the false teachers Peter rails against at 2:13, Christians awaiting the return of Christ strive *to be found . . . without spot or blemish*. Christ is the perfect Lamb of God without spot or blemish (cf. 1Pt 1:19; Lv 1:3). Living in the world while anticipating the return of Christ is a life lived *at peace* with God and neighbor. It is at peace with God because of what Christ has done to effect our salvation (cf. Rm 5:1). It is at peace with neighbor, in spite of persecution (1Pt 3:11) and because of the perfect peace given in Christ (1Pt 5:14). Life lived in light of the "new heavens and new earth" (v. 13) is a life that the God of peace Himself makes holy, as Paul prayed for the Thessalonians: "Now may the God of peace Himself sanctify you completely, and may your whole spirit and soul and body be kept blameless at the coming of our Lord Jesus Christ" (1Th 5:23).

3:15 Peter and his readers knew Paul and his writings and held him in regard and friendship. Early Christian history shows that there were churches devoted to the memory of both Peter and Paul in Rome in the first century. This fact supports our understanding of their interaction. As Paul had convinced his readers of his unity with the doctrine of the "pillar apostles" (cf. Gal 1–2), so Peter convinces his readers here of his unity with the doctrine of Paul. *Our beloved brother Paul* includes a similar argument about God's patience in Rm 2: "Or do you presume on the riches of His kindness and forbearance and patience, not knowing that God's kindness is meant to lead you to repentance? But because of your hard and impenitent heart you are storing up wrath for yourself on the day of wrath when God's righteous judgment will be revealed" (Rm 2:4–5). Judgment

Day has not yet come because God's *patience* is *salvation*—He is extending human history in order to extend His saving work to all who repent and believe. If God were not patient, all would be destroyed; Christians return to the Lord in repentance daily, trusting in His forgiveness. Luther wrote: "In this Christian church He daily and richly forgives all my sins and the sins of all believers" (SC, Third Article). Luther also wrote:

> We pray in this petition that our Father in heaven would not look at our sins, or deny our prayer because of them. We are neither worthy of the things for which we pray, nor have we deserved them, but we ask that He would give them all to us by grace, for we daily sin much and surely deserve nothing but punishment. So we too will sincerely forgive and gladly do good to those who sin against us. (SC, Fifth Petition)

3:16 Paul also spoke of *these matters*, that is, regarding false teachers and the Last Day, which indeed can be *things . . . hard to understand*. Peter is arguing that his own words should be read as a unified doctrine with Paul, and perhaps elucidating his words on the return of Christ, e.g., at 1Th 5:1–11 and 2Th 1:5–12. These, like other Scriptures, can be "twisted" by adding, subtracting, or reading contrary to context or sense. *The ignorant and unstable twist . . . other Scriptures* this way (cf. Rm 3:8; 6:1; Mt 5:17–19; Rv 22:18–19), and this is just what false teachers do as well (cf. 2:12, 17). Peter links Paul's letters here with *the other Scriptures*, indicating a recognition of inspiration (cf. 1:16–21).

3:17–18 The concluding sentence of the Letter has a negative and a positive: don't get *carried away* by the *error* of the false teachers I have warned you about, but do *grow in the grace and knowledge of our Lord*. Peter repeats his epithet for his hearers one last time before he leaves this world: *beloved* (3:1, 8, 14; cf. 1Pt 2:11; 4:12). He bequeaths to these friends the reminders in his Epistle (cf. 1:12–13; 3:1) and the warning to beware of false teaching. God's Word is the only sure way to remain on guard in the stability of salvation—Peter's entire Letter is a reminder of this fact. Remaining in God's Word is the substance of a relationship with Jesus Christ. Peter began the Letter by calling this relationship "knowledge of God" (1:2–3, 5–6, 8). He now closes the Letter on the same note, as he encourages his readers to *grow in the grace and knowledge*. Knowing God in Christ is the most important achievement in this life, one accomplished in

245

us by God the Holy Spirit in conversion as He proclaims God's Word to the sinner. God the Holy Spirit continues to proclaim that Word and grow Himself a people for the "now" and "not-yet," as Peter indicates in his doxology: *to Him be the glory both now and to the day of eternity.* Glory belongs to our God Jesus alone. Peter, all of the apostles, and all believers are His servants. Jesus is glorified and honored whenever believers witness to His grace with their words and actions, which is a practice for a lifetime. That our witness to Him changes throughout our life as we learn more of Him, "growing in grace and knowledge," is a fact that Luther explained:

> This teaching is not learned all at once, nor can it be understood speculatively. It must be learned by daily use and exercise amid the temptations of the world, the devil, and the flesh, amid despair, distrust, and innumerable other horrible things. And without these exercises it cannot be kept. Foolish people, therefore, are taken in. After reading one or more pages of Holy Scriptures and hearing maybe one sermon, they think they have already learned this teaching [of Christianity] completely. They can see that in other, lesser arts we do not immediately become masters. Much less can it happen in this greatest teaching of all, that we immediately trust in God from the heart and despise all the perils of the world, death, and the devil. These things cannot be learned in one day, but practice and immense exercise and a singular gift of God are required. (LW 12:248)

Wesley wrote:

> There may be, for a time, grace without growth; as there may be natural life without growth. But such sickly life, of soul or body, will end in death, and every day draw nigher to it. Health is the means of both natural and spiritual growth. If the remaining evil of our fallen nature be not daily mortified, it will, like an evil humour in the body, destroy the whole man. But "if ye through the Spirit do mortify the deeds of the body," (only so far as we do this,) "ye shall live" the life of faith, holiness, happiness. The end and design of grace being purchased and bestowed on us, is to destroy the image of the earthy, and restore us to that of the heavenly. And so far as it does this, it truly profits us; and also makes way for more of the heavenly gift, that we may at last be filled with all the fulness of God. The strength and well-being of a Christian depend on what his soul feeds on, as the health of the body depends on whatever we make our daily food. If we feed on

what is according to our nature, we grow; if not, we pine away and die. The soul is of the nature of God, and nothing but what is according to his holiness can agree with it. Sin, of every kind, starves the soul, and makes it consume away. Let us not try to invert the order of God in his new creation: we shall only deceive ourselves. It is easy to forsake the will of God, and follow our own; but this will bring leanness into the soul. It is easy to satisfy ourselves without being possessed of the holiness and happiness of the gospel. It is easy to call these frames and feelings, and then to oppose faith to one and Christ to the other. Frames (allowing the expression) are no other than heavenly tempers, "the mind that was in Christ." Feelings are the divine consolations of the Holy Ghost shed abroad in the heart of him that truly believes. And wherever faith is, and wherever Christ is, there are these blessed frames and feelings. If they are not in us, it is a sure sign that though the wilderness became a pool, the pool is become a wilderness again. (Wesley 628)

3:14–18 in Devotion and Prayer New and improved stain remover! Gets rid of mold and mildew! Diminish those wrinkles and age spots! Dark blotches? Scars? Blemishes? This product is sure to satisfy. Pimples, pustules, specks, and stains—we fight them on clothes, we fight them on our complexion, we fight them whether caused by ailment, illness, or age. But it seems that for every stain remover on the market, novelty and improvement never lead to perfection. Wrinkles, scars, and spots still show up; products still advertise as "even better than the last one." The imperfection of soaps and salves to fix our flaws is a hazy reflection of our spiritual condition. Peter, in the last chapter, talked about false teachers being a blot, a spot, a blemish on the good name by which God would call Himself a people. But you don't have to be a false teacher to suffer spots and stains: "though your sins are like scarlet . . . though they are red like crimson" (Is 1:18). Sin is a stain we have no ointment to address, no prescription or over the counter medicine, no chemical detergent or homeopathic remedy. The only thing that people so stained can hope for is something to cover the stain. Thanks be to God that such a covering has been given: an indelible mark that covers every stain of sin, an unerasable washing with Christ's righteousness, a clothing, a covering, that counts our blemishes concealed in Christ. "For as many of you as were baptized into Christ have put on Christ" (Gal 3:27). • Gracious Lord Jesus, You stained the wood of an executioner's cross

247

with Your holy blood. Stain me with Your indelible washing, that my sins, though scarlet, may be white as snow. Hide the stigma of my rebellion in Your own precious wounds. Look not at the spots on my record, past, present, or future, but according to Your abundant mercy blot out my transgressions, that I may be presented to You without spot or stain. Amen.

1, 2, 3 JOHN

INTRODUCTION TO
1, 2, 3 JOHN

Overview

Author

John, apostle and evangelist, called "the elder"

Date

AD 85–95

Places

Various churches, perhaps in Asia Minor

People

John the elder; the brethren (children, fathers, and young men); antichrists; false teachers; various "spirits"; the elect lady, her children, and her elect sister; deceivers; Gaius; brothers who are strangers; Gentiles; Diotrephes; Demetrius; friends

Purpose

To establish and encourage the faith of John's contemporaries in the wake of rising controversy because some had left Christian congregations or had troubled them

Law and Sin Themes

Sin; walking in darkness or light; God's commands; hatred; death; deceit; antichrist(s); love one another; lawlessness; deceivers; wicked works; imitate God, not evil

Grace and Gospel Themes

Christ, the atoning sacrifice; our advocate; eternal life; God perfects His love in us (sanctification); light; born of God; children of God; truth; fellowship; reward; abiding in Christ's teachings; Christ has come in the flesh

Memory Verses

Confession of sins (1Jn 1:7–9); Jesus, our advocate (2:1–2); the Son destroys the devil's work (3:8); God is love (4:7–12); true God and eternal life (5:20); beware of false teachers (2Jn 9–11)

Luther on 1, 2, 3 John

The first epistle of John is a genuine apostolic epistle and ought to follow right after his gospel. For as in the gospel he promulgates faith, so here he opposes those who boast of faith without works. He teaches in many different ways that works are not absent where faith is; and if they are absent, then faith is not genuine but is lies and darkness. He does this, however, not by harping on the law, as the epistle of James does, but by stimulating us to love even as God has loved us.

He also writes vigorously here against the Cerinthians, against the spirit of Antichrist, which was beginning even then to deny that Christ has come in the flesh, and which is today for the first time really in full sway. For although people do not now publicly deny with their lips that Christ has come in the flesh, they do deny it with their hearts, by their teaching and life. For he who would be righteous and saved by his own works and deeds is as much as denying Christ, since Christ has come in the flesh for the very purpose of making us righteous and saving us without our works, by his blood alone.

Thus the epistle fights against both parties: against those who would live in faith without any works, and against those who would become righteous by their works. It keeps us in the true middle way, that we become righteous and free from sin through faith; and then, when we are righteous, that we practice good works and love for God's sake, freely and without seeking anything else.

The other two epistles are not doctrinal epistles but examples of love and of faith. They too have a true apostolic spirit. (LW 35:393)

For more of Luther's insights on 1 John, see *Lectures on the First Epistle of St. John* (LW 30:217–327).

Calvin on 1 John

This Epistle is altogether worthy of the spirit of that disciple who, above others, was loved by Christ, that he might exhibit him as a friend to us. But it contains doctrines mixed with exhortations; for he speaks of the eternal Deity of Christ, and at the same time of the incomparable grace which he brought with him when he appeared in the world, and generally of all his blessings; and he especially commends and extols the inestimable grace of divine adoption.

On these truths he grounds his exhortations; and at one time he admonishes us in general to lead a pious and holy life, and at another time he expressly enjoins love. But he does none of these things in a regular order; for he everywhere mixes teaching with exhortation. But he particularly urges brotherly love: he also briefly touches on other things, such as to beware of impostors, and similar things. But each particular shall be noticed in its own place. (Calvin 156)

Calvin did not prepare commentary on 2 and 3 John.

Gerhard on 1, 2, 3 John

[1 John] too is called "catholic" because it was written to all Christians. Oecumenius calls it "encyclical." The ancients say that this Epistle was written to the Parthians, for this title is given it by Possidius (*Indiculus operum Augustini*) and by Augustine himself (*QQ. evang.*, bk. 2, c. 39) because in that area between the Tigris and Indus Rivers and in the places thereabouts there were many Jews from the ancient captivity and dispersion of the ten tribes. As a result they are again set in the first place (Acts 2:9); yet no less than Peter, John wanted this letter of his to belong also to those of the Gentiles who had been converted.

Eusebius (*Hist. eccles.*, bk. 3, c. 25) and Jerome (*Catalog.*) bear witness that "there never was any doubt in the Church concerning the authority and author of this Epistle." Indeed, the style and character, the constant inculcation of love, indicate sufficiently that John is the author of this Epistle, for which reason we put it among the canonical books of the first rank. In his commentary on this Epistle, Socinus claims: "The aim and theme of this letter are stated only by an exhortation to love, innocence of life, and the observation of Christ's precepts." The actual subject matter, however, shows that the theme of the Epistle extends more broadly.

It consists of five chapters and falls into three parts. The first is of teaching, concerning the person and office of Christ; the redemption performed through Christ; the benefits of Christ: adoption into sonship, the regeneration and indwelling of the Holy Spirit; about the coming of the Antichrist; the sin against the Holy Spirit; and the mystery of the Trinity. The second is of exhortation toward sanctity, purity, obedience, and especially to Christian love. The third is of warning about being wary of heretical seducers and antichrists. (E 1.279–282)

At one time there was no less doubt about 2 and 3 John than there was concerning Hebrews, James, and 2 Peter. Eusebius, bk. 3, c. 21: "The ancients, as well as the more recent, accept the first Epistle of John without any hesitation, but they speak against the other two." In the same book, c. 22: "Those that are spoken against, though they are well-known to many, are these: the Epistle attributed to James, etc., and 2 and 3 John, whether they are the work of that evangelist or of someone else with the same name as his." [Gerhard cites the opinions of other Fathers.]

It can be proved, however, that these Epistles, too, are apostolic and canonical. (1) Their author calls himself ["the elder"], which word often signifies ecclesiastical office but here seems rather to indicate his age. But now, it is evident that John reached an age greater than that of the other apostles.

(2) The salutation is fully apostolic: "Grace, mercy, and peace be with you from God our Father and from our Lord Jesus Christ, the Son of the Father, along with truth and concord."

(3) They agree in statements and words with the first Epistle, as a comparison shows. Bede, in his commentary on 2 John: "Some people think that this and the following Epistle are not the work of the apostle John but of a certain John the Elder, whose tomb can still be seen today in Ephesus. Now, however, the general consensus of the Church holds that the apostle John did write these Epistles because he indeed reveals a great similarity of words and of faith with his first Epistle and also admonishes the heretics with similar zeal." (Compare 1 John 2:7 with 2 John 5; 1 John 2:23 with 2 John 9; 1 John 3:6 with 3 John 11; 1 John 4:1–3 with 2 John 7; 1 John 5:3 with 2 John 6. Compare also those passages in both Epistles in which he encourages a love that is in truth.)

(4) The ancients cite these Epistles under John's name and list them with the canonical books: the third Council of Carthage (canon 47), the Council of Laodicea (last canon). . . . [Gerhard cites other Fathers.]

The fact that Papias (in Eusebius) and Jerome attribute these not to the apostle John but to John the Elder proves that these letters belong to the canonical books of the second order. You see, though a few people had doubts about their author while all the rest attribute them to John the apostle, this does not injure their canonical authority. . . .

The second Epistle appears to have been written especially against the wickedness of Basilides and of his adherents, who taught that "Christ was not true man but only a phantom; therefore He did and suffered none of those things He appeared to do and suffer" (Epiphanius, *Haeres.* 24). Therefore John congratulates "the elect lady," that is, a noble and outstanding woman who had been converted to Christ, and her sons, because they were holding the true faith concerning Christ Jesus. He encourages them to persevere in it, to adorn it with love and good works, and to watch out for heresies and the architects of heresies with great zeal.

The third Epistle commends Gaius for holding the correct faith regarding Christ and for adorning it with works of love. It encourages him to persevere faithfully in sincerity of faith and holiness of life and to follow the example of neither Diotrephes nor Demetrius in this matter. (E 1:285–86)

Bengel on 1, 2, 3 John

John writes his Epistle . . . in a simple style, without inscription or conclusion. He does not appear to have sent it abroad, but to have communicated it in person to his hearers. See ver. 4, compared with 2 John, ver. 12, at the end.

There are some who think that it is not easy to ascertain the design and arrangement of this Epistle: but if we examine it with simplicity, this will be laid open to us without any violence. In this letter, or rather treatise (for a letter is sent to the absent; but here the writer seems to have been among those to whom he was writing), St. John designs to confirm the happy and holy communion of the faithful with God and Jesus Christ, by showing the marks . . . of their blessed state. In the Exordium the apostle establishes authority for his own preaching and writing from the appearance of the Word of Life; and clearly points out his design. . . . The Conclusion (that we may at once clear out of the way this point) corresponds with the Exordium, more fully explaining the same design, a recapitulation of those Marks being made by the thrice-repeated *we know*, ch. v. 18, 19, 20. . . . The parts often begin and end in a similar manner; just as the Conclusion answers the Exordium. . . . Sometimes there is a previous allusion in some preceding part, and a recapitulation in a subsequent part. Every part treats of the Divine benefit by the most befitting inferences, of love towards God, of the imitation of Jesus Christ, of the love of the brethren: and although many things may appear to be repeated without order, yet these same inferences are formed in the most methodical manner, by regarding the subject in a different point of view from different causes.

The Elder . . . [in 2 John is] an appropriate title for a familiar Epistle, such as this, and the one that follows. And indeed the gravity of the argument, and the familiarity of the little Epistle, are wonderfully combined and adjusted. (Bengel 111, 141–42, 155)

Wesley on 1 John

> The great similitude, or rather sameness, both of spirit and expression, which runs through St. John's Gospel and all his epistles, is a clear evidence of their being written by the same person. In this epistle he speaks not to any particular church, but to all the Christians of that age; and in them to the whole Christian church in all succeeding ages. Some have apprehended that it is not easy to discern the scope and method of this epistle. But if we examine it with simplicity, these may readily be discovered. St. John in this letter, or rather tract, (for he was present with part of those to whom he wrote,) has this apparent aim, to confirm the happy and holy communion of the faithful with God and Christ, by describing the marks of that blessed state. (Wesley 601)

Challenges for Readers

Authorship. John the apostle and evangelist, who calls himself "the elder" (2Jn 1; 3Jn 1), most likely wrote these three books of Scripture. Early Christian writers describe John serving at Ephesus in Asia Minor for c. 30 years, which provides the likely setting for these books. In some passages, John refers to other eyewitnesses ("we," 1Jn 1:1, 3; 4:14) with whom he addresses his readers. Not written in the form of a letter, 1Jn reads more like a sermon, which could be sent with correspondence.

The Church as Family. Some expressions in John's letters have confused interpreters. For example, when John refers to his readers as "children" (1Jn 2:1, 12–13, 18, 28; 3:1–2, 7, 10, 18; 4:4; 5:2, 21; 2Jn 1, 4, 13; 3Jn 4), some have read this as an indication that he wrote the letters when he was old. This is to miss John's point about his relationship with the members of the congregations. It is not primarily an issue of age. John speaks to his readers as members of his family, the household of faith, for which he is a leader ("elder" or "parent"). The same emphasis on relationships is shown in descriptions of the churches as "the elect lady and her children" and "children of your elect sister" (2Jn 1, 13). Using family relationships to describe congregational relationships is characteristic of the Semitic culture from which the churches first sprang (see examples from Paul in Rm 8:16–17, 21; 9:8; 1Co 4:14, 17; 2Co 6:13; Gal 4:19; Eph 5:1; Php 2:15; 1Th 2:11; 1Tm 1:2, 18; 2Tm 1:2; 2:1; Ti 1:4; Phm 10).

Antichrists and Opponents. John describes his opponents as "antichrist(s)" (1Jn 2:18, 22; 4:3; 2Jn 7), "children of the devil" (1Jn

3:10), "false prophets" (1Jn 4:1), "liar(s)," and "deceivers" (1Jn 2:22; 4:20; 2Jn 7). Based on Church history, Luther associates these opponents with the followers of Cerinthus, who was described as one of the earliest Gnostic leaders to affect the Church at the end of the first century AD. This would indicate a late date for the letters: in the 90s. However, Cerinthus reportedly taught that Jesus was not true and eternal God and that God did not create the world. Cerinthus believed there was a low-ranking divine being, the Demiurge, who created the physical world and later descended to teach through the man Jesus. This dispute about the person of Christ fits some of the theological problems John attributes to his opponents (1Jn 2:18–25; 4:1–6; 2Jn 7–11) but does not fit his descriptions absolutely. In John's letters, the opponents seem focused on denying Jesus' human nature, which may describe an earlier or different heresy from the teachings of Cerinthus. In 3 John, he raises a second issue regarding "Diotrephes, who . . . does not acknowledge our authority" (v. 9). John does not describe this leader as a false teacher but perhaps refers to a congregational dispute.

Blessings for Readers

As you study the letters of John, pray for the peace and blessing of your congregation and fellowship. Greet your fellow Christians as beloved brothers and sisters, for whom Christ gave His life. Although John provides strong warnings against false teachers and their doctrines, he will also help you understand the true character of Christian love, faith, and good works.

Outline

1 John

   I.   Prologue (1:1–4)
  II. In the World, Not of It (1:5–3:12)
      A.   Because His Blood Cleanses Us from All Sin (1:5–2:2)
      B.   Because the True Light Is Already Shining (2:3–11)
      C.   Because the World Is Passing Away (2:12–17)
      D.   Because It Is the Last Hour (2:18–29)
      E.   Because Even Now We Are His Children (3:1–12)
 III. In Him Who First Loved Us (3:13–5:21)
      A.   So We Love and Do Not Hate (3:13–24)
      B.   For Ours Is the Spirit of Truth (4:1–6)
      C.   Ours Is a God Who First Loved Us (4:7–10)
      D.   So Our Love Is His Love (4:11–21)
      E.   For His Is the Testimony of the Spirit, the Water, and the Blood (ch. 5)

2 John

   I.   Greeting (1–3)
  II. Walking in Truth and Love (4–11)
 III. Final Greetings (12–13)

3 John

   I.   Greeting (1–4)
  II. Support and Opposition (5–12)
 III. Final Greetings (13–15)

1 JOHN

PART 1

PROLOGUE (1:1–4)

ESV	KJV
1 ¹That which was from the beginning, which we have heard, which we have seen with our eyes, which we looked upon and have touched with our hands, concerning the word of life—²the life was made manifest, and we have seen it, and testify to it and proclaim to you the eternal life, which was with the Father and was made manifest to us—³that which we have seen and heard we proclaim also to you, so that you too may have fellowship with us; and indeed our fellowship is with the Father and with his Son Jesus Christ. ⁴And we are writing these things so that our joy may be complete.	*1* ¹That which was from the beginning, which we have heard, which we have seen with our eyes, which we have looked upon, and our hands have handled, of the Word of life; ²(For the life was manifested, and we have seen it, and bear witness, and shew unto you that eternal life, which was with the Father, and was manifested unto us;) ³That which we have seen and heard declare we unto you, that ye also may have fellowship with us: and truly our fellowship is with the Father, and with his Son Jesus Christ. ⁴And these things write we unto you, that your joy may be full.

Introduction to 1:1–4 John's "letter" doesn't begin as ancient letters typically do, identifying the writer and the audience with a salutation. It is not addressed overtly to any particular congregation or person, and no specific occasion is explicitly mentioned. Rather, the beginning of 1Jn sounds more like the beginning of a sermon. These first four verses sound like a summary of the beginning of John's gospel (cf. Jn 1:18). Like Peter (2Pt 1:15–17), John's purpose and authority in writing have their source in the eyewitness of Christ (vv. 1–2). He teaches what he and others have witnessed in order to incorporate his audience into their fellowship and to fulfill their joy (vv. 3–4).

1:1 John writes about Jesus Christ, the Word of God, who is *from the beginning* (cf. Jn 1:1–3: "In the beginning was the Word, and the

Word was with God, and the Word was God. He was in the beginning with God. All things were made through him, and without him was not any thing made that was made"). Calvin wrote:

> As the passage is abrupt and involved, that the sense may be made clearer, the words may be thus arranged; "We announce to you the word of life, which was from the beginning and really testified to us in all manner of ways, that life has been manifested in him;" or, if you prefer, the meaning may be thus given, " What we announce to you respecting the word of life, has been from the beginning, and has been openly shewed to us, that life was manifested in him." But the words, That which was from the beginning, refer doubtless to the divinity of Christ, for God manifested in the flesh was not from the beginning; but he who always was life and the eternal Word of God, appeared in the fulness of time as man. Again, what follows as to the looking on and the handling of the hands, refers to his human nature. But as the two natures constitute but one person, and Christ is one, because he came forth from the Father that he might put on our flesh, the Apostle rightly declares that he is the same, and had been invisible, and afterwards became visible. (Calvin 157–58)

Jesus Christ is true God and true man. If there is a theological occasion for John's writing, it is this: to bear witness to the complete humanity, and the complete deity, of his Lord, Jesus Christ. John and others (*we* refers to other eyewitnesses) *heard* Jesus. Bengel wrote, "He appears to have written at a time, when many of the fathers were still alive. . . . They perceived the truth of His flesh, and in it the glory of the only begotten" (Bengel 112). They testify that they have *seen* Him. John recalls for his readers that he *looked* and *touched*. The testimony of John to the divinity of Christ is substantial, and corroborated by other apostles (cf. 2Pt 1:16); his witness is substantial regarding Christ's humanity as well, affirming that this was a Lord to touch. He had a physical, human nature (cf. Lk 24:39; Jn 20:27). The incarnation of Christ occurred according to God's plan so that sinful people like John, Peter, and you and me could trust in a God who locates Himself in time and space for us, as Luther affirmed: "By the grace of God I have learned not to turn my eyes away from that Person who was born to Mary, and not to seek or acknowledge another god. One's eyes must be fixed on that Person who was born of the Virgin Mary. Where the Son of God is, there Christ is; where Christ is, there the Father is" (LW 30:223).

1:2 Using language of revelation, John discloses the miracle of the incarnation: Christ was revealed in the flesh, *the life was made manifest*. In John's Gospel, Jesus identifies Himself as "the resurrection and the life" (Jn 11:25) and "the way, and the truth, and the life" (Jn 14:6), from which John can proclaim that "in Him was life, and the life was the light of men" (Jn 1:4). The "Life" who is Jesus is the great gift of God for all. He is a Savior who is eternal life for all who believe in Him: this is the central purpose of John's Letter. It delivers the good news of that eternal life in Christ (5:11–13). The incarnation of Christ is the means God uses to take away sins. This is why He was *made manifest* in human flesh, as Paul also repeats in the form of an early hymn: "Great indeed, we confess, is the mystery of godliness: He was manifested in the flesh, vindicated by the Spirit, seen by angels, proclaimed among the nations, believed on in the world, taken up in glory" (1Tm 3:16). Where the Son is, there is eternal life, and where the Son is, there is *the Father* (cf. Jn 14:9), always and eternally together in divine relationship. That divine relationship is delivered to those who believe this message. Not only was it *made manifest to us*, that is, to John and other eyewitnesses, but it is now being proclaimed *to you*, as John repeats in v. 3.

1:3 The audience for this Letter is *you*: not a specified congregation or group of individuals, but the plural *you*, meaning all Christians who read this Letter. John incorporates his audience into a *fellowship* (Gk *koinōnia*), referring to what (or rather, whom) Christians hold in common. As we have a share in Christ, we enjoy Christian fellowship. The fellowship to which John refers is far deeper than common interest or activities that might function under the "fellowship opportunities" section of a church bulletin; it is no less than *fellowship with the Father and with his Son Jesus Christ*. This fellowship, like the forgiveness of sins and eternal life (v. 2), has its source in Christ's incarnation. Our God, Jesus, took on a body of flesh and so shares a human nature with us, giving us fellowship with God through Christ. He incorporates us—places us in His own body!—and therefore we enjoy fellowship with one another as common members of one Body of Christ. This fellowship is "ecumenical," meaning that as believers, we share fellowship with all believers of all times and places, including the *us* of v. 3 (John and other eyewitnesses) and all others who have a share in Christ by trusting His promises (cf. Heb 11), past, present, and future.

1:4 John appears, as a father with children, to be overjoyed at sharing something he thinks is very special with the family he loves. Just as at 3Jn 4 ("I have no greater joy than to hear that my children are walking in the truth"), so here the apostle admits that writing this Letter brings great joy to him and other eyewitnesses. The verse's emphasis on complete joy is an interesting parallel to Jn 16:24, where Jesus invites John and others, "Ask, and you will receive, that your joy may be full." Undoubtedly, John prayed for his readers. God would give him joy in the answer to his prayer.

1:1–4 in Devotion and Prayer The incarnation of Christ is not just a narrative about Jesus, not just something John and the other Gospel writers wrote about so that we could celebrate Christmas. It is a story, no doubt, but one of greater import than can reside in a simple history text or theological tome: it is a story that involves you and me. The incarnation is our story, because we have something that Jesus came to trade, exchange, change out. If you recall one theological fact about Christmas, the incarnation, the enfleshment of the Son of God, please let it be this: the fact is, Jesus did not come to earth and become a baby and take on human flesh in order to save you from your flesh. Rather, Jesus took on human flesh to save you from your sin. He did not come to exchange your flesh for something esoteric or ascetic, to point you to more spiritual ideals or to give you some vain conceit of a spirit of giving. He didn't come to motivate you to go shopping or to encourage some other commercial desire. He came, quite simply, to exchange your sin for His righteousness. Your fall for His new creation. Your sickness for His health. Your ugliness for His beauty. Your death for His life. And He effects this glorious gift exchange in the blessed trade of His death for yours, a death that only a truly incarnate, real, flesh-and-blood man could have died—the Son of God who humbled Himself and suffered death, even death on a cross. That is why this is your story and my story, and not just any story. It is a story that gives you eternal life, life that depends on a God who took on flesh for you. • Receive my gratitude, dear Lord Jesus, for miraculous love that led You to wrap Yourself in my flesh and exchange my death for Your life. As You have shared in my humanity, so lead me this day to serve in Your body. Guide me to look, to hear, to see, and to touch those who are in need of God in the flesh with a promise from Your Word. And as You are risen from the dead, raise me also on the Last Day, in flesh imperishable, that I may glorify You forever. Amen.

PART 2

IN THE WORLD, NOT OF IT (1:5–3:12)

Because His Blood Cleanses Us from All Sin (1:5–2:2)

ESV	KJV
⁵This is the message we have heard from him and proclaim to you, that God is light, and in him is no darkness at all. ⁶If we say we have fellowship with him while we walk in darkness, we lie and do not practice the truth. ⁷But if we walk in the light, as he is in the light, we have fellowship with one another, and the blood of Jesus his Son cleanses us from all sin. ⁸If we say we have no sin, we deceive ourselves, and the truth is not in us. ⁹If we confess our sins, he is faithful and just to forgive us our sins and to cleanse us from all unrighteousness. ¹⁰If we say we have not sinned, we make him a liar, and his word is not in us. 2 ¹My little children, I am writing these things to you so that you may not sin. But if anyone does sin, we have an advocate with the Father, Jesus Christ the righteous. ²He is the propitiation for our sins, and not for ours only but also for the sins of the whole world.	⁵This then is the message which we have heard of him, and declare unto you, that God is light, and in him is no darkness at all. ⁶If we say that we have fellowship with him, and walk in darkness, we lie, and do not the truth: ⁷But if we walk in the light, as he is in the light, we have fellowship one with another, and the blood of Jesus Christ his Son cleanseth us from all sin. ⁸If we say that we have no sin, we deceive ourselves, and the truth is not in us. ⁹If we confess our sins, he is faithful and just to forgive us our sins, and to cleanse us from all unrighteousness, ¹⁰If we say that we have not sinned, we make him a liar, and his word is not in us. 2 ¹My little children, these things write I unto you, that ye sin not. And if any man sin, we have an advocate with the Father, Jesus Christ the righteous: ²And he is the propitiation for our sins: and not for ours only, but also for the sins of the whole world.

Introduction to 1:5–2:2 The first section of John's Letter addresses concerns similar to the overarching theme of 1Pt and 2Pt: believers live in a world that is opposed to them because it is opposed to Christ, a world that is darkness where He is light, a world that is facing imminent judgment as it passes away from its final hour. Under these circumstances, what ought the Christian to believe? How ought the Christian behave? In language tender with familial overtones, John exhorts believers to faith in Jesus Christ, the light of the world, who is God's answer to the darkness of false teachers who have afflicted congregations with teachings opposed to Christ and His apostles. Though Christians live in the world, they have a unique identity, distinct from the world: we are identified by Christ's blood that cleanses us from all sin, a fact that gives us fellowship with God and with each other (1:5–7). The reality of being a sinner exposed to the light leads the believer to confess and receive forgiveness (1:8–10). Though we sin, believers have good news to rely on: Jesus Christ is our advocate, the atoning sacrifice for our sins and the sins of the whole world (2:1–2).

1:5 *This is the message*, says John—here, in regard to who God is, and at 3:11, in regard to what our response to this God is to be (that we should love one another). In the first place: who is this God? What have we seen and heard and touched? John testifies that "the life was made manifest" (v. 2). In his Gospel, he wrote that this "life was the light of men. The light shines in the darkness, and the darkness has not overcome it" (Jn 1:4–5). Here he repeats the sentiment by saying that this is the message heard from *Him*, that is, Jesus, that *God is light, and . . . no darkness at all*. The apostle is not simply offering an abstract dualism. What makes this dichotomy between light and darkness concrete is the Word of God made flesh (Jn 1:14). Light and darkness have to do with God actually breaking into time and space in the incarnation of Christ, a historical moment that renders the world subject to judgment, as Jesus explains to Nicodemus: "And this is the judgment: the light has come into the world, and people loved the darkness rather than the light because their works were evil. For everyone who does wicked things hates the light and does not come to the light, lest his works should be exposed. But whoever does what is true comes to the light, so that it may be clearly seen that his works have been carried out in God" (Jn 3:19–21). When John talks about "light" and "darkness" in this brief section of 1Jn, he is referring to truth and falsehood for the sinner, as much as he is referring to the truth of God. Since Jesus is "the way, the truth, and the life" (Jn 14:6), we can trust that His promises are true, that His intentions are for good and not evil, and that He does not deceive.

1:6 John's repetition of the word *fellowship* (cf. note at v. 3) reminds his readers that the apostle is talking to people in a context, not just as individuals, but as members of a community, the Church. This is inclusive of John himself, other eyewitnesses, and all believers of all times and places. The apostle reminds his readers of the fact with his lively conditional conjunctions through the next many verses: "If *we* say"; "If *we* walk"; "If *we* confess"; etc. First, *if we . . . walk in darkness*, we are not living as children of the light, that is, we are living outside of the truth that has been revealed in Christ. Another word for this is sin. "Walk" is broadly metaphorical here, meaning the same thing as "conduct oneself" (cf. Is 2:5; Jn 12:35). The "walk" reveals the truthfulness of one's claims and confession. The Christian claims God's promise in Baptism and "walks" accordingly: "We were buried therefore with Him by baptism into death, in order that, just as Christ was raised from the dead by the glory of the Father, we too might walk in newness of life" (Rm 6:4; cf. 1 Jn 2:6; 2Jn 6).

1:7 Living in truth, trusting not in lies but only in the blood of Christ that washes away sin, is not to walk in darkness but to *walk in the light*. "Love covers a multitude of sin" (1Pt 4:8; cf. Pr 10:12). Lies that attempt to avoid confession of sins do not help. But fellow Christians who have *fellowship with one another* point to the only cure for sin: *the blood of Jesus*. Covering up our behavior in fear of judgment or with an intent to deceive is the silent heart of hypocrisy. Fellowship in the Church, however, encourages corporate and individual Confession and Absolution, an active sharing in the benefit that Christ's sacrificial, propitiatory, atoning blood has effected for us: His blood *cleanses us from all sin*. His blood alone can do this, for He alone is righteous (2:1); cf. Heb 1:3: "After making purification for sins, He sat down at the right hand of the Majesty on high." We readily confess that Christ's blood has power to forgive sins: the actual blood, dependent again upon the incarnation of Christ. Only the incarnate God could sacrifice Himself for all. The Lutheran reformers wrote:

> The Scriptures speak not merely in general of the Son of Man, but also indicate clearly His received human nature. . . . This is true

not only according to the merit ‹of Christ's blood› that was once attained on the cross. But in this place John means that in the work or act of justification, not only the divine nature in Christ but also His blood actually cleanses us from all sins. (FC SD VIII 59)

1:8 Some Christians, particularly tuned towards an inward striving after a goal of holiness, what they would consider perfection before God in this life, have claimed now and then to have reached a state in which they do not sin anymore. Any framework that suggests the possibility of temporal perfection, however, has become oblivious to the truth of the Christian life, which is lived in a state of being "*simul iustus et peccator*": at the same time sinful and declared righteous. As James reminded his readers (3:2, "we all stumble in many ways"), so John affirms in this memorable phrase: *If we say we have no sin, we deceive ourselves*—and not only so, but *we make Him a liar and His word is not in us* (v. 10)! Even Christians who strive after, and seem to achieve, some sort of victory over any actual sin, do well to remember that sin is far more than actions or omissions of thought, word, or deed that can be defined as our behavior. Sin is a state of being, "sinfulness," the inescapable reality of living in sinful flesh. This is why John articulates the sentence as precisely as he does. He does not say "we claim not to sin" but rather *we say we have no sin* (in Gk, literally "we do not have sin"). Anyone who claims not to have sin is indeed a liar, because sin is our possession, our state of being, our inheritance from Old Adam, our natural inclination, born in us from the beginning of our life (cf. Ps 51:5). The NT does not promote a theology of human perfection or a method of working one's way to holiness; Jesus taught that man's corrupted nature is incapable of doing any good (cf. Jn 6:63; 15:5). Luther commented:

> Although we have become a new creature, nevertheless the remnants of sin always remain in us. We still have sin, and the poison is still in us; and that sin incites us to the fruits of sin, as in the case of David, to whom inherent, encompassing, and indwelling sin said: "Slay Uriah" (cf. 2 Sam. 11:15). David consented and sinned. . . . Although we are Christians sprinkled with the blood of Christ, yet we often err. Therefore the true knowledge of Christ causes a person to feel that he has sin. Furthermore, it causes us to lament this. . . . Finally we should hold most firmly to this, that no one is or becomes righteous before God except through the blood of Jesus Christ. For God alone is righteous, truthful, and wise. Whatever we do out of faith, we should always say: "It is

sin" and "We are unworthy servants," Luke 17:10. But we gain salvation solely because of the righteousness of God, and it is because of this righteousness that we are saved. (LW 30:229)

1:9 The only thing left for the sinner faced with his sinfulness is to agree with God about it: to *confess our sins*. "Come now, let us reason together, says the LORD: though your sins are like scarlet, they shall be as white as snow; though they are red like crimson, they shall become like wool" (Is 1:18). The word "confess" (Gk *homologeō*) means to "same-say," that is, to agree, to say back to God what He has said about Himself and about the sinner. Coming clean before God means agreeing with His righteous judgment: as a lawbreaker and as an inheritor of sin, I am a sinner. And in Christ, I am a saint. God is *faithful and just*: not only is He righteous in all He does (including His condemnation of sin and sinfulness), but He is also trustworthy in regard to His promises and always keeps His Word. People who are "cleansed from all sin" (v. 7) can trust that He will daily *cleanse us* from sin by the all—and always—effective blood of Christ, which cleanses us *from all unrighteousness*. John's joy (v. 4) is our joy. All that we have done, all that we have failed to do; all that we know we have done, all that we are ignorant of; thought, word, deed; the guilt of our sins that looms ever over us to remind us of our sinfulness; even our very sinfulness itself—all is forgiven and washed clean in the blood of Christ.

1:10 "Homology"—the "same-saying" of confession—requires the trust that God speaks true, about Himself and about the sinner. To confess otherwise than that we are without sin makes *him a liar*, in other words, mistrusts what God has spoken true, and arrogates the sinful Adam over the righteous God. God has declared what fallen mankind cannot see: that all have sinned and fallen short of His glory (Rm 3:23). Being in Christ is not a personal choice of the sinner; God places us in Christ by delivering His Word into us. Standing in judgment of the righteous declaration of God about Himself and about the sinner is rejection of that Word, which is why John says that willful unrecognition of our sin means that His *word is not in us*. The Christian is called to abide in Christ for He is the living Word (cf. Jn 5:38; 8:31; 15:4–10). Christ promises to abide in those who abide in Him through faith. The rhythm of "homology," confession, "same-saying," operates on this dwelling with God through the Word that He has delivered, rather than relying on our own words or the opinions of men; God will not abide with lies (Rm 3:4: "Let God be true though every one were a liar"). Luther's thoughts operate on this distinction between what sinful man perceives versus God's perspective: "In the end God will prevail and gain the victory, either here by His goodness or hereafter by His severity. It will do no good to be justified before men or in our own eyes, for we must ignore this and wait with fear to learn what God thinks about it" (LW 14:168).

1:5–10 in Devotion and Prayer Confession and Absolution is a gem, a gift given by our God to assure us of His love, which is why Luther can say, "When I urge you to go to confession, I am simply urging you to be a Christian" (LC, Confession, 32). Like undressing for the doctor, exposing the sore bits, the wounded flesh, the sickness, and describing the symptoms (with all the attendant worry and anxiety), so that the physician can work responsibly, diagnosing and treating the malady, so we offer in confession our symptoms and hear the diagnosis. I have this sin, we say. And we hear back, yes, I've seen this before. I know this disease. It's called sinfulness. What's the prognosis, doc? Bad news. This one's fatal. How long do I have? You're dead as you stand there. Is there then nothing to be done? Here's where the analogy breaks down a bit—rather than a physician who might staunch the wound and give you a few more days, months, or years before he signs the last piece of paper on your medical chart (the death certificate), the dear confessor does one better. He speaks the name of God, the one that was signed on you in your Baptism; he points you to the signature of Christ's death, the cross, that was sealed on you to mark you as one redeemed by Christ the crucified. Our work in confession, revealing, exposing, admitting, coming clean with what's really going on in the sinful body, is answered by God's work: cleaning, healing, curing, ultimately announcing life in the name of Father, Son, and Holy Spirit! Holy Absolution absolves, dissolves, washes away sin in God's Name. It is not based on our work of confession. It is based on the work of the Great Physician of body and soul, the One whose death gives us life, the One whose blood is strong medicine, not effective for only another few months or years, but the medicine of immortality that brings life eternal. • Blessed is the one whose transgression is forgiven, whose sin is covered. Blessed is the man against whom the LORD counts no iniquity, and in whose spirit there is no deceit. For when I kept silent, my bones wasted away through my groaning all day long. For day and night Your hand was heavy upon me; my strength was dried up as by the heat of summer. I acknowledged my sin to You, and I did not cover my iniquity; I said, "I will confess my transgressions to the LORD," and You forgave the iniquity of my sin. Therefore let everyone who is godly offer prayer to You at a time when You may be found; surely in the rush of great waters, they shall not reach him. You are a hiding place for me; You preserve me from trouble; You surround me with shouts of deliverance. Amen. (Ps 32:1–7)

2:1 This is the first place in the Letter that John addresses his readers as *children* (cf. vv. 12–13, 18, 28; 3:1–2, 7, 10, 18; 4:4; 5:2, 21; 2Jn 1, 4, 13; 3Jn 4). Do these references mean John was an old man when he wrote this letter? Even if John was aged (he calls himself "the elder," the name of a church office that might ironically also refer to his age, at 2Jn 1 and 3Jn 1), the relative youth of these "children" is not the primary significance of the word, but rather the relationship established between the apostle and the Church, as all are "born of God" (3:9). The word is tender, indicating John loved these people. The identity extends naturally to members of Christ's Church considering each other as "brothers" (cf. 2:11; 3:10–17; 4:20–21; 5:16; 3Jn 3, 5, 10; also note at Jas 1:2; 1Pt 1:22–23).

In the face of grace, the human response tends to go one of two directions: the route of reception and grateful response on the one hand, or the path of licentiousness on the other. So Paul, after establishing the justification won by Christ's substitutionary sacrifice in Rm 5, picks up Rm 6 by anticipating the path of licentiousness: "What shall we say then? Are we to continue in sin that grace may abound? By no means! How can we who died to sin still live in it?" (Rm 6:1–2). The thrust of John's argument is similar. Believers have been brought out of darkness and into light (1:7). They have put away lies and come to truth (1:8–9). Sinfulness no longer defines the forgiven sinner! And so the apostle tenderly invites these Christians to hear the purpose of his words: *so that you may not sin*. Continuing in sin is not the appropriate response to grace. Nevertheless, Christians are "*simul iustus et peccator*," at the same time sinner and saint. The new identity of "forgiven," given by God for Christ's sake, gives believers the power to say no to sin. Rather than continuing on in darkness and lies, the Gospel motivates God's children to good works, to mutual love (vv. 7–14). The thought that follows is framed as a general condition: *if anyone does sin* should be read as "when anybody sins," or "whenever anyone sins." The good news is that in spite of the general, predictable condition (the fallen state of sinful man which will, in fact, result in actual sins), we have an *advocate* (Gk *paraklētos*, brought into English as "Paraclete"). We are used to thinking about the Holy Spirit when we hear the term "Paraclete," which literally means "encourager," or "comforter," but in this context, the word can also mean legal assistant or defender. As mediator between God and man (cf. 1Tm 2:5), Jesus is our intercessor, constantly representing us before God, making His plea on our behalf with evidence that guarantees our pardon in God's court of justice: His very death and resurrection, His blood shed on our behalf, which gives Jesus the title of *righteous* one. As the psalmist sang, "Call upon Me in the day of trouble; I will deliver you, and you shall glorify Me" (Ps 50:15). Melancthon wrote: "This is the worship that He approves above all other worship, that He be called upon in all afflictions" (AC XXI 3). Christ is the righteous advocate whom we call upon, as Luther commented:

> He is righteous and unstained. He is without sin. Whatever righteousness I have, this my Comforter has, He who cries out for me to the Father: "Spare him, and he has been spared! Forgive him! Help him!" The righteousness of Jesus Christ is standing on our side. For the righteousness of God in Him is ours. . . . This text should be written with golden letters and should be painted in the heart. Therefore you should get understanding and say: "Christ, I know Thee alone as the Advocate, the Comforter, and the Mediator; and I do not doubt that Thou art such a Person for me but cling firmly to this with my heart and believe." (LW 30:236)

2:2 The power of Confession and Absolution, of the blood of Christ that forgives sins (1:7), is not a feeling, not the emotions, not the relief of a burden shared or eliminated. The power of God's holy act of removing our sins is Christ Himself, *the propitiation*. Christ made sacrificial satisfaction for the demands of God's Law. Jesus actively fulfilled God's demands of perfect obedience; Jesus passively suffered in perfect payment for sins. In his active and passive obedience, in living a perfect life and in dying a perfect death, Jesus became the reconciliation of God and man. All who trust in Jesus' sacrificial work are justified before God, as Paul argues at Rm 3:25–26: "God put [Jesus] forward as a propitiation by His blood, to be received by faith. This was to show God's righteousness, because in His divine forbearance He had passed over former sins. It was to show His righteousness at the present time, so that He might be just and the justifier of the one who has faith in Jesus." This atonement is not selectively apportioned only for a group that God elected beforehand, willing others to destruction (cf. 1Tm 2:4; 2Pt 3:9), but is a universal atonement. Christ is the propitiatory sacrifice *for the sins of the whole world*. The objective fact of Christ making complete satisfaction for the sins of all mankind, from the beginning of the world to the Last Day, is what Christians of the Reformation refer to as "objective justification," distinguishing Christ's work from the terrible reality that not all people receive the benefits of His work in faith. This teaching of objection justification is a doctrine of comfort. Luther taught that Christ "does not sit at the right hand of the Father to terrify us, but He is the expiation. . . . Christ, who does not spurn a contrite and humble heart, wants to be the Lord and Author of life, not of sin" (LW 30:236–37). To go beyond this and conclude on the other hand that since not all are saved there is a capriciousness in God, that is, to assume that He must have predestined His creation to eternal damnation, flies in the face of clear Scriptures that teach that Jesus came in order to "taste death for everyone" (Heb 2:9)—even for those who reject Him, "denying the Master who bought them" (2Pt 2:1).

Because the True Light Is Already Shining (2:3–11)

ESV	KJV
[3]And by this we know that we have come to know him, if we keep his commandments. [4]Whoever says "I know him" but does not keep his commandments is a liar, and the truth is not in him, [5]but whoever keeps his word, in him truly the love of God is perfected. By this we may know that we are in him: [6]whoever says he abides in him ought to walk in the same way in which he walked. [7]Beloved, I am writing you no new commandment, but an old commandment that you had from the beginning. The old commandment is	[3]And hereby we do know that we know him, if we keep his commandments. [4]He that saith, I know him, and keepeth not his commandments, is a liar, and the truth is not in him. [5]But whoso keepeth his word, in him verily is the love of God perfected: hereby know we that we are in him. [6]He that saith he abideth in him ought himself also so to walk, even as he walked. [7]Brethren, I write no new commandment unto you, but an old

the word that you have heard. ⁸At the same time, it is a new commandment that I am writing to you, which is true in him and in you, because the darkness is passing away and the true light is already shining. ⁹Whoever says he is in the light and hates his brother is still in darkness. ¹⁰Whoever loves his brother abides in the light, and in him there is no cause for stumbling. ¹¹But whoever hates his brother is in the darkness and walks in the darkness, and does not know where he is going, because the darkness has blinded his eyes.

commandment which ye had from the beginning. The old commandment is the word which ye have heard from the beginning.

⁸Again, a new commandment I write unto you, which thing is true in him and in you: because the darkness is past, and the true light now shineth.

⁹He that saith he is in the light, and hateth his brother, is in darkness even until now.

¹⁰He that loveth his brother abideth in the light, and there is none occasion of stumbling in him.

¹¹But he that hateth his brother is in darkness, and walketh in darkness, and knoweth not whither he goeth, because that darkness hath blinded his eyes.

Introduction to 2:3–11 Confession and Absolution, forgiveness, propitiation: this is what defines the identity of John's readers. He can call them "little children," "brothers," (cf. note at v. 1) and "beloved" (v. 7), because Jesus' propitiation for sins and His perpetual advocacy for sinners (v. 2) draw us through God's love to an identity in Him: those who trust in Jesus for forgiveness of sins are not defined by sins anymore, but by relationship with Him who is the Light of the World (cf. note at 1:5). Christian action, good works, do not define our identity. God defines our identity in the blood of His Son, Jesus (1:7). But identity does translate into action. And action does reveal identity. John's argument through the next several verses outlines this Christian life as one that freely keeps God's Commandments. John proceeds by saying that walking in His Commandments shows the truth that we know Him (vv. 3–4), and that this reveals that God's love is being fulfilled in our life (v. 5). Christian behavior reveals that we are "in Christ" (v. 6). John's teaching is nothing new—his readers have known it from the beginning (v. 7)—but it is new because Christ the Light has come (v. 8). Therefore Christians walk not in darkness (which is hatred of the brother) but in the light of Christ (vv. 9–11).

2:3 God's *commandments* are not burdensome (5:3), because Christ's teaching (Jn 13:34) is based on the Gospel, not on condemnation. John here introduces an important truth: the Law does not motivate to action—in fact, it never provided the power to fulfill the things demanded of God's people (cf. Rm 3:20; Gal 2:16)! Rather, the Gospel of God's mercy in Christ motivates to holy action. Believers engage in holy action enlightened by the Light of the World. Cranmer wrote:

> All holy Scripture agreeably beareth witness, that a true lively faith in Christ doth bring forth good works; and therefore every man must examine himself diligently, to know whether he have the same true lively faith in his heart unfeignedly, or not; which he shall know by the fruits thereof. Many that professed the faith of Christ were in this error, that they thought they knew God and believed in him, when in their life they declared the contrary: which error St. John in his first Epistle confute[s]. (Cranmer 2:157–58)

2:4–5 Knowing or not knowing Christ, abiding in the truth or relying on lies—John's dualisms are on display through this section of his Letter. Keeping God's Commandments does not define the identity of believers, but it does reveal it; when one's living does not flow from love, it disproves all claims of knowing Jesus, who is God's very expression of love and truth.

2:5 When Christians read the word *perfected* in the Scriptures, they may be tempted to think of it as a challenge, that is, to interpret what John is saying here to mean "keeping God's Commandments pleases God." It is better to remember that words like "completion" and "perfection" have their root in the Gk word *telos* (literally "goal," "end"), and that the work of Christ was revealed to come to its completion in His final word from the cross: "It is finished" (Jn 19:30, Gk *tetelestai*). Rather than thinking that *the love of God is perfected* depending on our will, ability, and achievement in keeping His laws, John is encouraging his readers to understand that loving God is the goal of Christian life. Christians demonstrate this love, indeed can reflect that God's love has come to them as a finishing work, a completing work, in them, as their behavior reveals them to be God's own children. Do you love God? You will love His children. This is why we pray "forgive us our sins": "For if you forgive others their trespasses, your heavenly Father will also forgive you, but if you do

275

not forgive others their trespasses, neither will your Father forgive your trespasses" (Mt 6:14–15).

2:6 "In Christ" is the most important prepositional phrase for a sinner to remember. And John reinforces this with his description of Christian behavior. The one who *abides in* Christ is the one who has been brought into Christ by God. God works faith by giving us new birth in water and the Word of Christ. God works faith by proclaiming His Word and applying it to the sinner in many forms. God works faith, that it be no work of ours, but solely of God (Eph 2:8–9). As we trust "in Christ," we remain "in Christ," again, solely by God's grace. He gives us a word to trust, every day (cf. Jn 6:56: "Whoever feeds on My flesh and drinks My blood abides in Me, and I in him"; to which we confess with Peter the words of Jn 6:68–69: "Lord, to whom shall we go? You have the words of eternal life, and we have believed, and have come to know, that You are the Holy One of God"). John describes Christian conduct as walking *in the same way in which He walked*: as He has forgiven us, so we forgive others. As He has loved us, so we in turn show His love to others—this is what it means to say that His love has reached its goal in us (v. 5; cf. 1:7).

2:1–6 in Devotion and Prayer The Bible has some pretty big words in it. Words like "righteousness," "justification," and "sanctification" just scratch the surface, as we think of very big words in the KJV like "lovingkindnesses" (Ps 25:6) and "covenantbreakers" (Rm 1:31). In the original languages, there is some daunting diction like the Gk *prokekheirotonēmenos* ("chosen ones," Ac 10:41), not to mention some of the gargantuan names in Hbr like Mephibosheth (2Sam 4:4) and Maher-shalal-hash-baz (Is 8:1). But sometimes the biggest truths come in small packages. Little words like "but" are important, and we do well to sit confidently on the "big buts" of the Bible, like the one in the middle of Eph 2:3–5: we were children of wrath, "*but* God, being rich in mercy . . . made us alive together with Christ"! Just such a significant "little word" of the Bible is the word *in*. There is a significant truth in this small package. "*In* the beginning, God created the heavens and the earth" (Gn 1:1). "*In* the beginning was the Word" (Jn 1:1). Certainly significant, but more important by far is recalling that this same Word of God, Jesus Christ, has come to save you from sins "*in* which you acted" (Ezk 16:52), "*in* which you once walked" (Eph 2:2). Christ has now become the "messenger of the covenant *in* whom you delight" (Mal 3:1), because He is the one who died and rose again to forgive your sins. Now there is nothing *in* all creation that can separate us from God (Rm 8:38–39), because there is "now no condemnation for those who are *in* Christ Jesus" (Rm 8:1). Abide here, Christian. Abide *in Christ—in* His wounds, His open arms. His heart is open. He calls us not to live "with" Him, "beside" Him, owning Him as nothing more than companion, comrade, or copilot, but to abide *in* Him: "Therefore, if anyone is *in* Christ, he is a new creation. The old has passed away; behold, the new has come" (2Cor 5:17)! • From the state of sin, Lord, set me free, and move me to a new state, a new life, a new place in which to abide. Your cross has established a border between death and life, Lord Jesus. Move me across that border to dwell in life, to establish my citizenship in You. And while in residence here in this world, grant me the grace to live in the shadow of Your cross: "When I tread the verge of Jordan, Bid my anxious fears subside; Death of death and hell's destruction, Land me safe on Canaan's side. Songs of praises, songs of praises I will ever give to Thee." Amen. (*LSB* 918:3; *H82* 690:3; *TPH* 281:3; *TUMH* 127:3).

2:7 John's teaching is nothing new—his readers have known it from the beginning (cf. 1:1), which is why he can say that this is *no new commandment*. The same Word that gave us salvation, the very Word of God, Jesus Christ, gives us His words, which testify of Him (Jn 5:39). At the same time, the commands to which John refers are the "new command" that Jesus laid down for His disciples: "A new commandment I give to you, that you love one another: just as I have loved you, you also are to love one another. By this all people will know that you are My disciples, if you have love for one another" (Jn 13:34–35). John associates this with the eschatological hope of Christ's presence. The light of the world has come! This means the darkness is already passing away. Since this is the case, Christians are to work, knowing their deeds are seen by the light of Christ. Cf. Jn 9:4–5: "We must work the works of Him who sent me while it is day; night is coming, when no one can work. As long as I am in the world, I am the light of the world." The command all God's people have, from the source of their relationship with Him, established by being born of God, is to love one another (Lv 19:18; Jn 13:34).

2:8 This "old commandment" takes on new significance as it is fulfilled in Christ, someone who demonstrated true love for His neighbor: "This is My commandment, that you love one another as I have loved you. Greater love has no one than this, that someone lay down his life for his friends" (Jn 15:12–13); "God shows His love for us in that while we were still sinners, Christ died for us" (Rm 5:8). This is why John can at the same time call this exhortation to love one another *a new commandment*. God fulfills His love in Christians, that is, brings it to completion (cf. v. 5), by connecting this love of neighbor in Christ to the believer; this love for neighbor is *true in Him and in you*. This happens as the Gospel motivates the believer to actions in love for the neighbor, the love of Christ at work in the believer. Such Christian behavior is motivated also by knowing that the Last Day is at hand: *the darkness* and *the true light* are opposites in John's Gospel and letters. They define the world that Christians live in too. Though living in a world of darkness, Christians know that it is passing away; in the meantime we live in the light of Christ, which He applies to us tangibly through Word and Sacrament. Bengel wrote, "In Christ as things are always true, and were so from the beginning; but in Christ and in us, conjointly, the precept is then truth, when we acknowledge the truth, which is in Him, and have the same flourishing in us" (Bengel 117).

2:9–11 Like "darkness" and "light," "hate" and "love" are opposites that John employs as poles that reveal Christian identity. John calls Christians to love instead of hatred. So what does Christian love mean? What does it look like? It's common to hear platitudes in church like "Hate the sin but love the sinner." But other Scriptures paint a rather more uncomfortable picture: "You [God] hate all evildoers" (Ps 5:4–6). God is somehow able to hate the evildoer while also longing for his salvation (Jn 3:16; 2Pt 3:9). How then are Christians called to love? First, love is not toleration of evil behavior. Anyone who calls sin righteousness or vice versa is not acting "in Christ" (1:8–10; cf. 1Cor 5:4–8). Second, love and hatred are far more than emotions; they are actions motivated by God's own actions on behalf of sinners (cf. Rm 5:6–11). Love motivated by Christ's righteousness rather than self-righteousness results not in hatred for the brother, but in love that seeks to save his soul (cf. Mt 18:14–15). Love must prevail over hatred, because God has called us to the same family of believers, in which we regard the neighbor as *brother* (cf. note at v. 1). John's analogy to blindness and stumbling reflects Jesus' words found in his Gospel narrative: "If anyone walks in the day, he does not stumble, because he sees the light of this world" (Jn 11:9). The point of the analogy Jesus draws for His disciples is to trust in the works of the one who is the Resurrection and the Life, the one who would in a short time raise Lazarus from the dead. "See how He loved him!" say the Jews who saw Jesus weep (Jn 11:36). This kind of love—the kind that seeks life instead of death, indeed salvation instead of sin!—is the kind of love that John calls believers to in this Letter. John and the rest of the disciples did not immediately understand it (cf. Jn 11:8–16), but John understands it now and exhorts his readers not to act in blindness, darkness, hatred, and stumbling, but to show God's love by loving each other.

Because the World Is Passing Away (2:12–17)

ESV	KJV

12I am writing to you, little children,
    because your sins are forgiven for his name's sake.
13I am writing to you, fathers,
    because you know him who is from the beginning.
I am writing to you, young men,
    because you have overcome the evil one.
I write to you, children,
    because you know the Father.
14I write to you, fathers,
    because you know him who is from the beginning.
I write to you, young men,
    because you are strong,
    and the word of God abides in you,
    and you have overcome the evil one.
 	
15Do not love the world or the things in the world. If anyone loves the world, the love of the Father is not in him. 16For all that is in the world—the desires of the flesh and the desires of the eyes and pride of life—is not
	12I write unto you, little children, because your sins are forgiven you for his name's sake.
	13I write unto you, fathers, because ye have known him that is from the beginning. I write unto you, young men, because ye have overcome the wicked one. I write unto you, little children, because ye have known the Father.
	14I have written unto you, fathers, because ye have known him that is from the beginning. I have written unto you, young men, because ye are strong, and the word of God abideth in you, and ye have overcome the wicked one.
	15Love not the world, neither the things that are in the world. If any man love the world, the love of the Father is not in him.
	16For all that is in the world, the lust of the flesh, and the lust of the eyes, and the pride of life, is not of the Father, but is of the world.
	17And the world passeth away, and the lust thereof: but he that doeth the will of God abideth for ever.

from the Father but is from the world. ¹⁷And the world is passing away along with its desires, but whoever does the will of God abides forever.

Introduction to 2:12–17 God's people are in the world, but not of it. Though they are in the world, they are "in" Christ—abiding in His Word. This world is passing away (cf. v. 8), and so John encourages his readers in this section to consider it dead, an enemy of the Christian. He begins with a poetic exhortation to all members of God's family, children, fathers, youngsters (vv. 12–14). John continues with a defense against the world: the love of the world is opposed to love of the Father (v. 15), because the world is the location of desires contrary to the Father's (v. 16). Echoing Is 40:6–8, John concludes the section with a reminder that the world is passing away, but not so those who do God's will (v. 17).

2:12 John celebrates the Church as the family of God in this section. As at v. 1, John calls the believers *little children*, referring not only to the youth of his readers, but also to the relative maturity of those who enter God's kingdom, who receive it "as little children" (cf. Mt 18:4; Mk 10:15; Lk 18:17). Children rely on Christ for their sufficiency, depending on forgiveness that they know comes only from God; John reminds them that their *sins are forgiven for His name's sake*, echoing the divine truths of Christ's universal atonement (cf. v. 2) and its application to the believer in Holy Absolution (cf. 1:8–10).

2:13–14 Again, perhaps not simply referring to status of age and relative maturity, but also to function or roles in the Church, John reminds *fathers*, that is, teachers and leaders in the Church, of the blessing they possess, in that they *know Him who is from the beginning* (cf. 1:1). *Young men* constitute a third category in John's poetic excursus, and their blessing reminds them of their victory over Satan through faith in Christ. We probably do well not to read too much into these categories of people in the family of God, particularly as we come to the "young men"; the word that John employs may well have been chosen for its poetic punning power, as the word for "young men" (Gk *neaniskoi*) shares sounds with the word for *you have overcome* (Gk *nenikēkate*). John essentially repeats vv. 12–13a in vv. 13b–14, underscoring the significance of the blessings God's family possesses. The crescendo of blessings climaxes in the final verse, reinforcing his love for them as a fellow member of God's family.

2:7–14 in Devotion and Prayer Since the end of the nineteenth century, the *Nike of Samothrace* has been standing in the Louvre. Sculpted in the second century BC, the statue is an 8-foot tall representation of the winged goddess Victory, originally erected to celebrate a naval conquest, won by the Greek state of Rhodes. It is a celebrated sculpture—rightly so, as its masterful form and interplay between marble and empty space represents supernatural power struggling against sea and wind and other invisible forces in a way seldom paralleled in ancient art. Its discovery has won the acclaim of critics and the imitation of modern artists, imprinting "Nike" on the collective consciousness of the Western world in a way more beautiful and artistic than any "swoosh" on a brand of shoes. But for all of its artistic mastery, the *Nike of Samothrace* lacks something. Actually a few things. It has no arms. It has no head. It may be made of expensive marble and it may stand in the most famous museum of Europe, but it lacks its original limbs, its original glory, and most of all, it lacks life. "I am writing to you, young men, because you have overcome the evil one" (1Jn 2:13)—because you have the victory (Gk *nikē*). And this is no incomplete victory: it is the victory that has conquered all the Christian's enemies, swallowing up sin, death, and the devil (1Cor 15:54–57). And this victory has a head: Jesus Christ, the Righteous One. "For everyone who has been born of God overcomes the world. And this is the victory that has overcome the world—our faith" (1Jn 5:4). Trust in the Lord Jesus, who gives us a living victory!

• "In all these things we are more than conquerors through Him who loved us. For I am sure that neither death nor life, nor angels nor rulers, nor things present nor things to come, nor powers, nor height nor depth, nor anything else in all creation, will be able to separate us from the love of God in Christ Jesus our Lord" (Rm 8:37–39). Amen.

2:15 Christians live in the world, but they are not to *love the world*. That kind of affection is reserved for things of God, not for the ephemeral *things* of this earthly life (cf. Jn 1:10; 3:16). John forges a picture of an exclusive dichotomy here: the one who is filled with love of the world has no room for *love of the Father*; it *is not in him*. A love that drives towards "completion" and "perfection" (cf. 2:5) is hindered from its goal when distracted by the love of the world, which is passing away.

2:16 The world is an enemy of the Christian because it distracts believers from God's will, offering in its place the *desires of the flesh and the desires of the eyes* and *pride of life*. "At the same time sinner and saint," our sinful human nature yet clings to us and is tempted by the fleeting things of this world that make empty promises to satisfy our material, emotional, and spiritual needs. Lust, covetousness, selfishness, greed: all the itches our fallen nature suffers can be scratched with the things of this world. But such answers are ultimately dissatisfying, such security as the world might promise always ends up being false. The fallen sinful nature finds false security in wealth and is proud of accumulated possessions (the *pride of life* in this passage, which can also be translated "pride in possessions"), which show off that wealth (cf. Gn 3:6). This "pride" (Gk *alazoneia*) is referred to by John with a word that never means something honorable (like "taking pride in a job well done"), but rather means something empty, better understood as "conceit," "empty babble," or old Ebenezer Scrooge's word, which we could use more often in a context like this: "humbug." Such love does not endure, is not true, and will pass away, because such things are *not from the Father*. God is never the source of our temptations, and He's certainly not the source of sins or sinful desires (cf. Jas 1:13–15), as Luther taught:

> First, the lust of the flesh must be overcome, and this is done more easily. Second, and this is more difficult, the lust of the eyes, for it cannot be deserted all at once, like the first, but it fails gradually. Finally, the most difficult is the pride of life. It, too, is born of victory over vices. Therefore this is not overcome, though it be left desolate or fail, unless it perish altogether because of its iniquity. It is the most harmful kind of vice which unjustly divides between God's glory and self-confusion. (LW 10:429)

2:17 John echoes Is 40:6–8 here: "The grass withers, the flower fades. . . . but the word of our God will stand forever" (Is 40:8). Applied to the believer, it is not just God's Word that stands forever, but also those who have that Word applied to them, and who live through that "new command" by loving God, loving the neighbor, and not loving the world. After all, the world is *passing away* (cf. v. 8), but those who do the *will of God* live forever. This is not a call to trust in human works or a sinner's ability to save himself; rather

God's will is that "everyone who looks on the Son and believes in Him should have eternal life, and I will raise him up on the last day" (Jn 6:40). The one who is given eternal life like this *abides forever* with God, in a resurrection life starting now (cf. Rm 6:5) and continuing on to eternity where God will dwell with man in the resurrection of the flesh (cf. 1Cor 15:42–49).

2:15–17 in Devotion and Prayer This word "humbug" that describes the "boasting of possessions" in 1Jn 2:16 has popular play not only in the mouth of Dickens' Ebenezer, but also in that of L. Frank Baum's poor Wizard, who attempts to scare Dorothy and her friends the Scarecrow, the Tin-Man, and the Cowardly Lion. After warning the friends not to "pay any attention to that man behind the curtain," they discover that "Oz, the Great and Terrible!" is no more than a simple old man from Omaha, whose bluster is as much hot wind as was in the balloon that transported him to the Emerald City. False pretenses have been discovered, and he acknowledges that he's a fraud, an imposter, just a "humbug." This world with its lusts, its desires, its false boasting, can do some real damage. But Christians are called to see that there is a promise more real than the false pretenses and humbug of this world. We are called to pay attention not to the flattery, flash, and false promises of this world, but rather "to pay attention to the Man" who has passed through the curtain (Mt 27:51; Mk 15:38; Lk 23:45; Heb 6:19), to trust rather in the Man who has given us "confidence to enter the holy places by the blood of Jesus, by the new and living way that He opened for us through the curtain, that is, through His flesh" (Heb 10:19–20). In this Man we find not fraud but fact, not deception but a deliverer, and finally no "humbug" but a human, a real Jesus whose real promise and real presence brings us to an eternal reality in Him. • Dear Father in heaven, since we have a great priest over the house of God, Your Son, Jesus, grant us grace that we may draw near with a true heart, in full assurance of faith, with our hearts sprinkled clean from an evil conscience and our bodies washed with pure water. Grant us grace that we hold fast the confession of our hope without wavering, since You are faithful to Your promise. And grant us grace not to neglect meeting together, but to encourage one another, and all the more as You show us that the Day is drawing near. Amen.

Because It Is the Last Hour (2:18–29)

ESV	KJV
¹⁸Children, it is the last hour, and as you have heard that antichrist is coming, so now many antichrists have come. Therefore we know that it is the last hour. ¹⁹They went out from us, but they were not of us; for if they had been of us, they would have continued with us. But they went out, that it might become plain that they all are not of us. ²⁰But you have been anointed by the Holy One, and you all have knowledge. ²¹I write to you, not because you do not know the truth, but because you know it, and because no lie is of the truth. ²²Who is the liar but he who denies that Jesus is the Christ? This is the antichrist, he who denies the Father and the Son. ²³No one who denies the Son has the Father. Whoever confesses the Son has the Father also. ²⁴Let what you heard from the beginning abide in you. If what you heard from the beginning abides in you, then you too will abide in the Son and in the Father. ²⁵And this is the promise that he made to us—eternal life.	¹⁸Little children, it is the last time: and as ye have heard that antichrist shall come, even now are there many antichrists; whereby we know that it is the last time. ¹⁹They went out from us, but they were not of us; for if they had been of us, they would no doubt have continued with us: but they went out, that they might be made manifest that they were not all of us. ²⁰But ye have an unction from the Holy One, and ye know all things. ²¹I have not written unto you because ye know not the truth, but because ye know it, and that no lie is of the truth. ²²Who is a liar but he that denieth that Jesus is the Christ? He is antichrist, that denieth the Father and the Son. ²³Whosoever denieth the Son, the same hath not the Father: he that acknowledgeth the Son hath the Father also. ²⁴Let that therefore abide in you, which ye have heard from the beginning. If that which ye have heard from the beginning shall remain in you, ye also shall continue in the Son, and in the Father. ²⁵And this is the promise that he hath promised us, even eternal life.
²⁶I write these things to you about those who are trying to deceive you. ²⁷But the anointing that you received from him abides in you, and you have no need that anyone should teach you. But as his anointing teaches you about everything, and is true, and is no lie—just as it has taught you, abide in him. ²⁸And now, little children, abide in him, so that when he appears we may have confidence and not shrink from him in shame at his coming. ²⁹If you	²⁶These things have I written unto you concerning them that seduce you. ²⁷But the anointing which ye have received of him abideth in you, and ye need not that any man teach you: but as the same anointing teacheth

know that he is righteous, you may be sure that everyone who practices righteousness has been born of him.

you of all things, and is truth, and is no lie, and even as it hath taught you, ye shall abide in him.

²⁸And now, little children, abide in him; that, when he shall appear, we may have confidence, and not be ashamed before him at his coming. ²⁹If ye know that he is righteous, ye know that every one that doeth righteousness is born of him.

Introduction to 2:18–29 Christ is coming back; His return is imminent. This eschatological hope prompts John to warn his readers that the antichrist is also coming (v. 18). In fact, the antichrist has already come: false teachers who have pretended to be a part of the Christian community but in fact are distinct from the family of God (v. 19). John's readers know how to discern the truth and lies because of their anointing from God, which is John's word for the teaching of the apostles (vv. 20–21). The truth to which John refers is the identification of Jesus as Christ (v. 22). This has everything to do with the Trinitarian understanding of God: without the Son it is impossible to know the Father (vv. 23–24) and to have eternal life (v. 25). The true teaching of the apostles is the anointing that defines the Christian community in the face of false teaching (vv. 26–27), and it reveals itself in abiding in Christ and working righteousness (vv. 28–29).

2:18 John reminds his readers that Christ's second coming is near, proclaiming that it is the *last hour* (cf. Ac 2:17; Heb 1:2). Calvin wrote:

> But so many ages having passed away since the death of John, seem to prove that this prophecy is not true: to this I answer, that the Apostle, according to the common mode adopted in the Scripture, declares to the faithful, that nothing more now remained but that Christ should appear for the redemption of the world. But as he fixes no time, he did not allure the men of that age by a vain hope, nor did he intend to cut short in future the course of the Church and the many successions of years during which the Church has hitherto remained in the world. And doubtless, if the eternity of God's kingdom be borne in mind, so long

a time will appear to us as a moment. We must understand the design of the Apostle, that he calls that the last time, during which all things shall be so completed, that nothing will remain except the last revelation of Christ. (Calvin 189)

As James and Peter had to deal with false teachers (cf. Jas 3:1–5, 13–16; 2Pt 2:1), so John also warns his readers that they *have heard* about the appearance of false teachers who speak by the spirit of the antichrist (cf. 1Jn 4:3). Such false teachers, false shepherds, and false prophets originate from the source of their teaching—the father of lies, the devil (Jn 8:44). The appearance of these false teachers, whom John calls *many antichrists*, sets the stage for the coming of "the Antichrist," who will arise from within Christendom (2Th 2:1–11; cf. Rv 13). *Antichrist* means "instead of Christ" or "in place of Christ." As there are *many antichrists*, John is indicating that there are as many different antichrists as there are different ways of opposing Christ. One false teaching about Jesus is that He is not actually the Christ as the apostles have taught.

2:19 John insists that though the false teacher may talk about Jesus, *they*, the antichrists, are not teaching the same things as the apostles have taught. This, in spite of the fact that they *went out from us*. Though claiming authority to teach about Jesus, they in fact have separated themselves from the Christian Church (cf. 2Jn 7–11). John protests that *they all are not of us*. The issue that John and his readers face is an important reminder for Christians of all times and places: not everyone who claims to be a Christian really is a Christian. This is most significant when doctrine is at stake. God is at work in the Church even in the midst of divisions regarding doctrine, and believers can rely on His continuing care for His flock even in the midst of false teachers who would divide Christ's Church (cf. 1Cor 11:19: "there must be factions among you in order that those who are genuine among you may be recognized"). What do believers look to when disagreements over doctrine arise? John's teaching points to the self-exclusion of the false teachers: *they went out*. He expands his thoughts in later verses to indicate more specific differences between apostolic teaching and the teaching of the false teachers, namely, Jesus' identity as the Christ, the Son of God, and the Father's relationship with Him (cf. vv. 22–23). If Christians face doctrinal division in the Church, those who cling to Christ's Word and teaching prove themselves to be genuine believers (cf. 1Cor 12:2–3).

2:20–25 This section of John's Letter is an apostolic apologetic (or defense) for a Trinitarian understanding of God. The need for such a defense is just as significant today in the Christian Church as it was in the first several centuries of the early Church. God is one and reveals Himself in three Persons: Father, Son, and Holy Spirit. This is the orthodox, apostolic faith: "one Lord, one faith, one baptism, one God and Father of all" (Eph 4:5–6); it is therefore necessary for salvation to believe what God's Word teaches concerning the Father, the Son, and the Spirit. One cannot have the Father without holding to the Son and also to the Spirit. This truth is confessed in the three Ecumenical Creeds, which is one of the reasons why most Christians confess one of the Creeds in worship each week.

2:20 Believers are *anointed* with God's Holy Spirit at Baptism (cf. Jn 3:5), even as Jesus is the "anointed one" (which is what "Christ" means), anointed with the Holy Spirit at His Baptism (cf. Ac 10:38; Jn 1:32–33). God baptizes sinners into His Son's death with the Word of God that is His name: Father, Son, and Holy Spirit. This Word of our Baptism, the name of *the Holy One*, Jesus Christ (cf. Ac 2:38), is a strong teaching, giving believers *knowledge* (cf. note at 2Pt 1:2), the rich gift of knowing God in Christ (cf. 1:1–4).

2:21 Knowing *the truth* defines believers who have been baptized into God as He has revealed Himself in Christ, and who have been taught all things which Christ commanded to be taught, namely His Gospel; cf. Mt 28:19.20: "Go therefore and make disciples of all nations, baptizing them in the name of the Father and of the Son and of the Holy Spirit, teaching them to observe all that I have commanded you. And behold, I am with you always, to the end of the age." The baptizing and teaching ministry of the apostles is baptizing and teaching into the Word of Christ, and it is that Word that gives Christians the ability to distinguish the truth from false teaching (cf. 1Cor 12:2–3).

2:22 The one who denies that Jesus is Christ is the one *who is the liar*; failing to recognize Christ as God's Son is the failing of all who follow their "father the devil" (cf. Jn 8:44). Plenty of heresies accept various confessions of Christian faith, but fail to acknowledge one or more parts of God's revealed truth in the Gospel. *He who denies that Jesus is the Christ* is such a one, who denies what Christians like John and his readers had themselves seen and had been taught by Christ Himself: that Jesus Christ was born, lived, died, bodily rose, and physically ascended to the right hand of God the Father as the Son of Man and the Son of God.

2:23 "In Christ" is the most important prepositional phrase for a sinner to remember (cf. note at 2:6). Some might teach that Christ is unnecessary or insufficient for a relationship with a transcendent God. John reminds his readers that no one knows God except for knowing Him "in Christ." Some might teach that understanding God in terms of human relationship is to deny His transcendence. John insists that understanding God is understanding Him "in Christ." Some might teach that to talk about a Son and a Father somehow subordinates Jesus' status. In spite of all questions or other theories, John maintains that *no one who denies the Son has the Father*. It is all "in Christ." One cannot have the Father except through the Son and by the Spirit, and therefore the one who confesses the truth about God *confesses the Son*. And lest anyone think this is simply doctrine with no application, John's understanding of this truth has abundant import: the fellowship shared between Father and Son is the fellowship believers also share with God and with one another through the Son, "in Christ" (cf. 1:3).

2:24 "Abiding," "remaining" in Christ is what He calls all His disciples to do; cf. Jn 15:7–10: "If you abide in Me, and My words abide in you, ask whatever you wish, and it will be done for you. By this My Father is glorified, that you bear much fruit and so prove to be My disciples. As the Father has loved Me, so have I loved you. Abide in My love. If you keep My commandments, you will abide in My love, just as I have kept My Father's commandments and abide in His love." John's teaching in the Letter is consistent with Christ's teaching in his Gospel. His readers have known Christ *from the beginning*—it is not simply a narrative that abides in them, but the very Person of Jesus Christ (cf. 1:1; 2:7, 13–14; 3:11).

2:25 God has given *us*, all who believe in Jesus Christ, the promise of eternal life; cf. Jn 17:2–3: "You have given Him authority over all flesh, to give eternal life to all whom You have given Him. And this is eternal life, that they know You the only true God, and Jesus Christ whom You have sent."

2:26–27 John calls the false teachers *those who are trying to deceive you*. His readers, however, possess the *anointing* of the Holy Spirit (cf. v. 20), rich with the teaching about Christ, located in the Word of His name, and therefore have *no need* of false teachers, who deny God the Father by denying His Son. The sufficient teaching and warning from John is as it has been throughout the Letter: *abide* in Christ!

2:18–27 in Devotion and Prayer Which Jesus do you want? There are, after all, lots of Jesuses out there to devote yourself to. Do you prefer the teacher Jesus, the ethical instructor, the bearded-Buddha-in-Birkenstocks who simply offers his philosophical followers a route to reduce their suffering? How about the soft, tolerant Jesus who thinks like you, would vote like you, and simply opens his arms to embrace whatever evil you want to excuse, whose mantra is "judge not" and, turning a blind eye to the unwholesome, simply joins you in your "enlightened" opinions? Some may prefer the crusader Jesus, who spurs you to action for whatever social ill you want to eradicate or whatever political platform you want to support. Do you favor the god Jesus who gets you out of binds whenever you pray in his magical name, or do you favor the human Jesus who may have been a nice guy and all, but whose "miracles" were probably overly exaggerated by his followers? Will, finally, the Real Jesus please stand up? The fact, the reality, the very palpable wall of history that gets crashed into by all who look for the real Jesus is that He is none of these. He is, in fact, as His apostles confessed, "the Christ, the Son of the living God" (Mt 16:16). This is a Jesus who is bound to please none of the people none of the time—that God would be conceived by a virgin, born a man, suffer, and die is simply scandalous. But this is the real Jesus. That He would be not just human, but divine, ascribing to Himself titles, powers, authority, the very name of God Himself, this also is simply scandalous. But this is the real Jesus. In the final evaluation, it is no wonder that false teachers have abounded since the beginning of the Christian Church, because this scandalous teaching, "This is a hard saying; who can listen to it?" (Jn 6:60). Thank God the final decision does not rest on figuring out which Jesus to devote myself to. Thank God the final decision rests on Jesus Himself devoting Himself to me. Because it is this Jesus, the One who died and rose again, the divine One, the human One, the Savior, the One who laid down His life for me (1Jn 3:16): this is the only Jesus given to us to trust in. • Lord Jesus Christ, in the midst of false teachers, false shepherds, false prophets, and false promises, let God be true and all men liars! You are the way, the truth, and the life. Preserve me in Your way and give me eternal life, as I abide in Your Word of truth. Amen.

2:28–29 John's appeal to believers here is based on knowing that Christ's appearing is imminent (cf. v. 18). *Confidence . . . at His coming* is based on knowing "that when He appears we shall be like Him" (3:2), no less than a strong faith in the bodily flesh of Christ (4:2) raised incorruptible, guaranteeing that we will *not shrink from Him in shame*. Until that day, God's children are to *abide in Him*, which means to remain in Christ through faith in Him, through trust in His Word, and in a life conducted in *righteousness*, here referring to the natural response of the believer (cf. note at Jas 1:20). Christian conduct is not what defines the believer's identity, but it does reveal it; it shows that we are *born of Him* (cf. Jn 3:3–5).

Because Even Now We Are His Children (3:1–12)

ESV	KJV
3 ¹See what kind of love the Father has given to us, that we should be called children of God; and so we are. The reason why the world does not know us is that it did not know him. ²Beloved, we are God's children now, and what we will be has not yet appeared; but we know that when he appears we shall be like him, because we shall see him as he is. ³And everyone who thus hopes in him purifies himself as he is pure. ⁴Everyone who makes a practice of sinning also practices lawlessness; sin is lawlessness. ⁵You know that he appeared to take away sins, and in him there is no sin. ⁶No one who abides in him keeps on sinning; no one who keeps on sinning has either seen him or known him. ⁷Little children, let no one deceive you. Whoever practices righteousness is righteous, as he is righteous. ⁸Whoever makes a practice of sinning is of the devil, for the devil has been	*3* ¹Behold, what manner of love the Father hath bestowed upon us, that we should be called the sons of God: therefore the world knoweth us not, because it knew him not. ²Beloved, now are we the sons of God, and it doth not yet appear what we shall be: but we know that, when he shall appear, we shall be like him; for we shall see him as he is. ³And every man that hath this hope in him purifieth himself, even as he is pure. ⁴Whosoever committeth sin transgresseth also the law: for sin is the transgression of the law. ⁵And ye know that he was manifested to take away our sins; and in him is no sin. ⁶Whosoever abideth in him sinneth not: whosoever sinneth hath not seen him, neither known him. ⁷Little children, let no man deceive you: he that doeth righteousness is righteous, even as he is righteous.

sinning from the beginning. The reason the Son of God appeared was to destroy the works of the devil. ⁹No one born of God makes a practice of sinning, for God's seed abides in him, and he cannot keep on sinning because he has been born of God. ¹⁰By this it is evident who are the children of God, and who are the children of the devil: whoever does not practice righteousness is not of God, nor is the one who does not love his brother.

¹¹For this is the message that you have heard from the beginning, that we should love one another. ¹²We should not be like Cain, who was of the evil one and murdered his brother. And why did he murder him? Because his own deeds were evil and his brother's righteous.

⁸He that committeth sin is of the devil; for the devil sinneth from the beginning. For this purpose the Son of God was manifested, that he might destroy the works of the devil.

⁹Whosoever is born of God doth not commit sin; for his seed remaineth in him: and he cannot sin, because he is born of God.

¹⁰In this the children of God are manifest, and the children of the devil: whosoever doeth not righteousness is not of God, neither he that loveth not his brother.

¹¹For this is the message that ye heard from the beginning, that we should love one another.

¹²Not as Cain, who was of that wicked one, and slew his brother. And wherefore slew he him? Because his own works were evil, and his brother's righteous.

Introduction to 3:1–12 John celebrates the identity God has given us: we are His children (v. 1), who know that we will see Christ face to face, and therefore purify ourselves (vv. 2–3). A pure identity reveals itself in righteous behavior, which is the opposite of willfully sinning (vv. 4–6). Righteous people practice righteousness. It's a matter of our (new) birth: born of God's seed, we do not practice the works of the devil, but the works of God (vv. 7–10). John echoes Gn 3 to get at this Christian truth and continues from Gn 4, the story of Cain and Abel, to conclude the section with a negative example of a fraternal relationship that illustrates the irreconcilable dualism of good and evil (vv. 11–12).

3:1–3 God's purpose has become reality for John's listeners. *What kind of love* has the Father *given to us*? What is its quality? Whence did it come? The Father's love is described here primarily as gift, a gift with a purpose: *that we should be called children of God.* The sacrificial *agapē* love of God has been given to sinners so that He could call people mired in iniquity and selfishness to Himself.

291

God gives this kind of love to sinners, applying it in Holy Baptism to make Himself a people. This means more than a simple declaration or name change: God's will is that we should be *called* children of God, and that is what *we are*, truly birthed anew by God, who has recreated us in Christ (2Cor 5:17). "Giving" is grace language, and this is what makes God's love unique. Not only does God not treat us as our sins deserve, but He further lavishes on us a transformation of identity, of being. *We are* children of God. This is the promise of grace, over against all lies of the world and our sinful flesh (cf. 2:21, 27). The *agapē* love given by God is something that John frames in a context of words that sound slightly similar to *agapē* to underscore the distinction between believers and the world: the world *does not know us* (Gk *ou ginōskei*) because it *did not know Him* (Gk *ouk egnō*). Furthermore, those who have received this *agapē* are *beloved* (Gk *agapētoi*) and are called to purify ourselves (Gk *hagnizei*) even as *He is pure* (Gk *hagnos*). John could have used different words to express these truths, but employing these assonant terms reinforces the interdependence of all of these verses. God has lavished love on His children. This identity, rooted in God's *agapē* love, makes us unknown to the world, a fact anticipated by their ignorance of Christ. As we are similar to Christ in this way, so our hope is twofold: that we will also be like Him in His glorious revelation *when He appears*, and that we will be like Him until that day, as the believer *purifies himself as He is pure*. The glory to which John refers in these verses is a glory hidden from the world, but seen with the eyes of faith, a glory that has its root in the application of God's love delivered in Baptism, and that will be revealed to all in the Last Day, as Luther taught:

> God is infinite, but we are finite creatures. Moreover, the creature will never be the Creator. Yet we shall be like Him. God is life. Therefore we, too, shall live. God is righteous. Therefore we, too, shall be filled with righteousness. God is immortal and blessed. Therefore we, too, shall enjoy everlasting bliss, not as it is in God but the bliss that is suitable for us. (LW 30:268)

The life of glory hidden from the world is a life lived in hope. No longer slaves to sin, but having been purified in Baptism, we live a life transformed by God in holy conduct, free to serve our Savior and our neighbor because we have been born of God. Cranmer wrote, "St. John saith, that the lively knowledge and faith of God bringeth forth good works; so saith he likewise of hope and charity, that they cannot stand with evil" (Cranmer 2:158).

3:4 John defines *the practice of sinning* as *lawlessness* in this verse, diagnosing the symptom and the disease. God cares not only about our behavior, but also the state of man, the sinner's natural orientation and inclination to hate God and violate His Law. God's work in Christ is not simply to act as a moral guide to curb sin, but to cure the disease of lawlessness through His sacrificial death.

3:5 Both the disease of lawlessness and its symptoms, sins, are transgressions against God's divine Law. God addresses the problem in Christ. Jesus Christ *appeared*, as John testifies (cf. 1:2), and His appearance had a purpose: *to take away sins*. Whatever is taught about Jesus, the central message of the Gospel is the forgiveness of sins. The whole mission of God is wrapped up in the person and work of God the Son, as He is "the Lamb of God, who takes away the sin of the world" (Jn 1:29). This Lamb is perfect in every way, as the author of Heb reminds us: "For we do not have a high priest who is unable to sympathize with our weaknesses, but one who in every respect has been tempted as we are, yet without sin" (Heb 4:15). John anticipates the response of Christian behavior by reminding his readers that *in Him there is no sin*; those who are in Christ by faith are regarded by God as sinless as well: "There is therefore now no condemnation for those who are in Christ Jesus. For the law of the Spirit of life has set you free in Christ Jesus from the law of sin and death" (Rm 8:1–2).

3:6 Christ's blood has washed away all sins (1:7, 9). The disease of lawlessness has been cured! Therefore there is a problem with the one who *keeps on sinning*: John employs the continuative aspect of this verb to demonstrate the black and white distinction of the believer's identity. You have been brought from death to life! To go back to the things of death is to deny your identity. The person who *keeps on sinning* denies that the disease of sin has indeed been cured by Christ's blood and treats that strong medicine in a way that proves he has not *either seen Him or known Him*. Luther wrote: "If sin does what it wants, the Holy Spirit and faith are not present" (SA III III 44). John uses the words "seeing" and "knowing" to mean believing in Christ, based on God revealing Him to sinners: "No one has ever seen God; the only God, who is at the Father's side, He has made Him known" (Jn 1:18); "If you had known Me, you would have known My Father also. From now on you do know Him and have seen Him" (Jn 14:7).

3:7 John proceeds with his teaching on Christian behavior in light of the forgiveness of sins because false teachers have communicated a misleading message in this regard. He pleads with his readers: *let no one deceive you*. It is tempting to run with the forgiveness of sins in the direction of licentiousness on the one hand or in the direction of personal merit on the other. "Christ forgave me—it must have been something good in me that inspired Him to do that?" This is not *righteousness*. No, John knows what righteousness is and confesses that Christ *is righteous*, the one who in His righteousness serves as an "advocate" for poor sinners (2:1–2) in a forensic declaration of new life and salvation. "Great then. Christ forgave me. This must give me license to do whatever I want, then, including sinning?" No, this is not *righteousness* either. John points to the fact that Christ *is righteous* and shows that the believer is revealed to be *righteous* as he *practices righteousness*. The source of the saved sinner's righteous practice is the alien, imputed righteousness of Christ. Christ's righteousness is revealed in righteous living, a complete break with the old life of sin. This is no less and no more than simply the life of repentance, which has two parts: contrition (sorrow over sin) and faith (trust in Christ and His Word). The new birth Christ delivers to us gives us the gift of His Word, by which the Christian conducts his life.

3:8–10 The illustration John offers in these verses turns on the "protoevangelium," that is, the first promise of the Messiah's birth and victory over the devil, delivered in the context of God's curse of the serpent: "I will put enmity between you and the woman, and between your offspring and her offspring; He shall bruise your head, and you shall bruise His heel" (Gn 3:15).

3:8 God's curse is righteous judgment *of the devil* who has been *sinning from the beginning*. John argues that the one who continues in sin is no believer at all, because he goes back to works of the devil, whose works *the Son of God appeared . . . to destroy*. The one who continues in sin therefore is revealed to be not a child of God (3:1) but *of the devil*; everyone who sins serves the devil and continues his evil work (cf. Jn 8:34–47; Eph 2:1–3). The Lutheran reformers wrote: "God is not a creator, author, or cause of sin. By the instigation of the devil through one man, sin (which is the devil's work) has entered the world" (FC SD I 7). An ancient liturgical form is preserved yet today in asking baptismal candidates whether they renounce the devil, all his works, and all his ways. This confession of faith echoes John's teaching that *the Son of God appeared . . . to destroy the works of the devil*. Christ's appearance is effective for all epochs of human experience. The devil's corrupting works began in human history with the temptation and sin of our first parents, Adam and Eve, and brought sin into the world. Christ's sacrificial death takes away sins and purifies sinners still as they trust in Him. Christ's destruction of the devil's corrupting works will come to an end on the Last Day when we see at the resurrection that sin, the devil, and death are swallowed up in victory, as Luther taught: "Here you have the fulfillment of the first sermon of the Gospel. The Seed of the woman had to be born to destroy the works of the devil (Gen. 3:15). Now He has appeared in the flesh and has destroyed them" (LW 30:272). Melanchthon wrote:

> Just as the devil cannot be conquered except by Christ's help, so we cannot free ourselves from this slavery by our own strength. World history shows how great and powerful the devil's kingdom is. The world is full of blasphemies against God and wicked opinions. The devil keeps all tied up many hypocrites who appear holy and who are wise and righteous in the world's eyes. Even greater vices are seen in other people. Since Christ was given to us to remove both these sins and these punishments and to destroy the devil's kingdom, sin, and death [1 John 3:8], we will never be able to recognize Christ's benefits unless we understand our evils. (Ap II 48–50)

Calvin wrote: "He does not make the children of God wholly free from all sin; but he denies that any can really glory in this distinction, except those who from the heart strive to form their life in obedience to God" (Calvin 212).

3:9 John contrasts different births in this verse (cf. note at 3:8–10). Those who are of the seed of promise are *God's seed*, that is, God's "offspring." Jesus is certainly the primary referent when talking about God's offspring, and He refers to Himself as a seed (Jn 12:24). He also compares His Word to seed (Mt 13:19; Mk 4:14). But John's argument is that *God's seed abides in* forgiven sinners by faith, a seed that cannot sin. Just as plants, animals, and all other things in creation do not act contrary to birth, so those born of God's seed act according to the new birth: they have *been born of God* (cf. 1Jn 2:29; 4:7; Jn 3:5). St. Bernard of Clairvaux said, "Even tho they are seen to have sinned in time, their offenses do not appear in eternity, because the charity of their Father covers the multitude of sins" (*WDC*, p. 174). Cranmer wrote:

> Deceive not yourselves therefore, thinking that you have faith in God, or that you love God, or do trust him, or do fear him, when you live in sin: for then your ungodly and sinful life declareth the contrary, whatsoever ye say or think. It pertaineth to a Christian man to have this true Christian faith, and to try himself whether he hath it or no, and to know what belongeth to it, and how it doth work in him. It is not the world that we can trust to; the world, and all that is therein, is but vanity. It is God that must be our defence and protection against all temptation of wickedness and sin, errors, superstition, idolatry, and all evil. If all the world were on our side, and God against us, what could the world avail us? Therefore let us set our whole faith and trust in God, and neither the world, the devil, nor all the power of them shall prevail against us. Let us therefore, good Christian people, try and examine our faith, what it is: let us not flatter ourselves, but look upon our works, and so judge of our faith what it is. (Cranmer 2:161)

Bengel included an example from science: "The magnetic needle, which always points to the pole, is easily turned aside from this direction, but always reseeks the pole" (Bengel 128).

3:10 Works of love are not the source of believers' righteousness before God. But they do reveal believers' relationship with the God who has given them new birth, as surely as hatred reveals a kinship with the devil. The practice of righteousness shows that Christ's righteousness has been imputed to us. We are shown to be righteous, even as He has declared us to be so. Jesus taught that mutual love for one another would make *evident* to the world that believers have an identity in Him (Jn 13:34–35). Love has its source in truth (1Co 13:6) and reveals itself in forgiving each other and pointing to the truth about Christ who is the Truth (2:18–27; 4:1–6).

3:11–12 John's application of the Gn 3:15 promise of seed and salvation in the preceding verses reminds his readers of the fall narrative, the plot of which turns on the temptation to eat from the tree of knowledge of good and evil. When our parents ate and fell, the knowledge they were left with was that God was good and they were evil for not having feared, loved, and trusted in Him alone. The introduction of sin into the world continues its destructive effects, rippling into breakdown of human relationships, illustrated by the story from the next generation after Adam and Eve. The *message* Jesus taught *from the beginning* was that His followers should love one another (Jn 13:34), and this is the "message" that John and the other apostles were delivering as well (cf. 2:7–8). Application of this teaching demands a new behavior: fear, love, and trust of God instead of the evil of internecine strife, *like Cain* (cf. Gn 4:1–12). The NT teaches that Abel was shown to be righteous and that his blood testifies to God's acceptance of his gifts instead of Cain's (Heb 11:4). In John's language of good-evil dualism, this demonstrates that Cain *was of the evil one*, killing Abel simply because Abel was righteous in God's sight and righteous in sacrificial deed. Cain murdered because *his own deeds were evil*, an important distinction to consider in John's argument. Cain was not evil because he was a murderer; his sins of greed (Jude 11) led him to further great shame and vice. Our works flow from our identity. Born of the devil, we will sow only seeds of sin, but born of God, works proceed from faith (cf. Rm 14:23).

2:28–3:12 in Devotion and Prayer Behold what manner of love the Father has given unto us, to the end that we should be called children of God. And we are God's children! On account of this, the world doesn't know us—like a baby animal that has been found by a well-meaning heart who doesn't know what she is getting herself into when she scoops it up in a shoe box, or her skirt, or her hands, and brings it to mama saying, I found this dying squirrel. . . . I found this dying bird. . . . I found this dying kitten. . . . Can we keep it? And what does mama say? She repeats that old saying about the human smell on the baby bird, and says, Oh, honey, please don't touch it. If you do, its mother will not take it back. It's like that with the world. The world does not know us because we are called children of God, adopted as a kind of first fruits through faith in the resurrection of Christ, the Son of God. Like fuzzy fledglings handled by well-meaning human hands, our old parentage in the world may see and sniff and wonder, and finally conclude, this is not my child. This fuzzy fledgling has a different identity; it is parented by someone else now. I don't know who, I just know this kid is not my son, not my daughter, not my fledgling. The world does not know us because we have been transformed by Christ now, while yet in the world. He transforms us by touching us, not with a hand that secretes special oils or a new scent, not with pheromones that are unrecognizable by the mother bird, nothing so metaphorical and conceptual and allegorical. He touches us with real elements, with water and His holy Word, rich in grace, making it a life-giving water, a washing of regeneration in the Holy Ghost. That's how love has been poured into us: poured out on a cross where Jesus' wounds heal the wounds the world inflicts on us His children; poured down on us in the life-giving torrent of His baptismal washing, making us white, coming out of the great tribulation and washing our robes and making them white in the blood of the Lamb; poured into us through the Holy Spirit, given to us as a gift in that same Baptism. John can call his little flock "beloved" because they are loved by God. With well-meaning hands, this God truly has lifted you, fuzzy fledgling, out of the mire of the world and transformed you into an eagle who soars on alien wings—wings not your own, wings unknown to the world. He has transformed you into a bird who neither hungers nor thirsts anymore, and the sun will not strike you by day nor any scorching heat, for the Lamb in the midst of the throne will be your shepherd and guide you back to your Baptism—to springs of living water—and better than that, to a world made new where God will wipe away every tear from your eyes. (Rev 7:16–17) • Grant me grace, Lord Jesus Christ, that I may live unknown to the world, as the world did not know You. Keep me in the hope that when the world sees You as You are, I will be like You, and will see You as You are. Draw me ever to the promise given by You in Holy Baptism where You purified me, that I may be found holy and blameless, Your own child while yet in the world that does not know me. Amen.

PART 3

IN HIM WHO FIRST LOVED US (3:13–5:21)

So We Love and Do Not Hate (3:13–24)

ESV	KJV
¹³Do not be surprised, brothers, that the world hates you. ¹⁴We know that we have passed out of death into life, because we love the brothers. Whoever does not love abides in death. ¹⁵Everyone who hates his brother is a murderer, and you know that no murderer has eternal life abiding in him. ¹⁶By this we know love, that he laid down his life for us, and we ought to lay down our lives for the brothers. ¹⁷But if anyone has the world's goods and sees his brother in need, yet closes his heart against him, how does God's love abide in him? ¹⁸Little children, let us not love in word or talk but in deed and in truth. ¹⁹By this we shall know that we are of the truth and reassure our heart before him; ²⁰for whenever our heart condemns us, God is greater than our heart, and he knows everything. ²¹Beloved, if our heart does not condemn us, we have confidence before God; ²²and whatever we ask we receive from him, because we keep his commandments and do what pleases him. ²³And this is his commandment, that we believe in the name of his Son Jesus Christ and	¹³Marvel not, my brethren, if the world hate you. ¹⁴We know that we have passed from death unto life, because we love the brethren. He that loveth not his brother abideth in death. ¹⁵Whosoever hateth his brother is a murderer: and ye know that no murderer hath eternal life abiding in him. ¹⁶Hereby perceive we the love of God, because he laid down his life for us: and we ought to lay down our lives for the brethren. ¹⁷But whoso hath this world's good, and seeth his brother have need, and shutteth up his bowels of compassion from him, how dwelleth the love of God in him? ¹⁸My little children, let us not love in word, neither in tongue; but in deed and in truth. ¹⁹And hereby we know that we are of the truth, and shall assure our hearts before him. ²⁰For if our heart condemn us, God is greater than our heart, and knoweth all things. ²¹Beloved, if our heart condemn us not, then have we confidence toward God.

love one another, just as he has commanded us. ²⁴Whoever keeps his commandments abides in God, and God in him. And by this we know that he abides in us, by the Spirit whom he has given us.

²²And whatsoever we ask, we receive of him, because we keep his commandments, and do those things that are pleasing in his sight.

²³And this is his commandment, That we should believe on the name of his Son Jesus Christ, and love one another, as he gave us commandment.

²⁴And he that keepeth his commandments dwelleth in him, and he in him. And hereby we know that he abideth in us, by the Spirit which he hath given us.

Introduction to 3:13–24 A life "in Christ" is a life transformed by a new identity: we are children of God (v. 1). This new identity is the source of a life of love instead of hate. The Christian experience of hatred in this world is no surprise (v. 13), but the world does not claim the citizenship of believers: we have passed from the world to God's kingdom, from hatred to love, from death to life (vv. 14–15). Christ's sacrificial love activates sacrificial love for one another (v. 16), which reveals itself in charity, in actions rather than words (vv. 17–18). As children of God, Christians trust in the objective word that He delivers about that identity, the only thing that reassures a heart that doubts (vv. 19–21). Believers' identity as children of God leads them to prayer (v. 22), faith in Jesus Christ (v. 23), and an assurance of God's abiding presence through the Holy Spirit (v. 24).

3:13 What is characteristic of the devil's seed here describes *the world* in John's estimation: it hates the brothers and sisters that make up the community of believers. Jesus warned His disciples: "If the world hates you, know that it has hated Me before it hated you. If you were of the world, the world would love you as its own; but because you are not of the world, but I chose you out of the world, therefore the world hates you" (Jn 15:18–19; cf. Jn 17:14). The world's hatred is one more reason to take to heart John's warning at 2:15–17; the world does not love you, Christian, so what business have you in loving it?

3:14–15 John's dualisms are on display: this business of loving the neighbor is a matter of life or death! Our alliance is with God's kingdom rather than the world. This new citizenship reveals itself in love for one another rather than hatred, because our identity is changed, as *we have passed out of death into life*. The dynamic of death and new life is pioneered by Jesus' passing through the death of a cross into resurrected glory; His death and new life are applied to believers by faith: "Truly, truly, I say to you, whoever hears My word and believes Him who sent Me has eternal life. He does not come into judgment, but has passed from death to life" (Jn 5:24; cf. Eph 2:1, 5; Rm 5:6, 8, 10; 6:4). Believers have passed from death to life as surely as they have been "born of God" (2:29). In fact, it is this birth that keeps us acting in *love* with people that God has called our *brothers* by virtue of our common Father. The love we have for one another has its source therefore in the love that He first shows us, a point which John refers to at v. 16 and anticipates here. Not loving the brothers is really not a choice for the Christian, as the antitheses the apostle has outlined, hatred and love, death and life, reveal that the one who *does not love abides in death*. What is revealed in hatred for the neighbor is a sin that John calls murder (cf. the example of Cain, v. 12), even if such hatred has not yet escalated to what the world would define as the physical crime of homicide. The believer is called to love; those who do not love are therefore spiritually dead, unbelievers. The Lutheran reformers wrote: "Love is a fruit that surely and necessarily also follows true faith. The fact that a person does not love is a sure sign that he is not justified. He is still in death or has lost the righteousness of faith again, as John says" (FC SD III 27).

3:16 How do we know what love is? God shows us. "In this is love, not that we have loved God but that He loved us" (4:10). "The life I now live in the flesh I live by faith in the Son of God, who loved me and gave himself for me" (Gal 2:20). Jesus defined it and exemplified it: "Greater love has no one than this, that someone lay down his life for his friends" (Jn 15:13). Sacrificial love for the brother grows out of the source of God's love for us.

3:17 The *world's goods* (Gk *bion tou kosmou*, literally "life of the world") are things that can be used to help those in need. It is worth remembering that God gives such things to all people. Luther wrote: "He richly and daily provides me with all that I need to support this body and life" (SC, First Article). As all these gifts are from our heavenly Father, He calls us to share with our brother in need, and not to be one who *closes his heart against him,* or to say it in King James' English, *shutteth up his bowels of compassion from him,* a signal that "heart" in this verse (Gk *splangkhna*) is synonymous with, but distinct from, the word that is used in vv. 19–21 (Gk *kardia*). The difference in meaning between them is negligible, as both may be understood to be the center of affection, pity, and emotion; the image John impresses on his readers is that a brother's neediness ought to cause a visceral reaction. When we close the door of our "heart" to our brother, there is no passage, no entry point for *God's love* to *abide.* Luther commented:

> God is merciful. Yet He is not idle. He does not let sinners go unpunished. To the humble, who fear Him, He is merciful. . . . There are several degrees of love: an enemy must not be offended, a brother must be helped, a member of one's household must be supported. You know Christ's commandment concerning love for one's enemies. But you owe more to a brother who loves you in return. (LW 30:278)

3:18 Actions speak louder than words, and lip-service is no love at all. We are clumsy with words, things get lost in translation, and even the best of intentions can be misconstrued through misinterpretation of our communication mode: we speak in plain human language. God shows us His love by revealing Himself not only in words spoken to the prophets, words mediated through angels, or words written on the pages of Scripture. God wraps Himself in our humanity and reveals Himself as the Word made flesh. This is the Word in action, this is the Word of Truth, Jesus Christ. So we also ought to love *in deed and in truth,* and in such a way that the brother's needs are taken care of, as Luther taught:

> To love a brother who is kind and pleasant in return—this is a trivial matter. This is the way the world also loves. "The crowd judges friendships by their usefulness." Accordingly, John does not say: "Let us love those who are saintly, agreeable, and rich." No, he says: "Let us love the brethren," in such a way that then nothing but the brotherhood is loved and regarded; for a brother is loved out of a sense of duty, not because of usefulness and not because of praise. All the gifts we have should serve those who do not have them. For example, he who is learned should serve him who is not learned; he who is rich should serve him who is

poor; he who is sensible should serve him who is foolish, etc. (LW 30:278–79)

3:19 If there is a distinct nuance to the word *heart* (here, Gk *kardia* as opposed to *splangkhna* in v. 17), it is that the "heart" is the location of self-reflection, what we might also call the "mind," the seat of the conscience. On self-reflection, we who see God's love reflected in Christian action on behalf of the brother can *reassure our heart*, knowing that love for one another as Jesus loved us flows from genuine, saving faith. This is what it means to be *of the truth*, that is, believers have a source, a root, and the love they share starts there: the eternal Truth who is Jesus Christ. Cf. Jn 18:37: "For this purpose I was born and for this purpose I have come into the world—to bear witness to the truth. Everyone who is of the truth listens to My voice." Believers are reassured (Gk *peithō*, literally "persuade"), that is, "convinced," by the promise that comes from outside of themselves, the Lord who keeps His promises to bless them through His means of grace.

3:20 If on self-reflection the believer is "cut to the heart" (Ac 2:37), with God's Law condemning sin and burdening the *heart*, that is, the conscience (cf. note at v. 19), we have good news: *God is greater than our heart*. "Greater" does not simply refer to relative size, which would not of itself be good news. Rather, located in the middle of John's thoughts on "reassuring the heart" (v. 19) and "confidence before God" (v. 21), this "greater" is consistent with the other places he employs the word, to point the believer to God's Gospel (cf. 4:4; 5:9; Jn 1:50; 4:12; 5:36; 8:53; 10:29; 13:16; 14:28; 15:20). Our heart (conscience) may accuse us (Gk *kataginōskō*, that is, to know or observe something through a prejudicial lens), but God *knows everything* (Gk *ginōskō*, simply to know). John's wordplay is intended to drive the Gospel point home: He doesn't judge us "more" than our heart does, but knowing all things, He does judge in a different way, in a way that takes into account the person and work of Jesus Christ. God, who knows everything, gives our hearts confidence by affirming Christ's work on our behalf on the cross.

3:21–22 The Law always accuses, and the Gospel always pardons and comforts. *Confidence before God* is produced by the Gospel, the God who is greater than our heart (v. 20) forgiving us all our sin for the sake of Jesus. "Confidence" leads us to prayer. Luther wrote: "God tenderly invites us to believe that He is our true Father

303

and that we are His true children, so that with all boldness and confidence we may ask Him as dear children ask their dear father" (SC, First Petition). The prayer of faith is first and foremost prayer for God's will to be done (cf. Jas 4:3 and note). Such prayer, as all the behavior of the believer who lives according to His will and His Word, *pleases Him*, because what is done through God-given faith is done in Christ.

3:23 When John moves from the plural "commandments" (v. 22) to the singular *commandment* in this verse, he shows the preeminence of the most important commandment. Cf. Mk 12:28–31: "And one of the scribes came up and heard them disputing with one another, and seeing that He answered them well, asked Him, 'Which commandment is the most important of all?' Jesus answered, 'The most important is, "Hear, O Israel: The Lord our God, the Lord is one. And you shall love the Lord your God with all your heart and with all your soul and with all your mind and with all your strength." The second is this: "You shall love your neighbor as yourself." There is no other commandment greater than these.'" The vertical dimension of faith and the horizontal dimension of love for the neighbor have their source in God who delivers His gifts. Jesus sums up the commandment as singular as well at Jn 17:3: "And this is eternal life, that they know You the only true God, and Jesus Christ whom You have sent"; John repeats the thought here, saying that *this is His commandment, that we believe in the name of His Son Jesus Christ* (cf. 1:5).

3:24 "Abiding" *in God* is the natural result of God abiding in the believer. To be "in Christ" then means that the reciprocal is true: Christ is in you! This promise is confirmed *by the Spirit whom He has given us*, a promise Paul expounds on at Rm 8:9–11: "You, however, are not in the flesh but in the Spirit, if in fact the Spirit of God dwells in you. Anyone who does not have the Spirit of Christ does not belong to Him. But if Christ is in you, although the body is dead because of sin, the Spirit is life because of righteousness. If the Spirit of Him who raised Jesus from the dead dwells in you, He who raised Christ Jesus from the dead will also give life to your mortal bodies through His Spirit who dwells in you" (cf. 2:20–26).

3:13–3:24 in Devotion and Prayer The water drip, drip, drops from Pilate's hands as he washes himself clean: See, my hands are innocent of this Man's blood! I refuse to take the fall for this one! And the crowd answers back, Let His blood be on our hands, on our heads! We accept the blame! Let Him be crucified! His blood be on us and our children! So where is the fault? Where is the blame? Jesus is the guilty one! Jesus is the one condemned! But we know that He isn't really guilty. We know, as we hear the passion narrative, that a travesty of justice has been committed, that the law has condemned an innocent Man. So if we should speak honestly, where does the condemnation lie? Where is Jesus' blood? On Pilate's washed hands? On the crowd? It is on your hands. It is on your head. It is for our sins that the Lord laid down His life, for my hands that drip, drip, drop, in the same game of pass-the-buck that Pilate played; that drip, drip, drop with greed, selfishness, murder, even as I might protest my own innocence; that drip, drip, drop with stains that condemn me, because I know I am to blame for Christ's death. Our hearts condemn us! And we know there is nothing we can do to remove the spot. No works, no privilege, no excuse, no reparation—our hearts condemn us, and our God condemns us too, because that stain of sin on us is a spot that damns us, that shows us that we are the ones under judgment, facing the sentence of eternal wrath, eternal death, eternal separation from a God of justice. We are the ones who stand condemned, but for the drip, drip, drop of Jesus' blood, pouring from a cross. Jesus' blood is a cleansing that scours injustice from the world as surely as the drip, drip, drops of the flood of Noah's day, when God said I will punish, but I will not simply wash My hands of you like a problem I'm too important or busy to deal with. I will not wash My hands of you, but I will wash you clean, pouring out the drops of My very lifeblood for you. I will wash you clean, pouring water that drip, drip, drops over you, shouting through that water that I cleanse you of every stain, cleansing the very heart that condemns you. Our God pours Himself out for us in reassuring love, just as He did that night with a basin and a towel, washing His disciples and saying, because I have so served you, so you must serve one another. This God, greater than our hearts, promises no condemnation for those who are in Christ. This God, greater than our hearts, gives us confidence, reassuring us in love towards Him and love for each other. Drip, drip, drop: you were washed, you were sanctified, you were justified in the name of the Lord Jesus Christ and by the Spirit of our God. • Lord Jesus Christ, you promised that "an hour is coming, and is now here, when the dead will hear the voice of the Son of God, and those who hear will live." Silence the alarm and condemnation of my heart, and open instead my ears, that I may hear Your voice. You who know everything, speak a Word of comfort to me, that I may have confidence before You. Speak through Your Word this day in which You have called me forth from the grave of my sin. And keep me in faith until the Last Day, when all who are in the tombs will hear Your voice and come out. Amen.

For Ours Is the Spirit of Truth (4:1–6)

ESV	KJV
4 ¹Beloved, do not believe every spirit, but test the spirits to see whether they are from God, for many false prophets have gone out into the world. ²By this you know the Spirit of God: every spirit that confesses that Jesus Christ has come in the flesh is from God, ³and every spirit that does not confess Jesus is not from God. This is the spirit of the antichrist, which you heard was coming and now is in the world already. ⁴Little children, you are from God and have overcome them, for he who is in you is greater than he who is in the world. ⁵They are from the world; therefore they speak from the world, and the world listens to them. ⁶We are from God. Whoever knows God listens to us; whoever is not from God does not listen to us. By this we know the Spirit of truth and the spirit of error.	4 ¹Beloved, believe not every spirit, but try the spirits whether they are of God: because many false prophets are gone out into the world. 5 ²Hereby know ye the Spirit of God: Every spirit that confesseth that Jesus Christ is come in the flesh is of God: ³And every spirit that confesseth not that Jesus Christ is come in the flesh is not of God: and this is that spirit of antichrist, whereof ye have heard that it should come; and even now already is it in the world. ⁴Ye are of God, little children, and have overcome them: because greater is he that is in you, than he that is in the world. ⁵They are of the world: therefore speak they of the world, and the world heareth them. ⁶We are of God: he that knoweth God heareth us; he that is not of God heareth not us. Hereby know we the spirit of truth, and the spirit of error.

Introduction to 4:1–6 John concluded the last section with the assurance of the Holy Spirit that guarantees that God abides in believers as believers abide in Christ. But the Holy Spirit is not the only spirit at work in the world. There are false teachers that proclaim a different message to the congregations that John and the other apostles serve, teachers who speak by a different spirit than the One who proclaims the Gospel of Christ. John warns his readers to test the spirits (v. 1) and that the test has to do with whether the prophet will agree that Christ has come into the flesh (vv. 2–3). False prophets are of the world, that enemy of the Christians (vv. 4–5), but the apostolic message is God's message, proclaimed by the Spirit of truth instead of the worldly, false spirit of error (v. 6).

4:1–3 John warns his readers to *not believe every spirit*, just as Paul preaches to Timothy: "Now the Spirit expressly says that in later times some will depart from the faith by devoting themselves to deceitful spirits and teachings of demons" (1Tm 4:1). Far more substantive than the idea of "zeitgeist" or contemporary worldview, Paul, John, and the rest of the Early Church identified the source of false teachings as "spirits," that is, creatures created by God, who though lacking flesh and bones, yet serve God or Satan. This means that the Church is involved in spiritual battle, fought on the field of teachings about Christ. There is no neutral ground. John's dualisms continue to underscore this fact: everyone is either of God's seed or of the serpent's; of the light or of the dark; of God's kingdom or of the world; of the truth or of the lie. Where Paul was specifically warning Timothy about prophets preaching abstinence from marriage and certain foods, perhaps some kind of protognostic heresy (1Tm 4:2–3), John's warnings seem to address a possibly related, but distinct, heresy: the teaching that Jesus did not really *come in the flesh*. The answer for this and every heresy is to *test the spirits*, that is, to examine teachings, including words and actions of the teachers and followers, in light of the whole testimony of Scripture (cf. Dt 18:18–22; 1Co 14:29). We cannot boast in human intellect or effort (a "magisterial" use of human reason that puts human thinking above God), but must rely on the objective Word from Scripture, as Luther commented: "The emphasis is on the words 'test the spirits,' for with these words he touches their boasting as with a needle. It is as if he were saying: 'Those who boast of the Spirit will come to you. But test the spirits'" (LW 30:284). Calvin wrote:

> The word spirit I take metonymically, as signifying him who boasts that he is endowed with the gift of the Spirit to perform his office as a prophet. For as it was not permitted to any one to speak in his own name, nor was credit given to speakers but as far as they were the organs of the Holy Spirit, in order that prophets might have more authority, God honoured them with

this name, as though he had separated them from mankind in general. Those, then, were called spirits, who, giving only a language to the oracles of the Holy Spirit, in a manner represented him. They brought nothing of their own, nor came they forth in their own name. But the design of this honourable title was, that God's word should not lose the respect due to it through the humble condition of the minister. For God would have his word to be always received from the mouth of man no otherwise than if he himself had appeared from heaven. (Calvin 229–30)

4:2 One can *know the Spirit of God* by the content of one's confession (Gk *homologei*, to "same-say," to agree). The content of Christian confession is that Jesus Christ is Lord and is both true God and true man (cf. 1Cor 12:3: "Therefore I want you to understand that no one speaking in the Spirit of God ever says 'Jesus is accursed!' and no one can say 'Jesus is Lord' except in the Holy Spirit"). That *Jesus Christ has come in the flesh* is the eyewitness declaration of the apostles, who saw, heard, and touched the resurrected Christ (cf. 1:1 and note).

4:3 All false christs have this in common: none of them come as God in the flesh of Jesus Christ (cf. 2Jn 7–11). But spirits do speak through the teaching of people in the flesh, which is why John warns his readers about these false teachers. Everyone who denies Christ is against Christ, and therefore *antichrist*. This has everything to do with how the Church receives the gifts God would deliver; "testing the spirits" is a matter of congregational survival and confidence, as Hus taught about this verse: "Here the spirit is subtle and heretical, denying Jesus to be very God and very man" (*The Church*, p. 91).

4:4 The Church has no reason to fear antichrists. The Church has confidence in God's promises in Christ: "the gates of hell shall not prevail against it" (Mt 16:18); "In the world you will have tribulation. But take heart; I have overcome the world" (Jn 16:33). In the spiritual battle for the truth of Christ's message, John's readers *have overcome* false teachers through faith in Jesus (cf. 5:4–5). The source of victory is not a more accurate use of human reason or a more charismatic preacher, but *He who is in you*, namely Christ, who dwells within every believer (cf. 3:24 and note). The lines of battle are drawn, but victory is not in question. The victory of God over Satan, the world, and human sin is secure, because God is *greater than he who is in the world*. God's victory over Satan is secured by Christ's crucifixion and resurrection, which judged sin and its author, the world and its prince. This theology of the cross permeates Christian experience until the Last Day as well, as Luther taught:

> "Christ is stronger; He has overcome, is overcoming, and will overcome that strong man in us (Luke 11:21–22)." Still the devil does sometimes overcome us in the flesh, in order that even in this way we may experience the power of the Stronger against that strong man and say with Paul (2 Cor. 12:10): "When I am weak, then I am strong." (LW 26:193)

4:5–6 As citizens of God's kingdom, we live not only an earthly life in the world, but a spiritual life taught by the Holy Spirit (cf. Jn 3:6). The world is stuck listening only to false teachers; believers listen to the message that the Holy Spirit proclaims, that Jesus Christ is Lord. And whoever listens to this message listens to the apostles, whose teaching is the teaching of the Holy Spirit, as John says: *whoever knows God listens to us.* All who are in fellowship with God recognize and listen to the true teaching of Christ when they hear it. The battle being waged is much more than simply a battle "of ideas." It is a battle of real spirits (cf. Eph 6:12), which is why it is so important for the Church to discern between the Holy Spirit and the *spirit of error*: behind every false teaching and empty idol is a very real demon (cf. 1Co 10:20).

4:1–6 in Devotion and Prayer The word for "spirit" in the Bible is also a word that we can translate as "breath." And it turns out there's some pretty bad breath out there in the world. A sort of hellish halitosis, in fact. For those with a sense of smell, there's a simple test for finding out whether breath is foul or fresh, whether it's wholesome or unhealthy: just take a whiff! Bad breath is not so much a disease, however, as a symptom of something more sinister at the source. Perhaps it is from something as innocuous as a choice at lunch—the roasted garlic or the spicy chicken. Or perhaps its source is something potentially deadly, like decay and rot in the mouth or the gastrointestinal tract. Like bad breath, false teaching has its source as well. As innocuous as any particular message might seem, if it does not proclaim at its root Christ Jesus, crucified and risen for the sake of sinners, then it is coming from the sickness of Satan's school. No amount of masking the malady with mints or mouthwash or gum, or denial, dressing it up as "no big deal," will cure the problem this poses, though: the only cure for this kind of bad breath is a thorough cleaning and a regular regimen of care. We have a God who so cleanses us, going so far as to replace the bad breath with good, destroying the symptom and the disease with the curative of the cross and delivering to us the Spirit of God. So what does God's breath smell like? What does the teaching of God's Church smell like? Christian, what do you smell like? "But thanks be to God, who in Christ always leads us in triumphal procession, and through us spreads the fragrance of the knowledge of Him everywhere. For we are the aroma of Christ to God among those who are being saved and among those who are perishing, to one a fragrance from death to death, to the other a fragrance from life to life" (2Cor 2:14–16). • Grant me grace, Lord, to use the eyes, ears, nose, and all my members which You have given me, which You still take care of, to serve You and Your children. Awaken my senses to hear and trust You, to distinguish between the lies of the world and the truth of Your Word. Give to me Your Spirit, that the words of my mouth and the meditation of my heart be acceptable in Your sight. O Lord, open my lips, and my mouth will declare Your praise. Amen.

Ours Is a God Who First Loved Us (4:7–10)

ESV	KJV
[7]Beloved, let us love one another, for love is from God, and whoever loves has been born of God and knows God. [8]Anyone who does not love does not know God, because God is love. [9]In this the love of God was made manifest among us, that God sent his only Son into the world, so that we might live through him. [10]In this is love, not that we have loved God but that he loved us and sent his Son to be the propitiation for our sins.	[7]Beloved, let us love one another: for love is of God; and every one that loveth is born of God, and knoweth God. [8]He that loveth not knoweth not God; for God is love. [9]In this was manifested the love of God toward us, because that God sent his only begotten Son into the world, that we might live through him. [10]Herein is love, not that we loved God, but that he loved us, and sent his Son to be the propitiation for our sins.

Introduction to 4:7–10 This brief section is the beginning of John's final appeal, continuing on to 5:12, for the congregations to examine their faith and practice. As such, it bears similarities to the first half of the Letter (1:5–2:27). The introductory verses of this appeal call Christians to love one another (vv. 7–8), because God is love (vv. 7–8). God demonstrates this love by loving us first (v. 9), the pinnacle of that demonstration of love being Christ's substitutionary sacrifice (v. 10).

4:7 *Love* is the operative word through this section of John's Letter. While not laid out exactly metrically as a poem, there are sonorous elements in its rhythm. (For example, the first line "Beloved, let us love one another" in Gk is *agapētoi, agapōmen allēlous*, which ends with the easily recognizable "dum-ditty-dum-dum" that closes the Gk hexameter.) Furthermore, John's argument turns on a repetition and manipulation of the word "love" that reveals his wit and rhetorical purpose. John argues that *love is from God*, and an identity in Him results in active love for one another. This is not love as understood by the world, selfish and self-centered, but the sacrificial love of God, Gk *agapē*. As John argues at 2:15–17, believers are called not to love the world, but to love God. God's love purifies our own, leading us away from "love" of sinful pleasures, which is misplaced affection, corrupting what is good. John is not calling Christians to libertine affection, exploiting God-given desires in some sort of licentious freedom. Rather than such an identity that is shared by the world, love among Christians is sanctified by God, giving us a new identity: we are *born of God*. The new birth is effected by God alone (cf. Jn 1:12–13) through receiving His Word of life in all of its forms (cf. Jn 3:5; Rm 10:17). His Word alone allows us to be born of God; therefore the believer *knows God*, that is, not simply to know things about Him, but to exist in relationship with Him by faith.

4:8 John asserts that the one *who does not love* does not know God, and proves it by identifying God as love, down to His very nature. God is a God of giving (Rm 5:5–8, 15–17), of seeking and saving the lost (Lk 15:7, 10, 20). This is a God of love, whose love delivered even His Son, in flesh and blood, for the sins of mankind: "For God so loved the world, that He gave His only Son, that whoever believes in Him should not perish but have eternal life. For God did not send His Son into the world to condemn the world, but in order that the world might be saved through Him" (Jn 3:16–17).

4:9–10 God reveals His love to the world by sending His Son Jesus. This mission of God has a purpose: *that we might live through Him*. His love means life, and just as life has its source in God, the

311

author of life, so also is His love the source of our own love for Him and one another. We are saved not by our love for God, but by the love of God for us in sending Christ to be the atoning sacrifice for our sins, a *propitiation* (see 2:2 and note), a truth of scripture worth celebrating, affirming, and relying on for one's entire life. This is something Luther encourages: "Provide yourselves with armor from Scripture concerning justification, which takes place through faith. Collect, I say, a number of Scripture passages that ascribe righteousness to God. Then, if you put your reliance on these passages, you will be able to stand even after a fall, as, for example, after acts of fornication, murder, and other sins" (LW 30:295).

So Our Love Is His Love (4:11–21)

ESV	KJV
[11]Beloved, if God so loved us, we also ought to love one another. [12]No one has ever seen God; if we love one another, God abides in us and his love is perfected in us. [13]By this we know that we abide in him and he in us, because he has given us of his Spirit. [14]And we have seen and testify that the Father has sent his Son to be the Savior of the world. [15]Whoever confesses that Jesus is the Son of God, God abides in him, and he in God. [16]So we have come to know and to believe the love that God has for us. God is love, and whoever abides in love abides in God, and God abides in him. [17]By this is love perfected with us, so that we may have confidence for the day of judgment, because as he is so also are we in this world. [18]There is no fear in love, but perfect love casts out fear. For fear has to do with punishment, and whoever fears has not been perfected in love. [19]We love because he first loved us. [20]If anyone says, "I love God," and hates his brother,	[11]Beloved, if God so loved us, we ought also to love one another. [12]No man hath seen God at any time. If we love one another, God dwelleth in us, and his love is perfected in us. [13]Hereby know we that we dwell in him, and he in us, because he hath given us of his Spirit. [14]And we have seen and do testify that the Father sent the Son to be the Saviour of the world. [15]Whosoever shall confess that Jesus is the Son of God, God dwelleth in him, and he in God. [16]And we have known and believed the love that God hath to us. God is love; and he that dwelleth in love dwelleth in God, and God in him. [17]Herein is our love made perfect, that we may have boldness in the day of judgment: because as he is, so are we in this world. [18]There is no fear in love; but perfect love casteth out fear: because fear hath torment. He that feareth is not made perfect in love.

he is a liar; for he who does not love his brother whom he has seen cannot love God whom he has not seen. ²¹And this commandment we have from him: whoever loves God must also love his brother.

¹⁹We love him, because he first loved us.
²⁰If a man say, I love God, and hateth his brother, he is a liar: for he that loveth not his brother whom he hath seen, how can he love God whom he hath not seen?
²¹And this commandment have we from him, That he who loveth God love his brother also.

Introduction to 4:11–21 John expands his argument about the effects of God's love on the community of believers. God's love produces the response of love in His people (v. 11), and the love believers have for one another reveals God's love perfected in them (v. 12). The proof of God's love among us is His abiding with us by His Spirit (v. 13), who leads us to faith in Jesus as Savior and Son of God (vv. 14–16). God abiding with us in love gives us confidence for the Last Day instead of fear of judgment (vv. 17–18). John reaffirms the source of our love: God first loved us (v. 19), and His love demands a completely different identity in believers, who have been brought from lies to the Truth, from hatred to love (vv. 20–21).

4:11 John moves from a poetic excursus (vv. 7–10) to a systematic argument introduced by conditional clauses. There is no question whether God has loved us: we have the proof of the extent to which He has loved us, the quality of that love, to the point that "we should be called children of God" (3:1). This is vivid reality, and John gives his readers an equally true response: *If God so loved us, we also ought to love one another.*

4:12 The next several verses expound John's assertion from his Gospel: "No one has ever seen God; the only God, who is at the Father's side, He Has made Him known" (Jn 1:18). The incarnation of the Son of God made Him known, and His abiding presence with the Christian congregation, the body of Christ, continues to make Him incarnationally known as well, as Christians serve God by loving the neighbor through faith in Jesus. Here John repeats the lesson that *God abides in us* and that *His love is perfected in us* from 2:5–6 (see note there), connecting that "abiding" and "perfected love" with the love we show one another.

4:13 "Abiding" in Christ, and Christ's abiding in us, is guaranteed by the promise of His Holy Spirit. Christians flee here: *He has given us of His Spirit*, which creates and sustains faith in Christ. The Spirit only preaches Christ and Him crucified, which is why the apostles only preach Christ and Him crucified (cf. 1Cor 2:2).

4:14 The mission of God is seen clearly in this verse, which repeats John's purpose as apostolic eyewitness from 1:1–2: *the Father has sent His Son.* So also the Son sends the Spirit (v. 13) not only to reassure the Church, but also to equip and send the Church in love to serve Him, *the Savior of the world*, and to serve the world He came to save, by proclaiming the message of His love. Though the world exists in enmity to Christians, we are in fact called to love our enemies (Mt 5:44). The best way to do that is to point always to the source of "perfect love [that] casts out fear" (v. 18), as the entire world anticipates "the day of judgment" (v. 17).

4:15 John's Letter emphasizes confession in two ways: confession of sins and Holy Absolution that God delivers (1:8–10); and confession of faith, which is agreeing with, or "same-saying" (Gk *homologeō*), the truth of God that He has revealed in Christ. It is necessary for anyone who believes in God the way He has revealed Himself that he *confess . . . that Jesus is the Son of God.* Such confession is a fruit of true saving faith (cf. Rm 10:9).

4:16 John weaves together the threads of "love" and "abiding"— He in us, and we in Him—in this central verse. While doing so, John continues to proclaim that this profound truth depends on nothing but our trust in Him: *we have come to know and to believe the love that God has for us.* Luther expounded on this:

> These are simple words, but they are words that require faith in the highest degree—faith against which everything that is not of the Spirit of God fights. Conscience, the devil, hell, the judgment of God, and everything resist, in order that we may not believe that God is love but may believe that God is an Executioner and a Judge. By "the world" I also understand the adversaries of the Word and the sects. Here, therefore, it is taught in brief that one must cling to faith against these assaults. Consequently, he who has a true knowledge of God abides in Christ, and God abides in him. (LW 30:301)

4:17–18 "Perfection" language is purpose language, and John repeats this business of *perfected* love from his discussion at 2:5 (see note). The purpose or goal of God's love for us in Christ is that we believe it as objective fact. The effect this has is that we fear no punishment on *the day of judgment*. Does God punish sins? Yes indeed! Will God punish you for yours? The Christian on the Last Day will point to Christ's cross, His historical act of love on our behalf, and say boldly, He already did! We look not to our own works, but to the works of Christ for our assurance. In the same way, we do not look to any efforts or good will of our own, nor enumerate our good deeds and our misdeeds on some kind of eschatological ledger, but put our trust rather in the relationship He has established with us, which is one of adoptive sonship: *as He is so also are we.* God adopted us as His children through faith in Christ (cf. Rm 8:15–17). Because of this relationship, believers have confidence, by God's grace, to face judgment, knowing they are counted as perfectly righteous (cf. Mt 25:34, 40), so they have no *fear* of *punishment* (cf. Mt 25:46). God's *perfect love casts out fear*: it reaches its purpose as it seeks and saves instead of condemning (cf. Jn 3:18).

4:19 Life as a Christian has a rhythm: cause and effect, stimulus and response, gift and gratitude, sacrament and sacrifice. Here John summarizes the heartbeat of Christian identity: *we love because He first loved us*, not the other way round. We are able to love one another only because we have received love from Jesus, who loved us first. Melanchthon wrote:

> Our love for God, even though it is small, cannot possibly be separated from faith. For we come to the Father through Christ. When forgiveness of sins has been received, then we are truly certain that we have a God [Exodus 20:3], that is, that God cares for us. We call upon Him, we give Him thanks, we fear Him, we love Him as 1 John 4:19 teaches. . . . We love Him because He gave His Son for us and forgave us our sins. In this way John shows that faith comes first and love follows. (Ap V 20)

4:20–21 God does not need our good works, but our neighbor does. Just so, the way truly to show love for God is to deliver love to the neighbor! "No one has ever seen God" (v. 12), but John's argument has moved to this conclusion: God is indeed visible, not only in the incarnation of Christ, but in that incarnational love that the body of Christ demonstrates for one another. Love is palpable, tangible, real: God embodied it in Christ by taking on a body, and we embody it in Christ's body the Church by loving one another, according to Christ's command (cf. Jn 13:34).

4:7–21 in Devotion and Prayer The rhythm of the Christian life runs on the heartbeat of Christ's love for sinners. He loves, and we love in return. We love, and that proves His love has had an effect in our lives. It's like that time when Jesus dined with Simon the Pharisee, Lk 7:36–50. A woman wept on His feet, giving Jesus an opportunity to teach about the rhythm of love and forgiveness, the exchange in the economy of God's kingdom, and the currency that runs the show. The kingdom of heaven runs its economy on the blessed exchange: Christ becomes sin, and we become His righteousness, for any woman who is a sinner, for any man or child who is a sinner. The currency of this kingdom is need. This is why Jesus frequently talks about the kingdom of heaven in terms that resound with opposites and seeming paradoxes. It is a kingdom where the first are the last and the last are the first. It is a kingdom where the greatest are the least and the least are the greatest. It is a kingdom where Jesus demands, "Allow the tax collectors, the prostitutes, the children—those snot-nosed, marginalized brats, shuffled off to the edge of society—let those ones come to me. They have the greatest NEED, therefore they are the greatest in the kingdom of heaven." This is why He is the Jesus who will heal lepers, with or without a thank you. He will touch prostitutes and leave them with something better than they could ever offer Him. He will touch tax collectors and turn them into disciples. He will touch women who hemorrhage for years and know that power went out of Him for healing. He will touch blind men, deaf men, ugly men, poor men, sick men. "The exchange that's illustrated in My Gospel," says Jesus, "is a world in which the least are the greatest, the last are the first, the poor become rich, the dead become alive, the blind become sighted, the lame become whole, the ugly become beautiful, the broken become useful, and the one with the greatest need becomes My favorite kind of person. Because that is the one I can do the most for. Yes, that is the one who needs Me most. I've not come to call the healthy, but the sick. Not the rich, but the poor. Not the living, but the dead. Not the saint, but the sinner. Not the socially appropriate, winsome, charming, scrupled, and fastidious voting constituency who need me to kiss a baby for a picture. But rather a dirty little prostitute who has nothing to offer except for tears, tears that drip with the regret of a wasted life, tears that stream with the emptiness of human pursuits, imagined needs, fantasies of success or just survival, dashed to pieces at the foot of the bed every single time she's with a new John." Tears that now wet the feet of the Master in love, those feet that would be pierced for her and for you and me. He loves; she's forgiven. She's forgiven; that's why she loves. We love because He first loved us. • Dear Lord Jesus Christ, I need You. Grant me grace, that this day I shrink from protesting my own sufficiency and rely only on Your love and forgiveness. Lead me so to love as You have loved me and given Yourself for me. Amen.

For His Is the Testimony of the Spirit, the Water, and the Blood (ch. 5)

ESV	KJV
5 ¹Everyone who believes that Jesus is the Christ has been born of God, and everyone who loves the Father loves whoever has been born of him. ²By this we know that we love the children of God, when we love God and obey his commandments. ³For this is the love of God, that we keep his commandments. And his commandments are not burdensome. ⁴For everyone who has been born of God overcomes the world. And this is the victory that has overcome the world—our faith. ⁵Who is it that overcomes the world except the one who believes that Jesus is the Son of God? ⁶This is he who came by water and blood—Jesus Christ; not by the water only but by the water and the blood. And the Spirit is the one who testifies, because the Spirit is the truth. ⁷For there are three that testify: ⁸the Spirit and the water and the blood; and these three agree. ⁹If we receive the testimony of men, the testimony of God is greater, for this is the tes-	5 ¹Whosoever believeth that Jesus is the Christ is born of God: and every one that loveth him that begat loveth him also that is begotten of him. ²By this we know that we love the children of God, when we love God, and keep his commandments. ³For this is the love of God, that we keep his commandments: and his commandments are not grievous. ⁴For whatsoever is born of God overcometh the world: and this is the victory that overcometh the world, even our faith. ⁵Who is he that overcometh the world, but he that believeth that Jesus is the Son of God? ⁶This is he that came by water and blood, even Jesus Christ; not by water only, but by water and blood. And it is the Spirit that beareth witness, because the Spirit is truth. ⁷For there are three that bear record in heaven, the Father, the Word, and the Holy Ghost: and these three are one.

timony of God that he has borne concerning his Son. [10]Whoever believes in the Son of God has the testimony in himself. Whoever does not believe God has made him a liar, because he has not believed in the testimony that God has borne concerning his Son. [11]And this is the testimony, that God gave us eternal life, and this life is in his Son. [12]Whoever has the Son has life; whoever does not have the Son of God does not have life.

[13]I write these things to you who believe in the name of the Son of God that you may know that you have eternal life. [14]And this is the confidence that we have toward him, that if we ask anything according to his will he hears us. [15]And if we know that he hears us in whatever we ask, we know that we have the requests that we have asked of him.

[16]If anyone sees his brother committing a sin not leading to death, he shall ask, and God will give him life—to those who commit sins that do not lead to death. There is sin that leads to death; I do not say that one should pray for that. [17]All wrongdoing is sin, but there is sin that does not lead to death.

[18]We know that everyone who has been born of God does not keep on sinning, but he who was born of God protects him, and the evil one does not touch him.

[19]We know that we are from God, and the whole world lies in the power of the evil one.

[20]And we know that the Son of God has come and has given us understanding, so that we may know him who is true; and we are in him who

[8]And there are three that bear witness in earth, the Spirit, and the water, and the blood: and these three agree in one.

[9]If we receive the witness of men, the witness of God is greater: for this is the witness of God which he hath testified of his Son.

[10]He that believeth on the Son of God hath the witness in himself: he that believeth not God hath made him a liar; because he believeth not the record that God gave of his Son.

[11]And this is the record, that God hath given to us eternal life, and this life is in his Son.

[12]He that hath the Son hath life; and he that hath not the Son of God hath not life.

[13]These things have I written unto you that believe on the name of the Son of God; that ye may know that ye have eternal life, and that ye may believe on the name of the Son of God.

[14]And this is the confidence that we have in him, that, if we ask any thing according to his will, he heareth us:

[15]And if we know that he hear us, whatsoever we ask, we know that we have the petitions that we desired of him.

[16]If any man see his brother sin a sin which is not unto death, he shall ask, and he shall give him life for them that sin not unto death. There is a sin unto death: I do not say that he shall pray for it.

[17]All unrighteousness is sin: and there is a sin not unto death.

[18]We know that whosoever is born of God sinneth not; but he that is begotten of God keepeth himself, and that wicked one toucheth him not.

is true, in his Son Jesus Christ. He is the true God and eternal life. [21]Little children, keep yourselves from idols.

[19]And we know that we are of God, and the whole world lieth in wickedness.

[20]And we know that the Son of God is come, and hath given us an understanding, that we may know him that is true, and we are in him that is true, even in his Son Jesus Christ. This is the true God, and eternal life.

[21]Little children, keep yourselves from idols. Amen.

Introduction to 5:1–21 The final chapter of the Letter draws the threads of John's thoughts to a conclusion. Victory in faith (vv. 1–5) is confirmed by faith's object: the Son of God, to whom the Spirit testifies (v. 6), and who came by water and blood (vv. 7–8). God's testimony about His own Son is greater than man's testimony (vv. 9–11), giving believers confidence that they have life in the Son (v. 12). John proclaims the central purpose of his Letter: that believers may know they have eternal life (v. 13). The benefits of this gift include prayer, assured that God hears us (vv. 14–15); mutual intercession for our current sinful state (vv. 16–17); and confidence in an identity distinct from the world and Satan (vv. 18–19). That identity is known by the understanding given by God in Christ; believers rest assured that they are "in Him" (v. 20) and therefore listen to the final exhortation to avoid idolatry (v. 21).

5:1–2 John has advanced an argument throughout the Letter that locates Christian identity in new birth. Those who are born of God's seed are distinct from those of the world and those of Satan (2:29; 3:9; 4:7; cf. Jn 1:13; 3:3–8). He connects this new birth in faith, saying *everyone who believes . . . has been born of Him*, another way of saying what he affirms in his Gospel: "But to all who did receive Him, who believed in His name, He gave the right to become children of God, who were born, not of blood nor of the will of the flesh nor of the will of man, but of God" (Jn 1:12–13). The content of this faith is that *Jesus is the Christ*, a confession of Jesus as God in the flesh (cf. 2:22–23; 4:2–3, 15; 2Jn 7). Faith in Jesus as Christ translates into Christian action: the believer *loves whoever has been born of Him*, since we share a common birth, and believers *obey His command-ments*. This is a real brotherhood, revealed in action (cf. 2:5; 3:24): Christ, the only begotten Son, is the chief of the brothers, and we love each other because we share a common Father. Common faith embraces true fellowship, an objective reality based on God's actions in giving us new birth, birth from above, of His seed, received by faith in Jesus as the Christ.

5:3 Jesus says, "Take My yoke upon you, and learn from Me, for I am gentle and lowly in heart, and you will find rest for your souls. For My yoke is easy, and My burden is light" (Mt 11:29–30). *His com-mandments are not burdensome*, because Jesus did not come to be a new Moses, simply leaving a new set of difficult instructions to follow in a covenant by which human loyalty can be measured by fulfilling an impossible Law. Rather, Jesus fulfills God's holy Law on behalf of sinners. Faith in His perfect fulfillment incorporates sin-ners into the brotherhood of God's saints, who love Him and serve Him by loving and serving their brothers. As believers *keep His com-mandments*, they are revealed to be the children of God. Born of God's Gospel, believers cannot help but love one another; it is what children of God naturally do.

5:4 Feelings or faith? John offers an objective description of faith's benefits: the new birth marks the believer as one who *overcomes the world*; and the *victory* is *our faith*. This is a comfort only for those who sense how impossible such a victory seems because of human experience in tribulation and temptation. It is a comfort located in the victory of God Himself: "I have said these things to you, that in Me you may have peace. In the world you will have tribulation. But take heart; I have overcome the world" (Jn 16:33). Luther's commen-tary on this verse raises our human experience to the surface:

> This must happen through faith in Christ, which is the victory. For what could this fragile vessel accomplish against Satan, the god of the world (2 Cor. 4:4)? But God is greater. He always triumphs in us through Christ (cf. 2 Cor. 2:14). Therefore all glory of victory must be ascribed to God Himself, not by any means to us. We are far too insignificant for this. Here, however, the Word of God is required—the Word which promises and extends grace to the believers, so that when they have been hurled into so many great trials and are weighed down under such great and crafty spirits, they nevertheless fight their way out and triumph. But to be born of God is to believe in Jesus Christ. He who believes in Christ is

now a warrior. . . . For we are still engaged in the battle itself and are about to be victorious. . . . God has placed us in the midst of wolves, in the kingdom of the devil. As weapons He has given us His Word and Spirit, and He tells us to do battle and to conduct ourselves as bold warriors under Him Himself as our Prince while He Himself looks on and is also victorious. (LW 30:311)

5:5 Because Jesus overcame the world, sin, death, and the devil, so also Christians take comfort in their victory, a triumph that depends on faith—not strength of faith, size of faith, or any other quality of faith, but on the object of that faith. The only proper object of faith is Christ, for the one who *overcomes the world* is *the one who believes that Jesus is the Son of God.* Confession of faith in Jesus as the Son of God is the rock on which the Church stands, as Hus pointed out: "Peter confessed Christ to be very God and very man [Mt 16:16]. And among all the articles of faith, this one appertains most to the edification of the Church" (*The Church,* p. 84).

5:1–5 in Devotion and Prayer You're asked to bind yourself to a lot of things. You get tied down with things that are profitable and good, of course: family obligations, work responsibilities, civic duties. But we often fall in a trap of over-taxing ourselves with obligations that are unnecessary at best, and at worst harmful to ourselves and our neighbors. In a world that heaps more and more on you—physically, emotionally, and spiritually—finding a course to navigate those obligations can be trying. No worries, says the world, we have options to help you do everything yourself, to get you to succeed in life's demands. If you just follow my five-step plan, you will be free from that burden. If you just sign this contract, it will make your life easier. If you just commit to this class, that club; if you just make the time for this inward meditation or that outward public service; if you just follow my diet, if you just listen to these lectures; if you just have enough faith, you can get out of debt, be cured of every disease, have more charisma, be better looking, be a better parent, and all it will cost you is four easy payments of $19.95 (plus shipping and handling), if you just, if you just, if you just . . . The answers from the world's gurus are self-serving, leaving a burden impossible to bear. But those answers are easy to recognize, because they so often start with that future-less-vivid, saccharine lie: "if you just." In the midst of such a world, God plants His Son, Jesus, who humbly invites the weary: My commands are not burdensome.

321

Learn from Me. I am gentle and humble. Then you'll find shalom, true godly life with your neighbor, true communion with Me. It's not about "if you just"; it's about how I am just, how I justify you, how I just do all things for you. Stop looking to the guru, the leader, the motivational speaker, the example. Stop looking to the world for answers. And stop looking at Me the way the world looks at Me. Stop thinking I'm just any old prophet, priest, teacher, or king, and just actually trust in Me. Come to Me. Get to know Me. Walk with Me and let Me influence you. Walk with Me and let Me teach you justice and mercy. Not just how to be a better person, a more just person, a more merciful person, but let Me teach you what God has done in justice and mercy for YOU! Let Me change your life. Let Me be the most influential person in your life. For My yoke is easy and My burden is light. Don't be defeated, My dear child, by the weights you so want to heap on yourself or the burdens in disguise with which the world would weigh you down. Receive Me, receive release, receive victory that overcomes the world, even your faith. • "I bind unto myself today The pow'r of God to hold and lead, His eye to watch, His might to stay, His ear to hearken to my need, The wisdom of my God to teach, His hand to guide, His shield to ward, The Word of God to give me speech, His heav'nly host to be my guard." Amen. (*LSB* 604:3; *H82* 370:5)

5:6 "Jesus is the Christ" is the confession of Christians (v. 1), and John indicates that identity by naming Him as *He who came by water and blood*, referring on the one hand to Jesus' Baptism (cf. Mk 1:9–11), and on the other hand to His crucifixion (Jn 19:18). God's love is revealed in all of what Jesus did in His earthly ministry, but especially in His sacrificial death for the sins of the world. John gives the "water and blood" particular attention as he shows that Jesus' earthly ministry climaxes in His sacrificial death at Jn 19:31–34. John's narrative about the flow of blood and water when Jesus' side is pierced is important evidence for the Gospel writer: "He who saw it has borne witness—his testimony is true, and he knows that he is telling the truth—that you also may believe" (Jn 19:35). "Testimony" (Gk *martyria*) is related to the verb *testifies* (Gk *martyreō*); John's testimony is certain because *the Spirit is the one who testifies*. John heard the voice of the Father (cf. Mt 3:17; 17:5) and witnessed the testimony of the Spirit at Jesus' Baptism (Mt 3:16), marking Him as the Christ whose coming was foretold and as the Son of God (Jn 1:29–34). He is *the Spirit of truth* because Jesus is the Truth (Jn 14:6). The Holy Spirit teaches believers the truth and leads believers into all truth (Jn 14:26; 16:13–14). Christ's crucifixion and Baptism intimately connect with our own, as Luther noted:

> The water of Baptism is sanctified through the blood of Christ. Therefore it is not plain water; it is water stained with blood because of this blood of Christ which is given to us through the Word, which brings with it the blood of Christ. And here we are said to be baptized through the blood of Christ, and thus we are cleansed from sins. (LW 30:314)

Welsey saw in the water and the blood references to the Sacraments. For example, he wrote:

> Not by the water only—Wherein he was baptized. But by the water and the blood—Which he shed when he had finished the work his Father had given him to do. He not only undertook at his baptism "to fulfill all righteousness," but on the cross accomplished what he had undertaken; in token whereof, when all was finished, blood and water came out of his side. (Wesley 639)

5:7–8 There is an interesting problem in the textual history of these verses. The KJV translation *the Father, the Word, and the Holy Ghost* is the result, in part, of scholarly work done in the sixteenth century that produced the Gk text (known as the "*textus receptus*") that many translators followed until the nineteenth century. Translations since then have taken account of better manuscripts and critical scholarship, which is why the ESV translation omits the "witnesses from heaven" section of v. 7. (These words are often referred to as the "*comma Johanneum*.") John is outlining evidence that Jesus is the Christ, the divine Son of God, and draws his evidence from the narrative of His ministry on earth. The *three that testify* are the Holy Spirit, the water of Christ's Baptism, and the blood of His death on the cross. The significance of "three" is not overtly Trinitarian, but rather supports the notion of a legal claim with forensic certainty. Testimony established by two or three witnesses was testimony that could be considered trustworthy (Dt 17:6; Mt 18:16; cf. Jn 8:17–18). As an early practitioner of textual criticism, Bengel has a long excursus on the manuscript tradition for this passage. He devoted about fourteen pages to the issue in a commentary that is otherwise very pithy. Bengel noted the strong presence of the Trinitarian wording in the Latin tradition but virtual absence in the Greek tradition. Nevertheless, he defended the longer reading based on the internal argument of the text, sensing that it was necessary to John's Letter.

Luther reinforced the intimate connection between Christ's Baptism and sacrificial death and our own Baptism:

> The water cannot be proclaimed without the blood. Nor is the blood of Christ given without the water of Baptism. Besides, the blood and the water do not come to us except at the instance of the Holy Spirit, who is in the Word. Therefore those three cannot be separated, but the three do one thing. . . . For these three constantly accompany one another, and through the Word a daily immersion and a perpetual Baptism takes place, a perpetual shedding of the blood of Christ and of the Holy Spirit, a continual cleansing from sins. (LW 30:315)

Calvin wrote:

> He adds a third witness, the Holy Spirit, who yet holds the first place, for without him the water and blood would have flowed without any benefit; for it is he who seals on our hearts the testimony of the water and blood; it is he who by his power makes the fruit of Christ's death to come to us; yea, he makes the blood shed for our redemption to penetrate into our hearts, or, to say all in one word, he makes Christ with all his blessings to become ours. (Calvin 259)

5:9 John recalls God's own testimony about Jesus, as does Peter, who shared with John the experience of witnessing Jesus' transfiguration (cf. Mt 17:5; 2Pt 1:17). His repetition of the word *greater* (cf. note at 3:20) is resonant of Jesus' argument at Jn 5:34–37. Jesus needs no other to testify on His behalf; His Father bears witness that He is the Christ.

5:10–11 Believers are never put in a position of "taking a leap of faith" into the unknown, any more than a human court of law expects a judge to convict and sentence based on feelings, mood, or personal prejudices, instead of evidence and testimony. John lays out the evidence in his Gospel and points to the *testimony* that corroborates the evidence. We are called to trust the "testimony of God" (v. 9), and that trust means that the believer *has the testimony in himself.* This testimony is the objective Word of God that bears witness to the truth of His Son's death and resurrection on our behalf. Therefore, *whoever does not believe God has made Him a liar* (cf. notes at 2:22 and 2:23). We make God "a liar" if we fail to trust that

Jesus is the Son of God, that He is the Christ, and that in Him our sins are truly forgiven (1:10). Melanchthon wrote: "Absolution is the promise of the forgiveness of sins. Therefore, it necessarily requires faith. . . . If the heart doubts, it regards those things that God promises as uncertain and of no account" (Ap XIIA 61–62). The truth of God's *testimony* has a practical effect in the believer's life: it gives *eternal life . . . in His Son*. Only those who are "in Christ," who have faith in Him, have eternal life (cf. Jn 3:18, 36; 6:53; 20:31).

5:12 John sums up the exclusive claim of Christianity in this verse: *whoever has the Son has life*. Only in the God-man Jesus Christ is life found, through faith in His perfect life, death, and resurrection. Trusting God's testimony of His love in Christ results in eternal life. Faith in God's promise is a gift He freely gives to all (Eph 2:8–9). We possess the gift of eternal life now by believing in Jesus, which is why John writes this Letter, in order that his readers may believe and so know that they have eternal life (v. 13).

5:6–12 in Devotion and Prayer Winner or loser? John is intent on the question, because the world is the Christian's enemy and the battle is a spiritual battle. This is how our faith starts: with the question, victory or defeat? And this is how our faith starts, with a God who answers that question in defeat and victory. Our God shows us both, in water and blood. In a real, historical way, God showed water and blood pouring out at the cross, that symbol of defeat, in that last wound inflicted on our dead Lord, when His broken, holy heart bled out water mixed with blood after the soldier stabbed Him. That wound has particular significance to faith, as we see in the example of Thomas. This doubting disciple said, "Unless I see the nail prints, no, unless I touch them, and His side, I won't believe!" Jesus appears and speaks: "Peace. Thomas, come here. Stick your finger in here. Poke your fingers in My real flesh, thrust your sense of doubt into My wounded side, place your hand at the opening of My heart that cannot be closed in My real and glorified body! Stop being a loser in your unbelief. Here's proof! You don't have to lose anymore! Believe and gain victory over doubt, despair, the world! Remember, Thomas, in this life you will have troubles, but take heart, I have overcome the world! And because I have overcome, so you also will overcome the world! This wound is here so that you may be My child, washed in the water and blood that once flowed from it. This wound is here so that in all things you may be more than conquerors. This wound is here so that you may believe the words of My faithful servant, that he becomes a winner who believes simply that Jesus is the Son of God!" We believe. We believe in a God who died. We believe in a God who lives. Cling to it in faith: we believe, and so we have victory over the world. Whether we win or lose according to this world, we win. We conquer. And this is the victory: even our faith. Though we be concerned or doubt or despair of our standing here in this short-lived reality, even if we be concerned or despair of our standing as sinners and saints before the throne of our God, we win. • "At the Lamb's high feast we sing Praise to our victorious King, Who has washed us in the tide Flowing from His pierced side. Alleluia!" Amen. (*LSB* 633:1; *H82* 174:1)

5:13 Like the Gospel of John (Jn 20: 30–31; cf. 21:24–25), this Letter closes with a statement of purpose. John's purpose is that those *who believe* in the name of Jesus *may know* that they *have eternal life*, that is, that they may have confidence before God and the world.

5:14–15 *Confidence* before God means boldness in prayer. He Himself gives that confidence in calling us His own, finding us "in Christ" by faith. Prayer *according to His will* results in the confidence that *we have the requests that we have asked*, according to Jesus' promise: "If you abide in Me, and My words abide in you, ask whatever you wish, and it will be done for you" (Jn 15:7). We know that God gives good gifts to His children (Lk 11:13), and we pray according to His will, which is always for our salvation and for the salvation of all.

5:16–17 We have confidence to pray on behalf of our brothers and sisters in Christ as well. Such prayer is "intercession," and Christians find comfort and a holy example in the divine intercession of Christ on our behalf (cf. 2:1; Jn 17:9; Heb 7:25). Praying for our brothers and sisters activates and energizes the holy fellowship that God has called us to and saves us from great sin and vice (cf. Jas 5:15–16: "And the prayer of faith will save the one who is sick, and the Lord will raise him up. And if he has committed sins, he will be forgiven. Therefore, confess your sins to one another and pray for one another, that you may be healed. The prayer of a righteous person has great power as it is working"). John distinguishes between the *sins that do not lead to death* and the *sin that leads to death*. All sin can lead to death, but faith in Christ leads us to repent, to receive God's forgiveness, to be found in Christ; otherwise we die in our sins (3:8–9; cf. Jn 8:24). But faith in Christ receives the cleansing "from all sin" (1:7, 9; 2:1–2). So John's distinction has to do with repentance versus unrepentance, and not with particular sins, or kinds of sins, such as the false teaching about "mortal" (deadly) versus "venial" (forgivable) sins. The one who insists on sin in an unrepentant way is doomed—this is the *sin that leads to death*. Insisting on sin can take the form of rationalizing and self-justifying sinful behaviors, refusing to acknowledge that they are actually sins. This is the way of the idolaters John speaks against as false teachers (see 2:19, 26 and notes). The problem from the human side is not our sin for *all wrongdoing is sin*, and we sin daily, much, in many ways (Jas 3:2); the problem rather is what we do with the knowledge of our sin. We can deny it, rationalize it, justify ourselves, run from God, not acknowledge Him and His holy Law, and not trust in the promise of His Gospel. This leads to death. Or we can repent, confess, and receive the promise and pray for our brothers: *he shall ask, and God will give him life*. God will grant forgiveness of sins and life to the brother for whom we pray (cf. Jas 5:20). There is, however, no use in continually praying for deliberate, stubborn, unbelief which refuses God's love (Jn 3:18, 36); John calls this the "sin that leads to death" and says *I do not say that one should pray for that*. Such refusal of God's love amounts to self-exclusion from the Gospel, which is victory over sin, death, and the world (cf. Mt 18:15–20).

5:18 John's summary reprises the theme of new birth of God's seed (3:6, 9) as he describes the saints: *everyone who has been born of God does not keep on sinning*. While in the world, in spite of sin around us, and in spite of our very real sinfulness, Jesus, *who was born of God, protects* believers with the assurance that though we are sinners, we are saints at the same time (*"simul iustus et peccator"*). Being found in Christ, abiding in His Word, Jesus remains in us as a sure protection against the devil. Luther explored the paradox of being at the same time saint and sinner as he comments on these words:

> This is a strange thought. The same man sins, and at the same time he does not sin. It is here that those two statements of the apostle John are brought into harmony. The first is found in 1 John 1:8: "If we say we have no sin, we deceive ourselves"; the second occurs in 1 John 3:9 and 5:18: "No one born of God commits sin." All the saints, therefore, have sin and are sinners; yet no one of them sins. They are righteous in accordance with the fact that grace has

worked healing in them; they are sinners in accordance with the fact that they still must be healed. (LW 27:372)

5:19 While *the whole world lies* in Satan's power (Eph 2:1–3), God has rescued us (Col 1:13; Ac 26:18), just as He has always rescued His remnant and preserved it in the one true faith: "in the same way He calls, gathers, enlightens, and sanctifies the whole Christian Church on earth, and keeps it with Jesus Christ in the one true faith" (SC, Third Article). Those who have faith in Jesus as Christ, as Son of God, as the forgiveness of their sins, *are from God* (cf. 2:19; 4:13).

5:20 "Knowing" is a verb of special importance throughout the writings of John. He concludes his Letter with this summary: not only are we known by Christ (Jn 10:14), but also *we know that the Son of God has come and has given us understanding*. He gives us understanding of Himself, of His Scriptures, and understanding to know God because He reveals God to us (Jn 1:18). We know Jesus, *Him who is true* (Gk *alēthinon,* literally, "the genuine one"), that is, we know the real Christ (as opposed to the false christs taught by the spirit of the Antichrist, cf. 2:18, 22; 4:3; 2Jn 7). Biblical Christianity acknowledges the deity of Jesus Christ; John clearly states that *He is the true God* and that belief in Him is the only way to *eternal life.*

5:21 John's final appeal for the believers to *keep yourselves from idols* is the whole point of John's first Letter. Any teaching that presents Jesus as anything less than both true God and man in one person teaches idolatry. Likewise, any teaching that denies that Jesus is the Savior of all mankind, purely by God's grace alone, also presents an idol. Cf. Ac 15:20, 29; 21:25; Gal 5:19–20; 1Co 5:10; 6:9; Eph 5:5; Col 3:5.

5:13–21 in Devotion and Prayer We are always on dangerous ground when dealing with idols. It may seem a simple thing for Christians to stay away from "graven images" and feel confident in keeping the commandment "You will have no other gods." But we know that idols come in more forms than just pictures of "gods" made out of wood, gold, silver, bronze, or stone (Rv 9:20), than golden calves (Ex 32), Baals (1Ki 18:18–29), or Dagon (Jgs 16:23–24). Whatever we fear, love, or trust more than the triune God revealed in Christ becomes an idol, whether our money (Ps 115:4), our stomach (Php 3:19), or any earthly thing (Col 3:1–3). We do well to hear John's final appeal: protect yourselves from idols! Because when we find ourselves at odds with the world, the weakness of our own flesh, or dissatisfaction with the Church, we so quickly flee to those things that provide nothing less than temporary security, instant gratification, and the kind of soothing messages that tickle our ears with self-satisfaction, rationalizations, and a pat on the back that says, "I've got this handled. No need to bring this one to God. What does He know about modern life and my problems, anyhow?" How can we guard ourselves from that kind of seductive, sanctimonious self-confidence? The protection does not come from within. It comes from outside of us, from the Holy Spirit Himself, who covers us with protection. The belt of truth keeps us from false doctrine. The breastplate of righteousness is His own righteousness that covers us. We are fit and ready as we stand firmly on the Gospel of Jesus, extinguishing all the fiery darts of Satan with the shield of faith. The helmet of salvation and the sword of the Spirit complete the picture of one readily guarded against all forms of idolatry, for the Word of God is indeed a our trusty shield and weapon. • Lord Jesus Christ, "silence that evil spirit—the cruel backbiter, accuser, and magnifier of our sin—now and in our last hour, and in every torment of conscience. . . . Do not judge us according to the accusations the devil or our wretched conscience brings against us." Amen. (Luther, "Personal Prayer Book," *LW* 43:36)

1 John Article

The Doctrine of Sin

To envision how the reformers thought about sin, it is perhaps helpful to think first of a tree. The root of the tree, out of sight, is original sin—the inborn compulsion to do evil. The rest of the tree, above ground and in view, is actual sin. Actual sins are the day-by-day result of original sin, where we constantly do wrong and bring forth the deadly results of original sin in our lives. All the reformers cited here distinguished between original sin and actual sin. But there were differences in how they described actual sin.

In 1 John 5:16–17, the apostle distinguished between "sin that leads to death" and "sin not leading to death." Since the time of Augustine, Christian theologians distinguished these actual sins as mortal sins and venial sins. Mortal sins were deadly to a Christian, robbing him of faith and the blessing of eternal life. Venial sins were literally mercy-provoking sins (Lat. *venia* means "mercy"). They were the kinds of mistakes and faults in others that we find easy to forgive.

To help Christians think on their sins for the sake of avoiding them or confessing them, Gregory the Great listed seven principle sins, which became famously known as the seven deadly sins. But they are not a list you might immediately expect. Many today might think of sins like murder, idolatry, or adultery as deadly sins. But Gregory listed (1) pride, (2) covetousness, (3) lust, (4) envy, (5) gluttony, (6) anger, and (7) sloth. He reasoned that these were the poisonous root and branches from which all our day-by-day sins spring.

The medieval church expected Christians to confess their mortal sins when they sought private confession and absolution. Then in 1215, the Fourth Lateran Council ruled that all Christians must confess not only their mortal sins but also all their venial sins, including the circumstances in which they committed them! The confession of sins changed from a practice focused on help and comfort for sinners into an enormous burden on a Christian's conscience. No wonder Christians around this time took to the streets, whipping themselves, and the doctrines of purgatory and indulgences spread widely! People felt overwhelmed by their sins.

Although the late medieval penance system greatly troubled Luther, he saw value in retaining the long-standing distinction between mortal and venial sins, though emphasizing that all sin is damnable (cf. James 2:9–11). Melanchthon defined mortal sin as that which was incompatible with faith (Apology IV 109, 115), and Luther clarified this by teaching that when people fall into open, willful sin, then faith and the Holy Spirit depart from them (SA III III 43). Faith and the will were important for distinguishing mortal sins from venial sins. Lutherans continued to recommend that Christians troubled by their sins should go to their pastor for private Confession and Absolution. In place of the seven deadly sins, Lutherans used the Ten Commandments to prepare for confession.

Cranmer, like the Lutherans, recommended Confession and Absolution with a priest "at such time as [Christians] shall find their consciences grieved with mortal sin" (Cranmer 2:39). The Swiss Reformer J. H. Bullinger included the distinction between mortal and venial sins in the Second Helvitic Confession (Schaff 3:843).

Calvin took a different approach to the issue of sin due to his beliefs about predestination. He emphasized the deadliness of all sins (Institutes 2.8.58) like the Lutherans, but rejected the distinction between mortal and venial sins as arbitrary and Scholastic. For Calvin, predestination meant that God also gave to the elect the gift of perseverance or security so that they would not fall away, even if they committed heinous sins. The 1560 Geneva Bible included notes stating, "Although every sin is to death, yet God through his mercy pardons his [elect] in his Son Christ. . . . There [are those] whom God does so forsake that they fall into utter despair" (notes on 1 John 5:15–16; English updated).

Calvinists intended their emphasis on God's grace and election as comfort. But when people fell into sin, they struggled with wondering whether they were among the elect who would persevere or among the damned who would utterly despair. The controversial teacher Jacob Arminius tried to address the issue by changing Calvinistic teaching on predestination. In response, the Synod of Dort (1618–19) reintroduced something like the distinction between mortal and venial sins in its article on perseverance, distinguishing "daily sins of infirmity" and "enormous sins [that] incur a deadly guilt." Nevertheless, the article went on to maintain Calvin's view (Schaff, 3:592–93).

After the Reformation, Bengel also expounded 1 John 5 by moving the discussion away from sin to focus more on faith and the will.

> Any unrighteousness, which is committed in common life, is a sin not unto death. But sin unto death is not an ordinary or sudden sin, but a state of the soul, in which faith, and love, and hope, in short the new life, is extinguished: when anyone knowingly and willingly embraces death, not from the allurements of the flesh, but from the love of sin, as sin. It is a deliberate rejection of grace. (Bengel 151–52)

Wesley, who often worked closely from Bengel's commentary, defined the sin not unto death as "any sin but total apostasy from Christ" (Wesley 612). What started out as a discussion of different types of sin became a discussion about the state of the soul and faith. Wesley would distinguish himself from Lutherans, Anglicans, and Calvinists by teaching that a second work of grace could bring a Christian to the point of perfection in this life.

Conclusions

Although the emphasis on grace of Calvin and Wesley was intended to offer Christians comfort and confidence in the struggle against sin, it commonly resulted in frustration and even fear, since believers still found themselves falling into sin. The Lutherans and Cranmer took a more pragmatic approach, emphasizing the ongoing need for repentance and forgiveness in this life while looking forward to the bliss of heaven in the next. ∞

2 JOHN

PART 1

GREETING (1–3)

ESV	KJV
1 ¹The elder to the elect lady and her children, whom I love in truth, and not only I, but also all who know the truth, ²because of the truth that abides in us and will be with us forever: ³Grace, mercy, and peace will be with us, from God the Father and from Jesus Christ the Father's Son, in truth and love.	*1* ¹The elder unto the elect lady and her children, whom I love in the truth; and not I only, but also all they that have known the truth; ²For the truth's sake, which dwelleth in us, and shall be with us for ever. ³Grace be with you, mercy, and peace, from God the Father, and from the Lord Jesus Christ, the Son of the Father, in truth and love.

Introduction to 1–3 2Jn is the second-shortest book of the Bible. Like 3Jn, it may have accompanied 1Jn as an additional letter specifically addressed to a particular congregation, to be read in combination with the sermon that 1Jn comprises (see *Authorship* in introduction to 1, 2, 3 John, p. 256). John identifies himself as the "elder" and his audience as "the elect lady and her children" (v. 1), familial designations that suggest the theme of the Letter: Christian fellowship that arises from agreement in true doctrine which is called "the truth" (v. 2). The apostolic greeting takes the form of a promise that God's "grace, mercy, and peace will be with us" (v. 3).

1–2 Peter calls himself a "fellow elder" (1Pt 5:1), and John likewise names himself *the elder*, a common title for the spiritual leaders of Christian congregations (cf. notes at Jas 5:14; 1Pt 5:1–3). John is writing this congregation as their pastor. Consider Luther's explanation of the term: "'Elder' is 'presbyter' in Greek and is equivalent to 'priest.' So also Peter and John called themselves elders in their letters" (LW 10:19; sce also Tr 62). John describes the Church as *the elect lady and her children*, consistent with other NT descriptions of the Church as the chosen Bride of Christ (Eph 5:22–33; Rv 19:7;

cf. Gal 4:26). That John is describing a specific congregation is clear from his concluding appeal at v. 13, which delivers a greeting from another congregation which he calls "the elect sister." The Church is called *elect*, that is, "chosen," because they *know the truth* of the message of Christ, who is the Truth (Jn 14:6). *The truth that abides in us* is "in us" because we are "in Christ" (cf. notes at 1Jn 5:19–20).

3 John includes himself in the promise of his apostolic greeting: "God's grace *will be with us*" tenderly folds the apostle into the family of God along with the rest of the Church. True teaching (v. 2) confesses *Jesus Christ the Father's Son*. This confesses the true deity of the Son of God and opposes the teachings of the adoptionists and other false teachers who taught that Jesus was born only of human parents. Wesley wrote:

> Grace takes away guilt; mercy, misery: peace implies the abiding in grace and mercy. It includes the testimony of God's Spirit, both that we are his children, and that all our ways are acceptable to him. This is the very foretaste of heaven itself, where it is perfected. In truth and love—Or, faith and love, as St. Paul speaks. Faith and truth are here synonymous terms. (Wesley 642)

1–3 in Devotion and Prayer The Church as "lady" is an interesting metaphor. Men in the Church might chafe at a description like "elect lady," just as they might wince at being called the "Bride of Christ." But the NT authors do not have an emasculating agenda in mind; indeed, they do not describe individual members of the Church in such terms, but rather the whole Church, as a collective. And this is a great promise to confess, because God can, without reservation, reveal His love in terms quite natural to our human ears: "Christ loved the church and gave Himself up for her, that He might sanctify her, having cleansed her by the washing of water with the word, so that He might present the church to Himself in splendor, without spot or wrinkle or any such thing, that she might be holy and without blemish" (Eph 5:25–27). Paul calls this a great mystery, but we do well to find in this our glory: just as we take care of, respect, and celebrate our own bodies, whether men or women, so also our Savior Jesus cares for His own body, the Church—celebrated as the object of His dearest affection. You are the object of His affection. You are loved by Him! • "Thy heart now open wide, bid Christ with thee abide. He graciously will hear thee And be forever near thee. Hosanna, praise, and glory! Our King, we bow before Thee." Amen. ("O Bride of Christ Rejoice," *TLH* 57:5)

PART 2

WALKING IN TRUTH AND LOVE (4–11)

ESV	KJV
⁴I rejoiced greatly to find some of your children walking in the truth, just as we were commanded by the Father. ⁵And now I ask you, dear lady—not as though I were writing you a new commandment, but the one we have had from the beginning—that we love one another. ⁶And this is love, that we walk according to his commandments; this is the commandment, just as you have heard from the beginning, so that you should walk in it. ⁷For many deceivers have gone out into the world, those who do not confess the coming of Jesus Christ in the flesh. Such a one is the deceiver and the antichrist. ⁸Watch yourselves, so that you may not lose what we have worked for, but may win a full reward. ⁹Everyone who goes on ahead and does not abide in the teaching of Christ, does not have God. Whoever abides in the teaching has both the Father and the Son. ¹⁰If anyone comes to you and does not bring this teaching, do not receive him into your house or give him any greeting, ¹¹for whoever greets him takes part in his wicked works.	⁴I rejoiced greatly that I found of thy children walking in truth, as we have received a commandment from the Father. ⁵And now I beseech thee, lady, not as though I wrote a new commandment unto thee, but that which we had from the beginning, that we love one another. ⁶And this is love, that we walk after his commandments. This is the commandment, That, as ye have heard from the beginning, ye should walk in it. ⁷For many deceivers are entered into the world, who confess not that Jesus Christ is come in the flesh. This is a deceiver and an antichrist. ⁸Look to yourselves, that we lose not those things which we have wrought, but that we receive a full reward. ⁹Whosoever transgresseth, and abideth not in the doctrine of Christ, hath not God. He that abideth in the doctrine of Christ, he hath both the Father and the Son. ¹⁰If there come any unto you, and bring not this doctrine, receive him not into your house, neither bid him God speed: ¹¹For he that biddeth him God speed is partaker of his evil deeds.

Introduction to 4–11 The body of the apostle's Letter is brief, exhorting the congregation that they walk according the commandments they have received from the beginning (vv. 4–6). This appeal is important in light of false teachers seducing their hearers with antichristian doctrine (v. 7). Those who listen to such teaching run the risk of losing all that they have worked for, the true object of Christian faith, the Father and the Son (vv. 8–9). John warns them not to abide in false teaching, nor even to admit false teachers or greet them, lest they partake in the works of the antichristian teachers (vv. 10–11).

4–5 The good report John received about members of the congregation *walking in the truth* is a cause for him to rejoice. This encouraging word sets a foundation for his further exhortation to stand up against false teaching. *Walking in the truth* is living in conduct consistent with their calling as Christians, believing in Jesus as Christ, the Son of God, and loving the brothers as God has loved them in Christ. John reinforces the teaching of 1Jn 2:7 and 3:11 by repeating what he intended for all the churches: the *commandment* is not a *new* one, but the one that was *from the beginning—that we love one another.*

6 "We love because He first loved us" (1Jn 4:19): John's exhortation to the Church (*this is love*) has its source in God's love for us in Christ, which translates into love for one another (cf. 1Jn 2:5; 5:3; Jn 14:15). This is the commandment that John's readers *have heard from the beginning,* when they were first given the gift of faith in Jesus (cf. 1Jn 1:1; 2:7, 13–14, 24; 3:11).

7 John expands his warning against the *deceivers* he has in mind at 1Jn 4:1–6, noting that they teach by the spirit of *antichrist* and *do not confess the coming of Jesus Christ in the flesh.* Such denial refers to disbelief in the incarnation of the Son of God, as well as to a refusal to acknowledge the flesh of Christ delivered according to Christ's institution in the Lord's Supper. The issue among the churches to whom John addresses his appeal was known also in subsequent generations, as is evident in Ignatius: "They abstain from the Eucharist and from prayer, because they confess not the Eucharist to be the flesh of our Saviour Jesus Christ, which suffered for our sins, and which the Father, of His goodness, raised up again. Those, therefore, who speak against this gift of God, incur death in the midst of their disputes" (*ANF* 1:89). Luther confirms that the source of all heresy is a disbelief regarding what God has revealed about His Son:

I have also noticed that all error, heresy, idolatry, offense, misuse, and evil in the church originally came from despising or losing sight of this article of faith in Jesus Christ. And if one looks at it correctly and clearly, all heresies do contend against this dear article of Jesus Christ, as Simeon says of him, that he is "set for the fall and rising of many in Israel, and for a sign that is spoken against" [Lk 2:34]. . . . For whatsoever stumbles, certainly stumbles on this stone, which lies in everyone's way and is rejected by the builders. . . . St. John also gives no other or more certain sign for recognizing false and anti-Christian spirits than their denial of Jesus Christ [II John 7]. They have all wanted to reap honor at his expense and have instead garnered shame from it. (LW 34:207–8)

8 What is lost when an unsuspecting fish takes the bait of false teaching? All the things that the apostles, including John, *have worked for*, including fellowship with the Church, the Father and the Son (v. 9), indeed life itself. The Holy Spirit called the apostles to the singular mission of delivering the crucified and risen Christ to sinners through the proclamation of His holy Word. They spent their lives teaching the truth in Christ so that those who believe might remain faithful unto death and finally receive the crown of life. John's appeal is delivered vividly and emotionally because he cares for these "dear children" (cf. Jn 13:33; 21:5; 1Jn 2:1, 12–13, 18, 28; 3:7, 18; 4:4; 5:21), and because he does not want his life's work undone by deceivers who would cause Christians to lose their *full reward* (cf. Jn 4:36; Mt 5:12). Bengel wrote, "There is no half reward of the saints; it is either lost all together or received in full" (Bengel 157).

9 When John says *goes on ahead*, he means "transgresses" (cf. KJV, *whosoever transgresseth*). Christians who prefer a more "progressive" teaching than the one that the apostles have delivered, by inventing new teachings, will find themselves outside of orthodox teaching. This is why Paul taught Christians "not to go beyond what is written" (1Co 4:6). Christians are rather to *abide in the teaching of Christ*, that is, to remain faithful to what the Holy Spirit has delivered in His Word, through the apostles, and through the continued teaching and preaching of Jesus as Christ, the Son of God. The one who receives this teaching has what it promises: *both the Father and the Son*, because Jesus had promised, "No one comes to the Father except through me" (Jn 14:6).

10–11 The first century Church that John knew met in various locations; city churches often met in the houses of wealthy people as the center of public worship and distribution of money and food (cf. Rm 16:5; 1Co 16:19; Col 4:15; Phm 2). This is the context in which John employs language of hospitality. The Early Church had to deal with false teachers who came to congregations claiming special teaching directly from the Lord. Often these were itinerant preachers, looking for money, food, and lodging (cf. *Didache* 11–13). John's warnings include the admonition not to give such preachers hospitality, unless they *bring this teaching*, that Jesus Christ was God incarnate, true God and true man in one person. Not only should the congregation not allow such falsehood into their *house*, but they should also avoid giving such a false teacher *any greeting* and rather rebuke false teachers and warn others against their deceptions. This is exemplified in the narrative of John at the bathhouse, recorded by Eusebius: "John, the disciple of the Lord, going to bathe in Ephesus and seeing Cerinthus within, ran out of the bath-house without bathing, crying, 'Let us flee, lest even the bath fall, because Cerinthus, the enemy of the truth, is within'" (*NPNF2* 1:187). Luther noted that the rules of hospitality apply to the communion rail as well:

> We learn from all these sayings how the ban [from communion or congregation] should be used. First, we should seek neither vengeance nor our own gain—as is now the shameful custom everywhere—but rather the improvement of our neighbor. Second, punishment should stop short of his ruin or death, for St. Paul limits the goal of the ban to improvement, that he be put to shame because no one associates with him; and he adds in II Thessalonians 3[:15], "Do not look on him as an enemy, but punish him as a brother." At the present time, the ruthless tyrants deal with people as if they wished to cast them into hell, and do not seek their improvement at all. (LW 39:9)

This is why receiving the gifts of the Lord with the Church in common confession of faith is such serious business: Christian hospitality is not as facile and superficial as "let's just be nice to people." Rather, it is a matter of salvation. Giving the impression of communion with false teachers leads to assumptions of agreement with false doctrine. Such things are a matter of eternal life and death!

4–11 in Devotion and Prayer Christ coming in the flesh is the foundation of true Christian doctrine. And if the fact of God coming in flesh does not drive us truly to love our neighbor, then we are to be pitied above all sinners. If God coming down in love to become a human being for a sinner like me does not lead me to accept and to love the sinners around me that He also came to save, then I haven't really gotten it. I am still on the "outs" with God and His mission. I am not "in on it." If this message, that Christ has in fact become incarnate to be born, to suffer, to die, and to rise again for you, if this message doesn't change your attitude about the person sitting next to you or an enemy you hold a grudge against, then perhaps you know something that God doesn't. Perhaps you think that you are better than others, that you have a reason why God should honor you, merit you, above other people. "Chief of sinners though I be, at least that bozo is worse than me," or some such idea. The cure for this attitude is faith—a confession not only of our very grave sinfulness, but a confession also of our belief in a God who loves us so much that because of our sickness, He died to deliver a cure. The delivery of that cure occurs in the moment we receive the mystery of Christ incarnate: His flesh that suffered, died, and rose, that sits at the right hand of God, that flesh that enters your mouth and the blood that washes it down. Listen to the words that accompany that gift, and believe them. The most important words you will hear are the Gospel words, the words FOR YOU. That Christ was a baby, in the flesh, that He suffered, died, that He rose again in history—this, by itself, is no good news . . . unless it is FOR YOU. Receiving that gift in faith causes you to be "in on it." It is FOR YOU. Believe the promise, the mystery revealed: salvation has come, in the flesh, FOR YOU. • Lord and Savior Jesus Christ, let not my reception of Your Body and Blood, which I, all unworthy, presume to eat and drink, be to my judgment and condemnation; but by Your mercy may it be to me for protection and health both of soul and body; who with the Father and the Holy Spirit are one God, living and reigning now and forever. Amen.

PART 3

FINAL GREETINGS (12–13)

ESV	KJV
¹²Though I have much to write to you, I would rather not use paper and ink. Instead I hope to come to you and talk face to face, so that our joy may be complete. ¹³The children of your elect sister greet you.	¹²Having many things to write unto you, I would not write with paper and ink: but I trust to come unto you, and speak face to face, that our joy may be full. ¹³The children of thy elect sister greet thee. Amen.

Introduction to 12–13 John's final greetings anticipate a personal visit (v. 12) and relate greetings from a sister congregation (v. 13).

12 John states that he *would rather not use paper and ink*, though the "paper" he has in mind (Gk *khartēs*, literally "page") would be rather different than the paper we think about today—not as readily available, and therefore to be preserved from unnecessary or frivolous usage. Further communication from John could take place *face to face*, when questions could be answered and clarifications given (cf. 3Jn 14).

13 The language here, connecting the final greeting with the salutation of v. 1 and omitting any reference to a specific "lady," suggests strongly that John is relating a message from one congregation to another, and not two human female kinswomen. The churches are the *elect*, that is, "chosen," (cf. note at 1Pt 1:1) recipients of God's grace, in the family of God, and therefore called *children* (cf. note at v. 8).

12–13 in Devotion and Prayer Oh, to have more than just paper and ink! We live in a modern day of more than the printing press, not to mention handwritten copies of old texts. We use technology to record and broadcast sound, images, digital archives, and all manner of written data, and enjoy the ability to share such things with anyone, anywhere, in an instant. Wouldn't it be nice to have an audio or video recording of the events of the first century? We wouldn't have to be too picky—we wouldn't need digital quality; how about just some magnetic tape? But alas, we are stuck with just paper and ink. Ink and paper. But in that paper and ink is all that we need for the testimony of God's actions on our behalf in Christ. Rare as "paper" was in the first century, the words that have been delivered to us over the last two millennia were deliberate and precious indeed. God moved the recorders of His words deliberately and sufficiently to give you all you need to know about Him. And when we read His words, we are coming before Him face-to-face, because we are coming before His holy Word. And that Word is not a what, but a who: Jesus Christ speaks from every "jot and tittle," from every bit of ink on the page, pointing to your need for a savior, and pointing to Himself as that Savior. • Lord Jesus, You are my sufficiency. Thank You for revealing Yourself to me in just words—words that tell me enough about Your love for me, that draw me to faith in You, and that declare me truly just, righteous, and innocent before You. Grant me the grace to share Your just words with my neighbors, that they may also come face-to-face with Your all-sufficient love. Amen.

3 JOHN

PART 1

GREETING (1–4)

ESV	KJV
1 ¹The elder to the beloved Gaius, whom I love in truth.	*1* ¹The elder unto the wellbeloved Gaius, whom I love in the truth.
²Beloved, I pray that all may go well with you and that you may be in good health, as it goes well with your soul. ³For I rejoiced greatly when the brothers came and testified to your truth, as indeed you are walking in the truth. ⁴I have no greater joy than to hear that my children are walking in the truth.	²Beloved, I wish above all things that thou mayest prosper and be in health, even as thy soul prospereth. ³For I rejoiced greatly, when the brethren came and testified of the truth that is in thee, even as thou walkest in the truth. ⁴I have no greater joy than to hear that my children walk in truth.

Introduction to 1–4 The shortest book in the Bible, 3Jn, like 2Jn, may have accompanied 1Jn as an additional letter specifically addressed to a particular congregation, to be read in combination with the sermon that 1Jn comprises (cf. 2Jn 1–3 and notes; see *Authorship* in introduction to 1, 2, 3 John, p. 256). The Letter further expounds the emphasis on hospitality and guarding against false teaching that characterizes 2Jn and parts of 1Jn by praising the addressee of his Letter and condemning Diotrephes, another church leader whose pride John attacks. In the greeting, John addresses a specific individual, Gaius (v. 1), and shares a personal prayer for his good health (v. 2). As in 2Jn 3, John rejoices that his "children" (including Gaius) are "walking in the truth" (vv. 3–4).

1 On John's use of the term *elder*, see note at 2Jn 1–2. John writes this Letter, probably as an addendum to the sermon of 1Jn, addressed to a certain *Gaius*. It is unknown who this Gaius was (it was a very common Roman name in the first century; cf. Ac 19:29; 20:4; Rm 16:23; 1Cor 1:14). This Gaius was possibly a leader (a fellow elder perhaps?) in John's congregation or a faithful layman who gave hospitality to itinerant preachers and teachers.

2 Gaius' *soul* is healthy; things are going well there; John's prayer is that the health of Gaius' body may match that of his soul. God cares about the whole man: body, soul, mind, emotions, flesh, the whole lot. As the apostle prays for his friend's health, so also we ought to pray for the spiritual and physical health of our brothers and sisters in the faith.

3–4 John employs the familial vocabulary he used in 1Jn and 2Jn to talk about fellow believers, referring to them under the term *the brothers*. His apostolic ministry has been spent proclaiming *the truth* about Christ. As sinners came to faith in Jesus, John has cared for them spiritually, just as fathers look after their *children*. The Word John has preached has birthed a large family of brothers who together *are walking in the truth*. The Christian conduct that John points to in Gaius includes love for one another, as well as hospitality and support for those who teach the faith, according to the report that the brothers gave him. Wesley wrote:

> Gaius probably was converted by St. Paul. Therefore when St. John speaks of him, with other believers, as his children, it may be considered as the tender style of paternal love, whoever were the instruments of their conversion. And his using this appellation, when writing under the character of the elder, has its peculiar beauty. (Wesley 644)

1–4 in Devotion and Prayer My in-laws finish every correspondence—phone calls, emails, letters, even birthday cards—with two sentences: "stay faithful, and God keep you safe." For an "elder" like John, for a teacher, for a parent, the goal is the same: that the ones we teach and the ones we lead remain faithful to the truth. You may be familiar with an attitude that attempts to come off as rather more enlightened than such an old-fashioned ideal, a mindset that sounds something like, "I want my child or student to be free to come up with their own truth, to develop their own sense of reality." Every responsible teacher knows that the individuals in our care are different and will develop their own approach to the subject we teach, but in the final analysis, if they haven't received an objective truth from their teachers, they run the risk of devoting themselves to a lie. A palpable example is a mother who came to me distraught over her child, who had become a fanatic in a cult during his teenage years.

"How could this happen?" she asked. "I had raised him with no religion, so that he could make a rational decision when he was mature enough to decide for himself!" But we reap what we sow as we raise our young chicks; those chickens do indeed come home to roost. John's joy on the other hand, the joy shared by all teachers who point to a truth outside ourselves, is that children who have been brought up with the truth have something to rely on that is not based on lies, opinions, moods, or contemporary, ever-changing worldviews. They will grow up with opinions. They will grow up with challenges we cannot anticipate. They will grow up thinking, speaking, listening, and teaching differently. But if we insist, for ourselves and for the children we serve, ever and always and only on the objective truth of Christ dead for their sins, raised for their justification, and living to give them new life, they will grow up with Christ who is the Truth. And we, like John, "have no greater joy than to hear that my children are walking in the truth." • Dear Lord Jesus Christ, look with mercy on the ones I serve with Your truth. Amid the cacophony of voices in the world that attempt to draw them away, direct their ears to hear the voice of the Good Shepherd who knows His sheep, that they may know You. And bless me with understanding, care, and above all, faith, that I may be faithful to Your truth and lead Your lambs to be faithful to You. Amen.

PART 2

SUPPORT AND OPPOSITION (5–12)

ESV	KJV
[5]Beloved, it is a faithful thing you do in all your efforts for these brothers, strangers as they are, [6]who testified to your love before the church. You will do well to send them on their journey in a manner worthy of God. [7]For they have gone out for the sake of the name, accepting nothing from the Gentiles. [8]Therefore we ought to support people like these, that we may be fellow workers for the truth. [9]I have written something to the church, but Diotrephes, who likes to put himself first, does not acknowledge our authority. [10]So if I come, I will bring up what he is doing, talking wicked nonsense against us. And not content with that, he refuses to welcome the brothers, and also stops those who want to and puts them out of the church. [11]Beloved, do not imitate evil but imitate good. Whoever does good is from God; whoever does evil has not seen God. [12]Demetrius has received a good testimony from everyone, and from the truth itself. We also add our testimony, and you know that our testimony is true.	[5]Beloved, thou doest faithfully whatsoever thou doest to the brethren, and to strangers; [6]Which have borne witness of thy charity before the church: whom if thou bring forward on their journey after a godly sort, thou shalt do well: [7]Because that for his name's sake they went forth, taking nothing of the Gentiles. [8]We therefore ought to receive such, that we might be fellowhelpers to the truth. [9]I wrote unto the church: but Diotrephes, who loveth to have the preeminence among them, receiveth us not. [10]Wherefore, if I come, I will remember his deeds which he doeth, prating against us with malicious words: and not content therewith, neither doth he himself receive the brethren, and forbiddeth them that would, and casteth them out of the church. [11]Beloved, follow not that which is evil, but that which is good. He that doeth good is of God: but he that doeth evil hath not seen God. [12]Demetrius hath good report of all men, and of the truth itself: yea, and we also bear record; and ye know that our record is true.

Introduction to 5–12 John's Letter focuses on the ministry of the itinerant preachers of Asia Minor who serve the churches with apostolic endorsement. Gaius is praised for showing them hospitality and supporting them in the ministry (vv. 5–6), which is what the Church should be doing (vv. 7–8). But not everyone acknowledges apostolic authority; Diotrephes's influential leadership hinders the ministry of the preachers of the truth and divides the congregation (vv. 9–10). John's readers are encouraged not to imitate him, but rather to imitate the good (v. 11), and he recommends Demetrius as a teacher of the truth with the approval of all (v. 12).

5–6 From the body of the Letter, we get the sense that Gaius had received itinerant preachers or, as John calls them, *strangers*. Nevertheless, he recognized them from their teaching as brothers in Christ. John describes the hospitality Gaius gave them (*all your efforts*) as *a faithful thing*, and they in turn *testified* to Gaius' care: he wasn't doing them a personal favor, but performing the ministry of *the church*. This "church" was likely in Ephesus. Early Christian writers indicate that John served in Asia Minor, so this seems a likely setting for this Letter. That these are probably itinerant preachers is suggested also by John's reference to *their journey*, which would take them throughout Asia Minor to other churches and back to Ephesus. Christian hospitality supports the teachers of God's truth *in a manner worthy of God*, including things needful for such work, like food, money, and lodging. Such missionaries work not for their own benefit but to bring the Word of God to Gaius and his fellow Christians, and so are treated as Christ's ambassadors.

7 The preachers who have been supported by Gaius are not out to fleece the sheep, and they prove it by *accepting nothing from the Gentiles*. The verse suggests that less scrupulous preachers might attempt to swindle unconverted people, that is, non-Christians, looking for money from any source. The integrity of their mission is revealed by accepting support only from the Church, whose mission they are on, going out *for the sake of the name* of Jesus, teaching and preaching the love of Christ for all.

8 Jesus said, "The harvest is plentiful, but the laborers are few. Therefore pray earnestly to the Lord of the harvest to send out laborers into His harvest" (Lk 10:2). Missionaries who rely on God to provide every need are an answer to prayer! And since the mission of God is the Church's mission, the Church does well to support its teachers and preachers in whatever way it can to deliver the truth of Christ throughout the world. Gaius and the Asian congregations did their part, just as the church at Philippi did (cf. Php 1:5–6). John's encouragement is as true today as it was in his lifetime: *we ought to support people like these, that we may be fellow workers for the truth.*

9–10 Without more context, it is difficult to say anything definitive about *Diotrephes* or what John has in mind when he says *I have written something to the church.* From the brief reference in these verses, it seems that Diotrephes was in a congregation that received a message from John, and that he attempted to divide the church by claiming authority over John's teaching, *talking wicked nonsense,* because he *likes to put himself first,* showing himself to be an egotistical leader. Whether he was considered an "elder" or influential layman, Diotrephes held enough sway to refuse preachers approved by John, to keep others from welcoming them, and to expel them from the congregation. Influential leaders who do not acknowledge apostolic *authority* keep people from hearing teachers who preach the truth in Christ's name. This is the opposite of what a leader in the church should do, as Luther noted:

> [A bishop] should listen and answer gently. He should advise prudently, he should not insist on his own way. He should use good common sense so that it will be a pleasure to behold it. He is not noisy. He is not rash. Everything is done with good common sense. *philoxenos,* hospitable. He is a cheerful host to brothers who come from everywhere—from churches in other places. He gives them food and drink; he washes their feet. Indeed, the bishop's home should be open to foreign brethren, but not to just any vagrant. At the time of the Roman Empire this was not so, and the political community of the Jews in a very fine way wrote letters of recommendation for their brethren. We read about this in John's last epistle. (LW 28:285)

11–12 John follows up the negative example of church leadership resulting in division with the positive example of *Demetrius,* one of the teachers sent by John. Do not *imitate* the *evil* demonstrated by Diotrephes, he says, but *imitate good.* Do not imitate those who claw after personal influence and power, who want to be the supreme head, but those who point to the head of the Church, Christ. The one who *does good* is revealed to be *from God,* and the opposite is true also: the one who *does evil has not seen God* (cf. 1Jn 3:6–10). John sends Demetrius with his own recommendation and the recommendation of others (he *has received a good testimony*), and it is possible that he is the courier of John's letter to this congregation. But the best recommendation of Demetrius is the testimony *from the truth itself*: his teaching and actions were in accord with the truth of God's Word. As John advanced the three-fold testimony that Christ is the Son of God (cf. 1Jn 5:7–8), so also the recommendation of Demetrius is resonant with the same persuasive force: there are three testimonies, of John, of the Church, and of the truth of God's Word.

5–12 in Devotion and Prayer The kingdom of this world is shaped like a pyramid, like a big multi-level marketing scheme, where there's a lot of sheep on the bottom and only a few bigwigs up on top. The key to success in this world is waking up one day and being so dissatisfied with being a sheep that you claw your hoofs up the ladder. You climb over and onto and above your ovine brothers and sisters, make a little more cash, and earn a little more respect from those below you, whom you refer to in ever-increasingly pejorative terms as "sheep." You claw your way in the struggle of human ambition, otherwise known as a rat race, until you get a little further up and a little further in, calling it "evolution" or the "survival of the fittest." But all the while, you are willingly blind to the fact that you are buying into the lie that is modern-day secular humanism, which most of the rest of orthodox faith has only ever called by its oldest name: Satanism. It was Satan who said he would ascend to heaven to raise his throne above the stars of God. It was Satan who wanted to sit enthroned above all others and make himself like the Most High (Is 14:13–14). But this same Satan was brought down to the depths and has fallen from heaven. He who once laid low the nations has been cast down (Is 14:15–20). The kingdom of this world runs on pride, the glory of influencing people, gaining power, being first. This is how Diotrephes was acting. But we have been called to a different kingdom entirely, the kingdom of heaven, God's reign where the first are the last and the last are the first, where the greatest are the least and the least are the greatest. We do well to keep in mind this little Letter of John, this shortest book of the Bible, as a reminder of how God rules the show. Human pride is of the devil. We are called to serve in God's kingdom, even as the Son of Man came not to be served, but to serve, and give His life as a ransom for many (Mt 20:28). • "Lord, keep us steadfast in Your Word; Curb those who by deceit or sword Would wrest the Kingdom from Your Son And bring to naught all He has done." Amen. (*LSB* 655:1)

Part 3

Final Greetings (13–15)

ESV	KJV
¹³I had much to write to you, but I would rather not write with pen and ink. ¹⁴I hope to see you soon, and we will talk face to face. ¹⁵Peace be to you. The friends greet you. Greet the friends, every one of them.	¹³I had many things to write, but I will not with ink and pen write unto thee: ¹⁴But I trust I shall shortly see thee, and we shall speak face to face. Peace be to thee. Our friends salute thee. Greet the friends, each by name.

Introduction to 13–15 John concludes this brief Letter in a way very similar to the end of 2Jn. He notes his intention to write more (v. 13) and his hope to meet in person (v. 14). He then concludes with a personal salutation of peace, from friends, to friends (v. 15).

13–14 Instead of saying "ink and paper" (2Jn 12), John employs the phrase *pen and ink*, once again referring to the mode of writing correspondence in the first century. The similarity of the words that close 2Jn and 3Jn suggest that they may have been written together, to be delivered to specific audiences together with 1Jn as a longer teaching text.

14 Face-to-face meetings leave less room for questions or misinterpretation, as anyone who has had to explain an odd text message or email knows! Technology, whether it is instant messaging or pen and ink, can be just as much an obstacle as it is a help in communication. John leaves his future *hope* in the hands of the Lord *to see* his beloved friends (cf. Jas 4:13–16).

15 John ends the Letter with a prayer for *peace*, the common Hbr greeting of "shalom" (cf. note at 1Pt 5:14). Peace is found knowing that Christ is with us and that the name of Christ is on us (cf. Jn 20:19–23). As the itinerant preachers do their ministry "for the sake of the name" (v. 7), so also Christ gives His name to us in our Baptism.

The *friends* of Gaius in Ephesus greet the churches, and John's final plea is for the church to *greet the friends, each by name*, the name given at their Baptism. Such personal greetings would remind them that they were brothers and children of God by Baptism into Christ. Bengel wrote, "[Friend is] a title seldom found in the New Testament since it is absorbed by the greater one of brotherhood" (Bengel 161).

13–15 in Devotion and Prayer A name is great for a lot of things. When you are at the cemetery, for example, you can find someone's grave because the name is carved right there. For most of us, that may be the longest-lasting record of our personal name, outlasting friends, family, anyone at all who may have known us. A hundred years from now, perhaps centuries from now, your name may live on, on the gray stone of a grave marker. However, whatever we may do in this life to give ourselves a name of lasting significance, whatever name we might make for ourselves, the significance we might want to assign to any other saint living or dead, pales in comparison to the name that Christ puts on us. Christ is one who knows a thing or two about graveyards. He is the one who walked through His own, when Mary thought He was a gardener and who revealed Himself by calling her by name. Christ comes to the graveyard of our lives and sees our name, the name of the old Adam, and sees that we are dead in our sins, in our ambitions, in our sorrow, dead in our own opinions and works. He sees our names carved on our tombstones and erases them. Changes them. Writes over them His own living name. And as He does so, our lives change from a funeral to a new birth. He puts His name on us and it gives us new life. Christ meets you today and greets you, just as He did Mary, just as John does his fellow Christians, by name. Peace. I have called you by name. You are Mine. You belong to Me! • Dear Lord Jesus Christ, grant me the grace to honor the name that You have washed on me. Draw me ever to the waters of my Baptism, where You call me Your own. Kill the body of sin, and raise me up anew, that I may live to You in righteousness, innocence, and blessedness. Amen.

JUDE

INTRODUCTION TO
JUDE

Overview

Author

Jude

Date

c AD 68

Places

Egypt; Sodom and Gomorrah

People

Jude; James; false brothers and teachers; the apostles; doubters

Purpose

To warn fellow Christians about the dangers posed by the ungodly false teachers

Law and Sin Themes

The ungodly pervert God's grace; contend for the faith; God destroys unbelievers; blaspheming; eternal chains; gloomy darkness; stained by the flesh; judgment; eternal fire; way of Cain condemned

Grace and Gospel Themes

Called and beloved by God; peace; salvation; mercy of our Lord; present you blameless; God, our Savior

Memory Verse

Built up in the faith (vv. 20–23)

Luther on Jude

Reflecting on various statements from the Early Fathers, Luther concluded that St Jude did not write this letter. Many modern scholars would agree. However, one should note that Luther assumed the writer of Jude had copied 2 Peter. This is not necessarily the case (see "Relationship to Jude," p. 196).

> Concerning the epistle of St. Jude, no one can deny that it is an extract or copy of St. Peter's second epistle, so very like it are all the words. He also speaks of the apostles like a disciple who comes long after them [Jude 17] and cites sayings and incidents that are found nowhere else in the Scriptures [Jude 9, 14]. This moved the ancient fathers to exclude this epistle from the main body of the Scriptures. Moreover the Apostle Jude did not go to Greek-speaking lands, but to Persia, as it is said, so that he did not write Greek. Therefore, although I value this book, it is an epistle that need not be counted among the chief books which are supposed to lay the foundations of faith. (LW 35:397–98)

There is good reason to suppose that St Jude would have known Greek, which was commonly spoken in Judea and was also used in Persia.

For more of Luther's insights on this Book, see *Sermons on the Epistle of St. Jude* (LW 30:201–15).

Calvin on Jude

Though there was a dispute among the ancients respecting this Epistle, yet as the reading of it is useful, and as it contains nothing inconsistent with the purity of apostolic doctrine, and was received as authentic formerly, by some of the best, I willingly add it to the others. Its brevity, moreover, does not require a long statement of its contents; and almost the whole of it is nearly the same with the second chapter of the last Epistle [2 Peter].

As unprincipled men, under the name of Christians, had crept in, whose chief object was to lead the unstable and weak to a profane contempt of God, Jude first shews, that the faithful ought not to have been moved by agents of this kind, by which the Church has always been assailed; and yet he exhorts them carefully to beware of such pests. And to render them more hateful and detestable, he denounces on them the approaching vengeance of God, such as their impiety deserved. Now, if we consider what Satan has attempted in our age, from the commencement of the revived gospel, and what arts he still busily employs to subvert the faith, and the fear of God, what was a useful warning in the time of Jude, is more than necessary in our age. But this will appear more fully as we proceed in reading the Epistle. (Calvin 427)

Gerhard on Jude

The Epistle of Jude at one time was not placed beyond the uncertainty of doubt by all people. Eusebius, *Hist. eccles.*, bk. 2, c. 23: "Not many of the ancients mention the Epistle of James, just as they do not mention that which is ascribed to Jude, though it, too, is one of the seven that are called 'catholic.' Nevertheless we know that they, along with the rest, are read publicly in many of the churches." In bk. 3, c. 22, he lists the Epistle of Jude among the antilegomena. [Gerhard cites the opinions of other Fathers.]

The following, however, prove that this Epistle is apostolic: (1) The inscription. The author clearly calls himself "Jude, a servant of Jesus Christ and brother of James." (2) The subject matter. This Epistle agrees with both the thoughts and words of 2 Peter, of which it contains something like a brief summary and epitome. (3) The testimonies of the ancients. It is counted among the canonical books of the New Testament by the Council of Laodicea, the Council of Carthage, Athanasius, Augustine, and as many of the rest who listed a catalog of the sacred books. . . .

The stronger arguments in support of the contrary are as follows: (1) "In Holy Scripture there appear no traces of the accounts that this Epistle cites. Where is the account of the argument between the archangel Michael and the devil about the body of Moses?" We respond. Just as Paul cites the names of the mages Jannes and Jambres from tradition (2 Tim. 3:8), so also does Jude, regarding that argument of the archangel Michael and the devil. Furthermore, traces of that history are extant in a canonical book. Deuteronomy 34:6 mentions that the Lord buried the body of Moses in the valley of Mount Nebo and that the Israelites did not know the location of that tomb. The devil, therefore, seems to have wanted to reveal this to the Israelites so that they might establish an idolatrous worship of it, just as they later abused the golden serpent to the point of idolatry. The archangel Michael, however, prohibited the devil. At one time there was a writing called . . . "The Departure of Moses from This Life." . . . In it are contained the things cited in this passage about Moses' body. Some understand that argument as though the angel would have offered a service in burying Moses but that the devil was not willing to endure this; so the devil made the accusation that Moses belonged to him because of his murder of the Egyptian, and consequently the devil would not allow Moses to have an honorable burial. The earlier explanation, however, is more simple.

(2) "The author of this Epistle takes testimony from the Book of Enoch, which is apocryphal." We respond. . . . Nevertheless Jude did not consequently give his approval to the entire book, because the apostle proffers testimonies even from the heathen poets yet did not intend to assign canonical authority to them. . . .

(3) "The author does not call himself an apostle." We respond. Neither James nor John in their inscriptions call themselves "apostle." In the Epistle to the Philippians, Paul calls himself "a servant of Christ," which Jude also does here and adds "the brother of James," from which its apostolic authority is gathered clearly. In both letters to the Thessalonians, Paul omits the word "apostle," yet no one on this account doubts the authority of those Epistles.

(4) "The author signifies that he lived after the apostles: 'Be mindful of the words foretold by the apostles of our Lord Jesus Christ' (v. 17)." We respond. This proves that this Epistle was written after the Petrine and Pauline letters in which those prophecies are extant (1 Tim. 4:1; 2 Tim. 3:1; 2 Pet. 2:1). By no means, however, does he exclude himself from the number of the apostles with these words. Jude came after some of the apostles—Peter, Paul, and James—but not after them all, because John still survived.

(5) "Jude taught in Persia; therefore, he would have written in Persian, not in Greek, if he were the author of this Epistle." We respond. The Epistle of Jude is a catholic one, that is, written not to a particular church but to all the faithful. Therefore the author wanted to use the most common language of that time (that is, Greek) in his writing. . . .

Therefore we accept the Epistle of Jude among the canonical books, but of the second rank. Its author Jude had three names, for he was also called Thaddaeus and Lebbaeus (Matt. 10:3; Mark 3:[18]). This Epistle seems to have been written to the same people as 2 Peter, namely, to those especially who from their circumcision had believed the things he signified in v. 17: "Be mindful of the words foretold by the apostles of our Lord Jesus Christ. They told you that in the last days scoffers will come," words that are in 2 Pet. 2:1. He indicates this in v. 5: "I want to warn you, though at one time you knew all things." You see, this fits the Jews aptly, who were imbued with a knowledge of sacred history from the beginning of time. It also has the same theme as has 2 Peter, along with which it uses the same ideas and words.

Some people think that these Epistles of Peter and Jude were directed especially against the Gnostics. Their heresy, however, came after the times of the apostles, as is evident from Irenaeus and Epiphanius. Therefore it is more correct to claim that they were written against the followers of Simon Magus and the Nicolaitans, whose shameful heresy began to creep in far and wide after the deaths of the apostles. That is why Epiphanius (*Haeres.* on the Gnostics, who took their beginning from Simon Magus), after mentioning the wicked passions of that former sect, adds: "Disturbed as He was about these people, the Holy Spirit said to the apostle Jude: 'Whatever as mute spirits they knew naturally, such things are corrupted in them.' " In this Epistle, therefore, Jude exhorts those who were converted from Judaism to be steadfast in the faith, and he forewarns them of seducers who would corrupt the doctrine of the person of Christ, who would transfer the grace of God and spiritual freedom into license of the flesh, who would deny subjection to the magistracy, and who would stir up dissensions in the Church. Jude frightens them terribly and threatens God's judgment against them with the examples of the Israelites in the wilderness, of the wicked angels, and of the people of Sodom. Finally, he also teaches how they should be wary of deceits through their faith and prayers. (E 1:287–290)

Bengel on Jude

The epistle closely agrees with the Second of Peter, which Jude appears to have had before his eyes. Comp. ver. 17, 18, with 2 Pet. iii. 3. Peter wrote that at the end of his life: from which it may be inferred that St Jude lived longer, and saw, by that time, the great declension of all things in the Church, which had been foretold by St Peter. But he passes by some things mentioned by Peter, he expresses others with a different purpose and in different language, he adds others; while the wisdom of the apostle plainly shines forth, and his severity increases. Thus Peter quotes and confirms Paul, and Jude quotes and confirms Peter. (Bengel 161)

Wesley on Jude

In this introductory note, one can see the dependence of Wesley on Bengel.

This epistle greatly resembles the second of St. Peter, which St. Jude seems to have had in view while he wrote. That was written but a very little before his death; and hence we may gather that St. Jude lived some time after it, and saw that grievous declension in the church which St. Peter had foretold. But he passes over some things mentioned by St. Peter, repeats some in different expressions and with a different view, and adds others; clearly evidencing thereby the wisdom of God which rested upon him. Thus St. Peter cites and confirms St. Paul's writings, and is himself cited and confirmed by St. Jude. (Wesley 615)

Challenges for Readers

Authorship. The writer identifies himself as "a servant of Jesus Christ and brother of James" (v. 1). The names "James" and "Jude" (Gk *Judas*) were common among first-century Jews. The writer of Jude is not an apostle, but an associate with them (v. 17). Some early Christian writers associated the writer with the son of Mary and Joseph (cf. Mt 13:55; Mk 6:3; 1Co 9:5), making him a half-brother of Jesus. This tradition has persisted despite ancient and modern skepticism, in part because no other good alternative suggestion exists.

Relationship to 2 Peter. As Luther points out, there is a definite relationship between Jude and 2Pt 2. However, it is not clear that Jude depended on 2 Peter. See "Relationship to Jude," p. 196. This relationship to 2 Peter suggests a similar date of composition.

Citation of Jewish Legends/Writings. See notes, vv. 5–11; 8–9; 14–15.

Blessings for Readers

This short Letter is easy to overlook. Yet it contains important instruction that has always applied to Christians: false teachers are a constant threat. Jude will help you distinguish between false teachers, who are doomed to destruction, and wounded believers who are struggling with doubt and need fellow Christians to encourage them (vv. 22–23).

Outline

PART 1

GREETING (VV. 1–2)

ESV	KJV
1 ¹Jude, a servant of Jesus Christ and brother of James, To those who are called, beloved in God the Father and kept for Jesus Christ: ²May mercy, peace, and love be multiplied to you.	*1* ¹Jude, the servant of Jesus Christ, and brother of James, to them that are sanctified by God the Father, and preserved in Jesus Christ, and called: ²Mercy unto you, and peace, and love, be multiplied.

Introduction to 1–2 Jude introduces the Letter according to first century conventions of letter-writing. He identifies himself as "servant of Jesus Christ" and "brother of James," his audience as those who are "called" and "kept" for Jesus (v. 1), and a prayer for mercy, peace, and love (v. 2). Without more specific information, it is difficult to say with absolute certainty whether the James referred to is the half-brother of Jesus (the leader of the Jerusalem church) or the apostle (son of Zebedee, brother of the apostle John). The apostle John probably had no brother besides James, however (an inference drawn from, e.g., Mt 20:20 and 26:37), and he probably died earlier than the production of this letter (cf. Ac 12:2). Jude reminds his readers of "the predictions of the apostles" (v. 17) without identifying himself as an apostle or singling out other apostles by name. While Jude and James are common names in the first century (and in the NT; cf. Jn 14:22; Mt 10:3; Mk 3:18; Lk 6:16; Ac 1:13), early historical writers (such as the fourth century Eusebius) linked Jude to James, the half-brother of the Lord. Cf. the talk at Nazareth regarding Jesus and the other children in His family in Mk 6:3: "Is not this the carpenter, the son of Mary and brother of James and Joses and Judas and Simon? And are not his sisters here with us?" If this is the same Jude, he would also be a half-brother of Jesus. If so, he likely refers

365

to himself only as the "brother of James" out of humility, not presuming to call upon his familiar relationship to Jesus.

1 Jude calls himself a *servant* (Gk *doulos*, literally "slave"). Early Christians used this title, especially leaders of the Church (cf. note at Jas 1:1). Wesley wrote:

> [A servant of Jesus Christ—] the highest glory which any, either angel or man, can aspire to. The word servant, under the old covenant, was adapted to the spirit of fear and bondage that clave to that dispensation. But when the time appointed of the Father was come, for the sending of his Son to redeem them that were under the law, the word servant (used by the apostles concerning themselves and all the children of God) signified one that, having the Spirit of adoption, is made free by the Son of God. His being a servant is the fruit and perfection of his being a son. And whenever the throne of God and of the Lamb shall be in the new Jerusalem, then will it be indeed that "His servants shall serve him," Rev 22:3. (Wesley 646)

See Introduction to 1–2 for a brief consideration of Jude's identity as *brother of James*. Jude names his audience as the *called*, that is, the "elect," those chosen by God's grace to belong to Him (cf. note at 1Pt 1:1). Jude expands the description of their calling by adding that they are *beloved in God the Father* (cf. Rm 16:12; 1Cor 4:17) and *kept for Jesus Christ*. The word "kept" is the same word used in the NT for "keeping the Law," but as illustrated in this verse maintains the connotation of "cherish," or "treasure." The letter therefore begins with a tender comfort for saints awaiting the Day of Judgment with confidence, knowing that we are prized by Christ as His precious keepsake.

2 *Mercy, peace, and love* are delivered in this greeting, not as Christian virtues that saints are to embody, but as true promises that have their source in God and are delivered to them as the author prays.

1–2 in Devotion and Prayer Kept. There's something tender about that word, a promise of safety and security, preservation and protection. In a modern world filled with news about financial insecurity, political upheaval, natural disasters, wars and rumors of wars, a brief promise like that can be comforting. In a modern world that advertises products by sounding alarms about car theft, home theft, identity theft, a promise like that can also seem almost unbelievable. But the promise is sure: we are kept, preserved, possessed by our Lord Jesus Christ. Like a shepherd preserves his sheep, so does our Good Shepherd promise: "My sheep hear my voice, and I know them, and they follow me. I give them eternal life, and they will never perish, and no one will snatch them out of my hand. My Father, who has given them to me, is greater than all, and no one is able to snatch them out of the Father's hand" (Jn 10:27–29). This preservation is greater than a promise for a "not yet," however. It is a promise for the "now" of our daily life. Like fine china, preserved for a special occasion, so our Lord preserves us, sets us aside, sets us apart and keeps us for a special occasion, to serve up a banquet to our neighbor. As we open our hands, our hearts, our mouths to serve our neighbor with the Word of God, we share with them the Bread of Life, Jesus Himself. We are kept safe while in this world, we are kept by a God who promises never to leave us or forsake us, and we are kept for special use, sanctified to proclaim the salvation won for the world by Jesus. • O Holy Spirit, You have called me by the Gospel, enlightened me with Your gifts, sanctified me, and kept me in the true faith. Continue to preserve my life in Christ, that I may look forward with confidence to the last day when You raise up me and all the dead, and give to me and all believers in Christ everlasting life. Amen.

PART 2

JUDGMENT ON FALSE TEACHERS (vv. 3–16)

ESV	KJV
³Beloved, although I was very eager to write to you about our common salvation, I found it necessary to write appealing to you to contend for the faith that was once for all delivered to the saints. ⁴For certain people have crept in unnoticed who long ago were designated for this condemnation, ungodly people, who pervert the grace of our God into sensuality and deny our only Master and Lord, Jesus Christ. ⁵Now I want to remind you, although you once fully knew it, that Jesus, who saved a people out of the land of Egypt, afterward destroyed those who did not believe. ⁶And the angels who did not stay within their own position of authority, but left their proper dwelling, he has kept in eternal chains under gloomy darkness until the judgment of the great day—⁷just as Sodom and Gomorrah and the surrounding cities, which likewise indulged in sexual immorality and pursued unnatural desire, serve as an example by undergoing a punishment of eternal fire. ⁸Yet in like manner these people also, relying on their dreams, defile the flesh, reject authority, and blas-	³Beloved, when I gave all diligence to write unto you of the common salvation, it was needful for me to write unto you, and exhort you that ye should earnestly contend for the faith which was once delivered unto the saints. ⁴For there are certain men crept in unawares, who were before of old ordained to this condemnation, ungodly men, turning the grace of our God into lasciviousness, and denying the only Lord God, and our Lord Jesus Christ. ⁵I will therefore put you in remembrance, though ye once knew this, how that the Lord, having saved the people out of the land of Egypt, afterward destroyed them that believed not. ⁶And the angels which kept not their first estate, but left their own habitation, he hath reserved in everlasting chains under darkness unto the judgment of the great day. ⁷Even as Sodom and Gomorrha, and the cities about them in like manner, giving themselves over to fornication, and going after strange flesh, are set forth for an example, suffering the vengeance of eternal fire.

pheme the glorious ones. ⁹But when the archangel Michael, contending with the devil, was disputing about the body of Moses, he did not presume to pronounce a blasphemous judgment, but said, "The Lord rebuke you." ¹⁰But these people blaspheme all that they do not understand, and they are destroyed by all that they, like unreasoning animals, understand instinctively. ¹¹Woe to them! For they walked in the way of Cain and abandoned themselves for the sake of gain to Balaam's error and perished in Korah's rebellion. ¹²These are hidden reefs at your love feasts, as they feast with you without fear, shepherds feeding themselves; waterless clouds, swept along by winds; fruitless trees in late autumn, twice dead, uprooted; ¹³wild waves of the sea, casting up the foam of their own shame; wandering stars, for whom the gloom of utter darkness has been reserved forever.

¹⁴It was also about these that Enoch, the seventh from Adam, prophesied, saying, "Behold, the Lord comes with ten thousands of his holy ones, ¹⁵to execute judgment on all and to convict all the ungodly of all their deeds of ungodliness that they have committed in such an ungodly way, and of all the harsh things that ungodly sinners have spoken against him." ¹⁶These are grumblers, malcontents, following their own sinful desires; they are loud-mouthed boasters, showing favoritism to gain advantage.

⁸Likewise also these filthy dreamers defile the flesh, despise dominion, and speak evil of dignities.

⁹Yet Michael the archangel, when contending with the devil he disputed about the body of Moses, durst not bring against him a railing accusation, but said, The Lord rebuke thee.

¹⁰But these speak evil of those things which they know not: but what they know naturally, as brute beasts, in those things they corrupt themselves.

¹¹Woe unto them! for they have gone in the way of Cain, and ran greedily after the error of Balaam for reward, and perished in the gainsaying of Core.

¹²These are spots in your feasts of charity, when they feast with you, feeding themselves without fear: clouds they are without water, carried about of winds; trees whose fruit withereth, without fruit, twice dead, plucked up by the roots;

¹³Raging waves of the sea, foaming out their own shame; wandering stars, to whom is reserved the blackness of darkness for ever.

¹⁴And Enoch also, the seventh from Adam, prophesied of these, saying, Behold, the Lord cometh with ten thousands of his saints,

¹⁵To execute judgment upon all, and to convince all that are ungodly among them of all their ungodly deeds which they have ungodly committed, and of all their hard speeches which ungodly sinners have spoken against him.

¹⁶These are murmurers, complainers, walking after their own lusts; and their mouth speaketh great swelling words, having men's persons in admiration because of advantage.

Introduction to 3–16 Jude's purpose is to warn his readers about false teachers, against whom the Church is charged to fight (vv. 3–4). He spends the first half of the letter comparing their licentiousness and impending doom to OT (and extra-biblical) examples of God's righteous punishment of evildoers, much as Peter does in 2Pt 2:1–12. Jude's letter, in fact, bears many similarities with Peter's second letter. Jude mentions the exodus of the Israelites and notes that Jesus was their deliverer (v. 5), the fall and penalty of the evil angels (v. 6), and Sodom and Gomorrah (v. 7) as examples of punishment. He brings a charge of blasphemy against the false teachers he has in mind, noting that not even the archangel Michael dared blaspheme (vv. 8–10). Jude links the false teachers with the ancient sinners Cain, Balaam, and Korah (v. 11) and describes them creatively in terms that indicate their impotence (vv. 12–13). Referencing the Book of Enoch (*1En*), Jude identifies the false teachers as objects of God's wrath, following only their own desires and advantage (vv. 14–16).

3 Jude seems to have been motivated initially to write another kind of letter, having to do with their *common salvation*, that is, the saving work of Christ that is shared by all believers. The rise of false teachers has changed his course, however, compelling him to exhort the Church *to contend for the faith*. Most often, throughout the Scriptures, the word "faith" means "trust" or "belief," for example when we talk about one's trust in the saving work of Christ. Here Jude talks about "the faith" as that which is believed, namely, the objective content of Christ's salvific work. (This is sometimes referred to as *"fides quae creditur"*—the faith that is believed. cf. Gal 1:23; Php 1:27). This faith was *once for all delivered to the saints*: this is not just "once upon a time" but once (Gk *hapax*, literally "once,") for all time. Nothing will supersede this faith, so we rely not on any continuing revelation, but the Word as it was handed to the apostles, an attitude shared by the apostolic generation. Consider the words of the Early Church father, Polycarp: "Forsaking the vanity of many, and their false doctrines, let us return to the word which has been handed down to us from the beginning" (*ANF* 1:34). Luther likewise encouraged the *saints* of his own age and ours: "Wicked men will come, and they will not persevere. They always have this fault of teaching something different and new. A wicked spirit, not rooted in solid doctrine, causes this. It always looks for something new and a better doctrine" (LW 28:221). Again, Luther wrote:

We should labor over this faith and contend for it to the end. The flesh becomes sluggish; it sees to it that we forget the Word and grow tired of it. The bishop should not worry that he is often teaching the same thing. . . . [Paul] opposes diseases of doctrine; that is, doctrine should be right, stable, and constant. . . . Those who do not have a doctrine that is sure and constant do not teach. (LW 29:32)

These words are important for every generation including our own. We are called to believe, teach, and confess the faith that was once for all delivered to the saints.

4 Jude strikes the tone that will carry him through the rest of the letter by identifying the false teachers as *certain people* who are *ungodly*. The author suggests that although they *crept in unnoticed*, they are nevertheless recognizable because they *pervert the grace of our God into sensuality and deny . . . Jesus Christ*. Christian congregations are certainly made up of hypocrites, and all are sinners. The difference between saints and other sinners *designated for . . . condemnation* is not in degree of sinfulness or any other such quantification, but is solely a matter of repentance and faith. Hypocrites who continue in falsehood in the midst of God's Church are revealed in sinful action and sinful teaching, and present a real danger to the rest of God's flock. The danger is the temptation to change God's grace into something that it is not. When Jude calls this a perversion of God's grace *into sensuality*, he is referring to more than just sexual sin; indeed not receiving God's grace as the free, unmerited favor of God towards the sinner for the sake of Christ's person and work moves along two paths. One the one hand, a person might try to change God's Gospel into Law (what might more familiarly be understood as a "confusion" of Law and Gospel. This is the error that evolves naturally into Pietism). On the other hand, a person might imagine that the forgiveness of sins constitutes a license to ignore God's Law and is therefore a freedom to sin (antinomianism). Both errors are a denial of *our only Master and Lord, Jesus Christ*. So what ought Christians to do with such freedom as has been received by God's grace? Luther commented:

"Now you have obtained freedom through Christ. That is, you are far above all laws, both in your own conscience and in the sight of God; you are blessed and saved; Christ is your life. Therefore even though the Law, sin, and death may frighten you, they can neither harm you nor cause you to despair. This is your brilliant and inestimable freedom. Now it is up to you to be diligently on your guard not to use your freedom as an opportunity for the flesh." This evil is very widespread, and it is the worst of all the evils that Satan arouses against the teaching of faith: that in many people he soon transforms the freedom for which Christ has set us free into an opportunity for the flesh. . . . The flesh simply does not understand the teaching of grace, namely, that we are not justified by works but by faith alone, and that the Law has no jurisdiction over us. Therefore when it hears this teaching, it transforms it into licentiousness and immediately draws the inference: "If we are without the Law, then let us live as we please. Let us not do good, let us not give to the needy; much less do we have to endure any-thing evil. For there is no Law to compel or bind us." Thus there is a danger on both sides, although the one is more tolerable than the other. If grace or faith is not preached, no one is saved; for faith alone justifies and saves. On the other hand, if faith is preached, as it must be preached, the majority of men understand the teach-ing about faith in a fleshly way and transform the freedom of the spirit into the freedom of the flesh. This can be discerned today in all classes of society, both high and low. They all boast of being evangelicals and boast of Christian freedom. Meanwhile, how-ever, they give in to their desires and turn to greed, sexual desire, pride, envy, etc. (LW 27:48)

3–4 in Devotion and Prayer No Christian can put on the spe-cial "sheep and goats" spectacles that reveal what God alone can see, looking at the world (or the fellow-worshiper in the pew!), knowing how His righteous judgment will be revealed. Much as some might imagine they have a handle on those God loves and those He hates, we are bound to be shocked on the Last Day. "Wow, *she's* here? How did *he* make it?" We do well to point that prejudice back at ourselves, knowing that we are called to observe ourselves, "working out our salvation in fear and trembling" (Php 2:12), that is, cautious of our own judgment. And indeed, we do well moreover to recall that in the narrative of the "sheep and goats" in Mt 25, the sheep on the King's right hand are themselves shocked at what the Judge says. "When, Lord? When did we see you naked, hungry, in prison? When did we do any of these things?" We can say on that day, "Wow, *I'm* here too? How did *I* make it?" And the answer is clear: purely by the grace of God in Christ. This does not mean we can be anything less than vigi-lant in discerning error and right, in other people's teaching or our own. We cannot compromise the Gospel. Until the Day when Christ ultimately judges all, we rely on His grace to preserve His Church, heeding His call to divide His Word rightly, distinguishing Law and Gospel, receiving from Him every good gift, and trusting that when He looks at us, He does so through the lens of Christ's atoning blood shed for us. • Preserve us, Heavenly Father, from false teachers, and open our ears to hear the Word of the true Teacher, our Master and Lord, Your Son, Jesus Christ. Amen.

5 Jude enters on a series of OT examples that resemble Peter's illustrations from 2Pt 2 (see Introduction to 3–16). He begins with a narrative that we usually consider a salvation story: the exodus of the Israelites from Egypt. But where there is salvation, there is also judgment: *Jesus . . . saved* but *afterward destroyed those who did not believe.* Jude needs to *remind* his readers of the story because under the influence of false teaching, it is easy to forget the basics of the faith (cf. 1Cor 4:17). They knew the truth and needed to be faithful to the true Christian faith. *Jesus* is the one *who saved* God's people from Egypt, as Paul also notes: "For they drank from the spiritual Rock that followed them, and the Rock was Christ" (1Cor 10:4). This is a strong affirmation of Christ's deity. Jesus is the eternal Son of God. Pharaoh and his armies were destroyed in the Red Sea, but Jude is reminding his readers of the judgment on the Israelites *who did not believe* and therefore did not enter into the Promised Land, a sobering warning for Christians looking forward to their own exodus and entrance into heaven.

6 Jude's second example of divine punishment is the fall of the evil angels, a topic that the scriptures do not deal with directly in narrative form, but assume here and in other places (e.g., at Eph 6:12; cf. Rv 12:7–9; 2Pt 2:4, 10–11). The sin of the evil angels was arrogating their status above what had been given them; cf. the temptation of Adam and Eve (Gn 3). Because they were unwilling to *stay within their own position*, God righteously (and ironically) gives them their wish: they are now confined *in eternal chains under gloomy darkness*, the prison of hell, the darkness of which is the absence of Christ's light. It is a prison (cf. 1Pt 3:19; Rv 20:7) in which they are confined *until the judgment of the great day*, that is, Judgment Day, the great and terrible "day of the LORD," when Christ returns.

7 Like Peter (2Pt 2:6–8), Jude compares the destruction awaiting false teachers to the OT example of *Sodom and Gomorrah and the* *surrounding cities.* While God destroyed Admah and Zeboiim (Dt 29:23, cf. Gn 14:2–8), on Lot's behalf He spared Zoar (Gn 19:22), reminding the reader that God cares for His faithful remnant, even in the midst of judgment (cf. Hos 11:8–9). The narrative of Gn 19:4–11 outlines what Jude has in mind when he says *unnatural desire,* referring particularly to the sexual sin of the city of Sodom (cf. our English word "sodomy"). The example suggests that the "sensuality" (v. 4), into which the false teachers have transformed God's grace, includes sexual licentiousness and sin. Not only were Sodom and Gomorrah destroyed by fire, but Jude notes that this was only a foretaste of the *eternal fire* awaiting all who practice such sin. See notes at 2Pt 2:9–10a; 10b–12.

5–7 in Devotion and Prayer Our God is a gentleman; He will not always deny the wishes of those who prefer to exclude themselves from fellowship with Him. Certainly His great love for His creation compelled Him to send His Son on our behalf; certainly His Holy Spirit continues like the hound of heaven, ever chasing souls with the sword of the Spirit, the Word of God, calling out "Now is the day of salvation." The Gospel pleads with sinners, "Turn and be saved!" But the infection of sin can be ultimately lethal, turning the diseased victim against even the one who offers a cure, perverting the poisoned victim into perpetrator, hardening the harrowed into a calloused incorrigibility. The stern warning of a God who calls His creation to live within the bounds established by His Law is not a tease; He truly loves us enough to hedge us in, before and behind, that we know our place in His kingdom. Those who consistently make a habit of breaking through those hedges, tunneling for an escape from fellowship with God, will find a way away from Him. If a kid wants to run away from home, it will eventually happen. And God will grant that wish eventually—full emancipation, full freedom from His rules, from His chains, from an unwanted slavery to Him. He did it with angels. He did it with Pharaoh. And, if we insist, He will do it with us . . . though we are wise to consider the consequences. True freedom is never freedom *from* God in Christ, as attempts to be free from God's Law only ever shackle us to sin, to our selfishness, and ultimately to everlasting punishment—the gloomy darkness of those who in pride attempted to put themselves in God's place. No, true freedom is found only in Christ: if the Son sets you free, you will be free indeed. Anything other than freedom in Christ, being set free from sin and enslaved to righteousness, is a self-inflict-ed isolation from fellowship with God. They say the doors of hell are locked from the inside. Dear Christian, do not lock out the God who calls you today! • Dear Lord Jesus Christ, You were bound by soldiers and led to the death of a cross, to loose the shackles of my slavery to sin. As You are now risen from the dead, raise me this day to live in freedom for You. Hem me in, before and behind, that I not use my freedom in You to reach with hands, feet, eyes, speech, will, or intention, beyond what You have ordained for me. Take away any hardness of my heart, and give to me a heart of flesh, that I may serve You in truth. And bring me joyfully to Your table, where You freely feed me with the food of immortality, until the day when You feed me and all believers at the wedding feast in Your kingdom which has no end. Amen.

8–9 Jude's illustrations in the next section of the letter employ popular legends as well as biblical narratives to attack the false teachers. The first of these is a description of the *archangel Michael contending with the devil* over Moses' body, a popular Jewish legend, which is also recorded in the Assumption of Moses (a book writ-ten in the first century AD). Christians today find the reference odd; though it is likely that Christians of the first century found the story just as odd! Like the reference to Enoch (vv. 14–15), the illustration of Michael, the devil, and Moses' body may have been the stuff of speculation, just the sort of thing a false teacher might pick up and use as a foundation for teaching in competition with the apostles. If so, Jude cleverly turns the more "speculative" stories against those who would use them to steer people away from the truth. This does not amount to Jude endorsing such stories as inspired scripture, any more than Paul would when he refers to the classical poets Aratus (Ac 17:28) and Epimenides (Tit 1:12). Jude's point with the illustra-tion of the archangel Michael is that the false teachers forget their place, and therefore operate outside of what the Lord has given us to say. *Relying on their dreams* instead, they *blaspheme* God's servants, but even the angels, who have the right to speak on behalf of God, relaying His messages, do not presume so to curse. Speaking against God's servants is tantamount to speaking against God Himself (cf. 2Pt 2:10). Characterized as chief among God's servants, the *archan-gel Michael* (Hbr "who is like God?") is mentioned in Dn 10:21 and

12:1 as God's servant who watched over Israel (the only other mention of "archangel" in the NT is at 1Th 4:16).

Dt 34:5–6 briefly narrates the death of Moses: "So Moses the servant of the Lord died there in the land of Moab, according to the word of the Lord, and He buried him in the valley in the land of Moab opposite Beth-peor; but no one knows the place of his burial to this day." Since the Lord was responsible for Moses' burial, Jude brings up the assumption that Michael was the Lord's agent, who leaves the role of cursing to the Lord: *The Lord rebuke you.*

10 Jude's language attacks the blasphemy of the false teachers using the same images that Peter does at 2Pt 2:10, 12. Those who teach about God, on the other hand, should not *like unreasoning animals*, "curse, swear, use satanic arts, lie or deceive by His name, but call upon it in every trouble, pray, praise, and give thanks" (SC, Second Commandment).

11 Jude proceeds with three brief references to biblical narratives: Cain (Gn 4:5–8), Balaam (Nu 22–24; 31:16), and Korah (Nu 16:1–3, 31–35). The *way of Cain* is murder, as John teaches at 1Jn 3:12 (see note there), and greed, as Jude connects his narrative to Balaam's and all who are corrupted *for the sake of gain.* Any believer who falls into temptation of producing good works jealously striving with their brothers, or to line their own pockets, sins in the "way of Cain." The Lutheran reformers wrote: "As long as a person is not regenerate and guides himself according to the Law, he does the works because they are commanded. So from fear of punishment or desire for reward, he is still under the Law. . . . These are 'saints' after the order of Cain" (FC SD VI 16). *Balaam's error* is the same: seeking financial gain through cursing what God had blessed, namely His beloved Israel. *Korah* and his companions, before being swallowed up by the earth, likewise refused to hear what God had spoken through Moses and Aaron, God's elected mouthpieces for His nation. Speaking against His prophets is the same as speaking against the Lord Himself, as Moses reveals to Korah and his fellow conspirators: "Therefore it is against the Lord that you and all your company have gathered together. What is Aaron that you grumble against him?" (Nu 16:11; cf. also 21:4–9). All of Jude's OT examples point up the honor due God's Word and its messengers, and the punishment awaiting those who slander, misrepresent, or otherwise blaspheme God's name, whether for gain, jealousy, or any other vain reason.

12–13 Jude describes the ungodly false teachers with a series of vivid metaphors, beginning with the worship context of the Christian community: the *love feasts*, which is a reference to Early Church celebrations of the Lord's Supper and attendant meals. The object of Jude's invective are those who present themselves as *shepherds feeding themselves*—not pastors who feed their sheep, but pastors who fleece them! They are described in the ESV as *reefs*, but the Gk word (*spilades*) can also be translated as "blemishes" or "spots" (as in the KJV), like the "blots" (Gk *spiloi*) of 2Pt 2:13, which bears close resemblance to this verse. Like Peter, Jude's metaphors point up the impotence of these false shepherds' teachings. Rain *clouds* would normally be expected to produce rain, but they are *waterless. Trees in late autumn* would be expected to be laden with produce, but they are *fruitless* and *uprooted*. What good are they? Bombast and bluster characterize them as windbags; *swept along by winds . . . wild waves . . . wandering stars* also describe those who are double-minded, not like the "fixed stars," but like the planets which change their position in the night sky (cf. Jas 1:6–8). Like the evil angels, their punishment is nigh in the *gloom of utter darkness* (cf. v. 6; 2Pt 2:17–18).

14–15 *1 Enoch* is a book in the Jewish pseudepigrapha that is attributed to the OT figure Enoch (see. Gn 5:18–24; Heb 11:5–6). ("Pseudepigrapha" means that they are "falsely attributed," that is, they falsely claim to be written by a certain author.) Such books (like the Assumption of Moses, cf. note at v. 9) attempt to detail what other canonical books of the Bible may only refer to obliquely, such as the death of Moses or the career of Enoch. The bit that Jude quotes from this book may itself be derived from Moses' final blessing to Israel in Dt 33:2: "The Lord came from Sinai and dawned from Seir upon us; he shone forth from Mount Paran; he came from the ten thousands of holy ones, with flaming fire at his right hand." *1En* was well known enough for Jude's audience to be familiar with the reference. Enoch is counted as *the seventh from Adam* when counted inclusively. His prophecy of the Lord's judgment with His myriads of heavenly host is not good news; Jude includes the passage from *1En* to encompass *all* people, and to convict the wicked of their *deeds* and words: *all the harsh things that ungodly sinners have spoken against him.* Jude thus reinforces his earlier argument about blasphemy (vv. 8–10).

16 Jude concludes his portrayal of the false teachers by moving away from illustration and creative metaphor, and towards identifiable characteristics in the congregation. How can one spot one of these false teachers? They are *grumblers* (ESV), that is "whisperers," *murmurers* (KJV), people who divide the fellowship of Christians through their talk (cf. Pr 16:28; 26:20). The strife that gossip and grumbling causes is a cancer to the Church, and fuels what is false. They are *malcontents*, that is, they complain about the hand that they have been dealt. Dissatisfied with their station in the Church, they sour on its leadership when they are not in it (cf. 3Jn 9–10). They follow *their own sinful desires* (cf. 2Pt 2:10); they *are loud-mouthed boasters* (Gk *lalei hyperongka*, literally "talk big"); and they show *favoritism*, they are respecters of persons in order *to gain advantage*, flattering people so that they can gain their trust and support.

8–16 in Devotion and Prayer There is a time to plant, and a time to uproot (Ec 3:2). These Law words are repeated by Jude as he attacks false teachers, ungodly influences in Christ's Church: fruitless, twice-dead, uprooted (v. 12). They are similar to the words of Jesus talking about the Pharisees at Mt 15:12: "Every plant that My heavenly Father has not planted will be rooted up." What about you? What is your place in God's garden? We might think, speaking of gardens, that ever since our first parents' exile from the Garden of Eden, there is no one with any right to expect a place back in paradise. But where God uproots, He also plants. The seed that He planted in the earth was His Son: "Truly, truly, I say to you, unless a grain of wheat falls into the earth and dies, it remains alone; but if it dies, it bears much fruit" (Jn 12:24). Jesus died to give you new birth, to transplant you from a wilderness of sin to the greenhouse of His tender care, to take a wild olive that would have been cut down and graft you in to the cultivated tree of His choosing. Rejoice that when it is time for the weeding our Master gardener embarks on at the end of time, you will be found in Him as His chosen harvest through faith in Christ.
• Dear Jesus, You are the true vine, and have called me a branch. Grant me grace so to abide in You, as You abide in me. I cannot bear fruit of myself, but bear fruit in me, for apart from You I can do nothing. Look on me with mercy and love; prune me and care for me that I may keep Your commandments, and so glorify You. Amen.

PART 3

A CALL TO PERSEVERE (vv. 17–23)

ESV	KJV
¹⁷But you must remember, beloved, the predictions of the apostles of our Lord Jesus Christ. ¹⁸They said to you, "In the last time there will be scoffers, following their own ungodly passions." ¹⁹It is these who cause divisions, worldly people, devoid of the Spirit. ²⁰But you, beloved, building yourselves up in your most holy faith and praying in the Holy Spirit, ²¹keep yourselves in the love of God, waiting for the mercy of our Lord Jesus Christ that leads to eternal life. ²²And have mercy on those who doubt; ²³save others by snatching them out of the fire; to others show mercy with fear, hating even the garment stained by the flesh.	¹⁷But, beloved, remember ye the words which were spoken before of the apostles of our Lord Jesus Christ; ¹⁸How that they told you there should be mockers in the last time, who should walk after their own ungodly lusts. ¹⁹These be they who separate themselves, sensual, having not the Spirit. ²⁰But ye, beloved, building up yourselves on your most holy faith, praying in the Holy Ghost, ²¹Keep yourselves in the love of God, looking for the mercy of our Lord Jesus Christ unto eternal life. ²²And of some have compassion, making a difference: ²³And others save with fear, pulling them out of the fire; hating even the garment spotted by the flesh.

Introduction to 17–23 Jude shifts to encouragement in the last half of his letter, reminding his readers that false teachers were predicted by the apostles (vv. 17–18). Though they cause divisions in the Church (v. 19), Jude's readers are called to edify themselves in faith, prayer, and love as they wait on Jesus (vv. 20–21). He exhorts his readers to translate the love of God into love for the neighbor by showing mercy to those who doubt and are in danger of the fires of God's punishment (vv. 22–23).

17–18 Jude reminds his readers that they have been made aware of the *predictions of the apostles*. He possibly refers to the predictions of 2Pt, though his letter may precede Peter's. All of the apostles, and even our Lord Himself, warned their listeners that false teachers would come (cf. 2Pt 3:2–3; 2Cor 11:26; Mt 24:11, 24), and Jude's readers heard it from mouths of the apostles themselves, as he reminds them, *They said to you*.

19 Jude encourages the believers on the basis of their distinction vis-à-vis the false teachers. Where they distinguish themselves as causing *divisions*, believers work towards edification in communion with Christ and one another (cf. v. 20). Where the false teachers are *worldly*, the believers are spiritual (cf. Jas 3:13–18). Where the false teachers do not have the *Spirit*, the believers do; cf. Rm 8:9: "You, however, are not in the flesh but in the Spirit, if in fact the Spirit of God dwells in you. Anyone who does not have the Spirit of Christ does not belong to Him."

20–21 Paul also employed the image of *building* while addressing specifically the problem of divisions in the church at Corinth (1Cor 3:10, 12, 14; cf. v. 19). In light of the image of "uprooted trees" at v. 12, being built up in faith is the polar opposite (cf. Col 2:6–7; Eph 2:19–22). Calvin wrote:

> Since the whole perfection of man consists in faith, it may seem strange that he bids them to build upon it another building, as though faith were only a commencement to man. This difficulty is removed by the Apostle in the words which follow, when he adds, that men build on faith when love is added; except, perhaps, some one may prefer to take this meaning, that men build on faith, as far as they make proficiency in it, and doubtless the daily progress of faith is such, that itself rises up as a building. Thus the Apostle teaches us, that in order to increase in faith, we must be instant in prayer and maintain our calling by love. (Calvin 446–47)

Jude reminds his readers that incorporation into such faith is *most holy*—not "perfect," but rather "set apart" from the world in its unbelief. As if describing this *most holy faith,* Jude traces a trinitarian creedal outline in these verses as well: *praying in the Holy Spirit* (according to the Word He inspired; cf. 2Tm 3:16–17; Eph 6:18); abiding *in the love of God*; and *waiting for the mercy of our Lord Jesus Christ*. Paul outlines a corresponding trinitarian doctrine motivated by a similar discussion about "prayer" at Rm 8:26–30. Bengel wrote, "Jude makes mention of the Father, the Son, and the Holy Spirit: he also makes mention of faith, of love and hope, in this and the following verses" (Bengel 169).

22–23 The horizontal dimension of loving the neighbor involves more than good works that simply edify them materially and physically. Jude encourages spiritual service to the neighbor, the love of God for the Church translating into mercifully serving *those who doubt*, patiently delivering the gifts that produce faith, namely the Word of God. Jude seems to build his case by crescendo as he demands believers notice those who are in danger of *fire* as well, and need to be snatched out, a metaphor pregnant with the threat of future eternal punishment if those who commit sin are not urged to repent (cf. Jas 5:20; 1Pt 4:8). A mission post near the lake of fire, trying to snatch those who would exclude themselves from God's grace, is not a safe and secure place to do the work of a missionary, however Jude even urges the climax of his crescendo, to *show mercy*, but *with fear*, lest believers become subject to the stain of the world as they minister to doubters and sinners in need of God's Word.

17–23 In Devotion and Prayer Mark Twain wrote a novel about a prince and a pauper trading places. Far better than this fiction, Christians enjoy the glorious exchange of the Prince of Peace, Jesus, trading places with us and the our poverty of our sin. Exchanging my sin for His righteousness—a glorious exchange indeed. Nobody understood this point better than the apostle Paul, who was led to cry out in joy, that God "made him to be sin who knew no sin, so that in Him we might become the righteousness of God" (2Cor 5:21). That glorious exchange that Jesus made for him and for us all led the apostle to a corresponding vicarious wish, willing to suffer damnation if only his brothers could be saved: "For I could wish that I myself were accursed and cut off from Christ for the sake of my brothers, my kinsmen according to the flesh" (Rm 9:3). This is the voice of a man who has a lot of love for his fellow people and also understands a thing or two about trading places. He knows that he cannot just go and give someone else salvation. He knows that the key is that God is the one who traded places with us in Christ. Does Paul's love parallel yours? It reflects God's love. It is loving others so much that the response is lavish, an almost too extraordinary sentiment: I would be willing to risk hell, if only they would believe in the Lord of heaven! Is there someone you love so much that you would be willing to walk with them until they too know the Lord? Someone you love so much that you are unwilling to stop sharing until you are convinced that they will be in heaven with you? Be merciful with those who doubt; snatch others from the fire; trade places, walk in their shoes a bit, and be willing to share the love of God in Christ with those who yet need to trust in Jesus. • Holy Spirit, You brought me to faith in Jesus Christ by delivering Your Word to me. You killed me in Christ's death and raised me up to new life in Him. Lead me into all truth, that I may ever be prepared to show mercy to those in need of answers to their doubts, and to give to all who ask and answer for the hope that I have in Christ. Lead me boldly to share Your Word with those who need to hear it, for Jesus' sake. Amen.

PART 4

CLOSING DOXOLOGY (VV. 24–25)

ESV	KJV
²⁴Now to him who is able to keep you from stumbling and to present you blameless before the presence of his glory with great joy, ²⁵to the only God, our Savior, through Jesus Christ our Lord, be glory, majesty, dominion, and authority, before all time and now and forever. Amen.	²⁴Now unto him that is able to keep you from falling, and to present you faultless before the presence of his glory with exceeding joy, ²⁵To the only wise God our Saviour, be glory and majesty, dominion and power, both now and ever. Amen.

Introduction to 24–25 Jude's letter ends with one of the most lovely doxologies in all scripture. God is ascribed majesty and glory in connection with His saving work; He is the one who presents believers blameless before Himself.

24 Amid myriad false teachers, and beset by temptations and enemies in the world, the devil, and our sinful flesh, how is it that any one sinner is able to be saved? How is it that any believer may be preserved in the one true Church? As Jesus says, with man this is impossible, but with God all things are possible (Mk 10:27); so Jude's summary doxology begins: God *is able to keep you from stumbling*. Though we all stumble in many ways (Jas 3:2), God regards us on account of the perfect work of Christ, through whom we are presented *blameless* (cf. Eph 5:27; Col 1:22).

25 God is *our Savior*, known as savior *through Jesus Christ our Lord*. God particularly reveals Himself, His nature, and His character through the person and work of Jesus Christ. To this God are ascribed the *glory* that is due to God alone: that is praise for His salvation, as well as the comprehensive reign over all things. The final verse of the letter includes a time designation that is oddly specific—God is ascribed glory and honor through Jesus *before all time and now and forever*. It is as if Jude takes advantage of one final opportunity to address any false teacher who might argue against the eternal pre-existence of Christ. It also caps this brief letter with a reminder of its audience, the Christian congregation who would pray liturgically, "as it was in the beginning, is now, and ever shall be, unto the ages of ages. Amen."

24–25 in Devotion and Prayer It used to be that the older I got, the better I got at walking. When I was, say 4 months old, I certainly wasn't winning any races. By two and a half, I was still just toddling in a diaper. I hit high school age, and a growth spurt had me tripping over myself here and there, but I can safely say I knew how to walk without stumbling. Nevertheless, I think I have hit my peak. I am not getting better at walking anymore. I might in fact be getting ever so gradually worse. I'm getting to the age now, where bones are creaking and cracking a little more than they used to. I can imagine a day when my children will be worrying about whether a trip will send me to the hospital with fracture, a broken bone, or a hip replacement. What can keep me from stumbling? A whole lot of care, good preventative measures, extra calcium? Even with the help of a cane, a walker, a wheelchair, depending on need, there are no guarantees of stability that can prevent stumbling of any kind. Except one. We don't keep ourselves from stumbling in the Christian walk. Our God is the only one who can do that. No matter whether I feel fit enough to run a marathon or unable to do more than crawl, bleeding, senseless, and dying, our God is as sure as His promise. He is the one able to keep you from stumbling; He is the one who is able to make you stand. • Grant me grace, Lord Jesus Christ, to rely on You. You walked to Your death to lay down Your life for me. Now You are risen from the dead. Give new life to my imperfect limbs and strengthen me that I may serve You in the ways You have prepared, that I may walk in You without stumbling. Amen.

BIOGRAPHICAL SKETCHES

The following brief sketches introduce preachers and commentators cited or referenced in this volume. They appear in chronological order by the date of their death or era of influence. Although some of them are ancient and medieval Church Fathers respected by the reformers, they are primarily writers of the Reformation era and heirs of the Reformation approach to writing biblical commentary. This approach includes:

(1) Interpreting Scripture in view of Scripture and by faith, so that passages are understood in their literary and in their canonical contexts;

(2) Emphasis on the historic and ordinary meaning of the words and literary expressions;

(3) Careful review of manuscripts and texts in search of greater accuracy;

(4) Faith in the canonical Scripture as divinely inspired, truthful, and authoritative;

(5) Respect for the ancient, ecumenical creeds (Apostles', Nicene, and Athanasian) as touchstones of faithful interpretation and application of Scripture; and most importantly

(6) Focus on Christ and justification through Him as the chief message of Holy Scripture (e.g., the distinction of Law and Gospel or sin and grace in interpretation and application).

For more information about these figures, see Edward A. Engelbrecht, gen. ed., *The Church from Age to Age: A History from Galilee to Global Christianity* (St. Louis: Concordia, 2011).

Ancient and Medieval Fathers

Clement of Rome. (Late first century) An early bishop of Rome. Clement wrote to the congregation at Corinth in an effort to settle a dispute in that congregation.

Ignatius of Antioch. (c. 35–c. 107) Bishop of Antioch and martyr. As Ignatius was led captive from Antioch to Rome, where he would stand trial, he wrote seven letters to churches and church leaders, which resemble the letters of the apostle Paul in style and content.

Polycarp of Smyrna. (c. 69–c. 155) Bishop of Smyrna, a student of the apostle John, and a martyr. An account of his martyrdom illustrates the steadfastness of early Christians in the face of persecution.

Eusebius of Caesarea. (c. 260–c. 340) Bishop of Caesarea. Known as the Father of Church History. He participated as a moderating theologian in the Council of Nicea and was trusted by Emperor Constantine.

Augustine. (354–430) Bishop of Hippo Regius, near Carthage, North Africa. His extensive and profound writings, including commentary on Genesis, the Psalms, and the Gospels, made him the most influential theologian in western Christendom. The reformers drew constantly upon his insights.

John Chrysostom. (c. 347–407) Bishop of Constantinople and a key figure in the early Christological controversies. He was called "golden-mouthed" because of his brilliant oratory style. His commentaries on Scripture are sermons, valued by the church from ancient times.

Cassiodorus Senator. (c. 485–c. 580) Founder of Vivarium monastery where he established an educational program known as the seven liberal arts. Cassiodorus transmitted the learning of Augustine and other Fathers in late antiquity, making it available to medieval Christians.

Bede. (c. 673–735) Benedictine monk, biblical scholar, and historian. Bede's sermons and commentaries embodied the learning of the early Fathers who were admired in the western churches.

Bernard of Clairvaux. (1090–1153) Cistercian Abbot and Preacher. Bernard's sermons often beautifully proclaim Christ and God's grace, which made him a favorite medieval Father in the eyes of the reformers.

Hus, John. (c. 1372–1415) Priest and martyr. Lecturer and rector at the University of Prague, an enormously popular preacher and writer, greatly influenced by Augustine's theology and John Wycliffe's writings. Hus was falsely accused of heresy and condemned at the Council of Constance when the medieval church was sorely divided. His efforts heralded the Reformation.

Reformers

Luther, Martin. (1483–1546) Augustinian friar and preeminent reformer, lecturer on the Bible at the University of Wittenberg. Luther's preaching, teaching, and writing renewed biblically based piety in western Christendom. His translation of the Bible influenced the work of Bible publication throughout Europe, notably William Tyndale and the King James translators.

Cranmer, Thomas. (1489–1556) Archbishop of Canterbury and martyr. Cranmer served as a writer and editor for the Book of Common Prayer, one of the most influential works of the Reformation.

Melanchthon, Philip. (1497–1560) Lecturer on classical literature and languages at the University of Wittenberg. Melanchthon's *Commonplaces* and the Augsburg Confession laid the foundation for all subsequent works of Protestant dogmatic theology. He also wrote significant biblical commentaries.

Calvin, John. (1509–64) Preacher and lecturer on theology, founder of the Academy of Geneva. Calvin organized reformation efforts for Swiss, French, Dutch, and English Protestants. Calvin's *Institutes of the Christian Religion* and his extensive commentaries on Scripture are the most influential works of the second generation reformers.

Knox, John. (c. 1513–72) Scottish preacher and reformer. Knox edited the Book of Common Order used in Scottish churches and wrote a history of the Reformation in Scotland.

Chemnitz, Martin. (1522–86) Pastor and theologian at Brunswick, Germany. Chemnitz was largely responsible for the Formula of Concord that unified churches in Lutheran territories following the deaths of Luther and Melanchthon. His *Examination of the Council of Trent* equipped Protestant churches for responding to the Roman Catholic Counter Reformation.

Heirs of the Reformation

Gerhard, Johann. (1582–1637) Professor of theology at Jena and devotional writer. Gerhard wrote the most extensive dogmatic of the Protestant age of orthodoxy, the *Theological Commonplaces*, and was widely regarded for his knowledge of biblical Hebrew.

Bengel, Johann Albrecht. (1687–1752) New Testament scholar and professor. Bengel wrote the first scientific study of Greek New Testament manuscripts. His *Gnomon* on the New Testament is an influential, succinct commentary of enduring value.

Wesley, John. (1703–91) Missionary preacher. Wesley preached throughout England, Scotland, Ireland, and the American colonies. His *Explanatory Notes upon the New Testament* is a classic evangelical commentary, which drew upon principles and emphases of the Reformers